BLACK HAMMER™

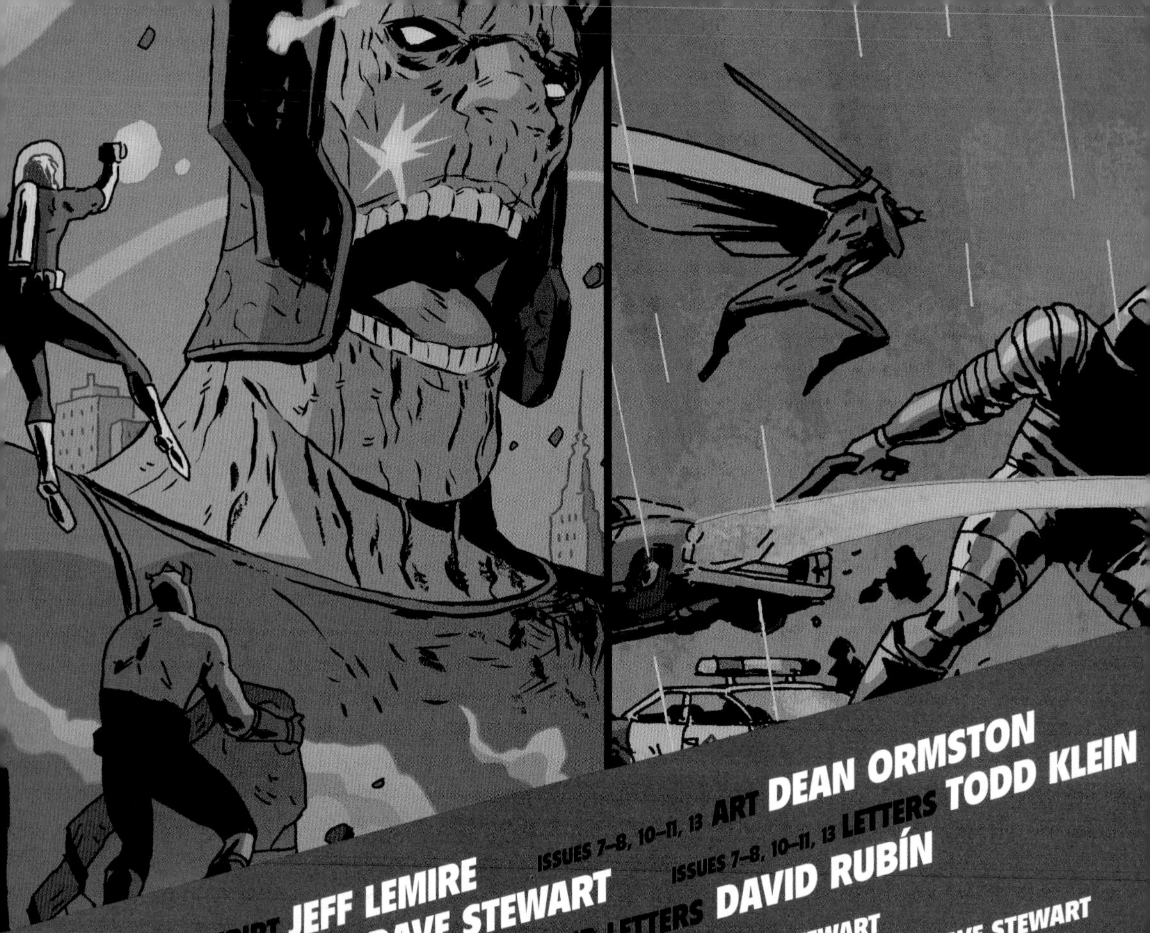

SCRIPT **JEFF LEMIRE**

ISSUES 7–8, 10–11, 13 ART **DEAN ORMSTON**

ISSUES 7–8, 10–11, 13 COLORS **DAVE STEWART**

ISSUES 7–8, 10–11, 13 LETTERS **TODD KLEIN**

ISSUE 9 ART, COLORS, AND LETTERS **DAVID RUBÍN**

COVER BY **DEAN ORMSTON WITH DAVE STEWART**

CHAPTER BREAKS BY **DEAN ORMSTON, JEFF LEMIRE, DAVID RUBÍN, AND DAVE STEWART**

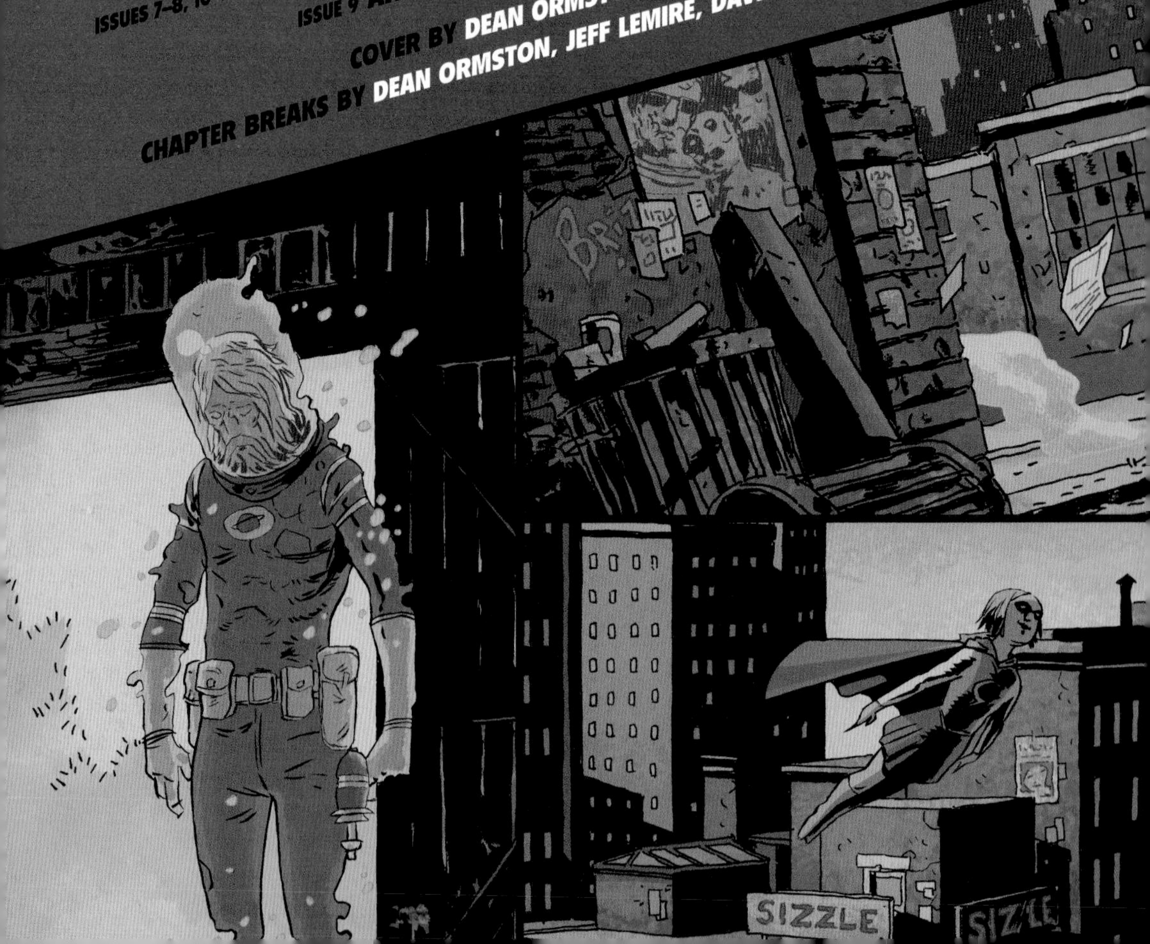
S!ZZLE
SIZZLE

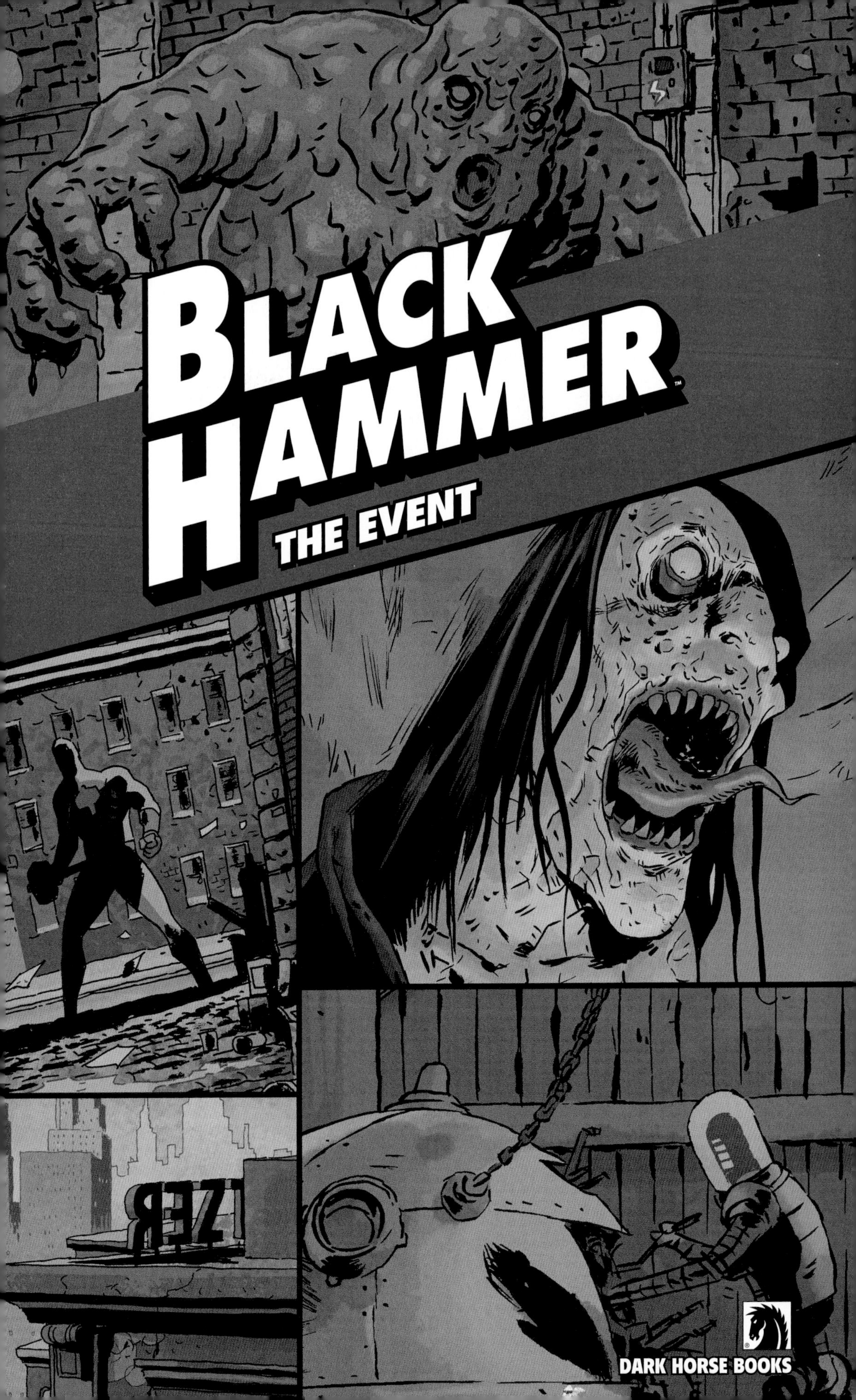
BLACK HAMMER™
THE EVENT
DARK HORSE BOOKS

PRESIDENT AND PUBLISHER
MIKE RICHARDSON

SERIES EDITORS
DANIEL CHABON
BRENDAN WRIGHT

DESIGNER
ETHAN KIMBERLING

COLLECTION EDITOR
DANIEL CHABON

ASSOCIATE EDITOR
CARDNER CLARK

DIGITAL ART TECHNICIAN
CHRISTINA McKENZIE

SPECIAL THANKS TO DIANA SCHUTZ

BLACK HAMMER VOLUME 2: THE EVENT

Black Hammer™ © 2017 171 Studios, Inc., and Dean Ormston. Dark Horse Books® and the Dark Horse logo
are registered trademarks of Dark Horse Comics, Inc. All rights reserved. No portion of this publication may be
reproduced or transmitted, in any form or by any means, without the express written permission of Dark Horse
Comics, Inc. Names, characters, places, and incidents featured in this publication either are the product of
the author's imagination or are used fictitiously. Any resemblance to actual persons (living or dead), events,
institutions, or locales, without satiric intent, is coincidental.

This volume collects issues #7–#11 and #13 of the Dark Horse Comics series *Black Hammer*.

Library of Congress Cataloging-in-Publication Data

Names: Lemire, Jeff, author, artist. | Ormston, Dean, artist. | Stewart,
  Dave, colourist. | Klein, Todd, letterer. | Rubín, David, 1977- artist.
Title: The event / script by Jeff Lemire ; issues 7-8, 10-11, 13 art by Dean
  Ormston, colors by Dave Stewart, letters by Todd Klein ; issue 9 art,
  colors, and letters by David Rubín, cover by Dean Ormston with Dave
  Stewart ; chapter breaks by Dean Ormston, Jeff Lemire, David Rubín, and
  Dave Stewart.
Description: First edition. | Milwaukie, OR : Dark Horse Books, 2018. |
  Series: Black Hammer ; Volume 2 | "This volume collects issues #7-#11 and
  #13 of the Dark Horse Comics series Black Hammer."
Identifiers: LCCN 2017029480 | ISBN 9781506701981 (paperback)
Subjects: LCSH: Comic books, strips, etc. | BISAC: COMICS & GRAPHIC NOVELS /
  Superheroes. | COMICS & GRAPHIC NOVELS / Science Fiction. | COMICS &
  GRAPHIC NOVELS / Fantasy.
Classification: LCC PN6728.B51926 L43 2018 | DDC 741.5/973--dc23
LC record available at https://lccn.loc.gov/2017029480

Published by
Dark Horse Books
A division of Dark Horse Comics, Inc.
10956 SE Main Street
Milwaukie, OR 97222

DarkHorse.com

To find a comics shop in your area, visit comicshoplocator.com
International Licensing: (503) 905-2377

First edition: December 2017
ISBN 978-1-50670-198-1

10 9 8 7 6 5 4 3 2
Printed in Canada

NEIL HANKERSON Executive Vice President TOM WEDDLE Chief Financial Officer RANDY STRADLEY Vice
President of Publishing MATT PARKINSON Vice President of Marketing DAVID SCROGGY Vice President of
Product Development DALE LaFOUNTAIN Vice President of Information Technology CARA NIECE Vice President of
Production and Scheduling NICK McWHORTER Vice President of Media Licensing MARK BERNARDI Vice President
of Digital and Book Trade Sales KEN LIZZI General Counsel DAVE MARSHALL Editor in Chief DAVEY ESTRADA
Editorial Director SCOTT ALLIE Executive Senior Editor CHRIS WARNER Senior Books Editor CARY GRAZZINI
Director of Specialty Projects LIA RIBACCHI Art Director VANESSA TODD Director of Print Purchasing MATT DRYER
Director of Digital Art and Prepress MICHAEL GOMBOS Director of International Publishing and Licensing

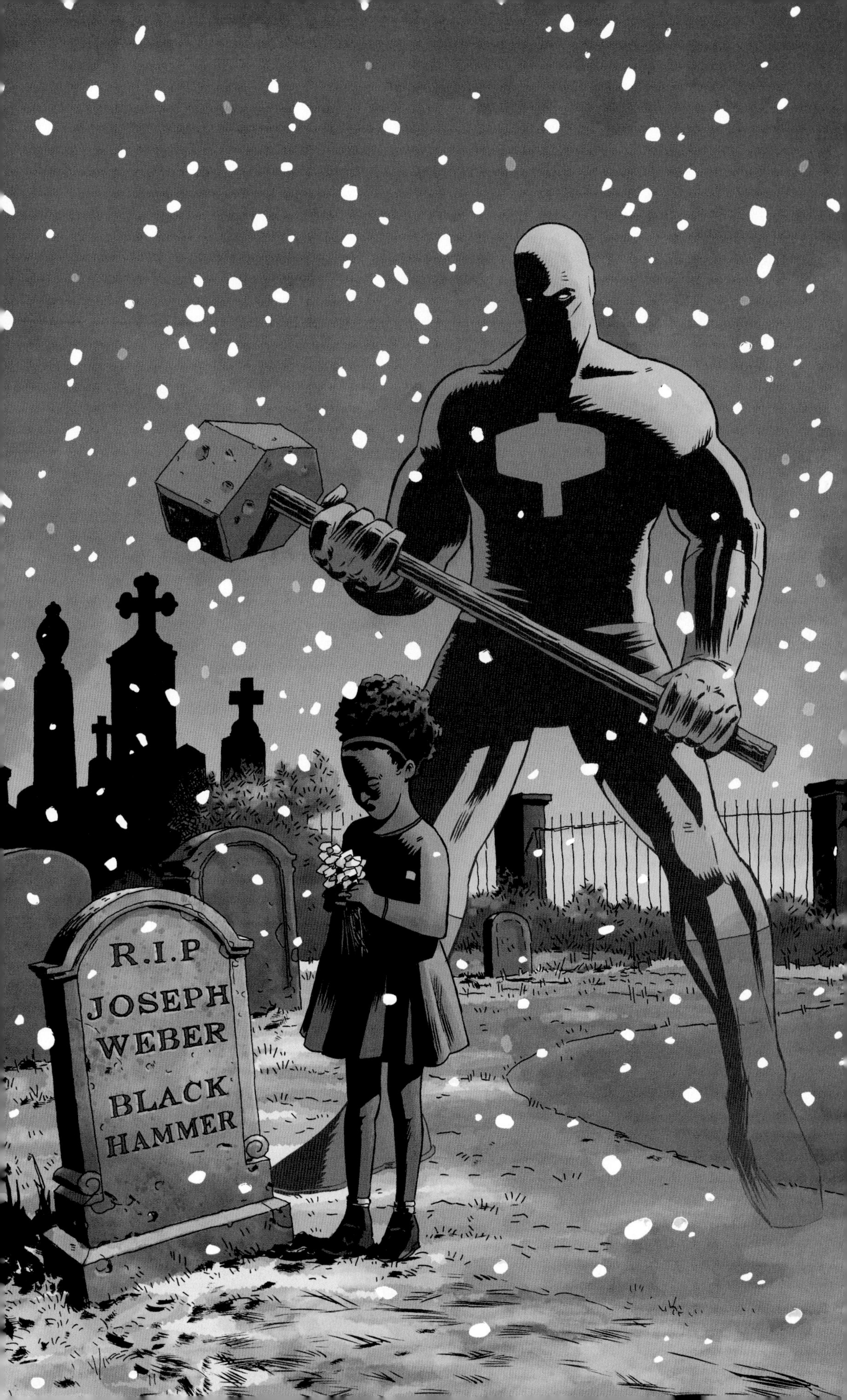
R.I.P
JOSEPH
WEBER
BLACK
HAMMER

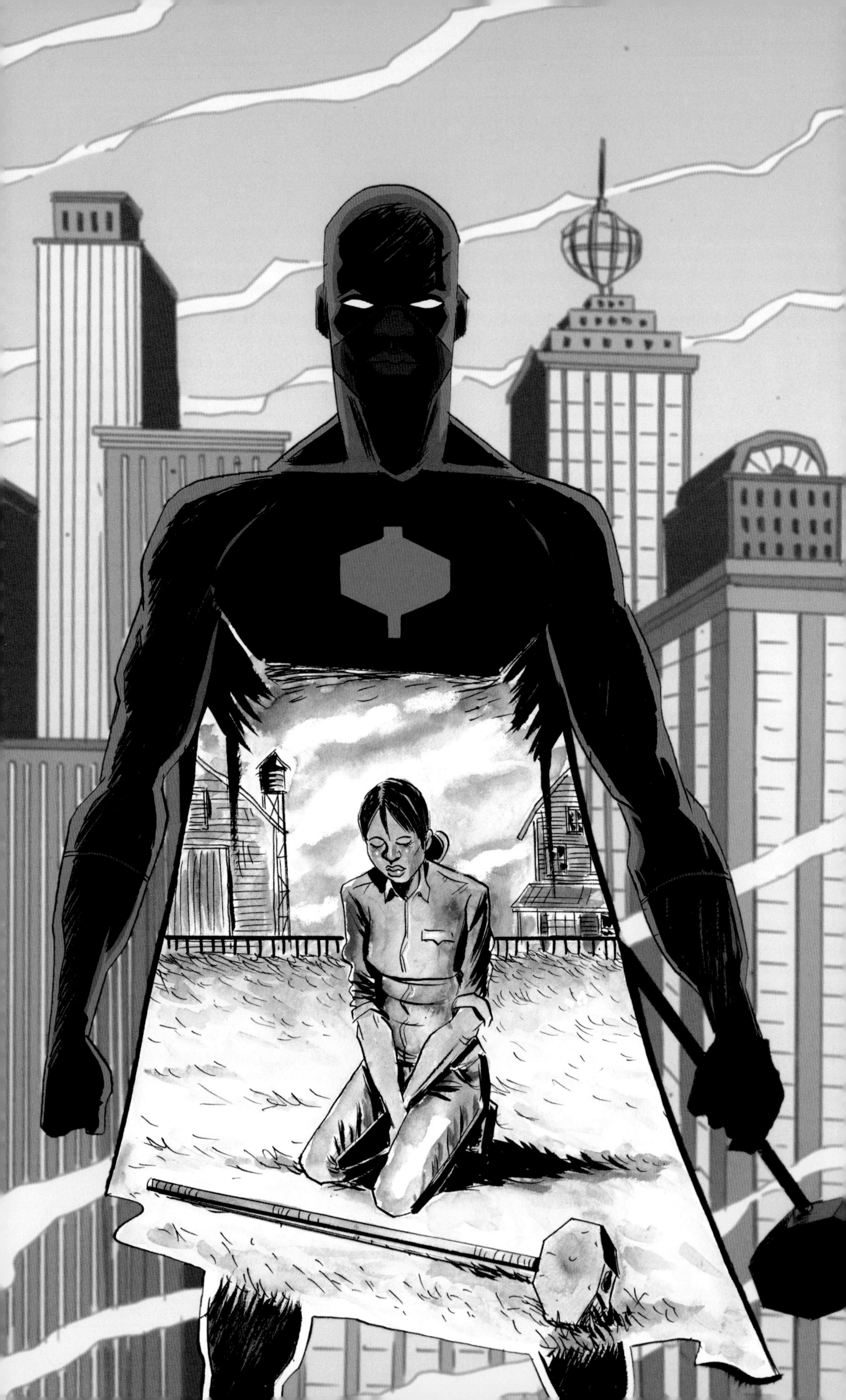

BLACK HAMMER FALLS!

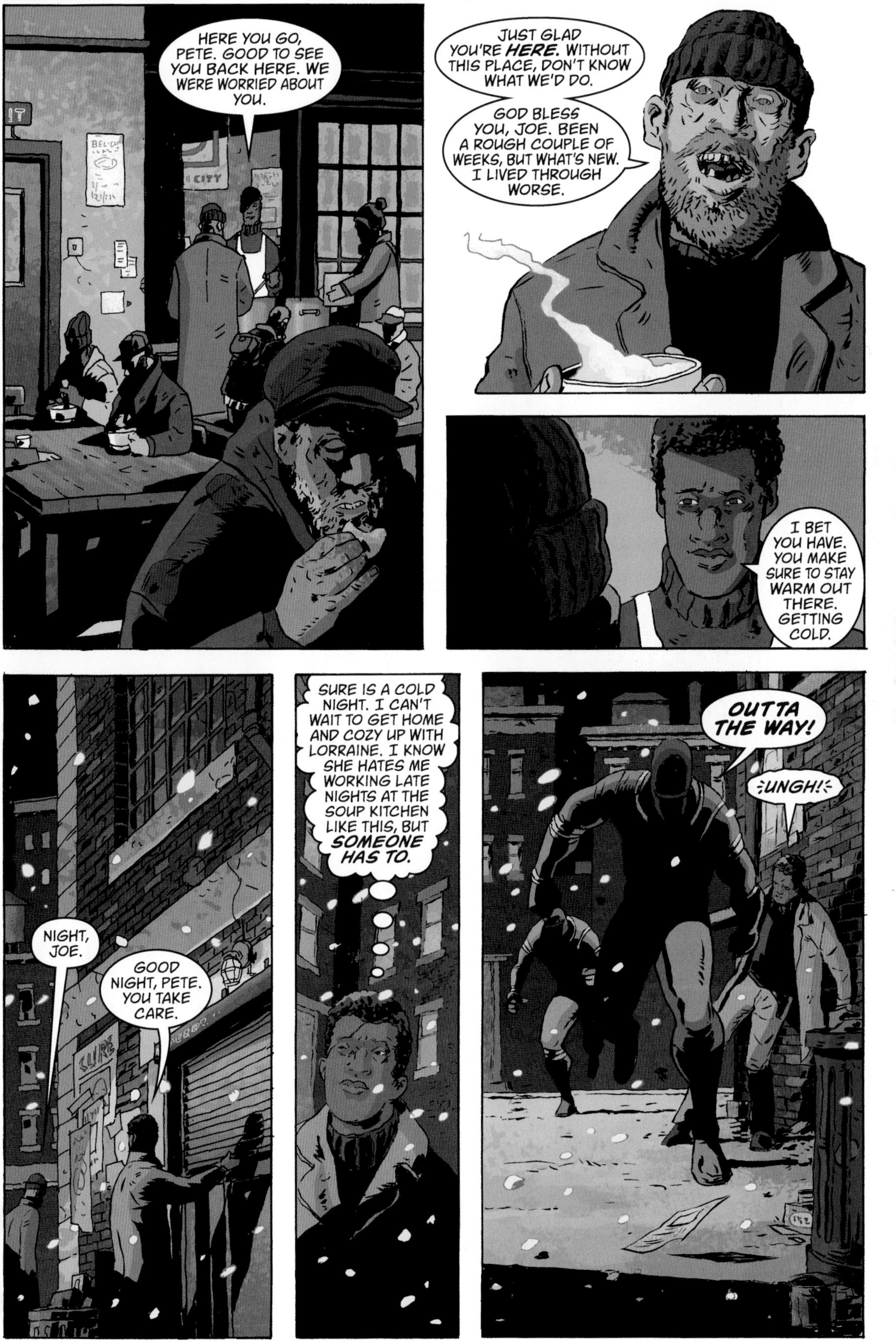

HERE YOU GO, PETE. GOOD TO SEE YOU BACK HERE. WE WERE WORRIED ABOUT YOU.
JUST GLAD YOU'RE HERE. WITHOUT THIS PLACE, DON'T KNOW WHAT WE'D DO.
GOD BLESS YOU, JOE. BEEN A ROUGH COUPLE OF WEEKS, BUT WHAT'S NEW. I LIVED THROUGH WORSE.
I BET YOU HAVE. YOU MAKE SURE TO STAY WARM OUT THERE. GETTING COLD.
NIGHT, JOE.
GOOD NIGHT, PETE. YOU TAKE CARE.
SURE IS A COLD NIGHT. I CAN'T WAIT TO GET HOME AND COZY UP WITH LORRAINE. I KNOW SHE HATES ME WORKING LATE NIGHTS AT THE SOUP KITCHEN LIKE THIS, BUT SOMEONE HAS TO.
OUTTA THE WAY!
UNGH!

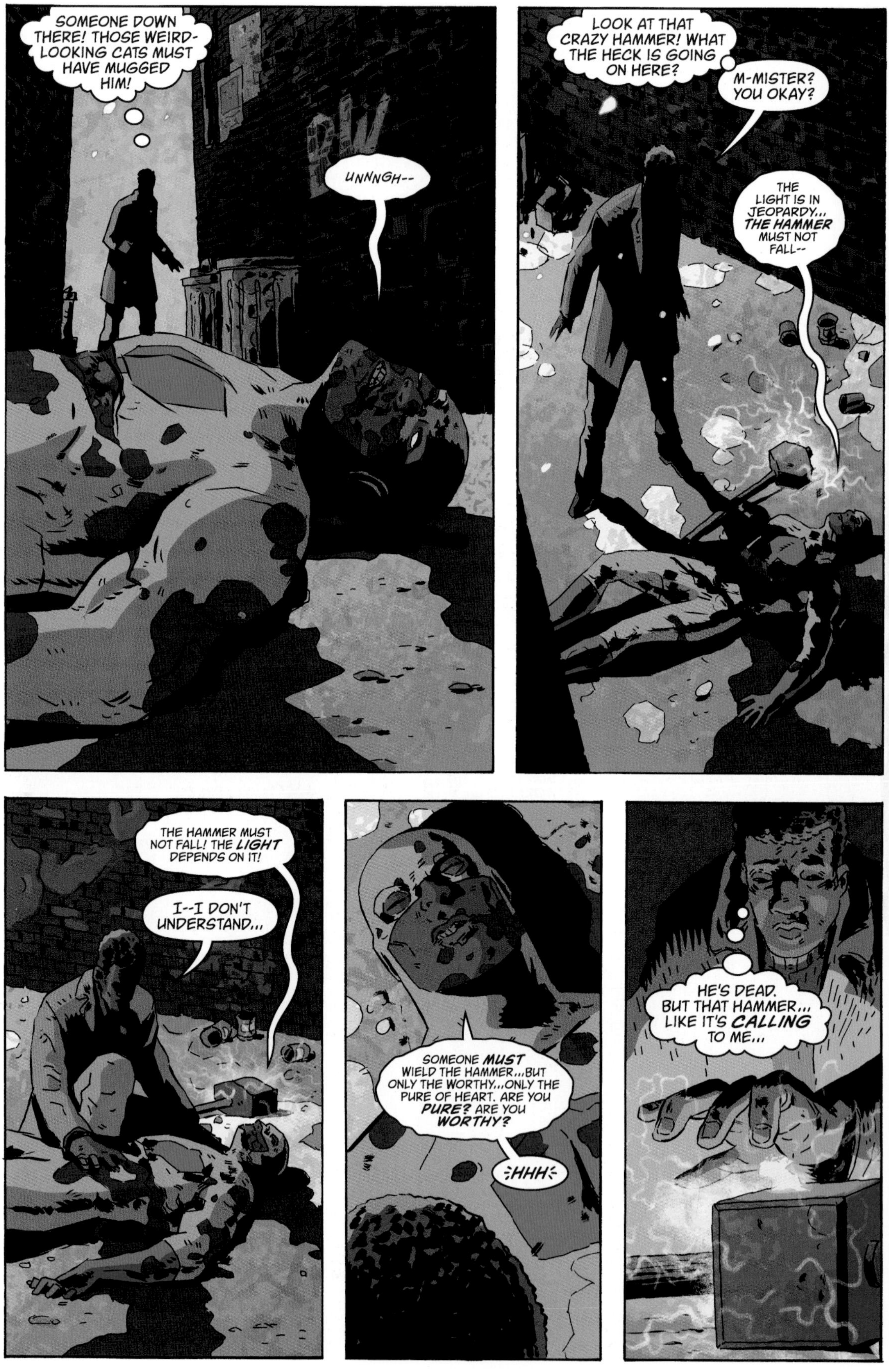
SOMEONE DOWN THERE! THOSE WEIRD-LOOKING CATS MUST HAVE MUGGED HIM!
UNNNGH--
LOOK AT THAT CRAZY HAMMER! WHAT THE HECK IS GOING ON HERE?
M-MISTER? YOU OKAY?
THE LIGHT IS IN JEOPARDY... THE HAMMER MUST NOT FALL--
THE HAMMER MUST NOT FALL! THE LIGHT DEPENDS ON IT!
I--I DON'T UNDERSTAND...
SOMEONE MUST WIELD THE HAMMER...BUT ONLY THE WORTHY...ONLY THE PURE OF HEART. ARE YOU PURE? ARE YOU WORTHY?
HHH
HE'S DEAD. BUT THAT HAMMER... LIKE IT'S CALLING TO ME...

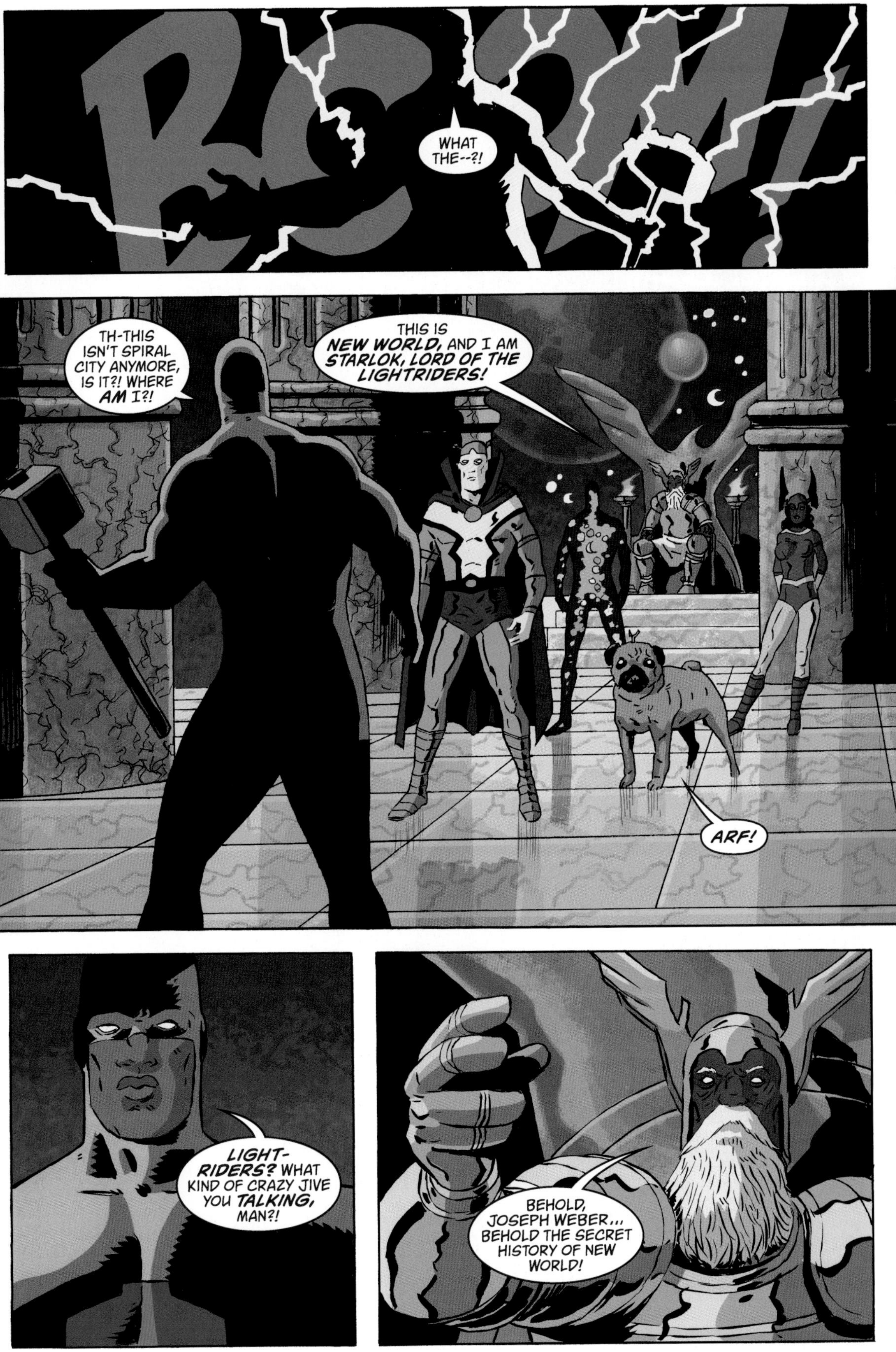
WHAT THE--?!
TH-THIS ISN'T SPIRAL CITY ANYMORE, IS IT?! WHERE AM I?!
THIS IS NEW WORLD, AND I AM STARLOK, LORD OF THE LIGHTRIDERS!
ARF!
LIGHT-RIDERS? WHAT KIND OF CRAZY JIVE YOU TALKING, MAN?!
BEHOLD, JOSEPH WEBER... BEHOLD THE SECRET HISTORY OF NEW WORLD!

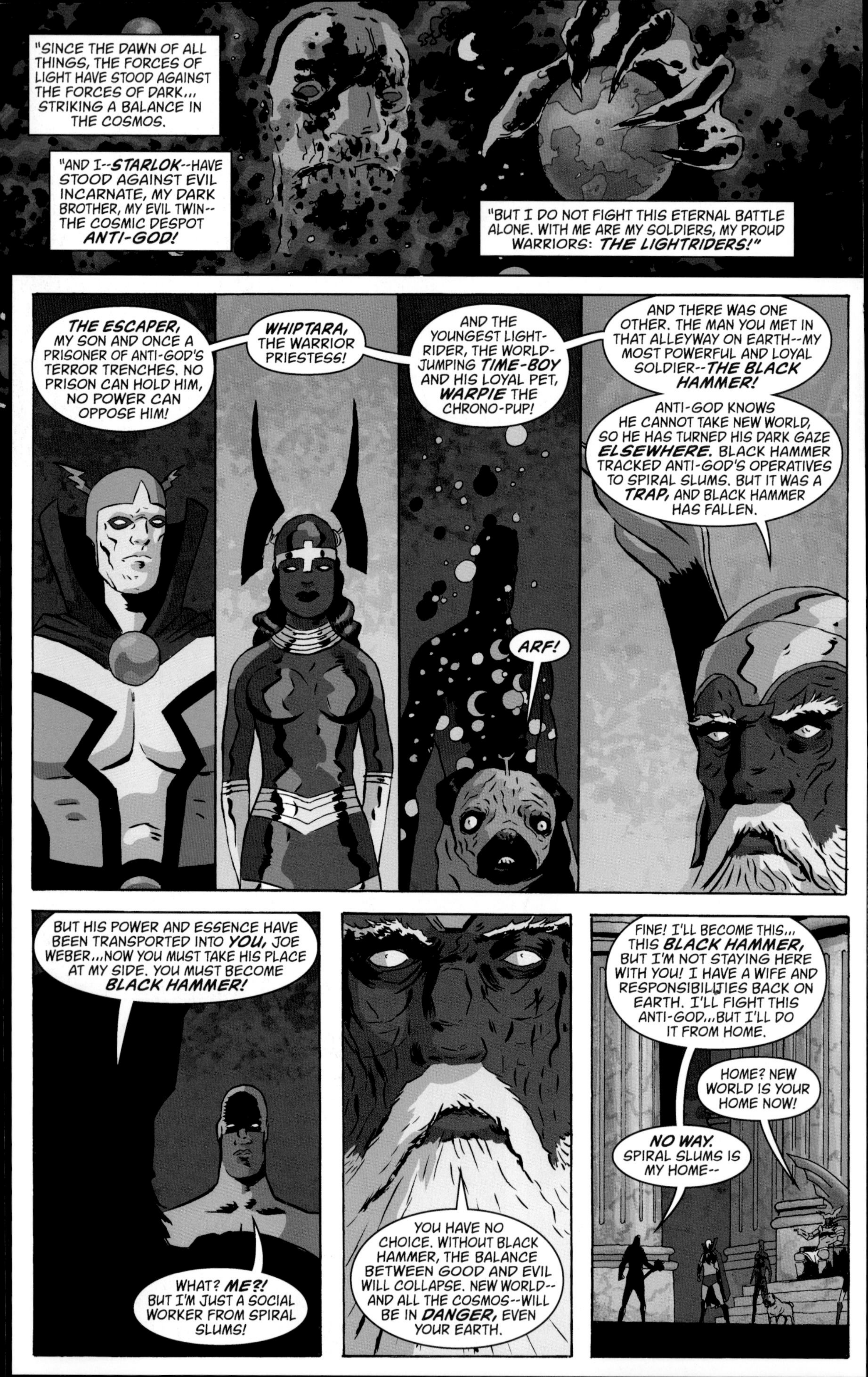
"SINCE THE DAWN OF ALL THINGS, THE FORCES OF LIGHT HAVE STOOD AGAINST THE FORCES OF DARK... STRIKING A BALANCE IN THE COSMOS.
"AND I--STARLOK--HAVE STOOD AGAINST EVIL INCARNATE, MY DARK BROTHER, MY EVIL TWIN--THE COSMIC DESPOT ANTI-GOD!
"BUT I DO NOT FIGHT THIS ETERNAL BATTLE ALONE. WITH ME ARE MY SOLDIERS, MY PROUD WARRIORS: THE LIGHTRIDERS!"
THE ESCAPER, MY SON AND ONCE A PRISONER OF ANTI-GOD'S TERROR TRENCHES. NO PRISON CAN HOLD HIM, NO POWER CAN OPPOSE HIM!
WHIPTARA, THE WARRIOR PRIESTESS!
AND THE YOUNGEST LIGHT-RIDER, THE WORLD-JUMPING TIME-BOY AND HIS LOYAL PET, WARPIE THE CHRONO-PUP!
ARF!
AND THERE WAS ONE OTHER. THE MAN YOU MET IN THAT ALLEYWAY ON EARTH--MY MOST POWERFUL AND LOYAL SOLDIER--THE BLACK HAMMER!
ANTI-GOD KNOWS HE CANNOT TAKE NEW WORLD, SO HE HAS TURNED HIS DARK GAZE ELSEWHERE. BLACK HAMMER TRACKED ANTI-GOD'S OPERATIVES TO SPIRAL SLUMS. BUT IT WAS A TRAP, AND BLACK HAMMER HAS FALLEN.
BUT HIS POWER AND ESSENCE HAVE BEEN TRANSPORTED INTO YOU, JOE WEBER...NOW YOU MUST TAKE HIS PLACE AT MY SIDE. YOU MUST BECOME BLACK HAMMER!
WHAT? ME?! BUT I'M JUST A SOCIAL WORKER FROM SPIRAL SLUMS!
YOU HAVE NO CHOICE. WITHOUT BLACK HAMMER, THE BALANCE BETWEEN GOOD AND EVIL WILL COLLAPSE. NEW WORLD--AND ALL THE COSMOS--WILL BE IN DANGER, EVEN YOUR EARTH.
FINE! I'LL BECOME THIS... THIS BLACK HAMMER, BUT I'M NOT STAYING HERE WITH YOU! I HAVE A WIFE AND RESPONSIBILITIES BACK ON EARTH. I'LL FIGHT THIS ANTI-GOD...BUT I'LL DO IT FROM HOME.
HOME? NEW WORLD IS YOUR HOME NOW!
NO WAY. SPIRAL SLUMS IS MY HOME--

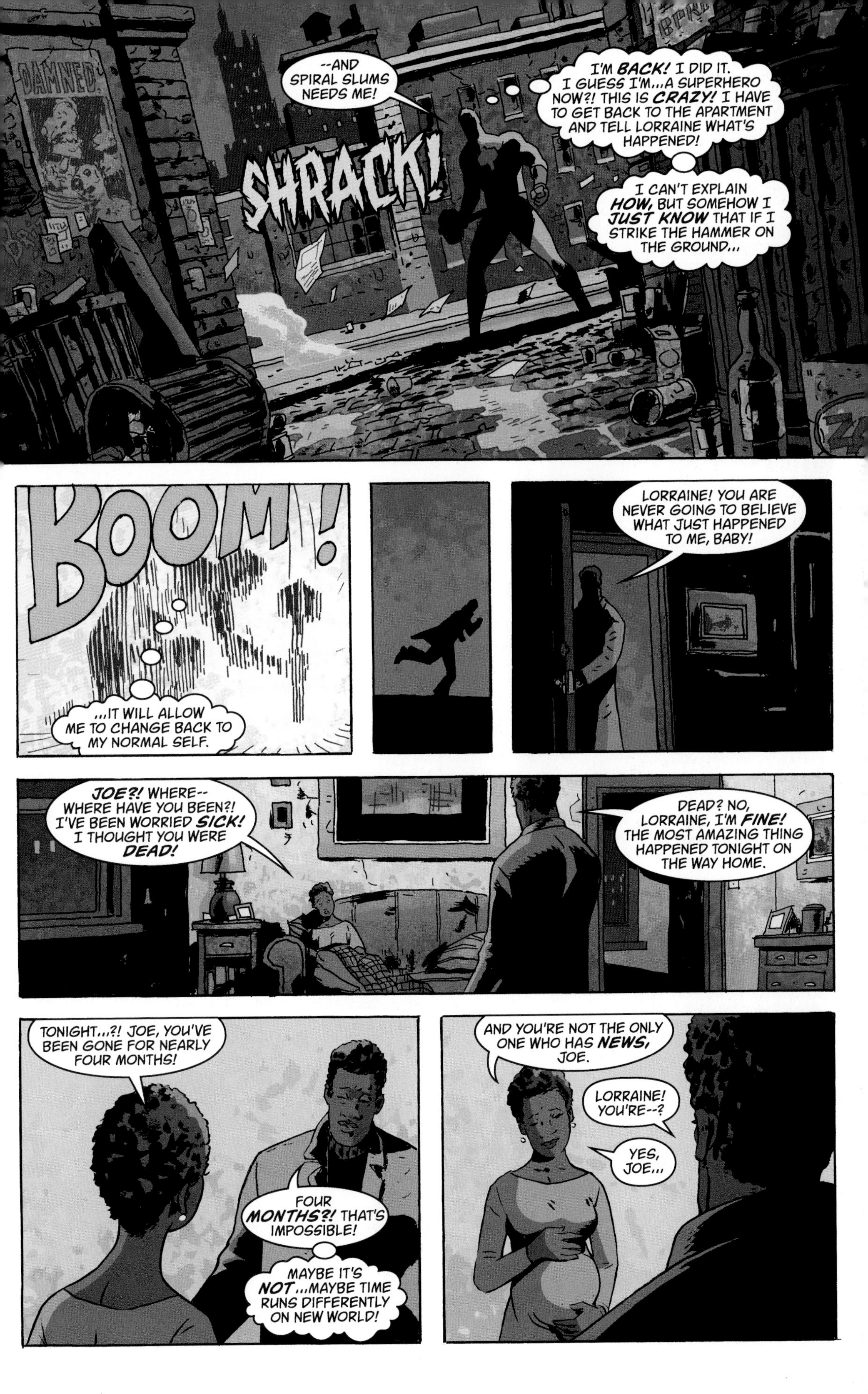
DAMNED
BPR
--AND SPIRAL SLUMS NEEDS ME!
I'M BACK! I DID IT. I GUESS I'M...A SUPERHERO NOW?! THIS IS CRAZY! I HAVE TO GET BACK TO THE APARTMENT AND TELL LORRAINE WHAT'S HAPPENED!
I CAN'T EXPLAIN HOW, BUT SOMEHOW I JUST KNOW THAT IF I STRIKE THE HAMMER ON THE GROUND...
SHRACK!
BOOM!
...IT WILL ALLOW ME TO CHANGE BACK TO MY NORMAL SELF.
LORRAINE! YOU ARE NEVER GOING TO BELIEVE WHAT JUST HAPPENED TO ME, BABY!
JOE?! WHERE-- WHERE HAVE YOU BEEN?! I'VE BEEN WORRIED SICK! I THOUGHT YOU WERE DEAD!
DEAD? NO, LORRAINE, I'M FINE! THE MOST AMAZING THING HAPPENED TONIGHT ON THE WAY HOME.
TONIGHT...?! JOE, YOU'VE BEEN GONE FOR NEARLY FOUR MONTHS!
FOUR MONTHS?! THAT'S IMPOSSIBLE!
MAYBE IT'S NOT...MAYBE TIME RUNS DIFFERENTLY ON NEW WORLD!
AND YOU'RE NOT THE ONLY ONE WHO HAS NEWS, JOE.
LORRAINE! YOU'RE--?
YES, JOE...

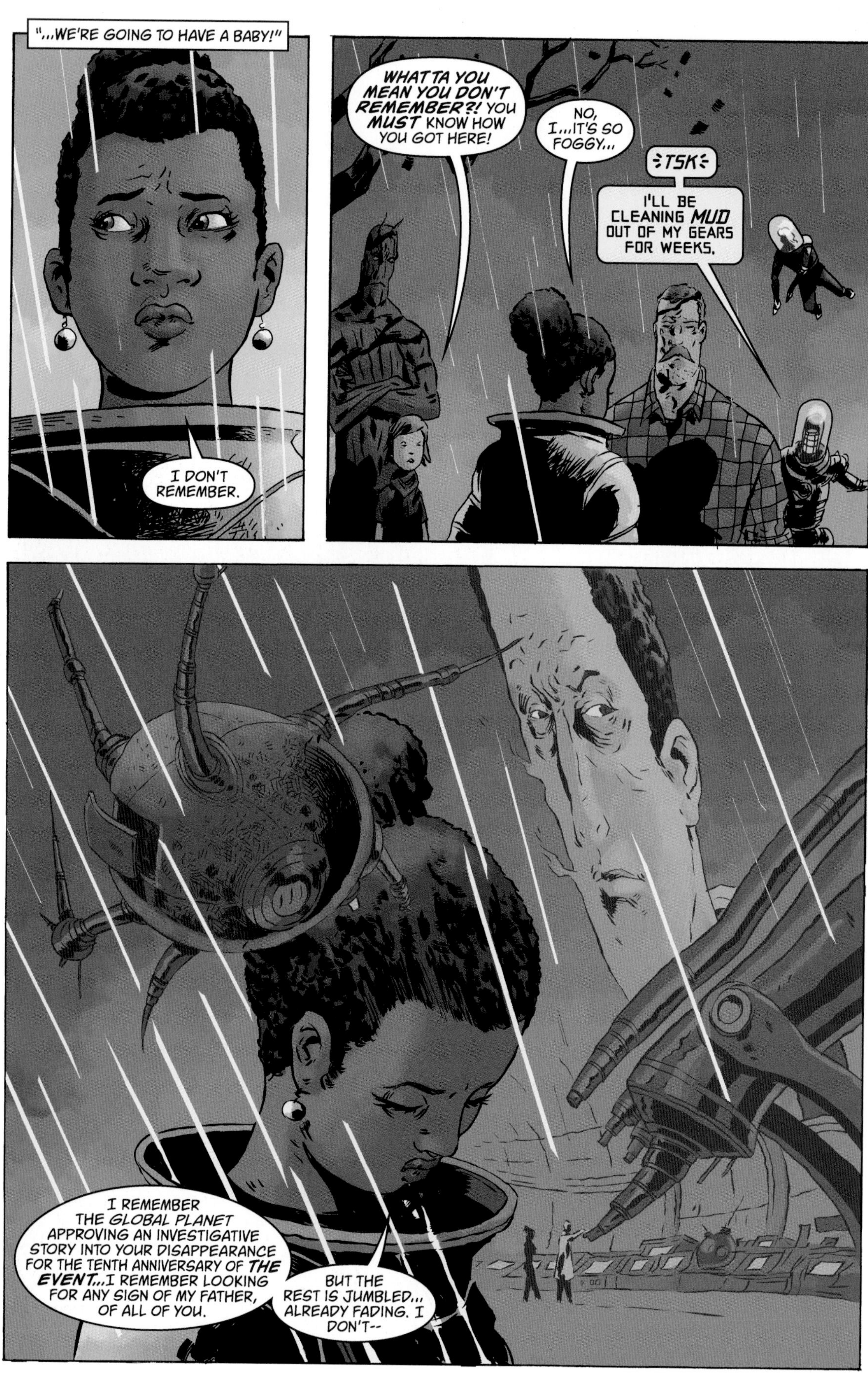
"...WE'RE GOING TO HAVE A BABY!"
I DON'T REMEMBER.
WHATTA YOU MEAN YOU DON'T REMEMBER?! YOU MUST KNOW HOW YOU GOT HERE!
NO, I...IT'S SO FOGGY...
TSK
I'LL BE CLEANING MUD OUT OF MY GEARS FOR WEEKS.
I REMEMBER THE GLOBAL PLANET APPROVING AN INVESTIGATIVE STORY INTO YOUR DISAPPEARANCE FOR THE TENTH ANNIVERSARY OF THE EVENT...I REMEMBER LOOKING FOR ANY SIGN OF MY FATHER, OF ALL OF YOU.
BUT THE REST IS JUMBLED... ALREADY FADING. I DON'T--

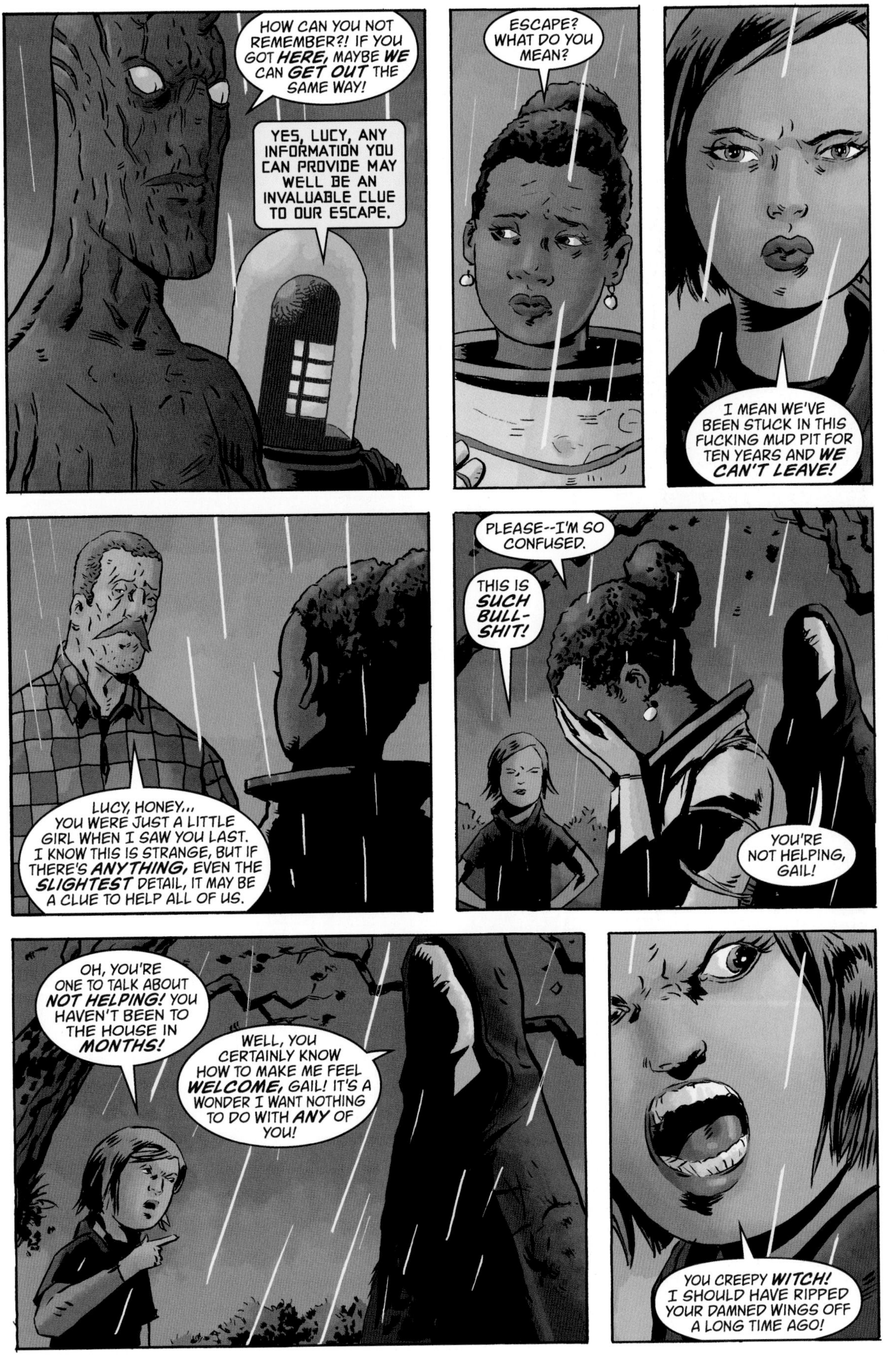
HOW CAN YOU NOT REMEMBER?! IF YOU GOT HERE, MAYBE WE CAN GET OUT THE SAME WAY!
YES, LUCY, ANY INFORMATION YOU CAN PROVIDE MAY WELL BE AN INVALUABLE CLUE TO OUR ESCAPE.
ESCAPE? WHAT DO YOU MEAN?
I MEAN WE'VE BEEN STUCK IN THIS FUCKING MUD PIT FOR TEN YEARS AND WE CAN'T LEAVE!
LUCY, HONEY... YOU WERE JUST A LITTLE GIRL WHEN I SAW YOU LAST. I KNOW THIS IS STRANGE, BUT IF THERE'S ANYTHING, EVEN THE SLIGHTEST DETAIL, IT MAY BE A CLUE TO HELP ALL OF US.
PLEASE--I'M SO CONFUSED.
THIS IS SUCH BULL-SHIT!
YOU'RE NOT HELPING, GAIL!
OH, YOU'RE ONE TO TALK ABOUT NOT HELPING! YOU HAVEN'T BEEN TO THE HOUSE IN MONTHS!
WELL, YOU CERTAINLY KNOW HOW TO MAKE ME FEEL WELCOME, GAIL! IT'S A WONDER I WANT NOTHING TO DO WITH ANY OF YOU!
YOU CREEPY WITCH! I SHOULD HAVE RIPPED YOUR DAMNED WINGS OFF A LONG TIME AGO!

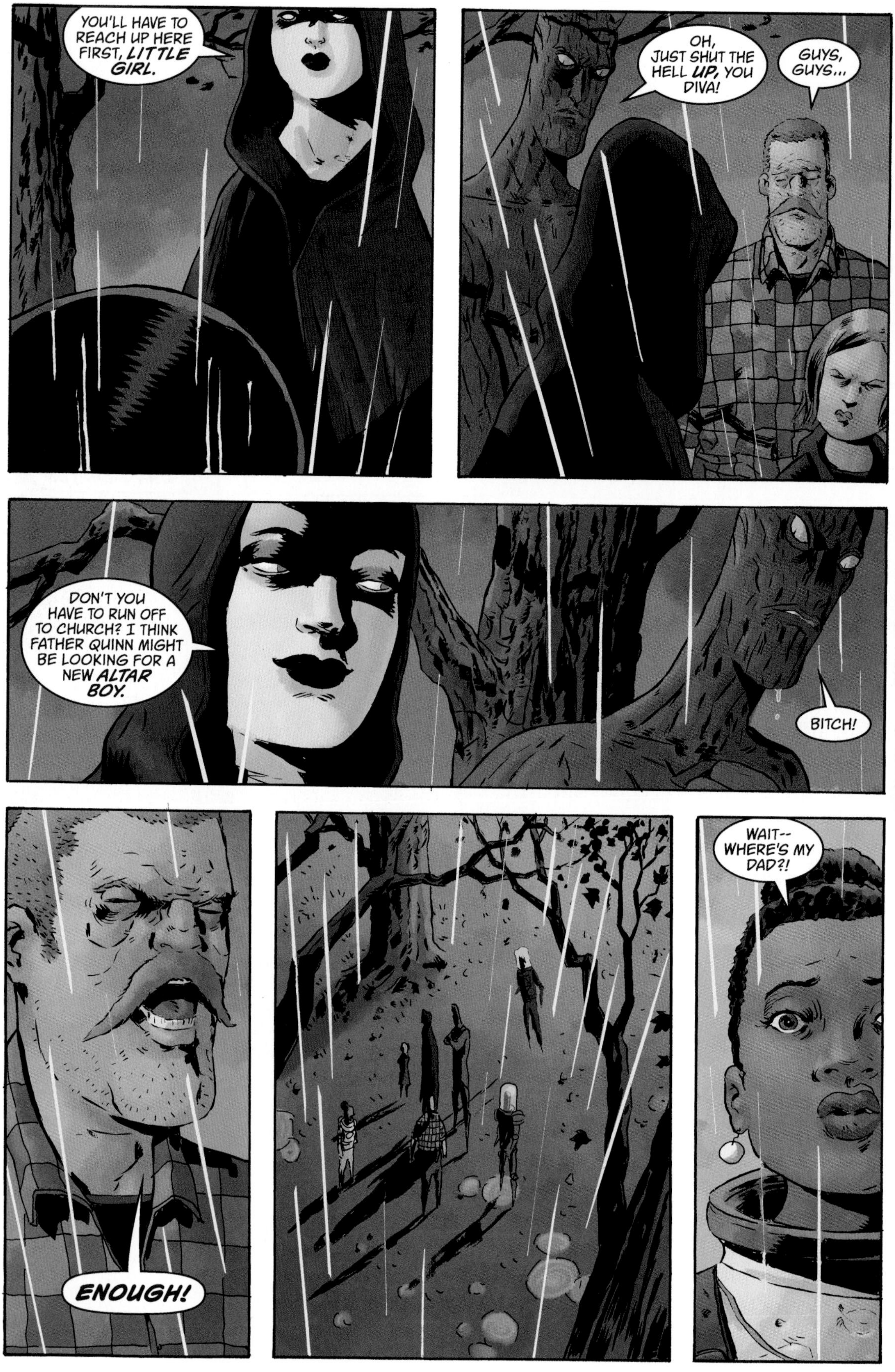
YOU'LL HAVE TO REACH UP HERE FIRST, LITTLE GIRL.
OH, JUST SHUT THE HELL UP, YOU DIVA!
GUYS, GUYS...
DON'T YOU HAVE TO RUN OFF TO CHURCH? I THINK FATHER QUINN MIGHT BE LOOKING FOR A NEW ALTAR BOY.
BITCH!
ENOUGH!
WAIT-- WHERE'S MY DAD?!

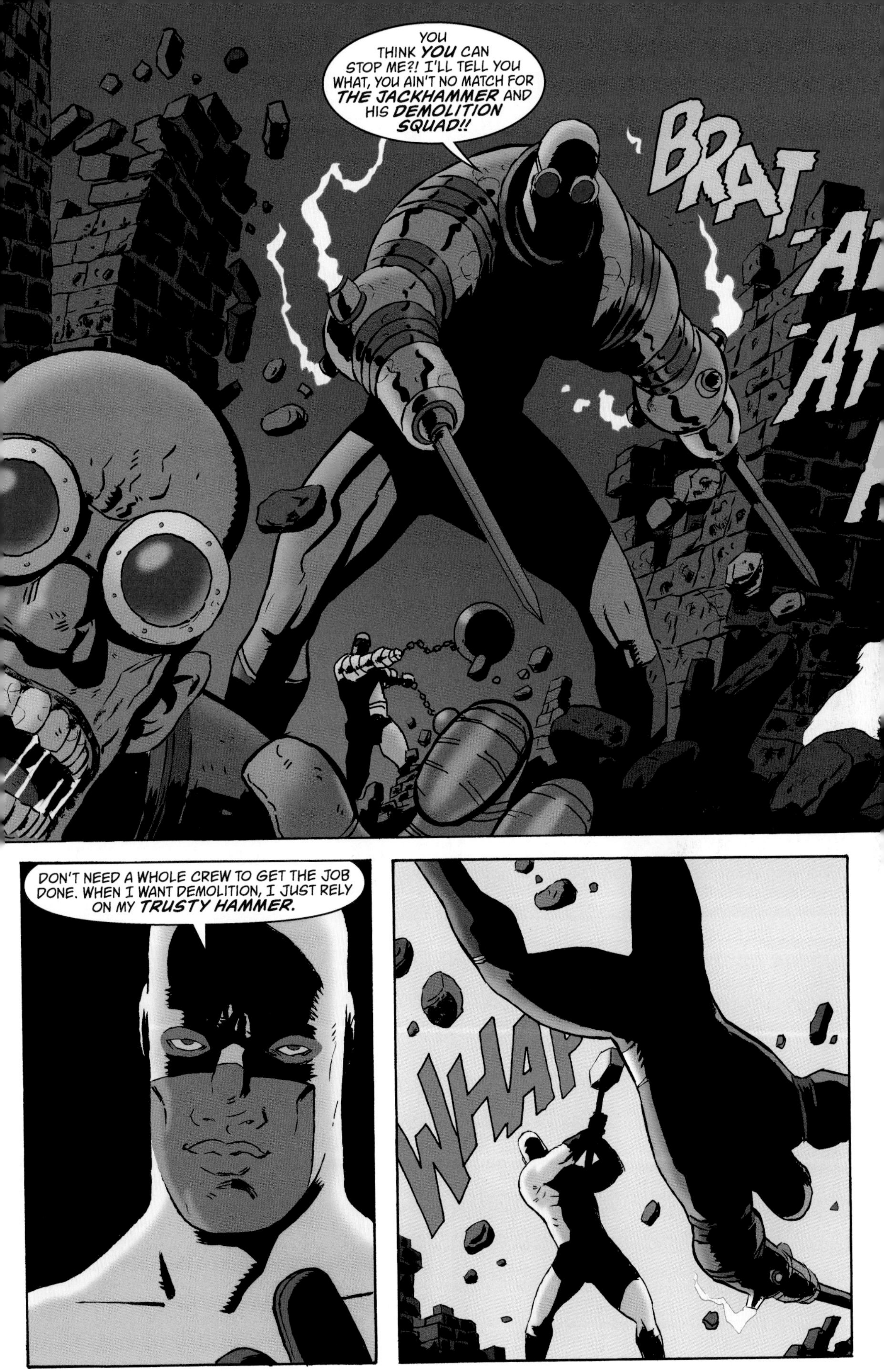
YOU THINK *YOU* CAN STOP ME?! I'LL TELL YOU WHAT, YOU AIN'T NO MATCH FOR *THE JACKHAMMER* AND HIS *DEMOLITION SQUAD!!*
BRAT-
DON'T NEED A WHOLE CREW TO GET THE JOB DONE. WHEN I WANT DEMOLITION, I JUST RELY ON MY *TRUSTY HAMMER.*
WHAP

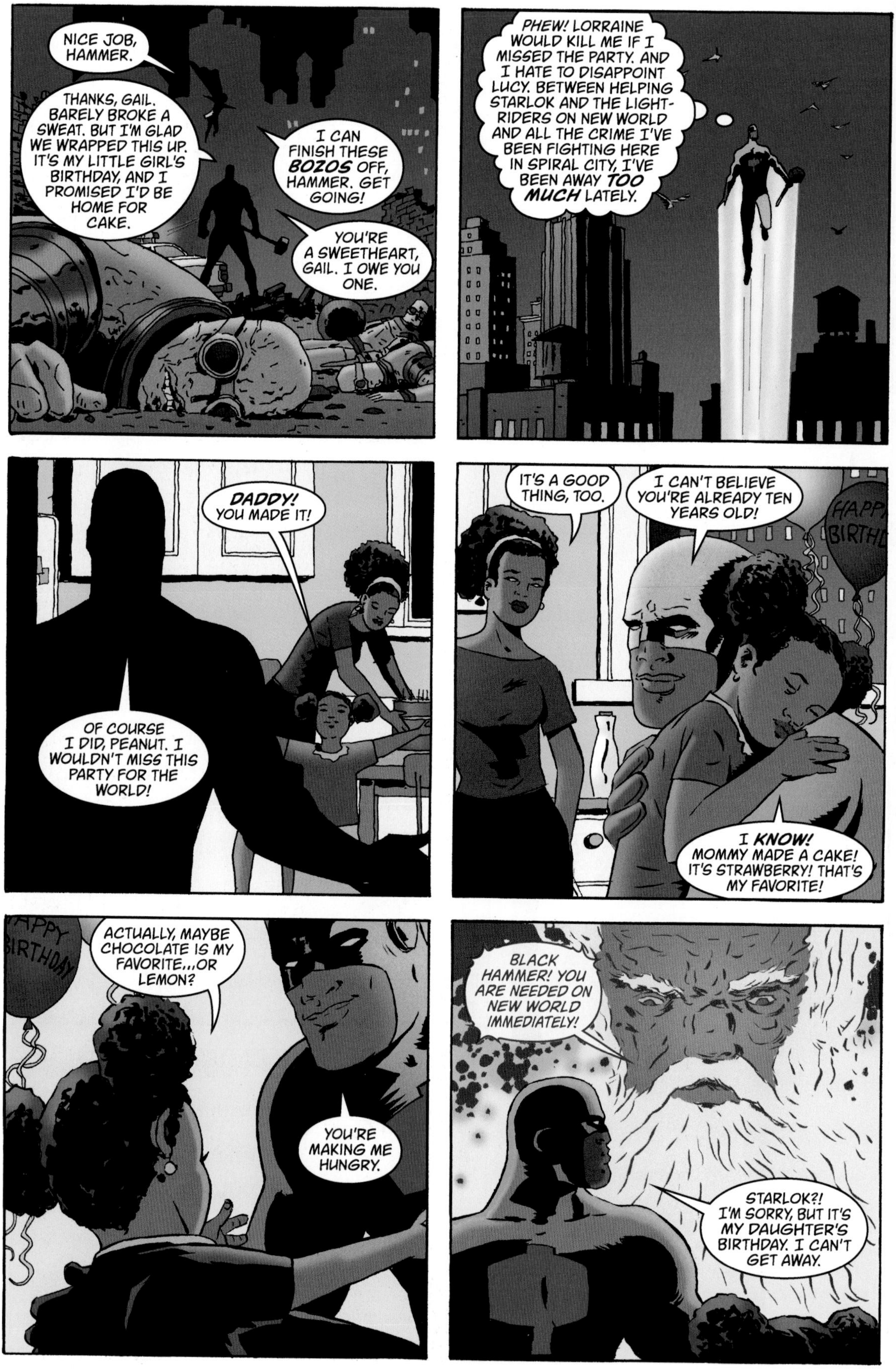
NICE JOB, HAMMER.
THANKS, GAIL. BARELY BROKE A SWEAT. BUT I'M GLAD WE WRAPPED THIS UP. IT'S MY LITTLE GIRL'S BIRTHDAY, AND I PROMISED I'D BE HOME FOR CAKE.
I CAN FINISH THESE BOZOS OFF, HAMMER. GET GOING!
YOU'RE A SWEETHEART, GAIL. I OWE YOU ONE.
PHEW! LORRAINE WOULD KILL ME IF I MISSED THE PARTY. AND I HATE TO DISAPPOINT LUCY. BETWEEN HELPING STARLOK AND THE LIGHT-RIDERS ON NEW WORLD AND ALL THE CRIME I'VE BEEN FIGHTING HERE IN SPIRAL CITY, I'VE BEEN AWAY TOO MUCH LATELY.
DADDY! YOU MADE IT!
OF COURSE I DID, PEANUT. I WOULDN'T MISS THIS PARTY FOR THE WORLD!
IT'S A GOOD THING, TOO.
I CAN'T BELIEVE YOU'RE ALREADY TEN YEARS OLD!
HAPPY BIRTH
I KNOW! MOMMY MADE A CAKE! IT'S STRAWBERRY! THAT'S MY FAVORITE!
APPY BIRTHDAY
ACTUALLY, MAYBE CHOCOLATE IS MY FAVORITE...OR LEMON?
YOU'RE MAKING ME HUNGRY.
BLACK HAMMER! YOU ARE NEEDED ON NEW WORLD IMMEDIATELY!
STARLOK?! I'M SORRY, BUT IT'S MY DAUGHTER'S BIRTHDAY. I CAN'T GET AWAY.

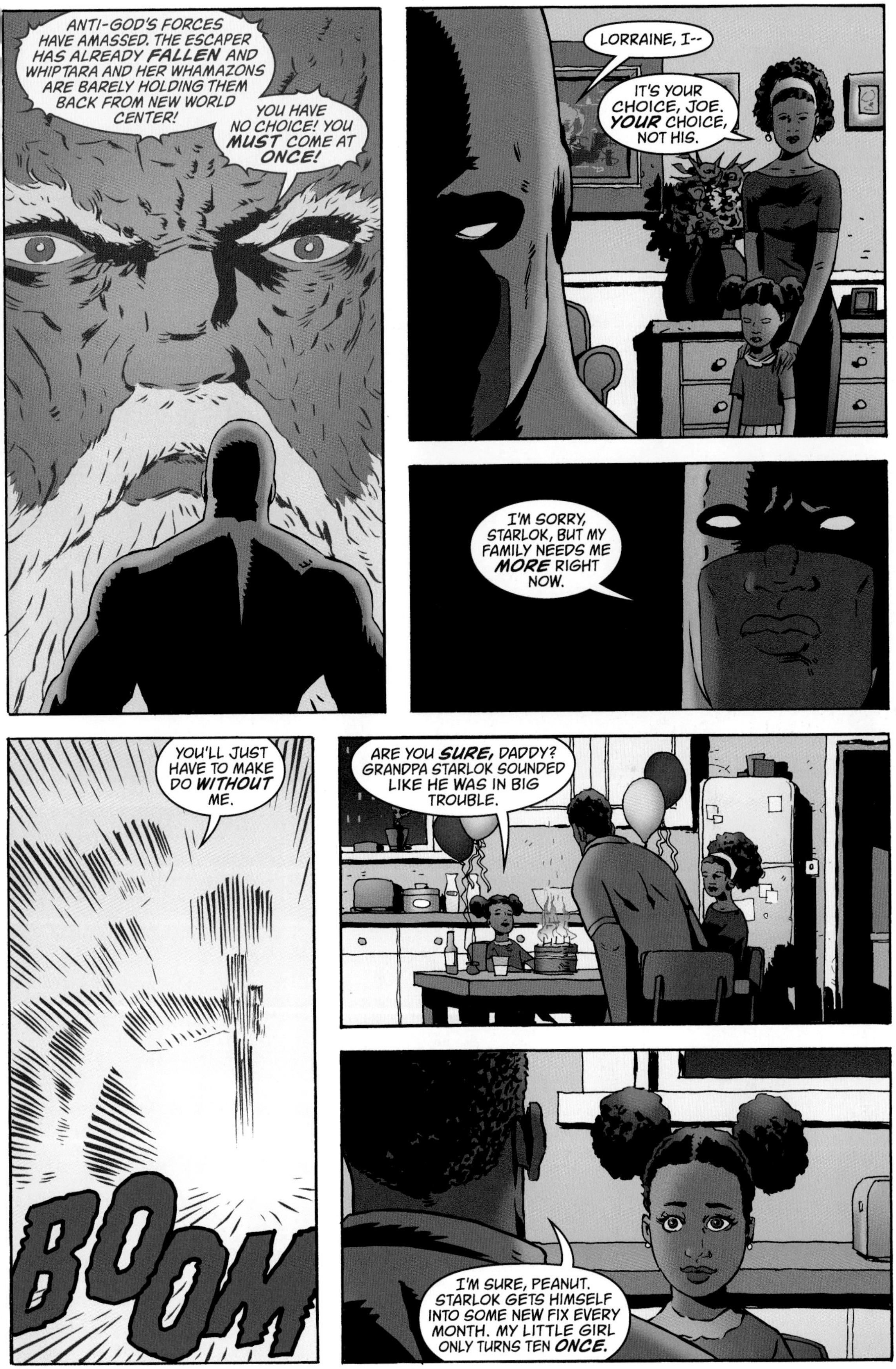
ANTI-GOD'S FORCES HAVE AMASSED. THE ESCAPER HAS ALREADY FALLEN AND WHIPTARA AND HER WHAMAZONS ARE BARELY HOLDING THEM BACK FROM NEW WORLD CENTER!
YOU HAVE NO CHOICE! YOU MUST COME AT ONCE!
LORRAINE, I--
IT'S YOUR CHOICE, JOE. YOUR CHOICE, NOT HIS.
I'M SORRY, STARLOK, BUT MY FAMILY NEEDS ME MORE RIGHT NOW.
YOU'LL JUST HAVE TO MAKE DO WITHOUT ME.
BOOM
ARE YOU SURE, DADDY? GRANDPA STARLOK SOUNDED LIKE HE WAS IN BIG TROUBLE.
I'M SURE, PEANUT. STARLOK GETS HIMSELF INTO SOME NEW FIX EVERY MONTH. MY LITTLE GIRL ONLY TURNS TEN ONCE.

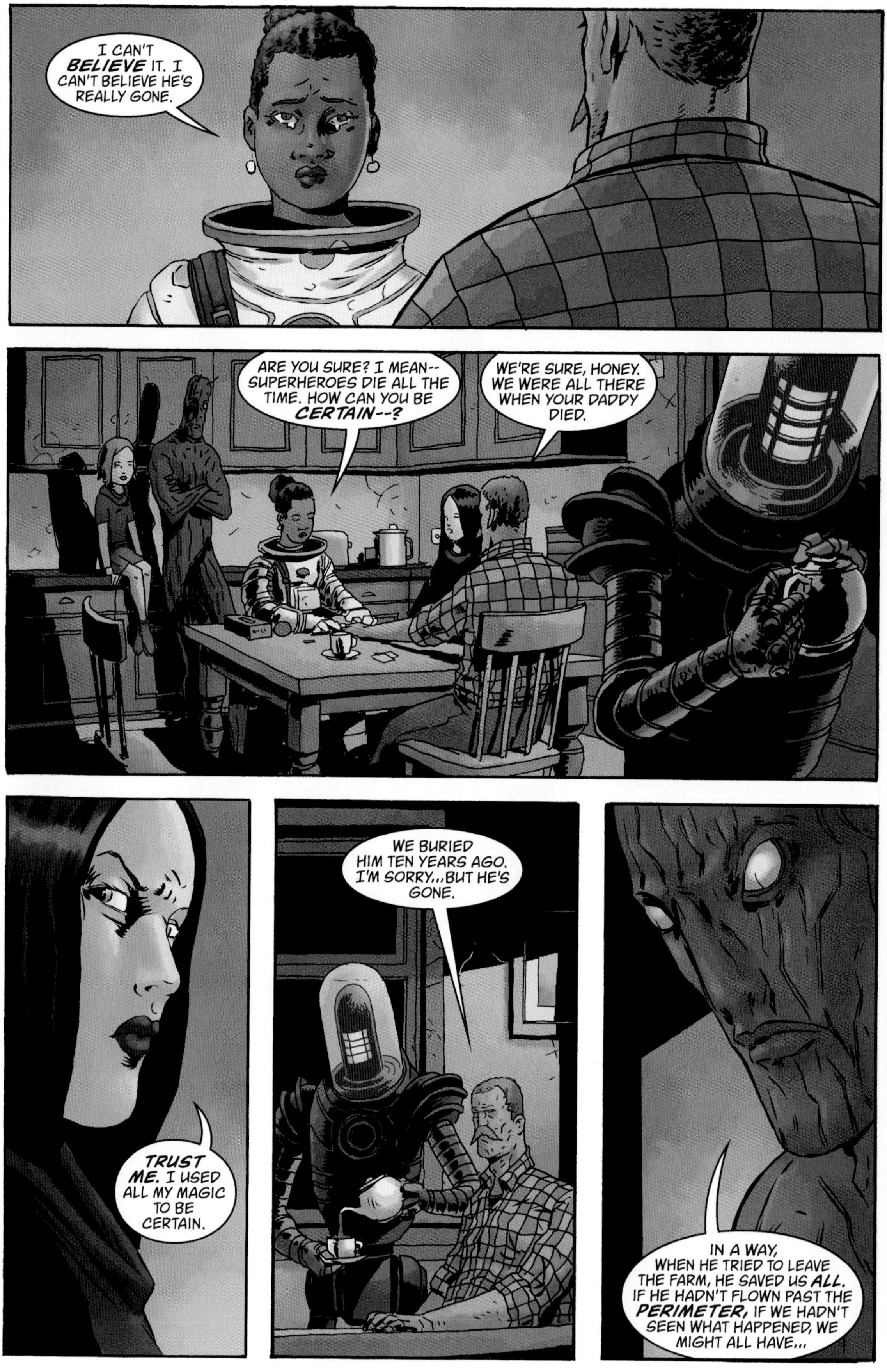
I CAN'T *BELIEVE* IT. I CAN'T BELIEVE HE'S REALLY GONE.
ARE YOU SURE? I MEAN-- SUPERHEROES DIE ALL THE TIME. HOW CAN YOU BE *CERTAIN--?*
WE'RE SURE, HONEY. WE WERE ALL THERE WHEN YOUR DADDY DIED.
TRUST ME. I USED ALL MY MAGIC TO BE CERTAIN.
WE BURIED HIM TEN YEARS AGO. I'M SORRY...BUT HE'S GONE.
IN A WAY, WHEN HE TRIED TO LEAVE THE FARM, HE SAVED US *ALL.* IF HE HADN'T FLOWN PAST THE *PERIMETER,* IF WE HADN'T SEEN WHAT HAPPENED, WE MIGHT ALL HAVE...

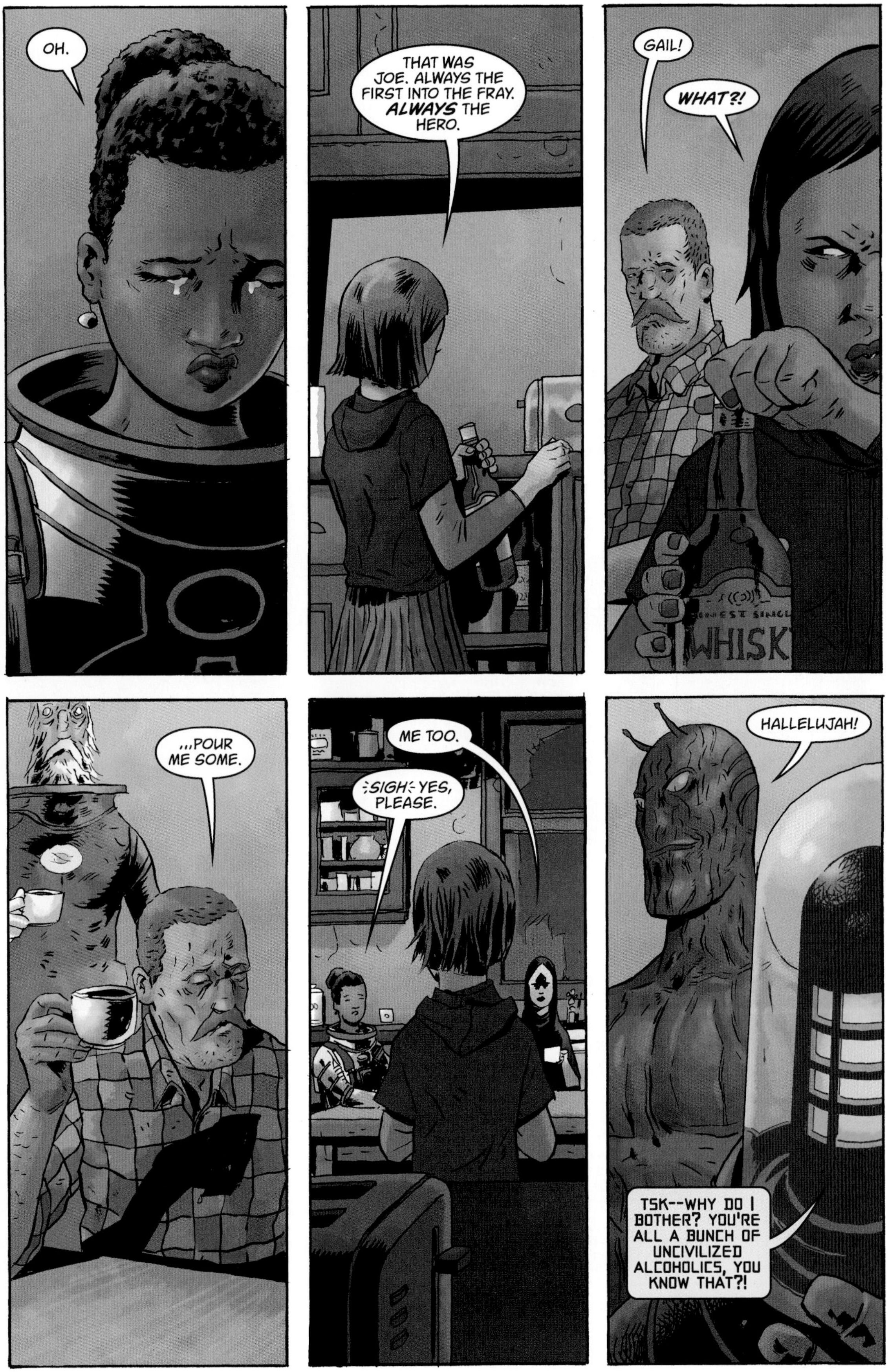
OH.
THAT WAS JOE. ALWAYS THE FIRST INTO THE FRAY. ALWAYS THE HERO.
GAIL!
WHAT?!
...POUR ME SOME.
ME TOO.
SIGH YES, PLEASE.
HALLELUJAH!
TSK--WHY DO I BOTHER? YOU'RE ALL A BUNCH OF UNCIVILIZED ALCOHOLICS, YOU KNOW THAT?!

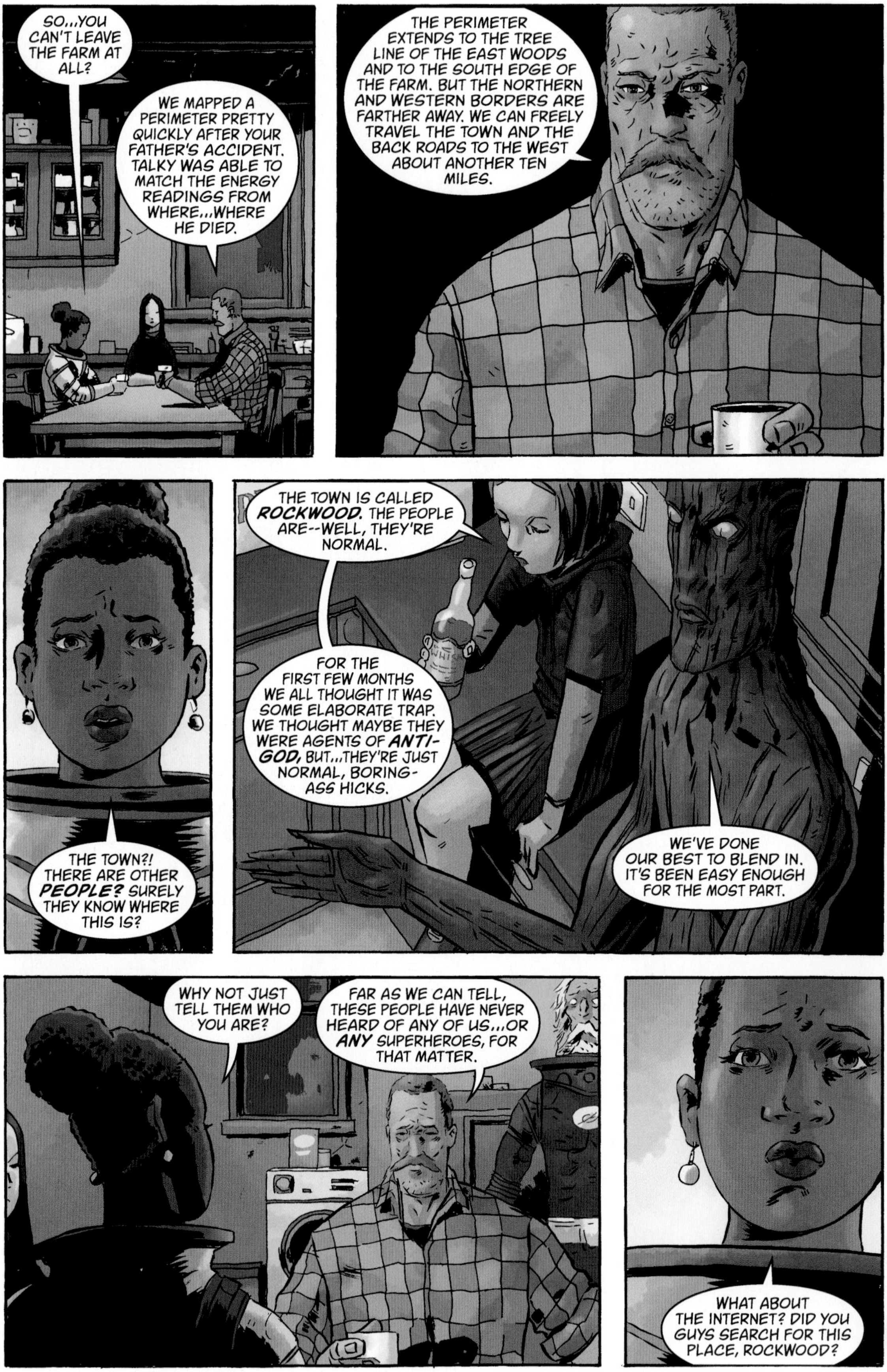
SO...YOU CAN'T LEAVE THE FARM AT ALL?
WE MAPPED A PERIMETER PRETTY QUICKLY AFTER YOUR FATHER'S ACCIDENT. TALKY WAS ABLE TO MATCH THE ENERGY READINGS FROM WHERE...WHERE HE DIED.
THE PERIMETER EXTENDS TO THE TREE LINE OF THE EAST WOODS AND TO THE SOUTH EDGE OF THE FARM. BUT THE NORTHERN AND WESTERN BORDERS ARE FARTHER AWAY. WE CAN FREELY TRAVEL THE TOWN AND THE BACK ROADS TO THE WEST ABOUT ANOTHER TEN MILES.
THE TOWN?! THERE ARE OTHER PEOPLE? SURELY THEY KNOW WHERE THIS IS?
THE TOWN IS CALLED ROCKWOOD. THE PEOPLE ARE--WELL, THEY'RE NORMAL.
FOR THE FIRST FEW MONTHS WE ALL THOUGHT IT WAS SOME ELABORATE TRAP. WE THOUGHT MAYBE THEY WERE AGENTS OF ANTI-GOD, BUT...THEY'RE JUST NORMAL, BORING-ASS HICKS.
WE'VE DONE OUR BEST TO BLEND IN. IT'S BEEN EASY ENOUGH FOR THE MOST PART.
WHY NOT JUST TELL THEM WHO YOU ARE?
FAR AS WE CAN TELL, THESE PEOPLE HAVE NEVER HEARD OF ANY OF US...OR ANY SUPERHEROES, FOR THAT MATTER.
WHAT ABOUT THE INTERNET? DID YOU GUYS SEARCH FOR THIS PLACE, ROCKWOOD?

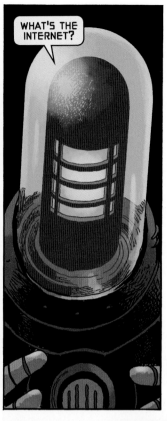

WHAT'S THE INTERNET?

ARE YOU JOKING, TALKY? OH BOY...THE WORLD HAS CHANGED A BIT SINCE THE EVENT, GUYS.

YOU DON'T KNOW HOW RELIEVED I AM JUST TO HEAR THE WORLD'S STILL *THERE!* AFTER WE BEAT ANTI-GOD IN SPIRAL...WELL, THERE WAS A FLASH OF WHITE *LIGHT,* THEN WE WERE HERE.

I WAS SO WORRIED IT WAS THE END OF *EVERYTHING.* I ADMIT, ONE OF MY THEORIES WAS THAT THIS WAS--SOUNDS STUPID TO SAY IT NOW--BUT THAT THIS WAS *HEAVEN.* THAT WE'D ALL *DIED.*

YOU REALLY THINK THIS FUCKING DUMP IS HEAVEN, ABE? MORE LIKE *HELL.*

LET'S NOT BE OVERLY HARSH...MAYBE PURGATORY.

NO. THE WORLD IS STILL THERE. *THAT* MUCH I AM SURE OF.

YOU ARE LIVING PROOF OF THAT, LUCY.

I--I WANT TO SEE WHERE YOU BURIED HIM...

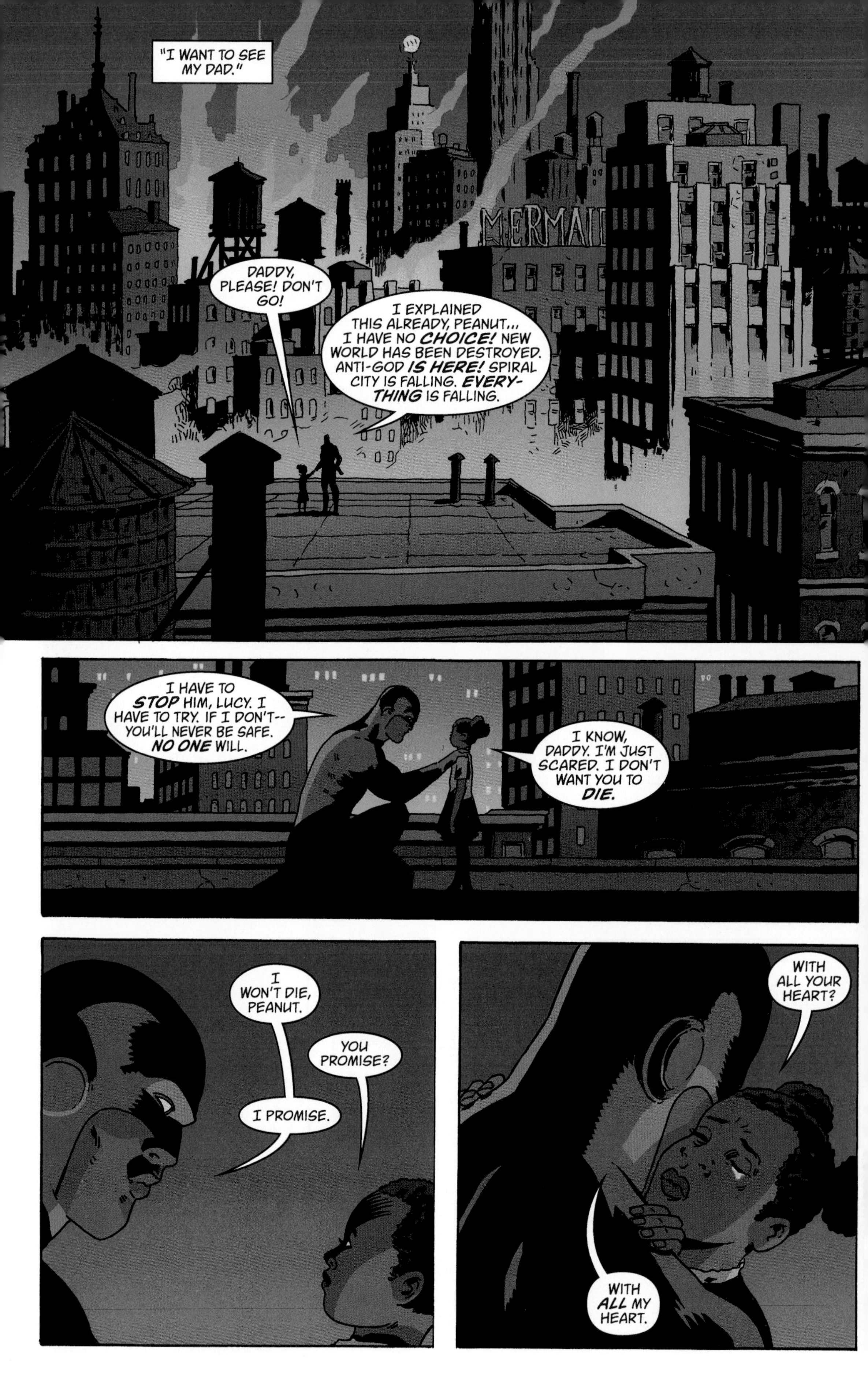
"I WANT TO SEE MY DAD."
MERMAID
DADDY, PLEASE! DON'T GO!
I EXPLAINED THIS ALREADY, PEANUT... I HAVE NO CHOICE! NEW WORLD HAS BEEN DESTROYED. ANTI-GOD IS HERE! SPIRAL CITY IS FALLING. EVERY-THING IS FALLING.
I HAVE TO STOP HIM, LUCY. I HAVE TO TRY. IF I DON'T-- YOU'LL NEVER BE SAFE. NO ONE WILL.
I KNOW, DADDY. I'M JUST SCARED. I DON'T WANT YOU TO DIE.
I WON'T DIE, PEANUT.
YOU PROMISE?
I PROMISE.
WITH ALL YOUR HEART?
WITH ALL MY HEART.

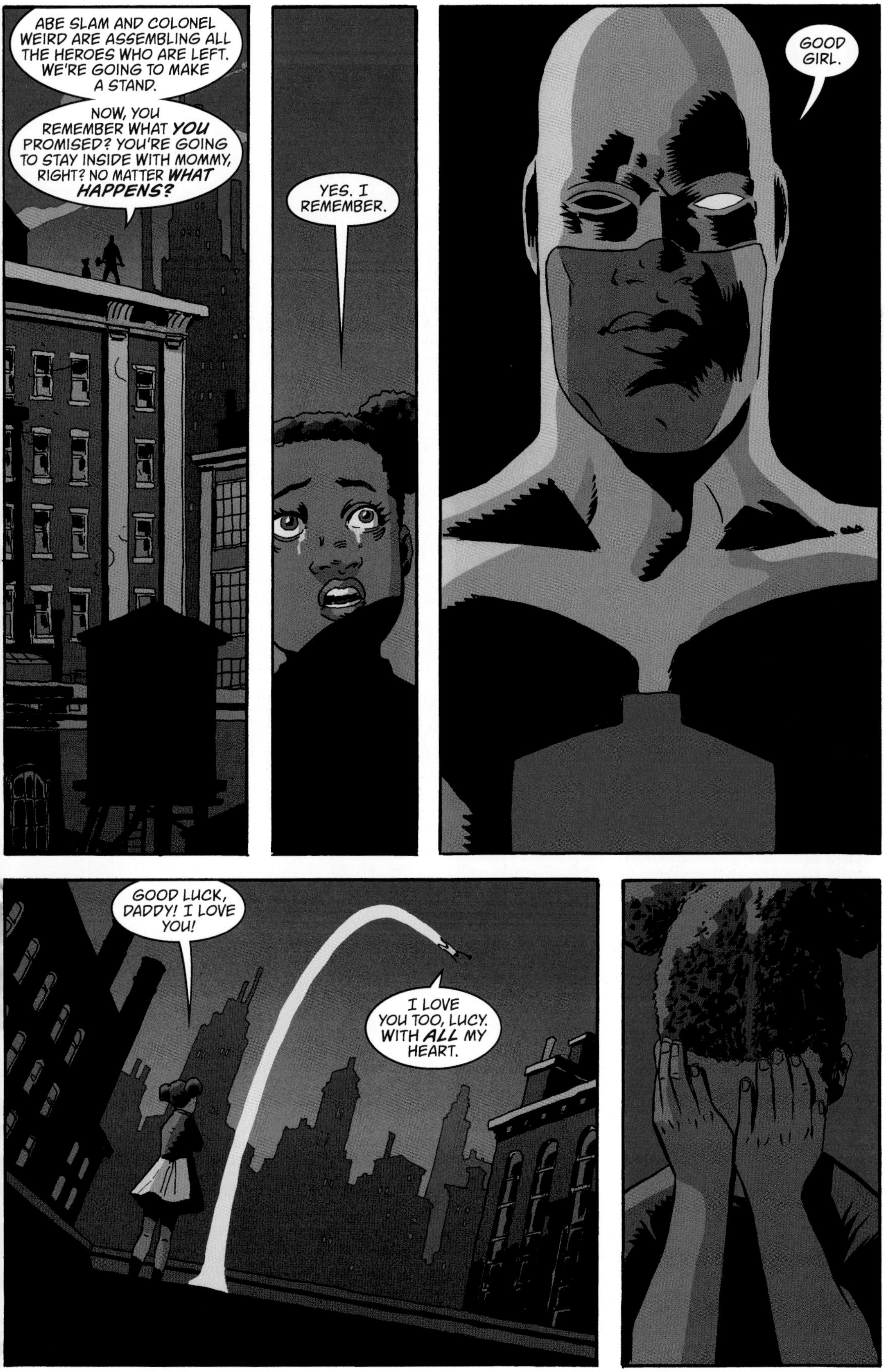
ABE SLAM AND COLONEL WEIRD ARE ASSEMBLING ALL THE HEROES WHO ARE LEFT. WE'RE GOING TO MAKE A STAND.
NOW, YOU REMEMBER WHAT *YOU* PROMISED? YOU'RE GOING TO STAY INSIDE WITH MOMMY, RIGHT? NO MATTER *WHAT HAPPENS?*
YES. I REMEMBER.
GOOD GIRL.
GOOD LUCK, DADDY! I LOVE YOU!
I LOVE YOU TOO, LUCY. WITH *ALL* MY HEART.

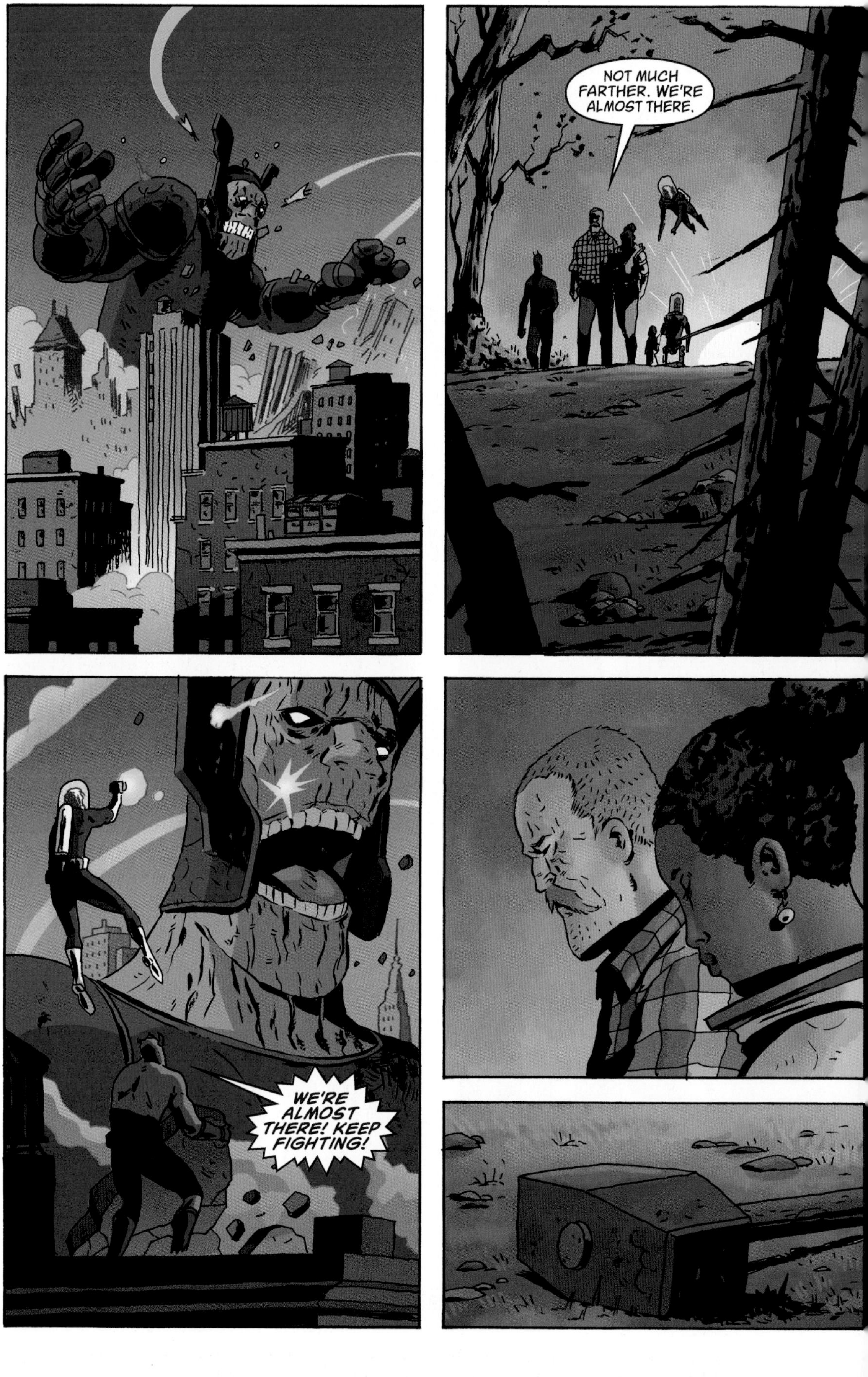
NOT MUCH FARTHER. WE'RE ALMOST THERE.
WE'RE ALMOST THERE! KEEP FIGHTING!

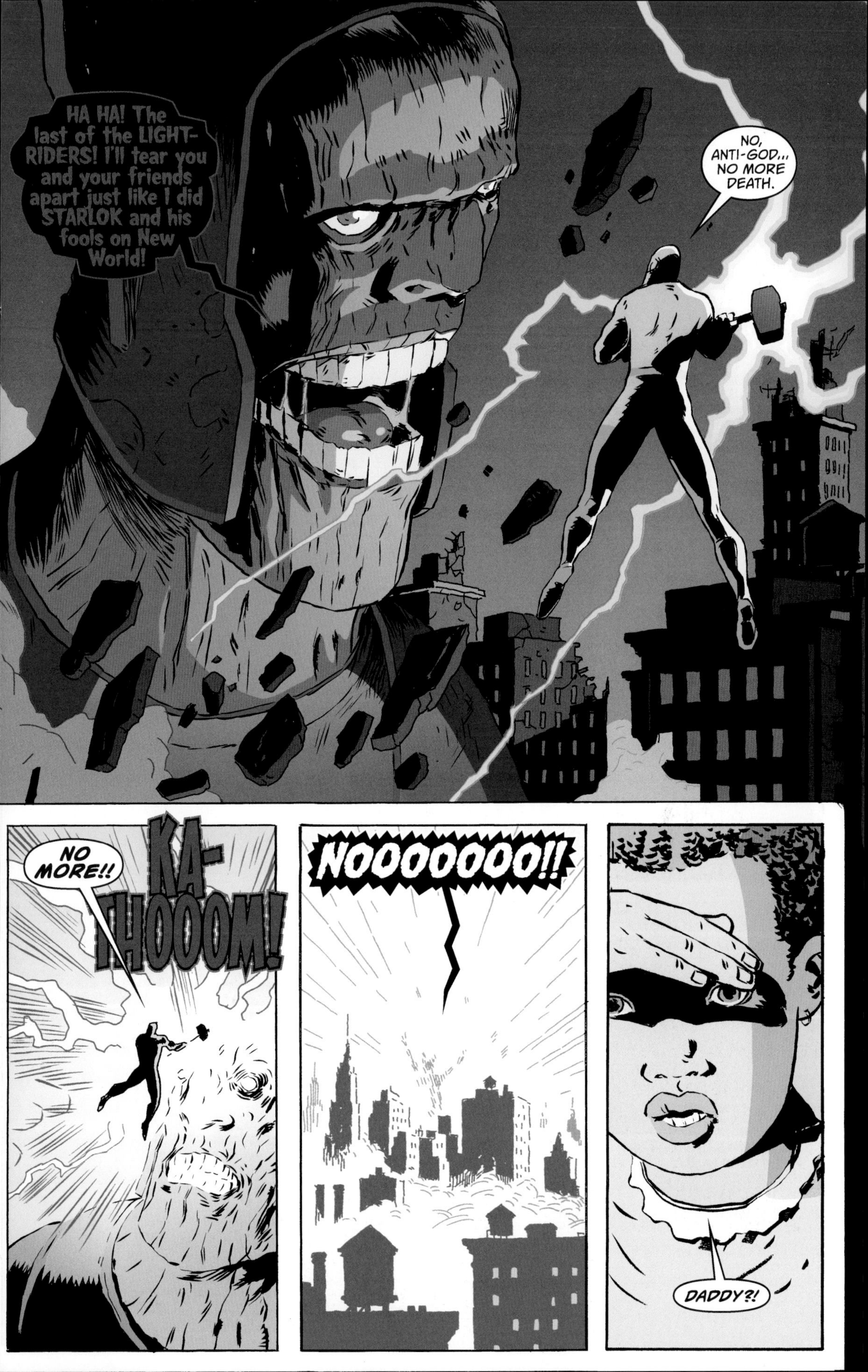
HA HA! The last of the LIGHT-RIDERS! I'll tear you and your friends apart just like I did STARLOK and his fools on New World!
NO, ANTI-GOD... NO MORE DEATH.
NO MORE!!
KA-THOOOM!
NOOOOOOO!!
DADDY?!

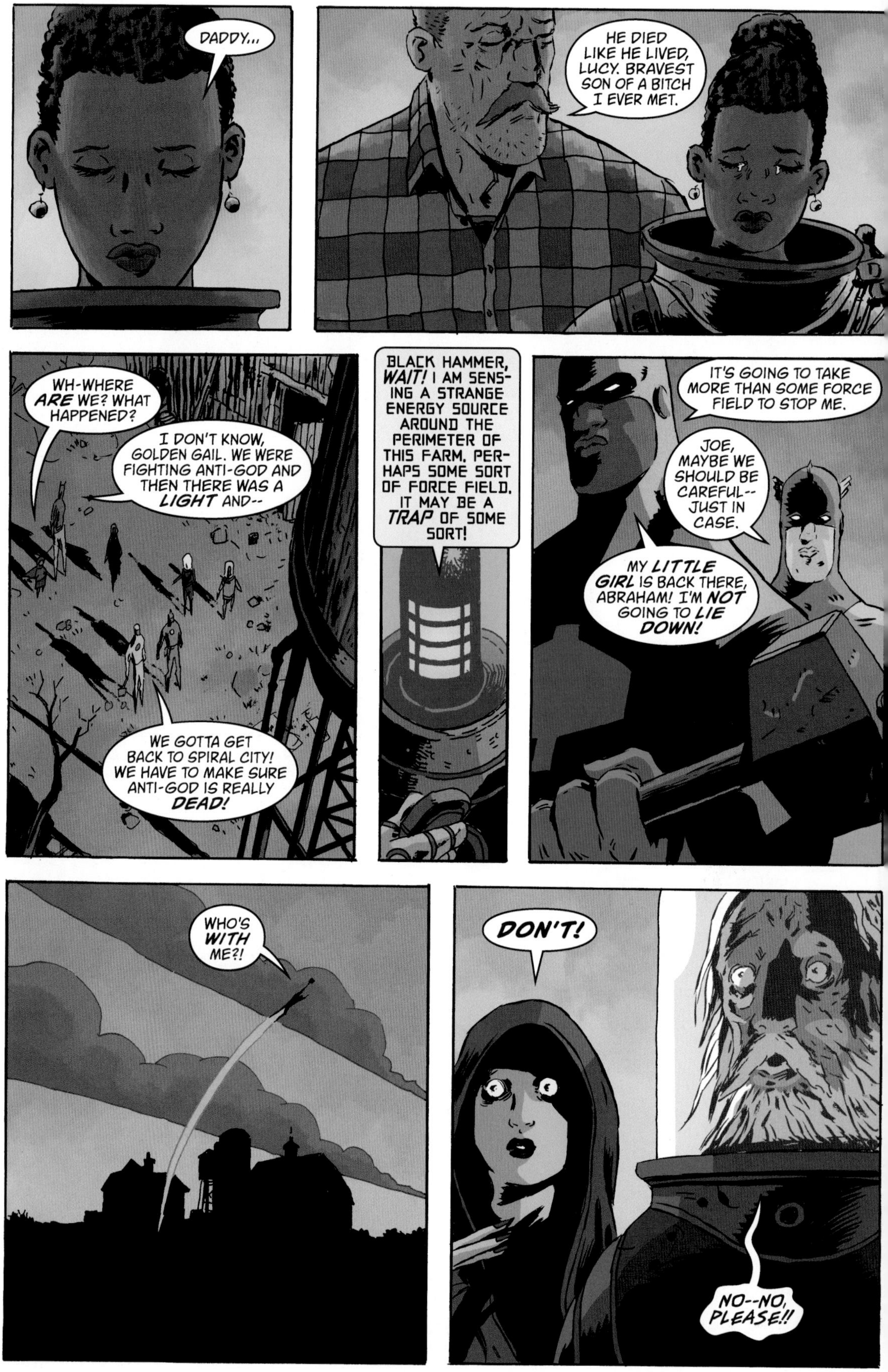
DADDY...
HE DIED LIKE HE LIVED, LUCY. BRAVEST SON OF A BITCH I EVER MET.
WH-WHERE ARE WE? WHAT HAPPENED?
I DON'T KNOW, GOLDEN GAIL. WE WERE FIGHTING ANTI-GOD AND THEN THERE WAS A LIGHT AND--
WE GOTTA GET BACK TO SPIRAL CITY! WE HAVE TO MAKE SURE ANTI-GOD IS REALLY DEAD!
BLACK HAMMER, WAIT! I AM SENSING A STRANGE ENERGY SOURCE AROUND THE PERIMETER OF THIS FARM. PERHAPS SOME SORT OF FORCE FIELD. IT MAY BE A TRAP OF SOME SORT!
IT'S GOING TO TAKE MORE THAN SOME FORCE FIELD TO STOP ME.
JOE, MAYBE WE SHOULD BE CAREFUL-- JUST IN CASE.
MY LITTLE GIRL IS BACK THERE, ABRAHAM! I'M NOT GOING TO LIE DOWN!
WHO'S WITH ME?!
DON'T!
NO--NO, PLEASE!!

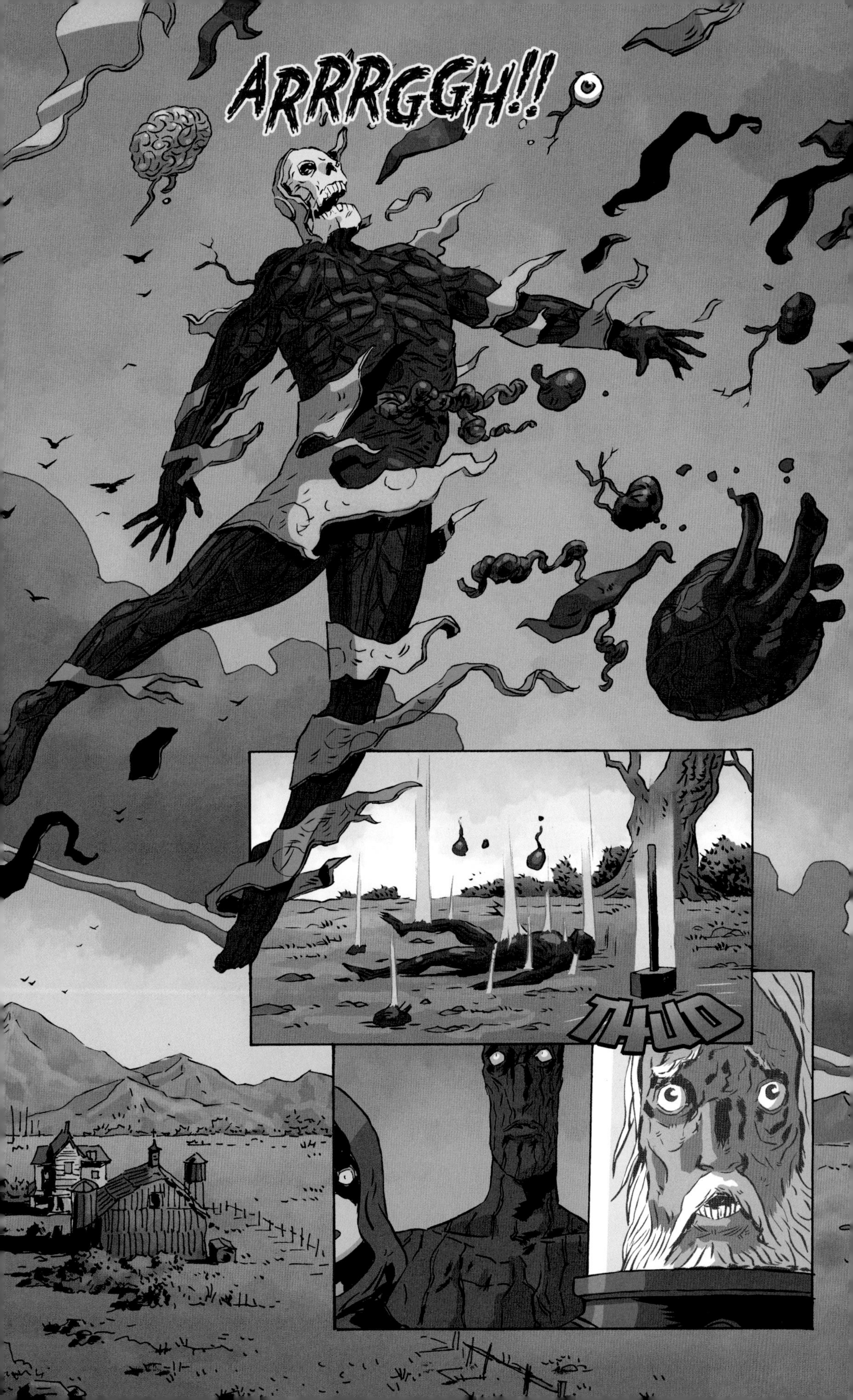
ARRRGGH!!
THUD

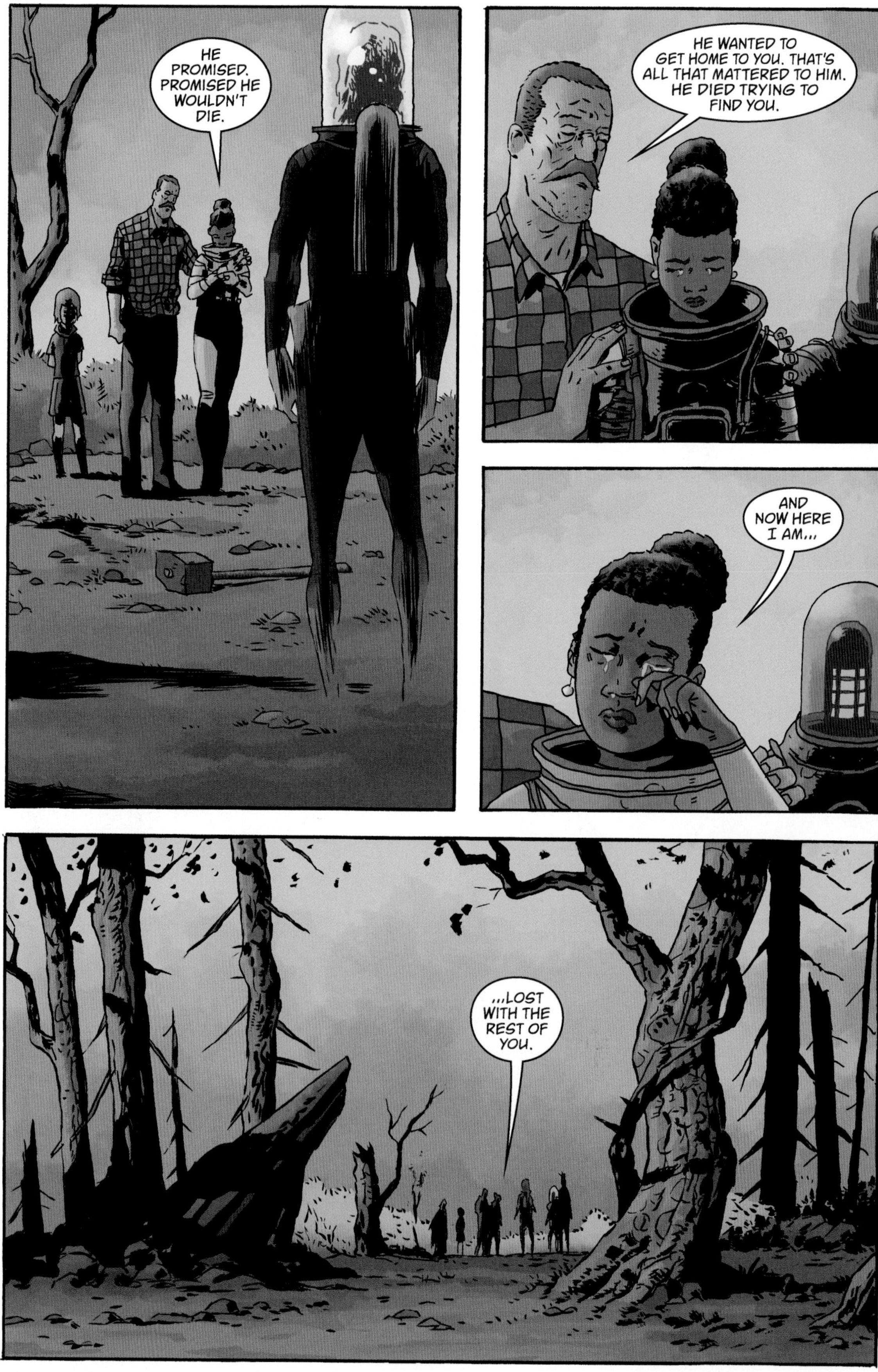
HE PROMISED. PROMISED HE WOULDN'T DIE.
HE WANTED TO GET HOME TO YOU. THAT'S ALL THAT MATTERED TO HIM. HE DIED TRYING TO FIND YOU.
AND NOW HERE I AM...
...LOST WITH THE REST OF YOU.

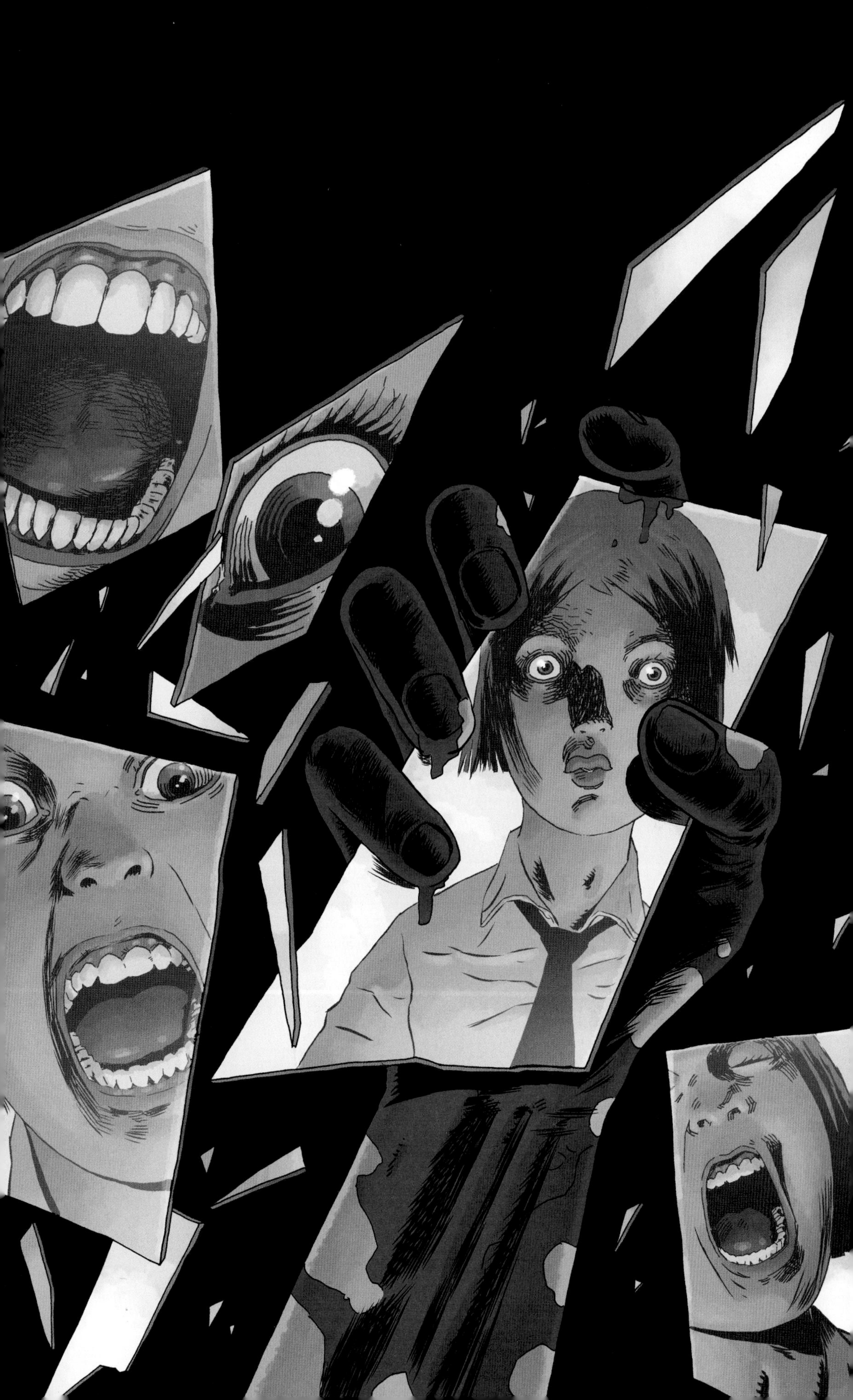

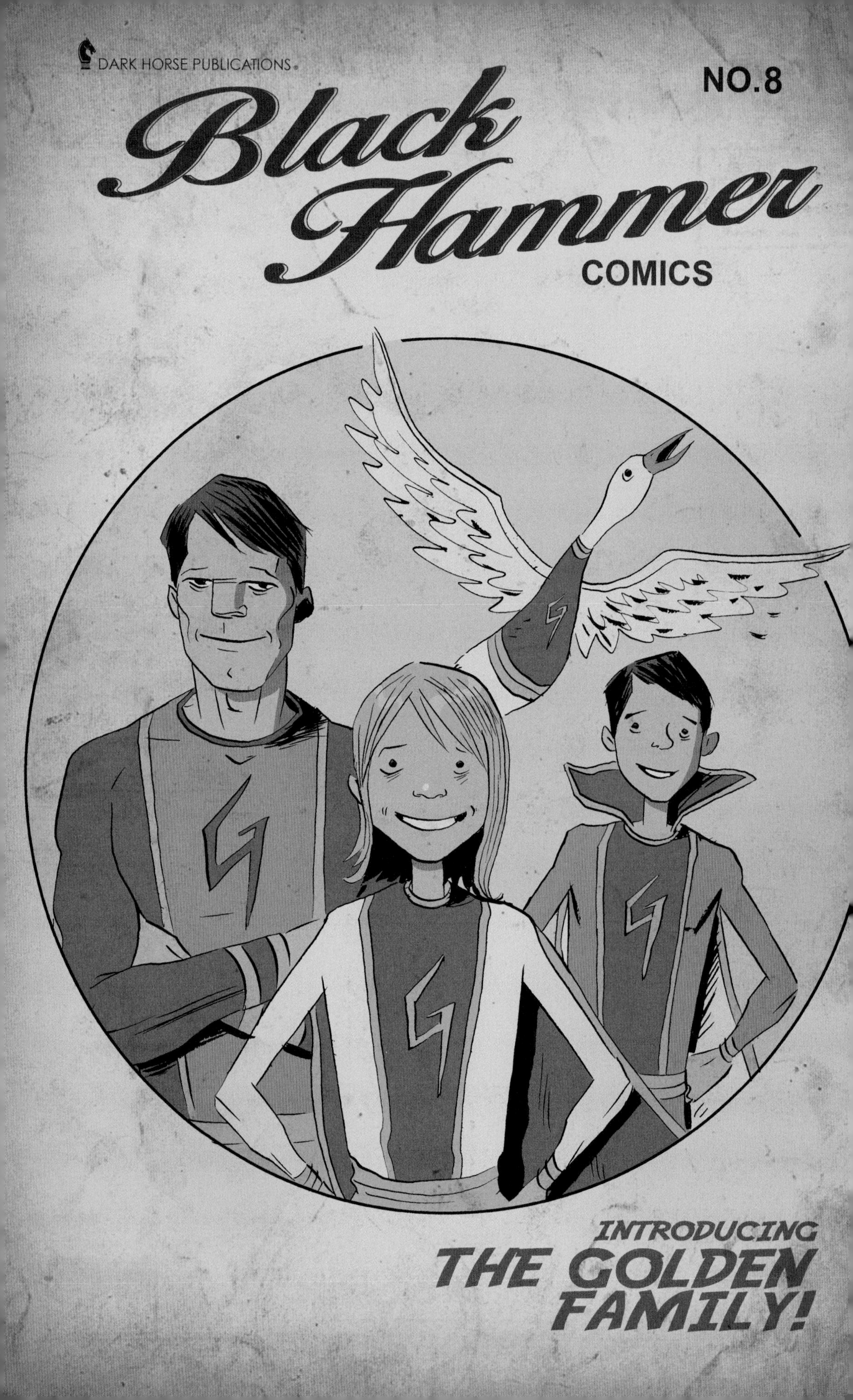

DARK HORSE PUBLICATIONS
NO.8
Black Hammer
COMICS
INTRODUCING
THE GOLDEN FAMILY!

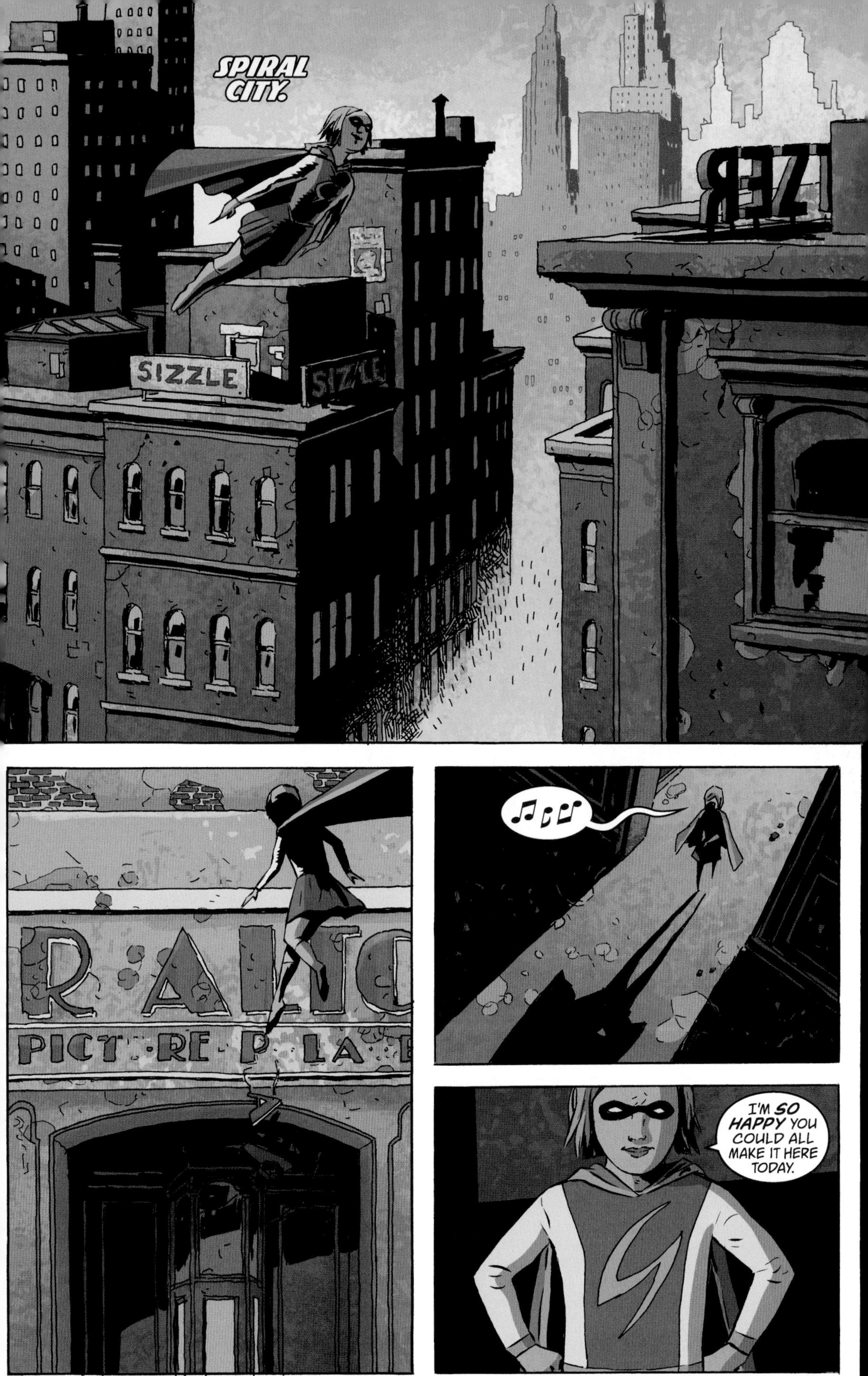
SPIRAL CITY.
SIZZLE
SIZZLE
ZER
R A IO
PICT RE P LA
♫♪♫
I'M SO HAPPY YOU COULD ALL MAKE IT HERE TODAY.

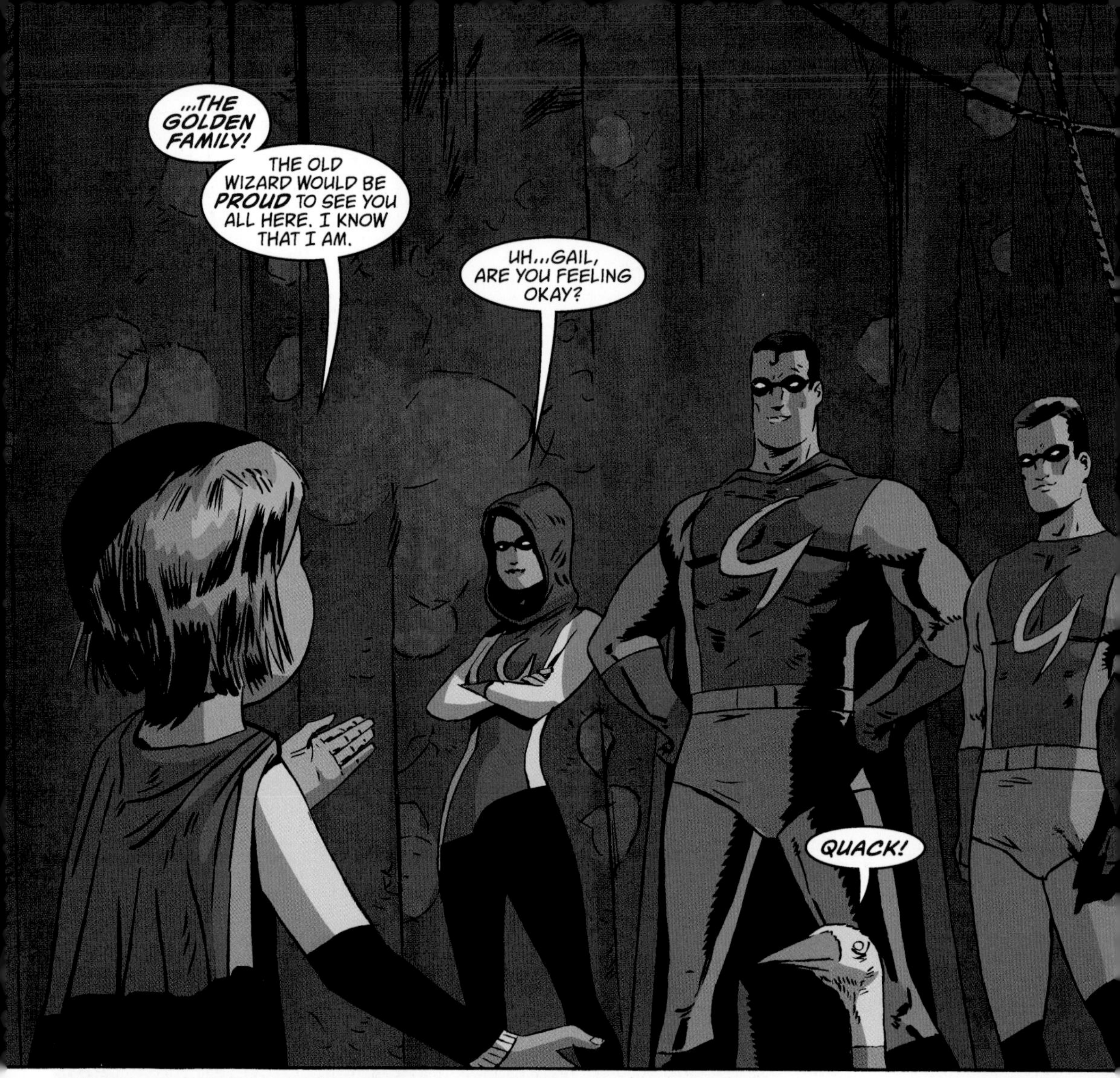
...THE GOLDEN FAMILY!
THE OLD WIZARD WOULD BE PROUD TO SEE YOU ALL HERE. I KNOW THAT I AM.
UH...GAIL, ARE YOU FEELING OKAY?
QUACK!

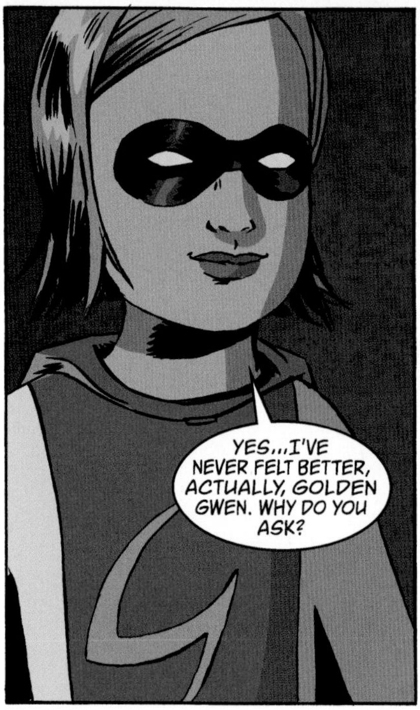
YES...I'VE NEVER FELT BETTER, ACTUALLY, GOLDEN GWEN. WHY DO YOU ASK?

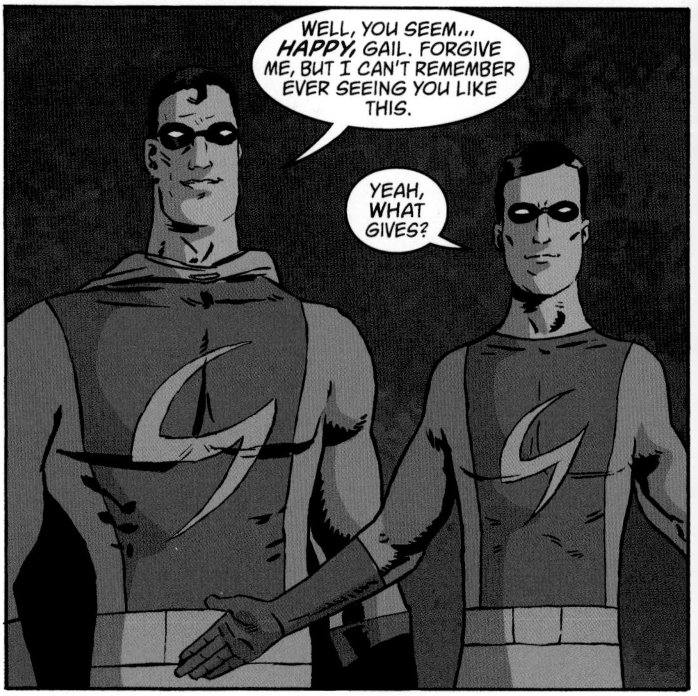
WELL, YOU SEEM... HAPPY, GAIL. FORGIVE ME, BUT I CAN'T REMEMBER EVER SEEING YOU LIKE THIS.
YEAH, WHAT GIVES?

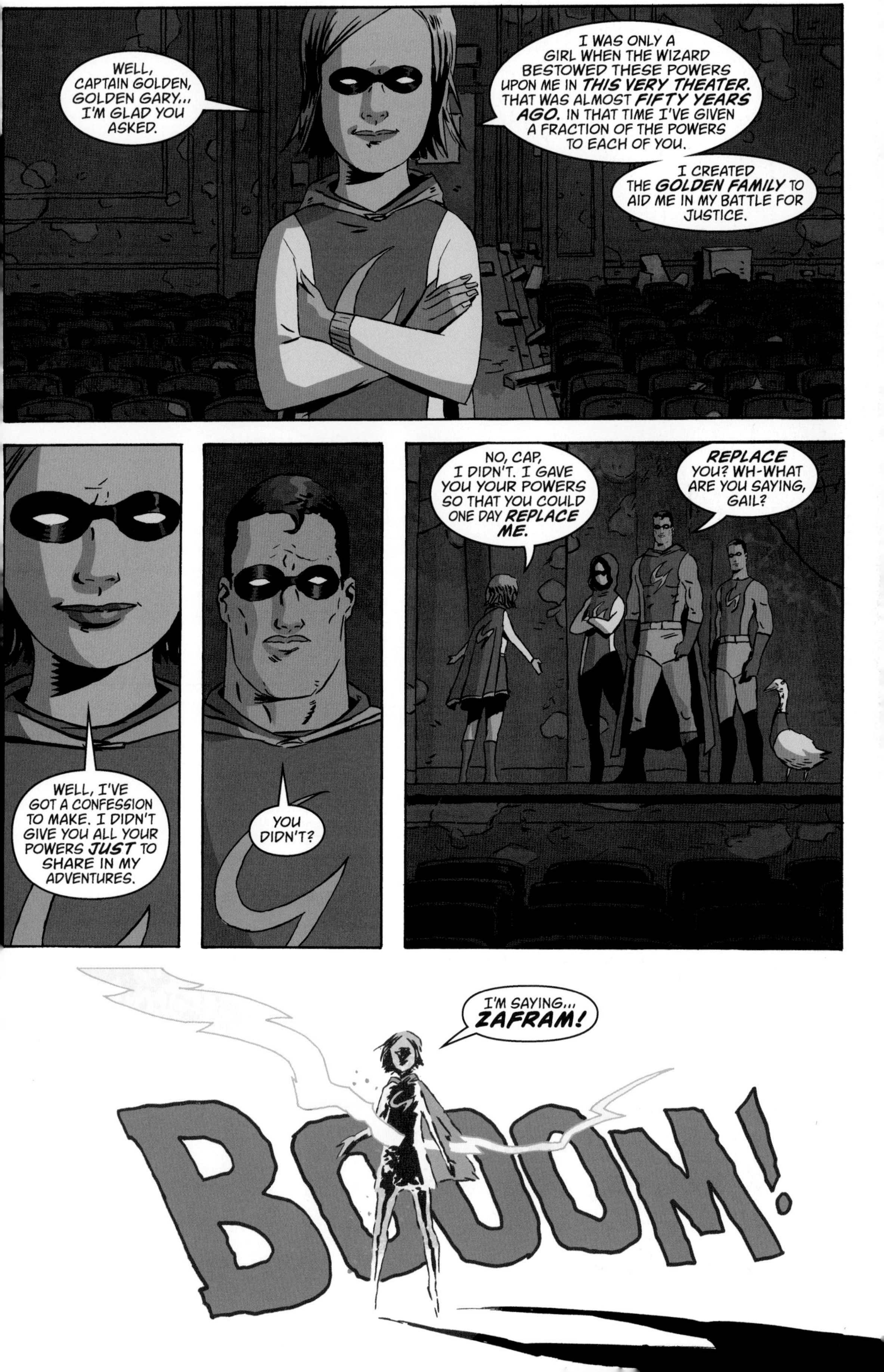
WELL, CAPTAIN GOLDEN, GOLDEN GARY... I'M GLAD YOU ASKED.
I WAS ONLY A GIRL WHEN THE WIZARD BESTOWED THESE POWERS UPON ME IN **THIS VERY THEATER.** THAT WAS ALMOST **FIFTY YEARS AGO.** IN THAT TIME I'VE GIVEN A FRACTION OF THE POWERS TO EACH OF YOU.
I CREATED THE **GOLDEN FAMILY** TO AID ME IN MY BATTLE FOR JUSTICE.
WELL, I'VE GOT A CONFESSION TO MAKE. I DIDN'T GIVE YOU ALL YOUR POWERS **JUST** TO SHARE IN MY ADVENTURES.
YOU DIDN'T?
NO, CAP, I DIDN'T. I GAVE YOU YOUR POWERS SO THAT YOU COULD ONE DAY **REPLACE ME.**
REPLACE YOU? WH-WHAT ARE YOU SAYING, GAIL?
I'M SAYING... **ZAFRAM!**
BOOOM!

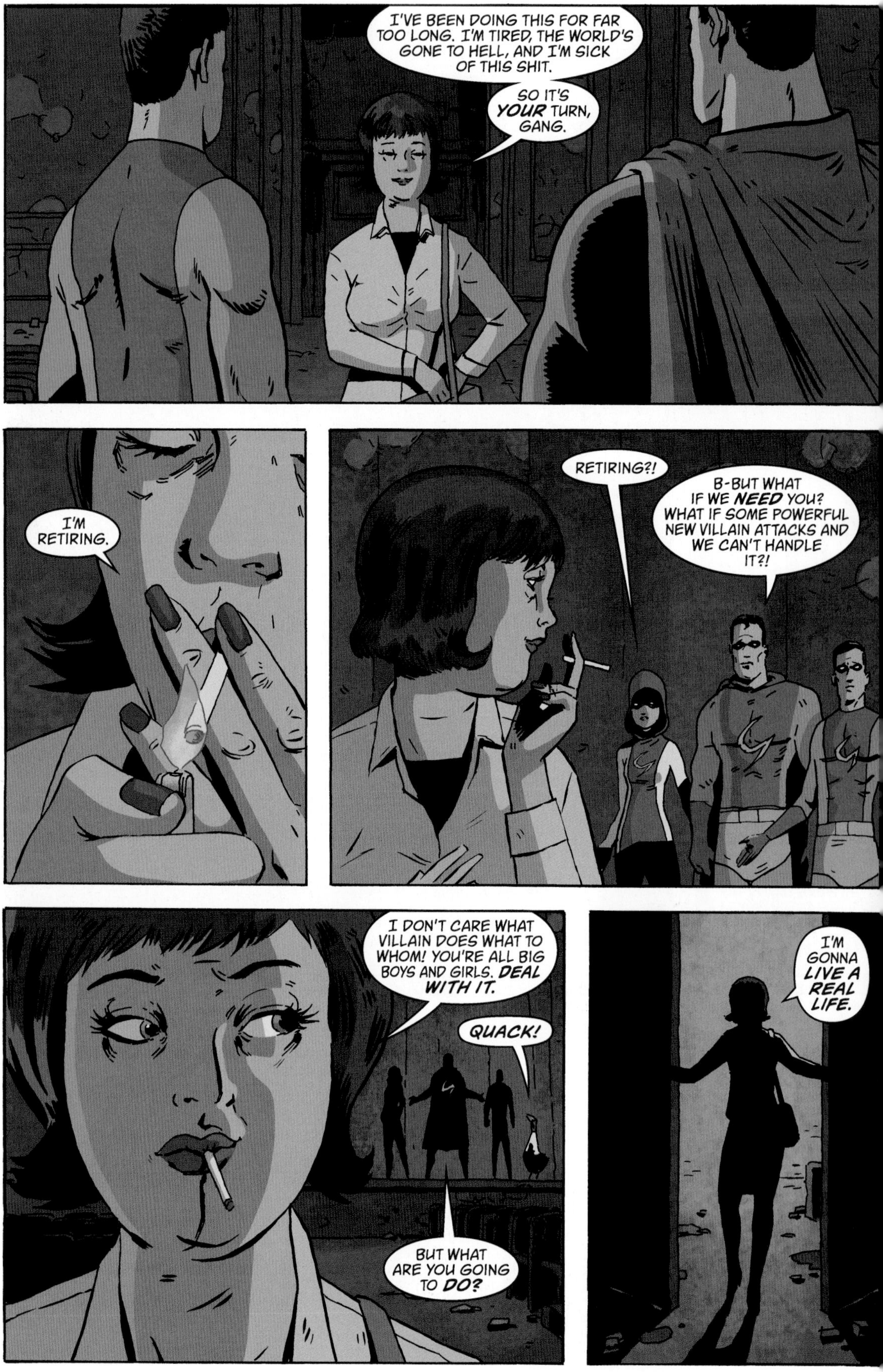
I'VE BEEN DOING THIS FOR FAR TOO LONG. I'M TIRED, THE WORLD'S GONE TO HELL, AND I'M SICK OF THIS SHIT.
SO IT'S YOUR TURN, GANG.
I'M RETIRING.
RETIRING?!
B-BUT WHAT IF WE NEED YOU? WHAT IF SOME POWERFUL NEW VILLAIN ATTACKS AND WE CAN'T HANDLE IT?!
I DON'T CARE WHAT VILLAIN DOES WHAT TO WHOM! YOU'RE ALL BIG BOYS AND GIRLS. DEAL WITH IT.
QUACK!
BUT WHAT ARE YOU GOING TO DO?
I'M GONNA LIVE A REAL LIFE.

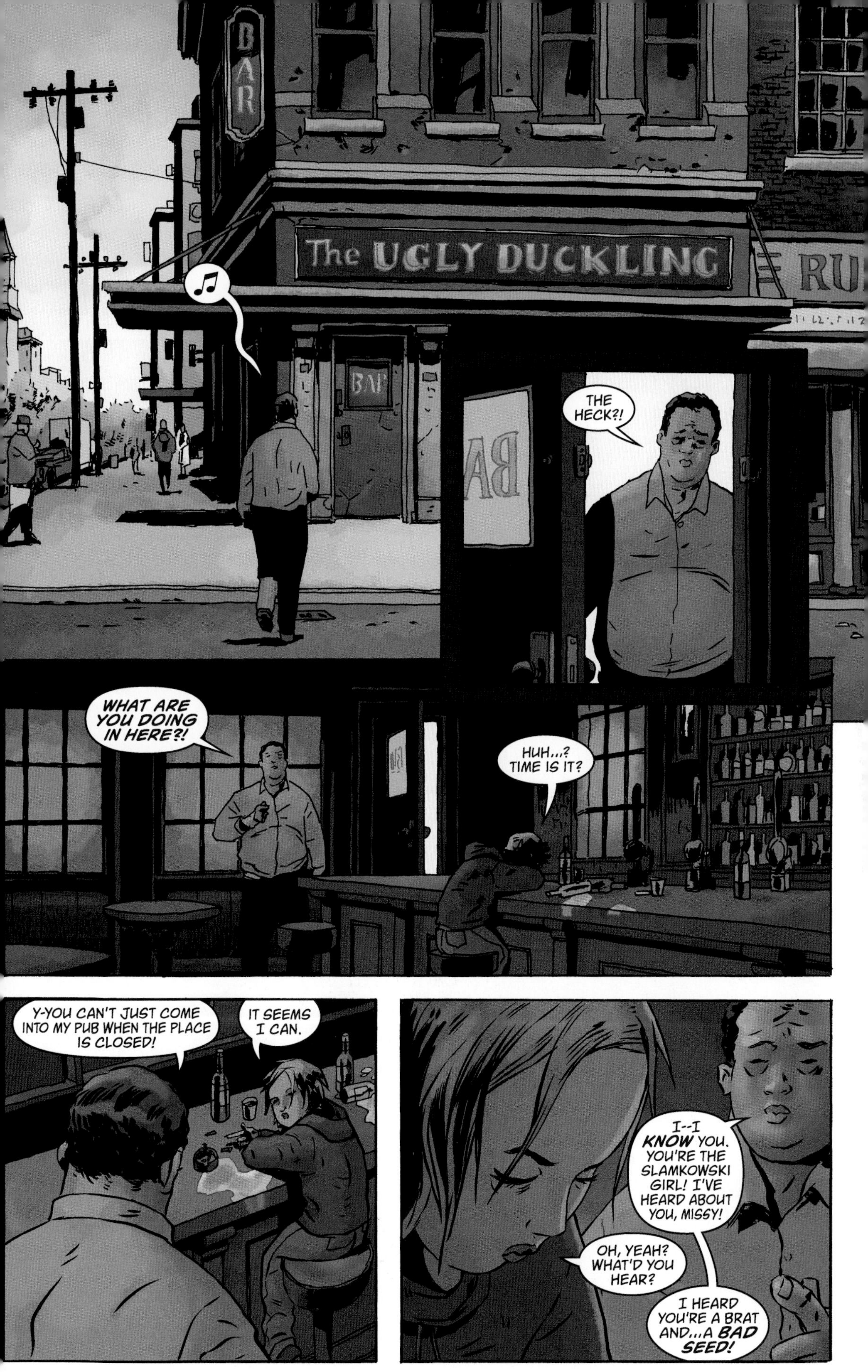
BAR
The UGLY DUCKLING
♫
THE HECK?!
WHAT ARE YOU DOING IN HERE?!
HUH...? TIME IS IT?
Y-YOU CAN'T JUST COME INTO MY PUB WHEN THE PLACE IS CLOSED!
IT SEEMS I CAN.
I--I **KNOW** YOU. YOU'RE THE SLAMKOWSKI GIRL! I'VE HEARD ABOUT YOU, MISSY!
OH, YEAH? WHAT'D YOU HEAR?
I HEARD YOU'RE A BRAT AND...A ***BAD SEED!***

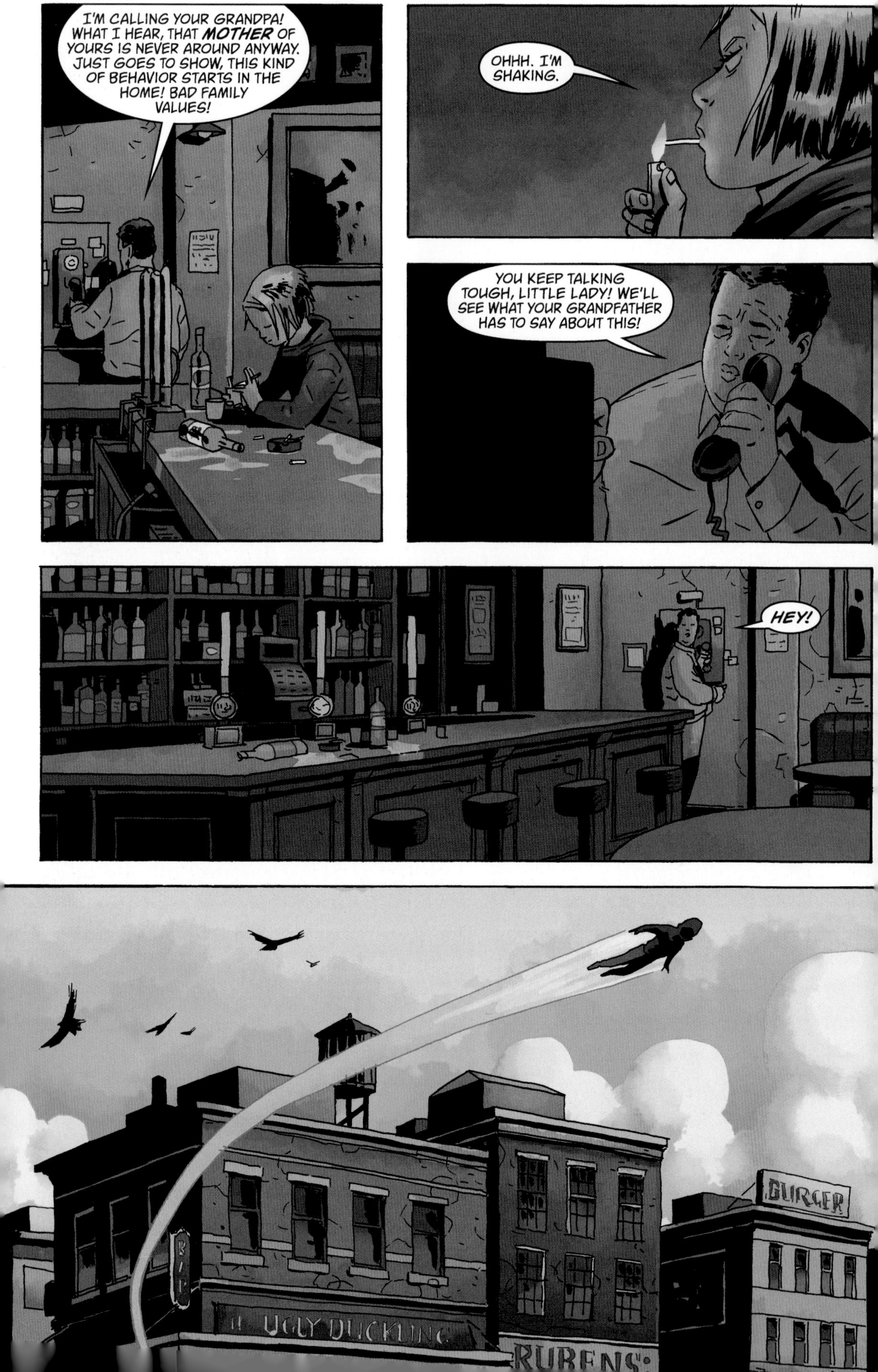
I'M CALLING YOUR GRANDPA! WHAT I HEAR, THAT MOTHER OF YOURS IS NEVER AROUND ANYWAY. JUST GOES TO SHOW, THIS KIND OF BEHAVIOR STARTS IN THE HOME! BAD FAMILY VALUES!
OHHH. I'M SHAKING.
YOU KEEP TALKING TOUGH, LITTLE LADY! WE'LL SEE WHAT YOUR GRANDFATHER HAS TO SAY ABOUT THIS!
HEY!
BURGER
UGLY DUCKLING
RUBENS

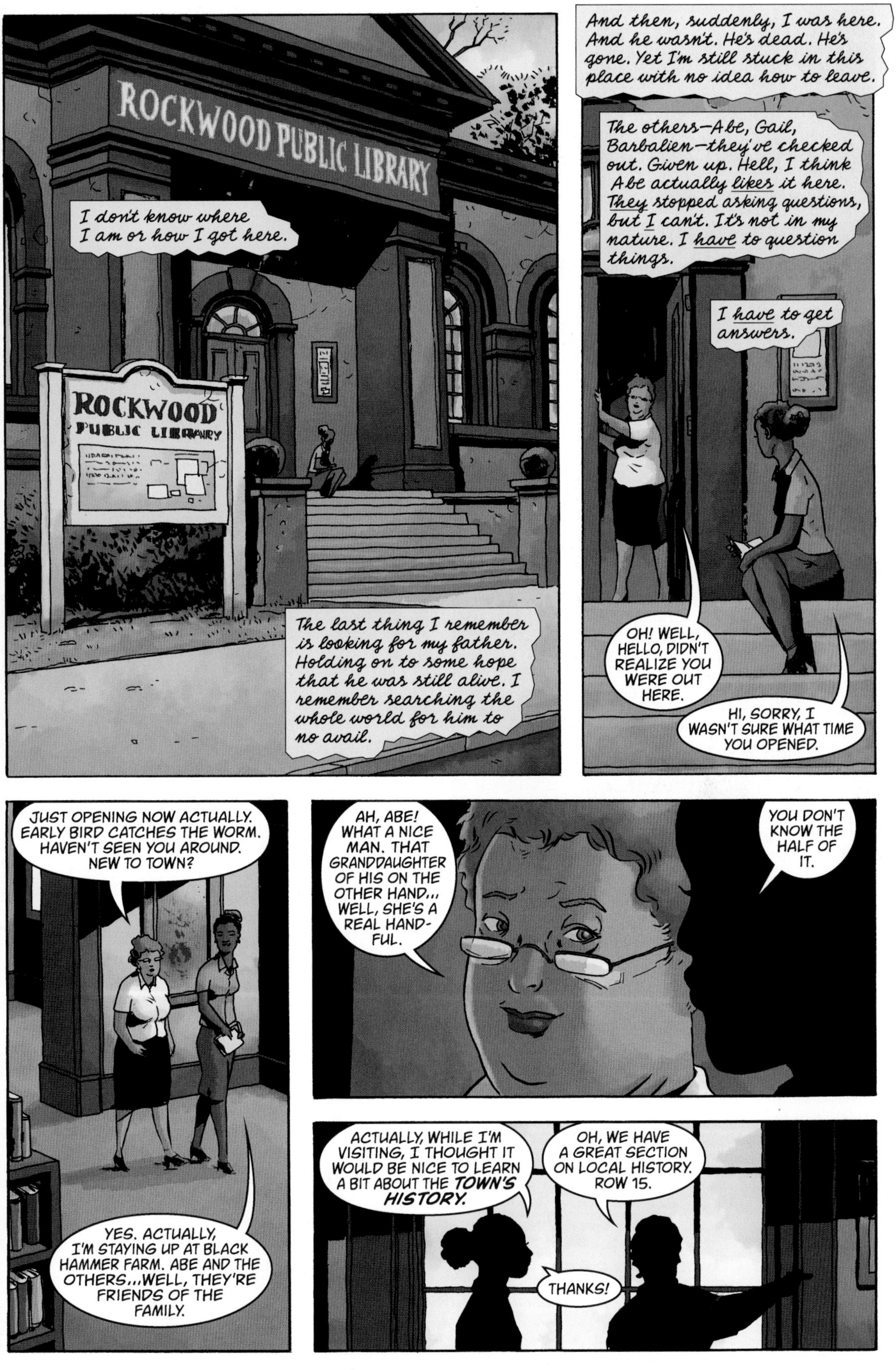
ROCKWOOD PUBLIC LIBRARY
I don't know where I am or how I got here.
ROCKWOOD PUBLIC LIBRARY
The last thing I remember is looking for my father. Holding on to some hope that he was still alive. I remember searching the whole world for him to no avail.
And then, suddenly, I was here. And he wasn't. He's dead. He's gone. Yet I'm still stuck in this place with no idea how to leave.
The others—Abe, Gail, Barbalien—they've checked out. Given up. Hell, I think Abe actually likes it here. They stopped asking questions, but I can't. It's not in my nature. I have to question things.
I have to get answers.
OH! WELL, HELLO, DIDN'T REALIZE YOU WERE OUT HERE.
HI, SORRY, I WASN'T SURE WHAT TIME YOU OPENED.
JUST OPENING NOW ACTUALLY. EARLY BIRD CATCHES THE WORM. HAVEN'T SEEN YOU AROUND. NEW TO TOWN?
YES. ACTUALLY, I'M STAYING UP AT BLACK HAMMER FARM. ABE AND THE OTHERS...WELL, THEY'RE FRIENDS OF THE FAMILY.
AH, ABE! WHAT A NICE MAN. THAT GRANDDAUGHTER OF HIS ON THE OTHER HAND... WELL, SHE'S A REAL HAND-FUL.
YOU DON'T KNOW THE HALF OF IT.
ACTUALLY, WHILE I'M VISITING, I THOUGHT IT WOULD BE NICE TO LEARN A BIT ABOUT THE TOWN'S HISTORY.
OH, WE HAVE A GREAT SECTION ON LOCAL HISTORY. ROW 15.
THANKS!

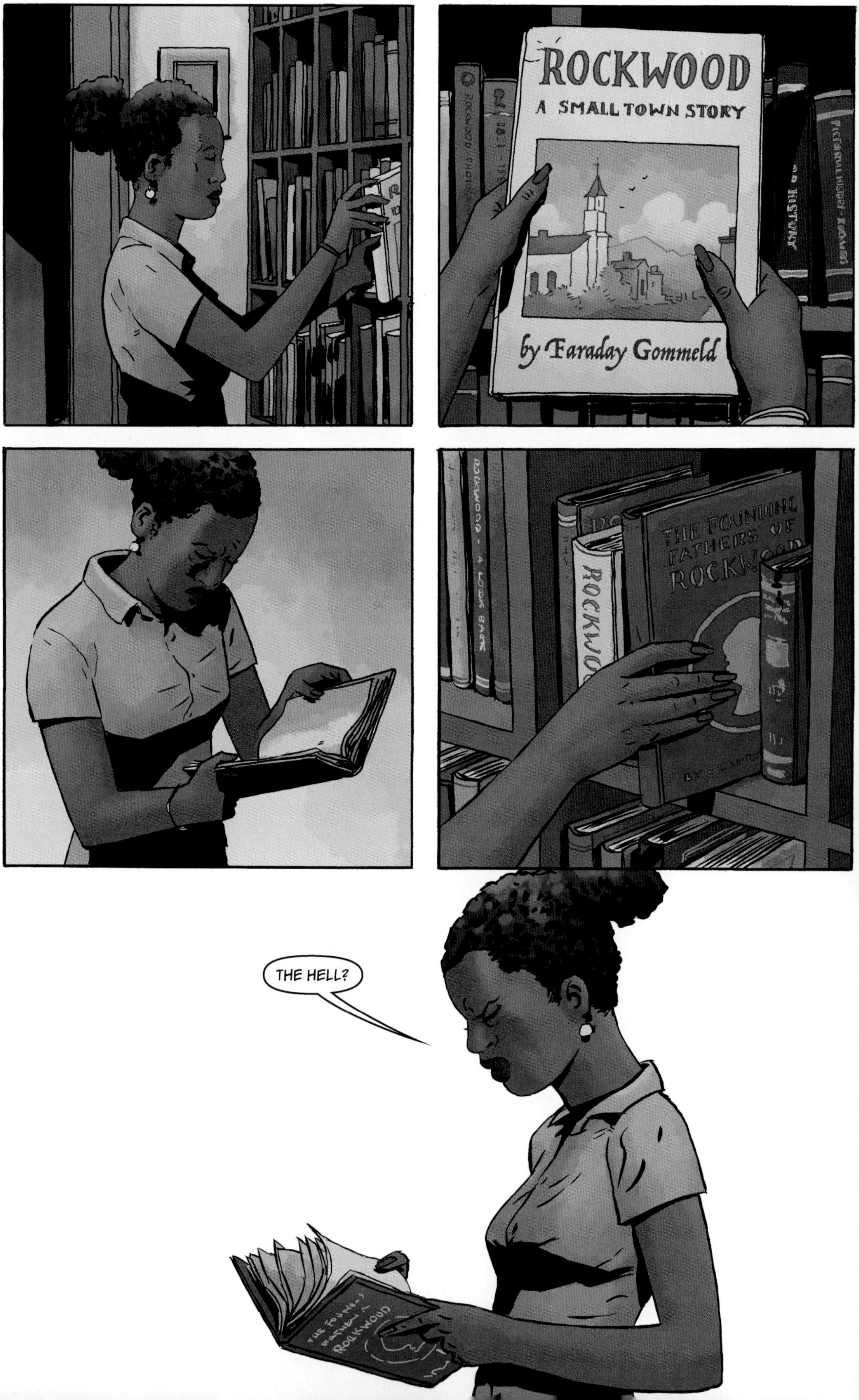
ROCKWOOD
A SMALL TOWN STORY
by Faraday Gommeld
ROCKWOOD - A LOOK BACK
THE HELL?

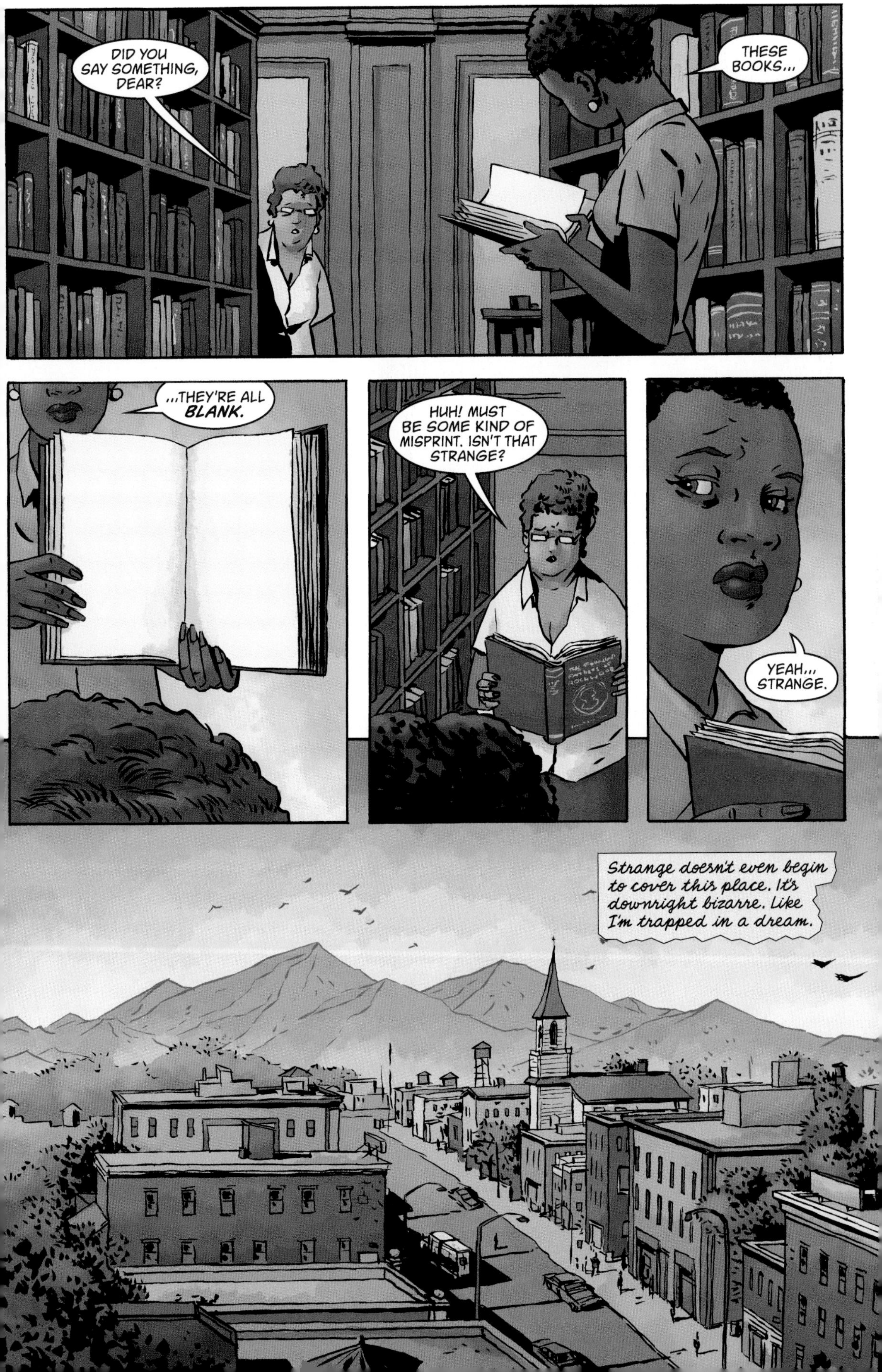
DID YOU SAY SOMETHING, DEAR?
THESE BOOKS...
...THEY'RE ALL BLANK.
HUH! MUST BE SOME KIND OF MISPRINT. ISN'T THAT STRANGE?
YEAH... STRANGE.
Strange doesn't even begin to cover this place. It's downright bizarre. Like I'm trapped in a dream.

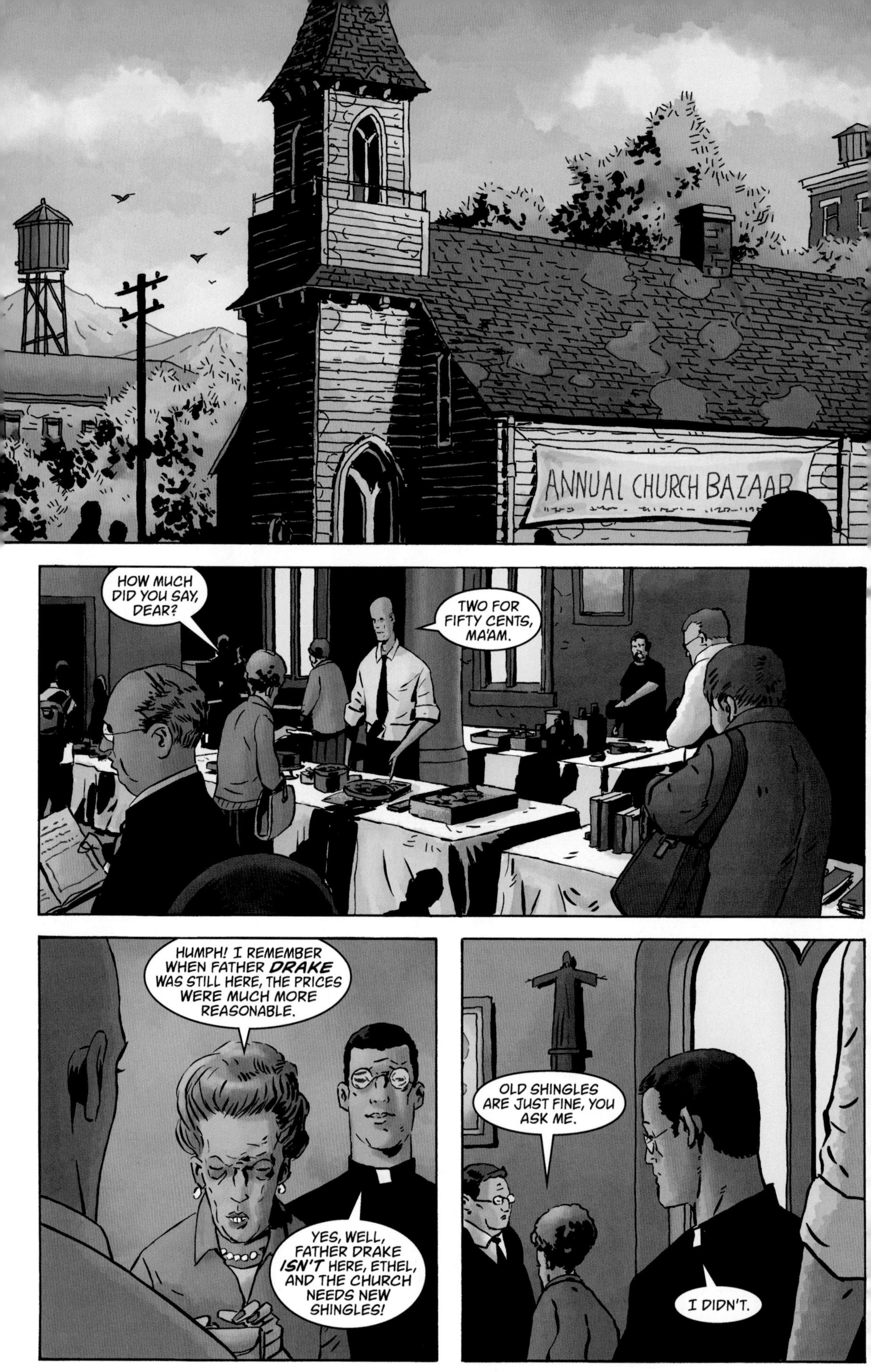
ANNUAL CHURCH BAZAAR
HOW MUCH DID YOU SAY, DEAR?
TWO FOR FIFTY CENTS, MA'AM.
HUMPH! I REMEMBER WHEN FATHER DRAKE WAS STILL HERE, THE PRICES WERE MUCH MORE REASONABLE.
YES, WELL, FATHER DRAKE ISN'T HERE, ETHEL, AND THE CHURCH NEEDS NEW SHINGLES!
OLD SHINGLES ARE JUST FINE, YOU ASK ME.
I DIDN'T.

YOU'RE TERRIBLE.

AH, SHE CAN TAKE IT. SHE'S A TOUGH OLD BIRD. BESIDES, SOME OF THESE OLD-TIMERS ARE SO SET IN THEIR WAYS. SO OLD FASHIONED. IT'S GOOD TO SHAKE THE TREE A BIT. WAKE THEM UP.

SPEAKING OF WHICH, I WANTED TO THANK YOU AGAIN FOR HELPING OUT, MARK.

OF COURSE. IT'S NOTHING.

MAYBE, BUT GETTING TO KNOW YOU HAS BEEN REALLY GOOD FOR ME. WHEN I CAME TO THIS PARISH A MONTH AGO, I WAS OUTNUMBERED. THE NEW GUY...

...IT'S NICE TO HAVE SOME-ONE ELSE TO TALK TO. I'M GLAD YOU'RE HERE, MARK.

I--

I'M GLAD, TOO.

STOP BY THE RECTORY FOR A DRINK LATER?

UH, SURE. YEAH.

AFTER YOU'VE SOLD ALL THOSE COOKIES. ROOF NEEDS NEW SHINGLES, YOU KNOW.

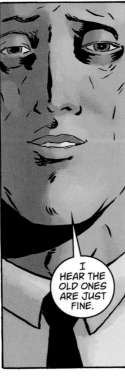

I HEAR THE OLD ONES ARE JUST FINE.

DON'T *YOU* START ON ME NOW.

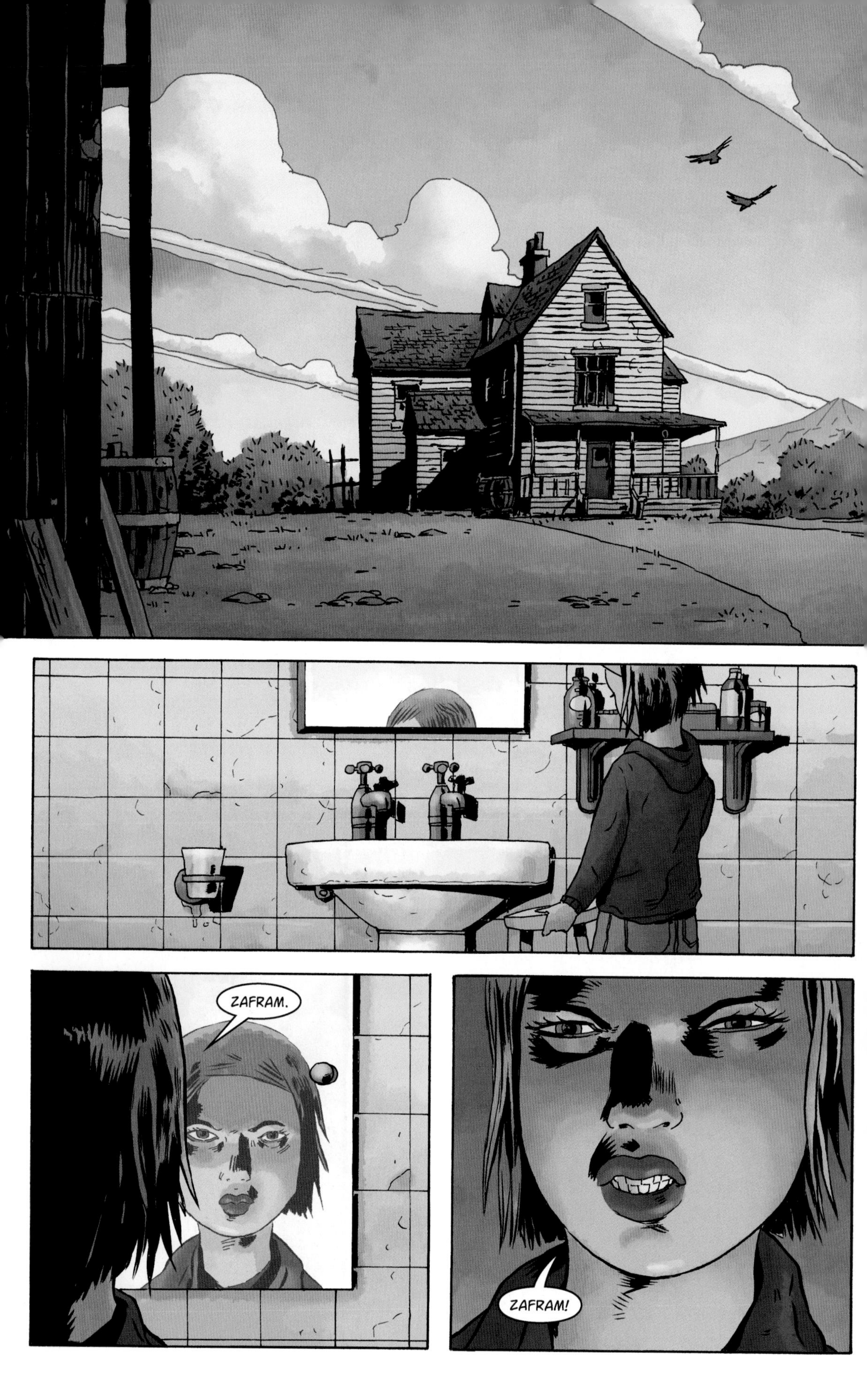

ZAFRAM.
ZAFRAM!

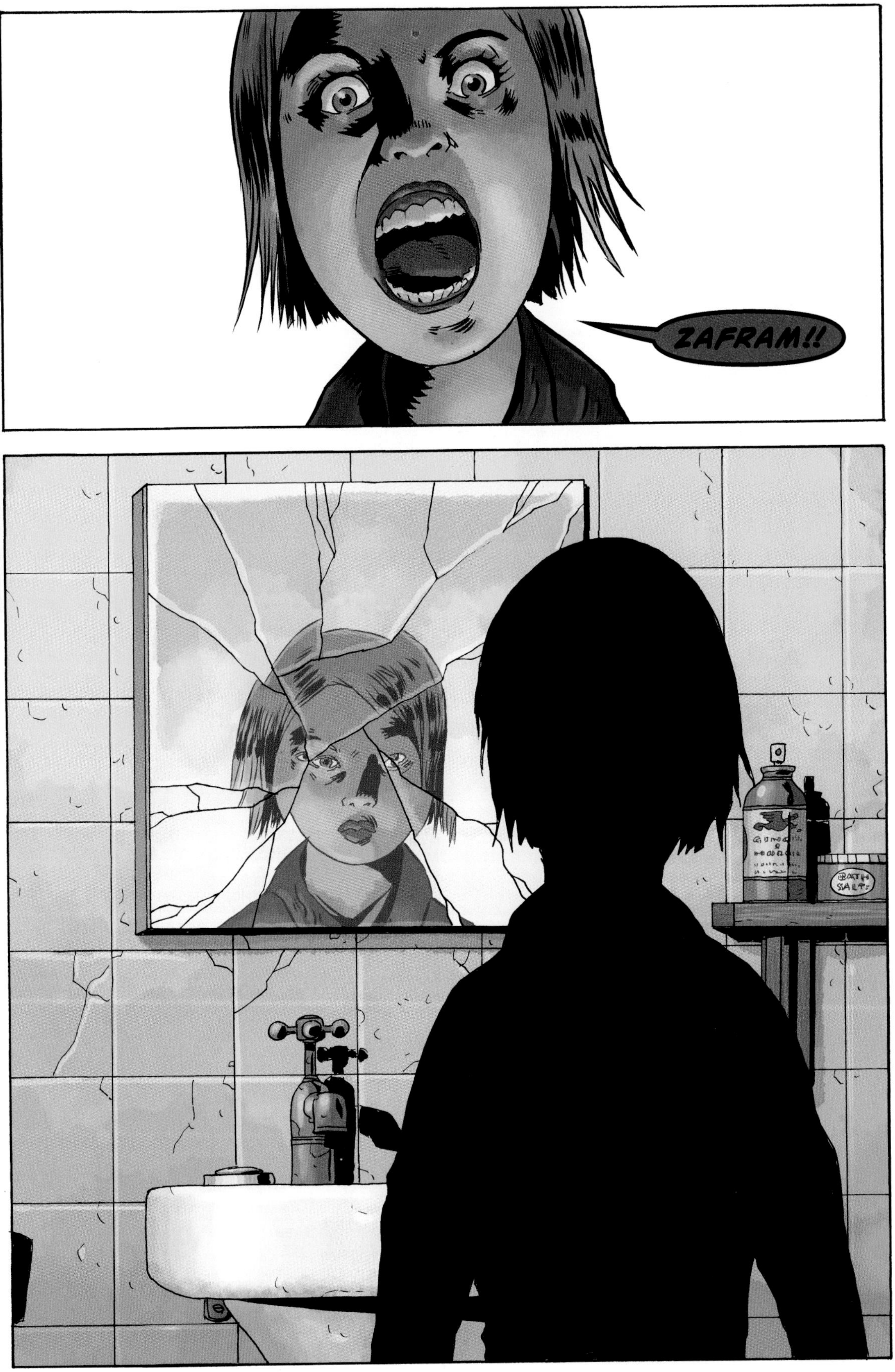
ZAFRAM!!
BATH SALTS

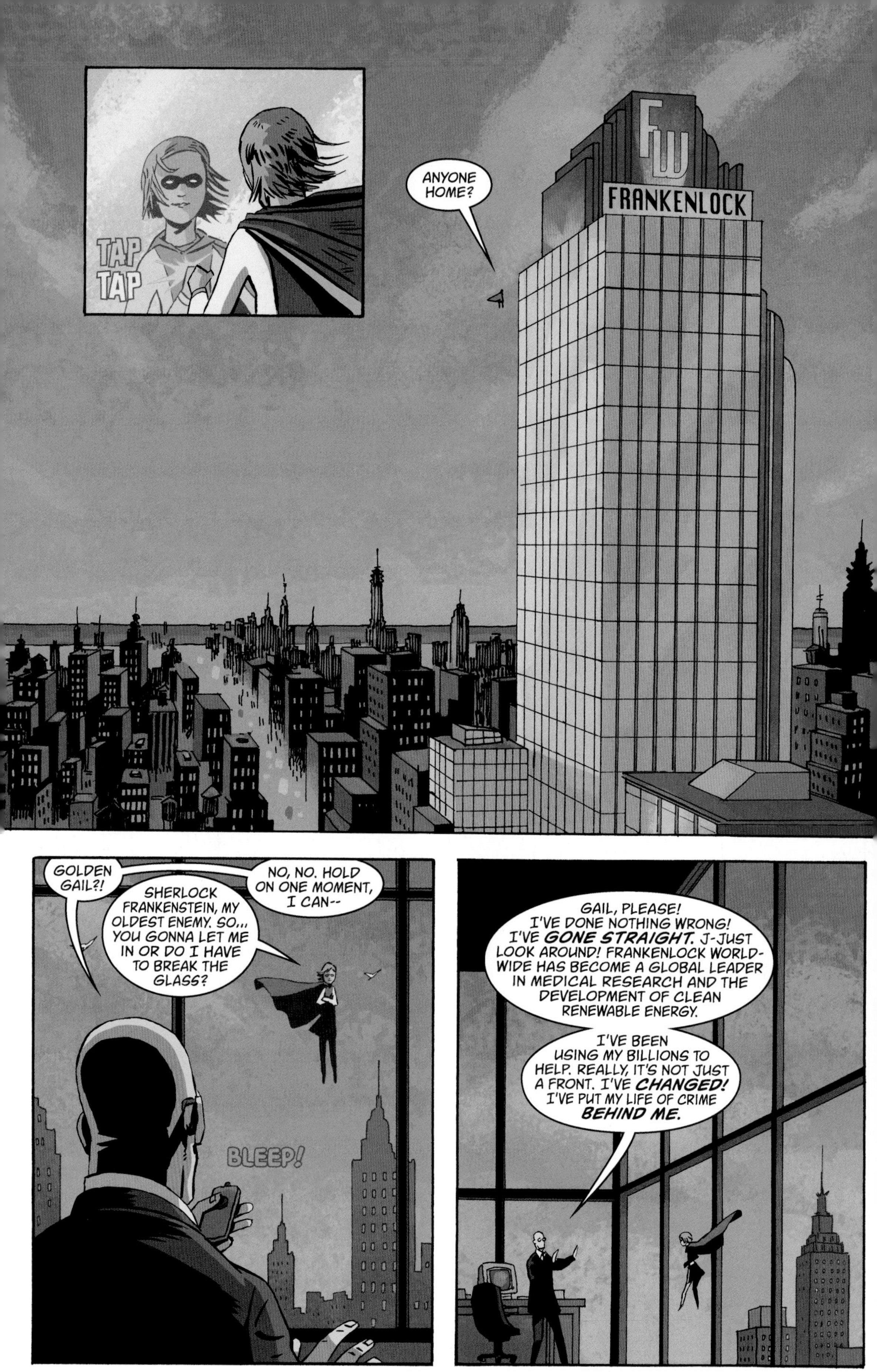

TAP TAP
ANYONE HOME?
FW
FRANKENLOCK
GOLDEN GAIL?!
SHERLOCK FRANKENSTEIN, MY OLDEST ENEMY. SO... YOU GONNA LET ME IN OR DO I HAVE TO BREAK THE GLASS?
NO, NO. HOLD ON ONE MOMENT, I CAN--
BLEEP!
GAIL, PLEASE! I'VE DONE NOTHING WRONG! I'VE GONE STRAIGHT. J-JUST LOOK AROUND! FRANKENLOCK WORLD-WIDE HAS BECOME A GLOBAL LEADER IN MEDICAL RESEARCH AND THE DEVELOPMENT OF CLEAN RENEWABLE ENERGY.
I'VE BEEN USING MY BILLIONS TO HELP. REALLY, IT'S NOT JUST A FRONT. I'VE CHANGED! I'VE PUT MY LIFE OF CRIME BEHIND ME.

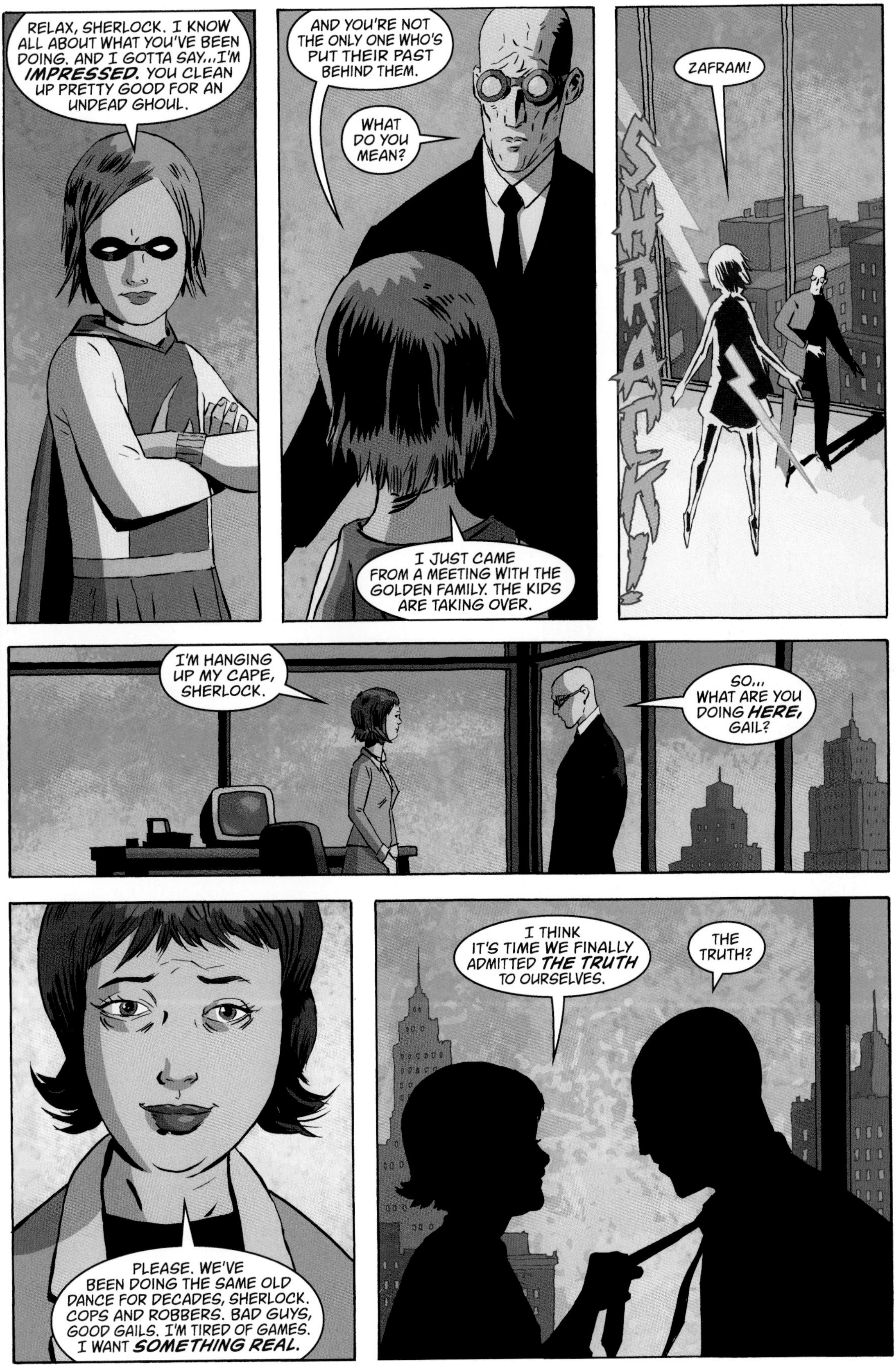

RELAX, SHERLOCK. I KNOW ALL ABOUT WHAT YOU'VE BEEN DOING. AND I GOTTA SAY...I'M IMPRESSED. YOU CLEAN UP PRETTY GOOD FOR AN UNDEAD GHOUL.
AND YOU'RE NOT THE ONLY ONE WHO'S PUT THEIR PAST BEHIND THEM.
WHAT DO YOU MEAN?
I JUST CAME FROM A MEETING WITH THE GOLDEN FAMILY. THE KIDS ARE TAKING OVER.
ZAFRAM!
SHRACK
I'M HANGING UP MY CAPE, SHERLOCK.
SO... WHAT ARE YOU DOING HERE, GAIL?
PLEASE. WE'VE BEEN DOING THE SAME OLD DANCE FOR DECADES, SHERLOCK. COPS AND ROBBERS. BAD GUYS, GOOD GAILS. I'M TIRED OF GAMES. I WANT SOMETHING REAL.
I THINK IT'S TIME WE FINALLY ADMITTED THE TRUTH TO OURSELVES.
THE TRUTH?

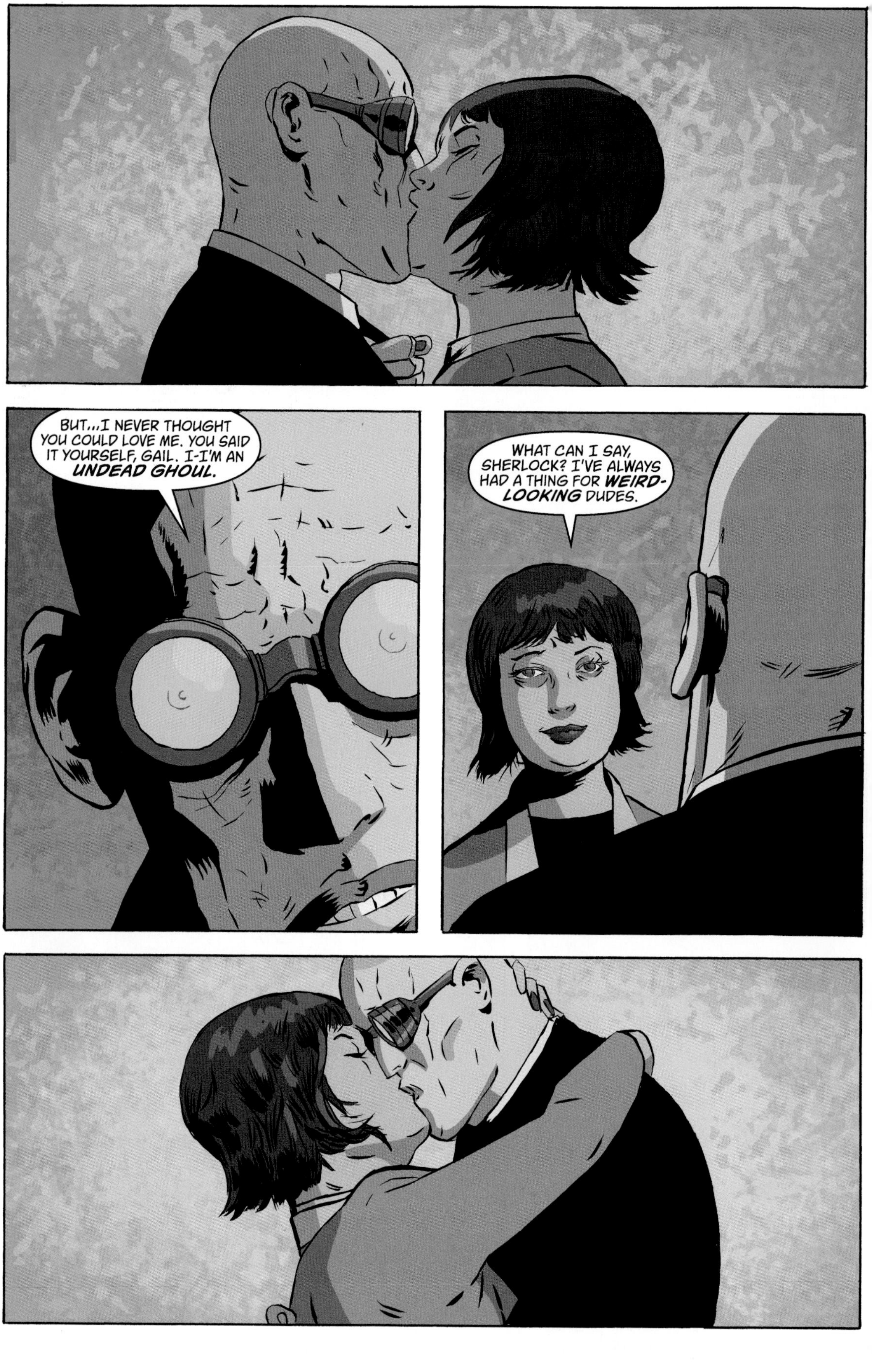
BUT...I NEVER THOUGHT YOU COULD LOVE ME. YOU SAID IT YOURSELF, GAIL. I-I'M AN UNDEAD GHOUL.
WHAT CAN I SAY, SHERLOCK? I'VE ALWAYS HAD A THING FOR WEIRD-LOOKING DUDES.

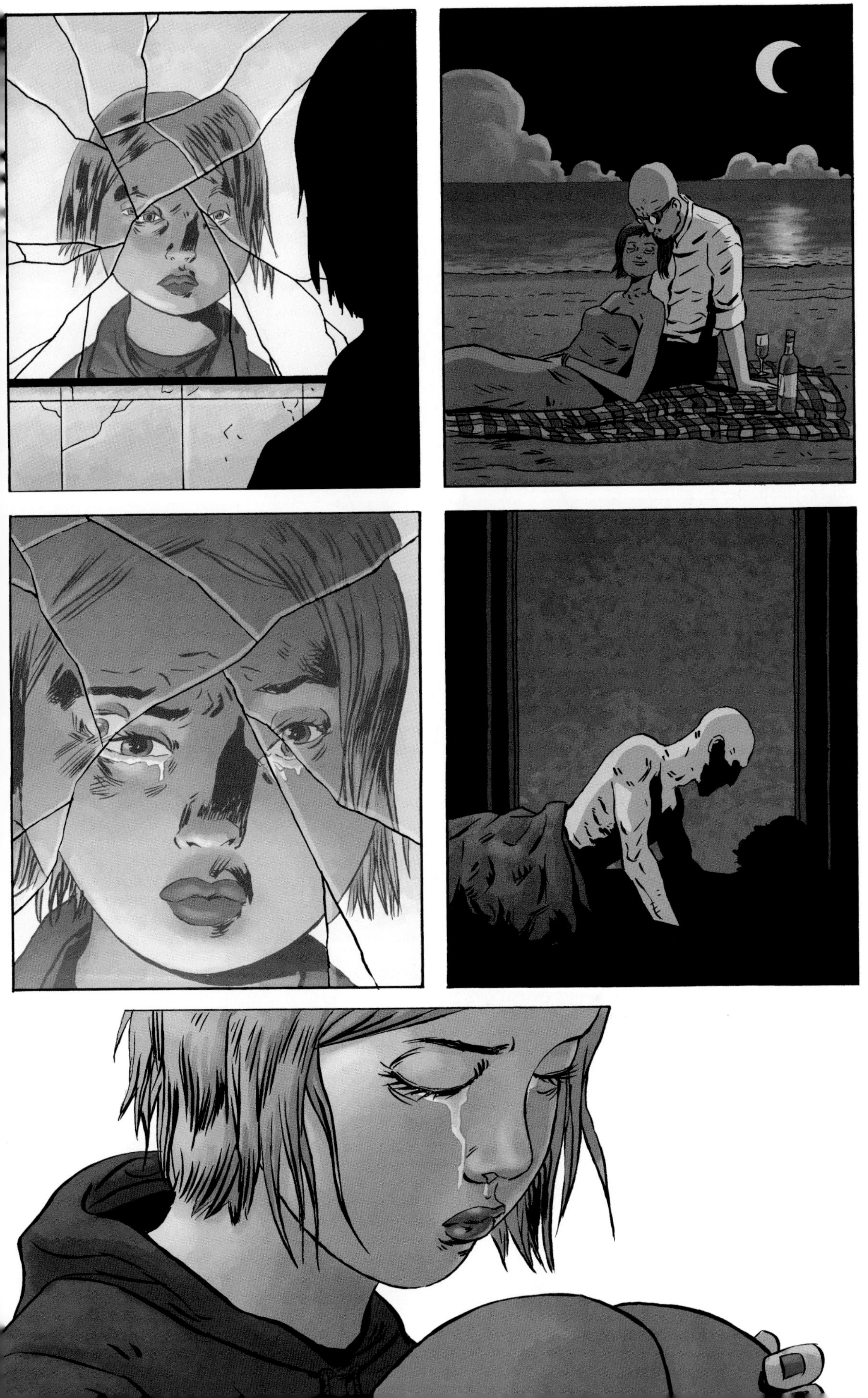

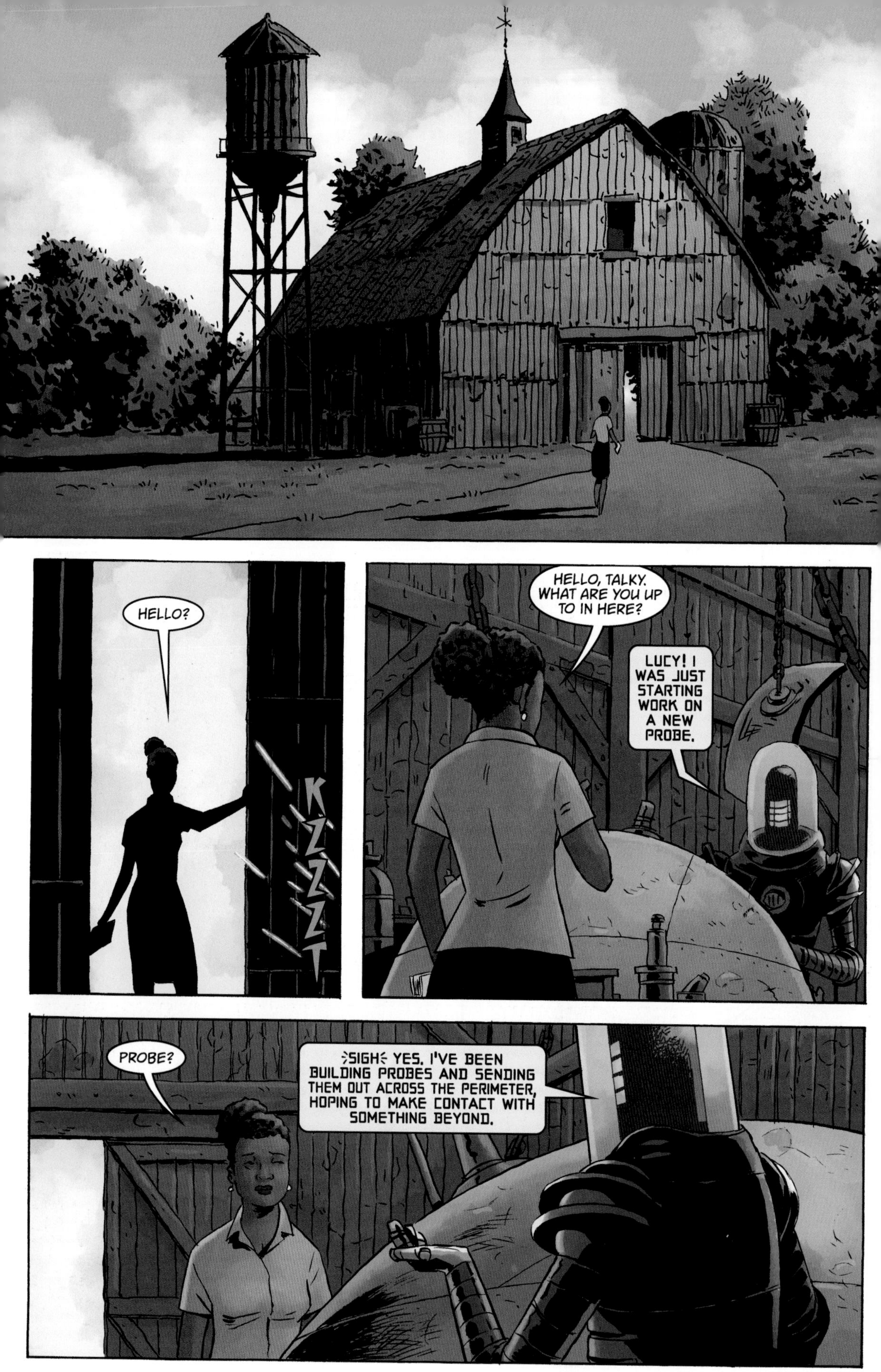
HELLO?
KZZZT
HELLO, TALKY. WHAT ARE YOU UP TO IN HERE?
LUCY! I WAS JUST STARTING WORK ON A NEW PROBE.
PROBE?
SIGH YES. I'VE BEEN BUILDING PROBES AND SENDING THEM OUT ACROSS THE PERIMETER, HOPING TO MAKE CONTACT WITH SOMETHING BEYOND.

SO FAR
I'VE HAD
NO LUCK.

LUCY?

LUCY? ARE YOU
ALL RIGHT?

WHA--? OH.
YEAH, SORRY. JUST
HAD A WEIRD FLASH OF
DÉJÀ VU OR SOMETHING.

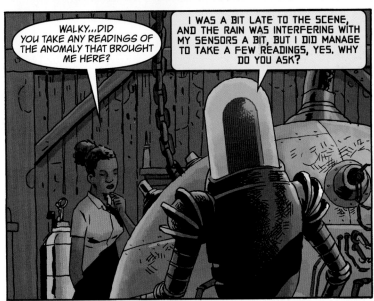

WALKY...DID
YOU TAKE ANY READINGS OF
THE ANOMALY THAT BROUGHT
ME HERE?

I WAS A BIT LATE TO THE SCENE,
AND THE RAIN WAS INTERFERING WITH
MY SENSORS A BIT, BUT I DID MANAGE
TO TAKE A FEW READINGS, YES. WHY
DO YOU ASK?

WHAT IF IT
CAN GO BOTH WAYS?
WHAT IF WHATEVER
BROUGHT ME HERE
HOLDS THE SECRET OF
GETTING US--OR AT THE
VERY LEAST, ONE OF
YOUR PROBES--OFF
THE FARM?

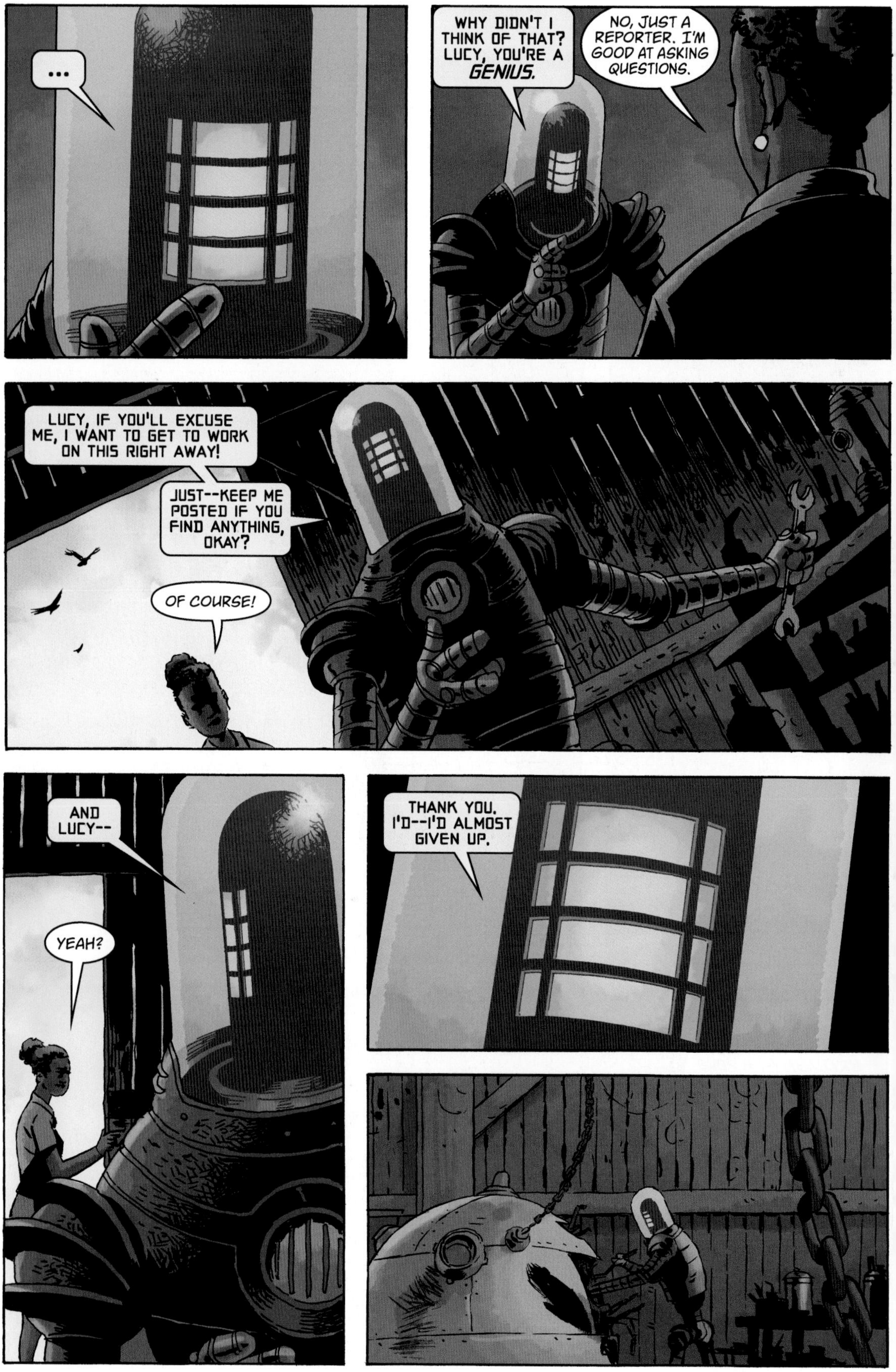
...
WHY DIDN'T I THINK OF THAT? LUCY, YOU'RE A *GENIUS.*
NO, JUST A REPORTER. I'M GOOD AT ASKING QUESTIONS.
LUCY, IF YOU'LL EXCUSE ME, I WANT TO GET TO WORK ON THIS RIGHT AWAY!
JUST--KEEP ME POSTED IF YOU FIND ANYTHING, OKAY?
OF COURSE!
AND LUCY--
YEAH?
THANK YOU. I'D--I'D ALMOST GIVEN UP.

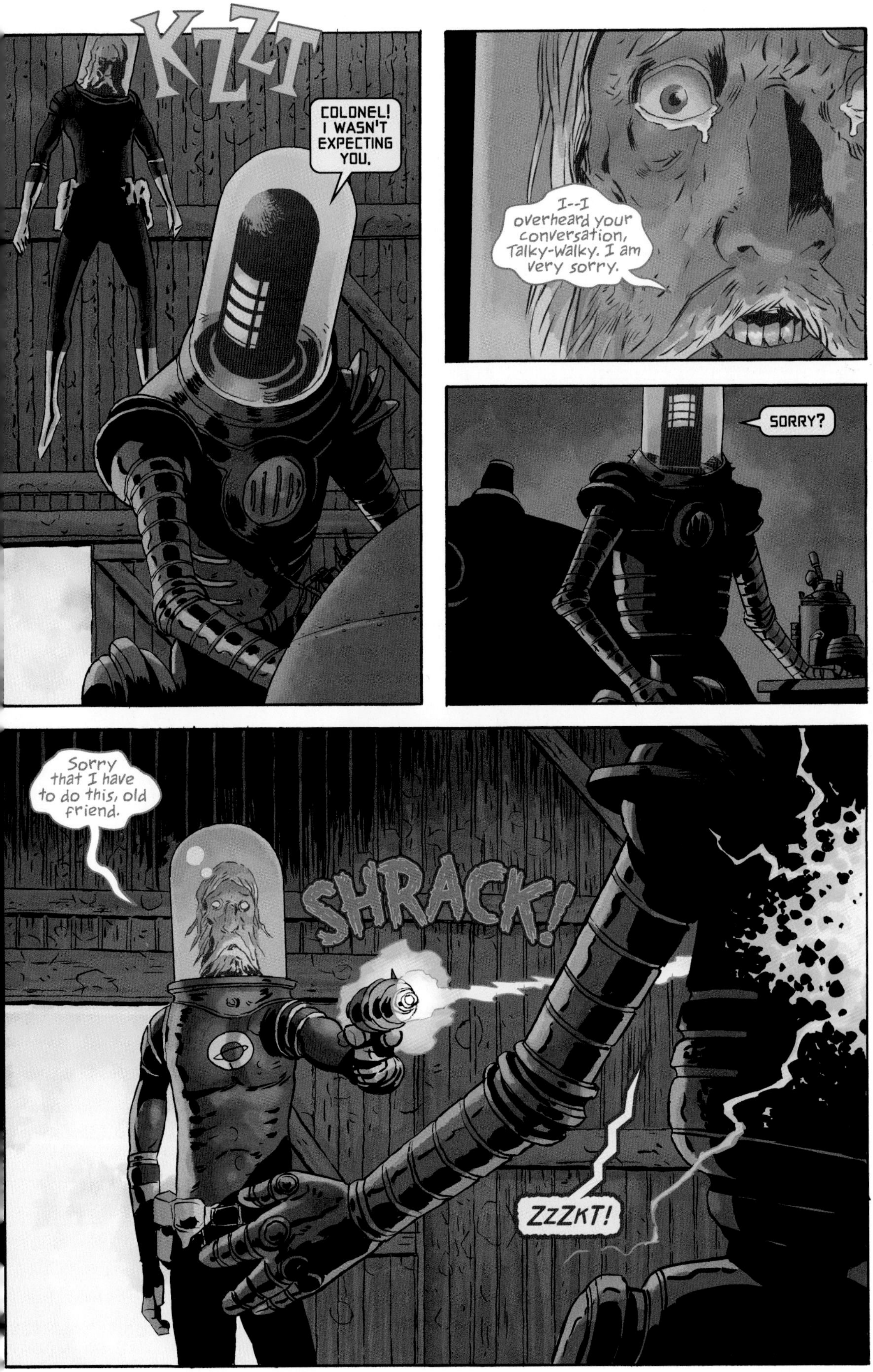
KZZZT
COLONEL! I WASN'T EXPECTING YOU.
I--I overheard your conversation, Talky-Walky. I am very sorry.
SORRY?
Sorry that I have to do this, old friend.
SHRACK!
ZZZKT!

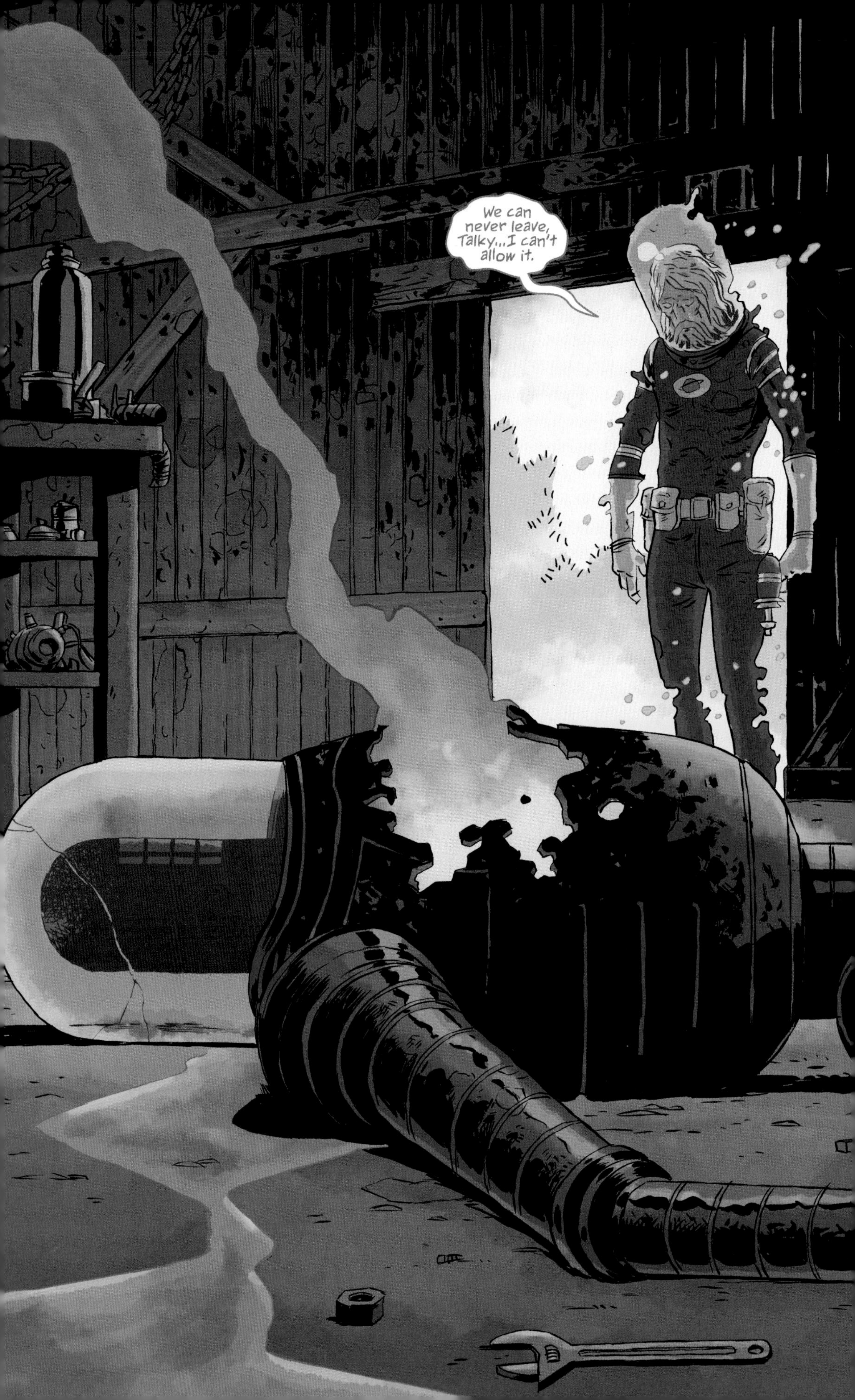
We can never leave, Talky...I can't allow it.

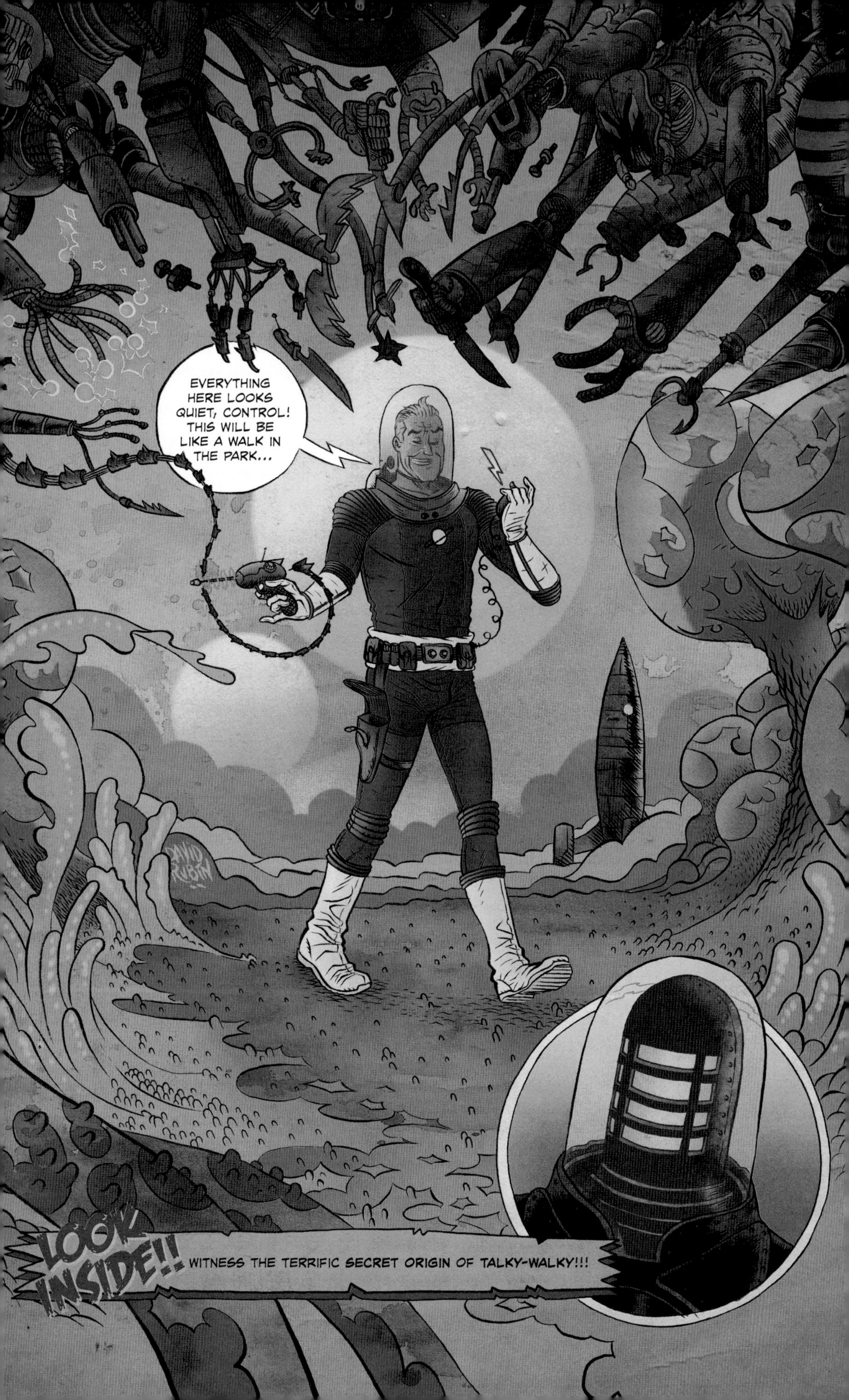
EVERYTHING HERE LOOKS QUIET, CONTROL! THIS WILL BE LIKE A WALK IN THE PARK...
DAVID RUBIN
LOOK INSIDE!!
WITNESS THE TERRIFIC SECRET ORIGIN OF TALKY-WALKY!!!

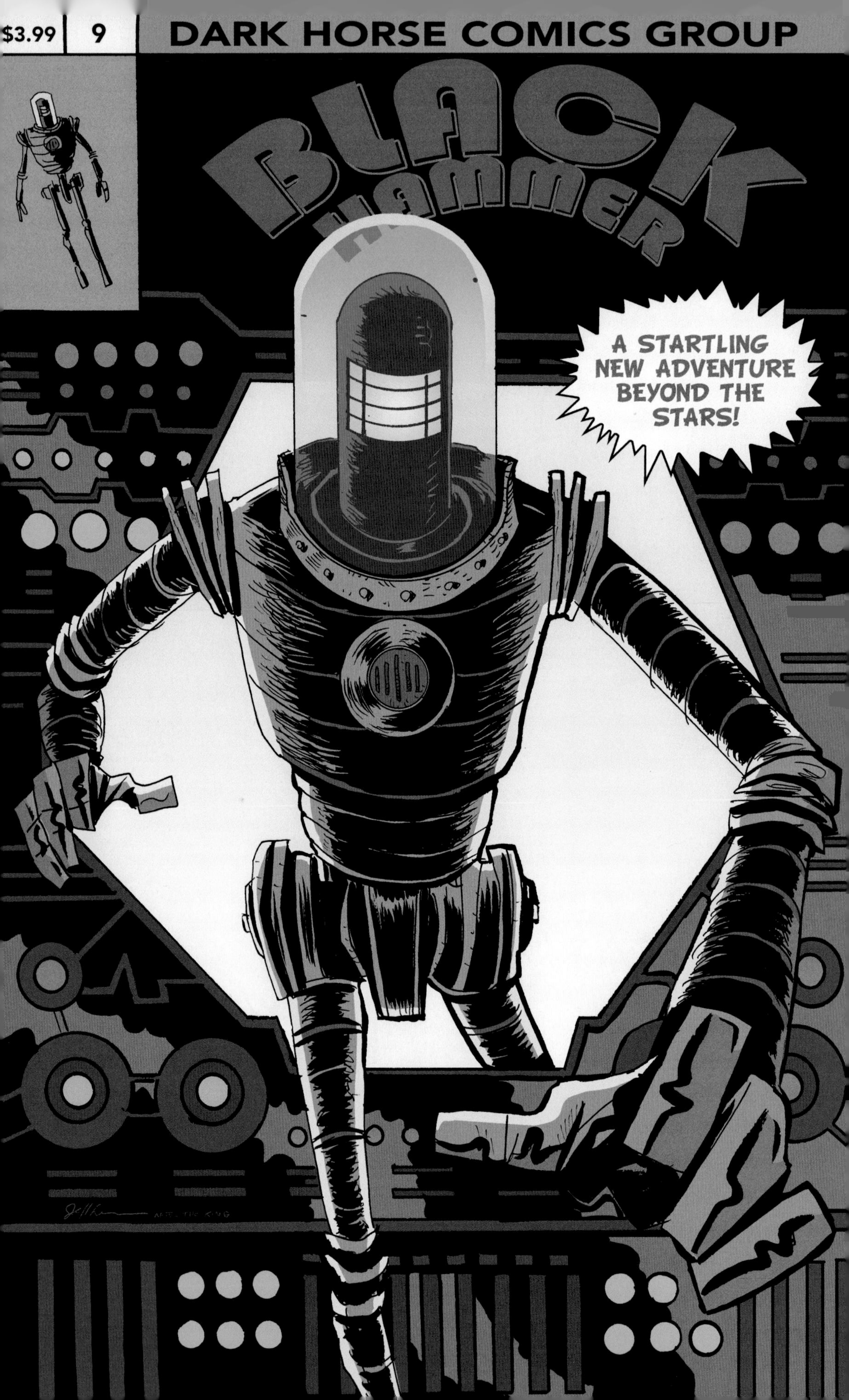
$3.99
9
DARK HORSE COMICS GROUP
BLACK HAMMER
A STARTLING NEW ADVENTURE BEYOND THE STARS!

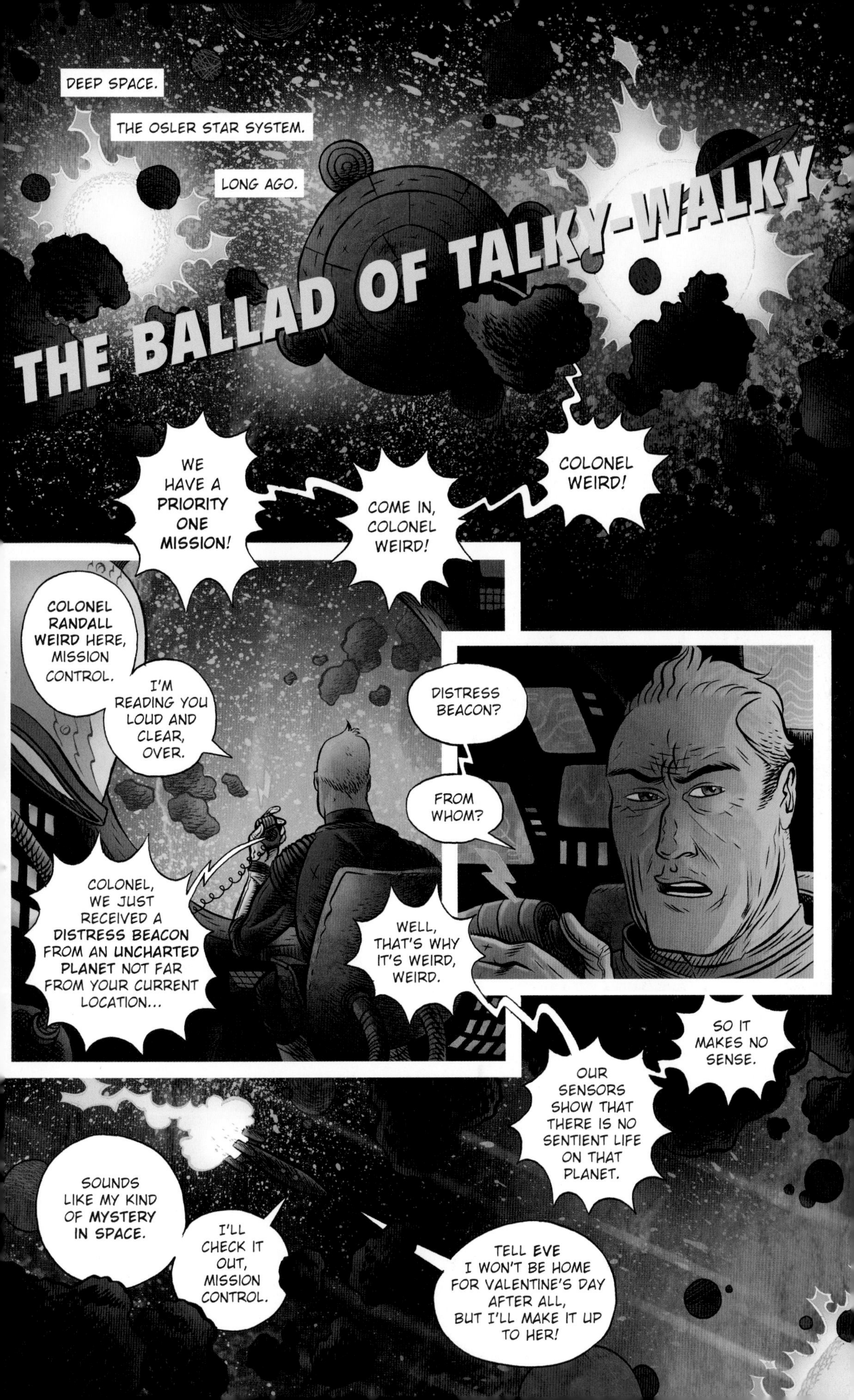
DEEP SPACE.
THE OSLER STAR SYSTEM.
LONG AGO.
THE BALLAD OF TALKY-WALKY
COLONEL WEIRD!
COME IN, COLONEL WEIRD!
WE HAVE A PRIORITY ONE MISSION!
COLONEL RANDALL WEIRD HERE, MISSION CONTROL.
I'M READING YOU LOUD AND CLEAR, OVER.
COLONEL, WE JUST RECEIVED A DISTRESS BEACON FROM AN UNCHARTED PLANET NOT FAR FROM YOUR CURRENT LOCATION...
DISTRESS BEACON?
FROM WHOM?
WELL, THAT'S WHY IT'S WEIRD, WEIRD.
OUR SENSORS SHOW THAT THERE IS NO SENTIENT LIFE ON THAT PLANET.
SO IT MAKES NO SENSE.
SOUNDS LIKE MY KIND OF MYSTERY IN SPACE.
I'LL CHECK IT OUT, MISSION CONTROL.
TELL EVE I WON'T BE HOME FOR VALENTINE'S DAY AFTER ALL, BUT I'LL MAKE IT UP TO HER!

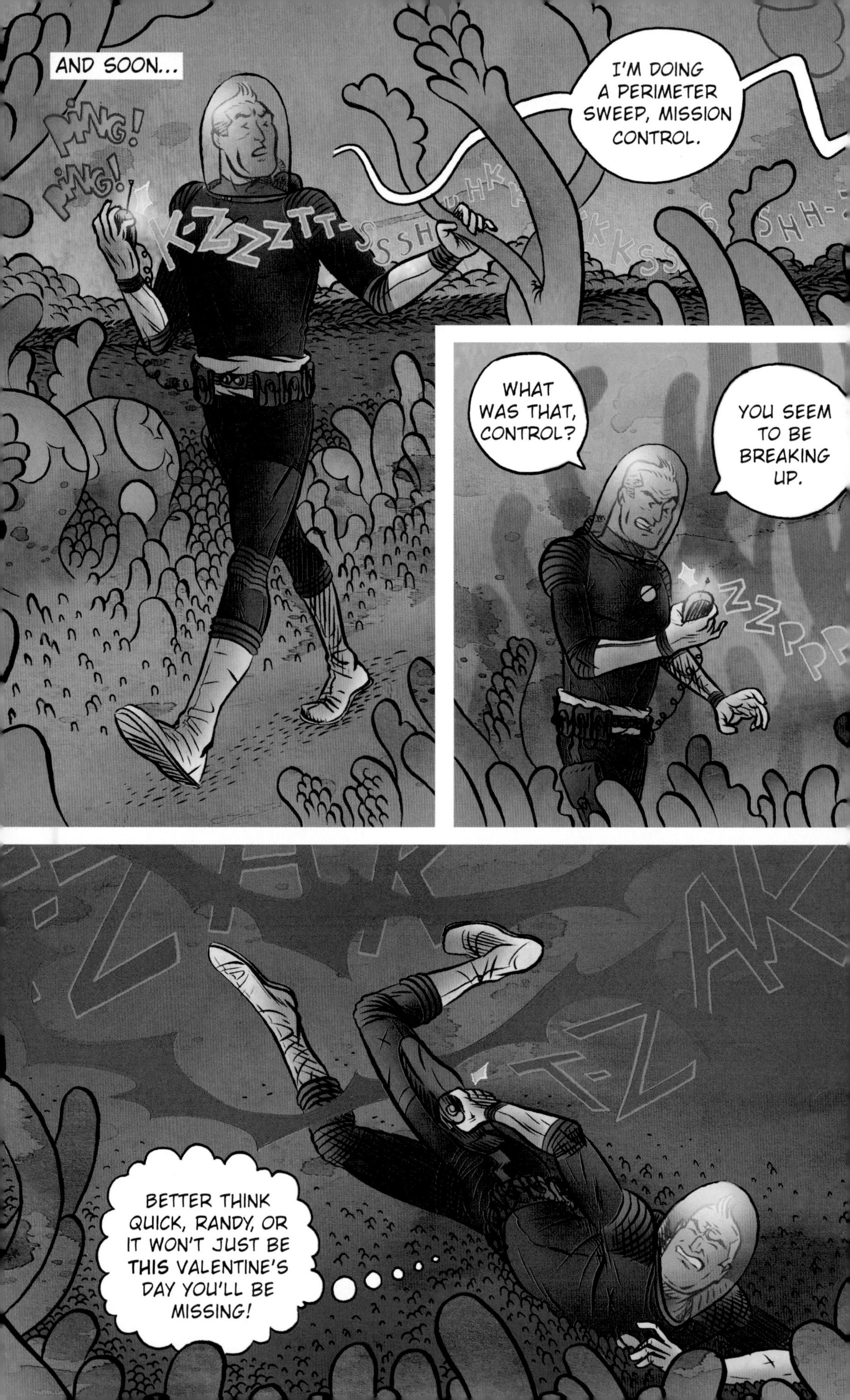
AND SOON...
PING!
PING!
K-ZZZTT-SSSH
I'M DOING A PERIMETER SWEEP, MISSION CONTROL.
WHAT WAS THAT, CONTROL?
YOU SEEM TO BE BREAKING UP.
ZZPPP
T-Z
BETTER THINK QUICK, RANDY, OR IT WON'T JUST BE THIS VALENTINE'S DAY YOU'LL BE MISSING!

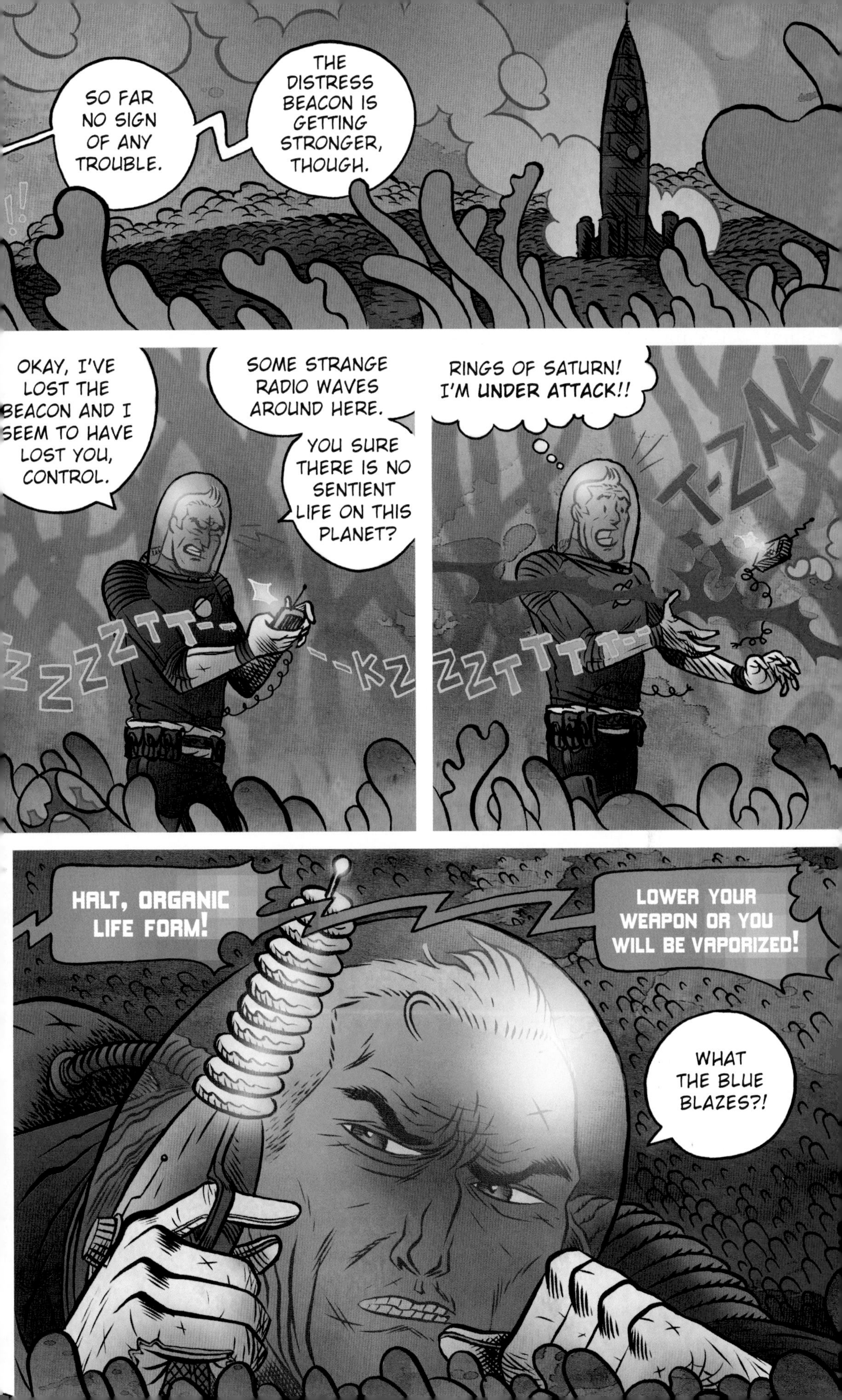
SO FAR NO SIGN OF ANY TROUBLE.
THE DISTRESS BEACON IS GETTING STRONGER, THOUGH.
OKAY, I'VE LOST THE BEACON AND I SEEM TO HAVE LOST YOU, CONTROL.
SOME STRANGE RADIO WAVES AROUND HERE.
YOU SURE THERE IS NO SENTIENT LIFE ON THIS PLANET?
ZZZZZTTT---KZ
RINGS OF SATURN! I'M UNDER ATTACK!!
T-ZAK
ZZZTTTT--
HALT, ORGANIC LIFE FORM!
LOWER YOUR WEAPON OR YOU WILL BE VAPORIZED!
WHAT THE BLUE BLAZES?!

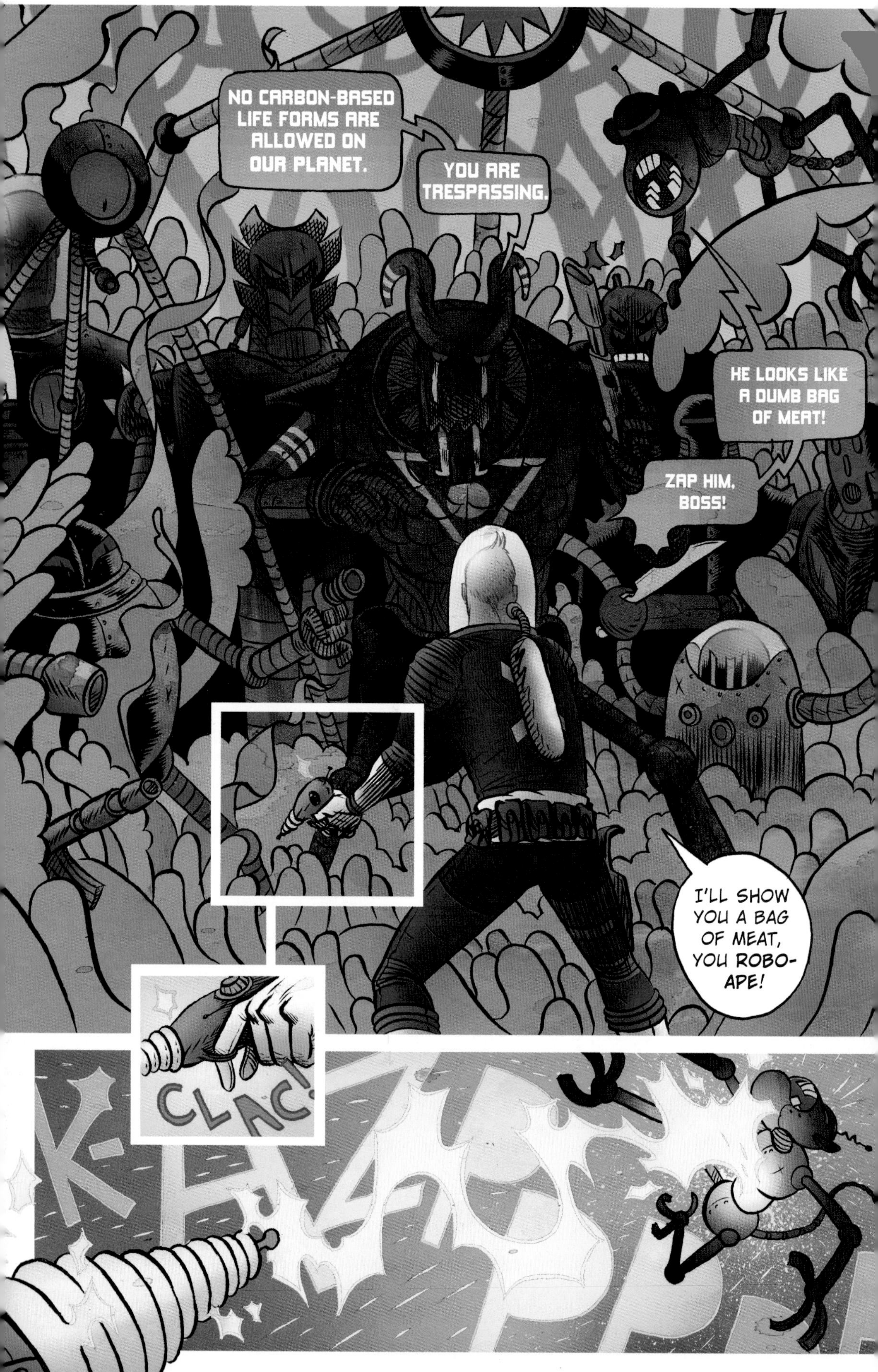
NO CARBON-BASED LIFE FORMS ARE ALLOWED ON OUR PLANET.
YOU ARE TRESPASSING.
HE LOOKS LIKE A DUMB BAG OF MEAT!
ZAP HIM, BOSS!
I'LL SHOW YOU A BAG OF MEAT, YOU ROBO-APE!
CLAC!
K-

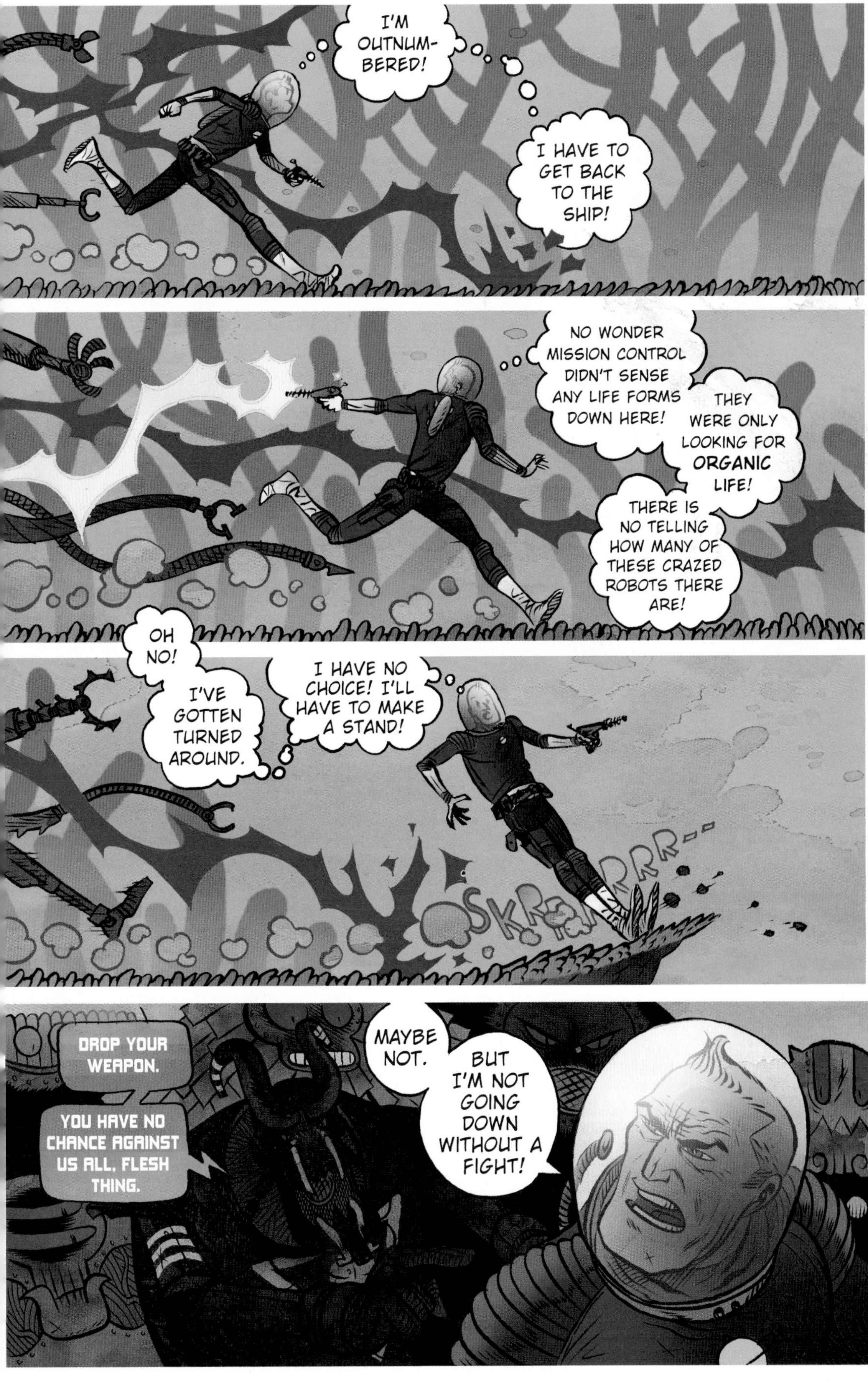
I'M OUTNUMBERED!
I HAVE TO GET BACK TO THE SHIP!
NO WONDER MISSION CONTROL DIDN'T SENSE ANY LIFE FORMS DOWN HERE!
THEY WERE ONLY LOOKING FOR ORGANIC LIFE!
THERE IS NO TELLING HOW MANY OF THESE CRAZED ROBOTS THERE ARE!
OH NO!
I'VE GOTTEN TURNED AROUND.
I HAVE NO CHOICE! I'LL HAVE TO MAKE A STAND!
SKRRRRR--
DROP YOUR WEAPON.
YOU HAVE NO CHANCE AGAINST US ALL, FLESH THING.
MAYBE NOT.
BUT I'M NOT GOING DOWN WITHOUT A FIGHT!

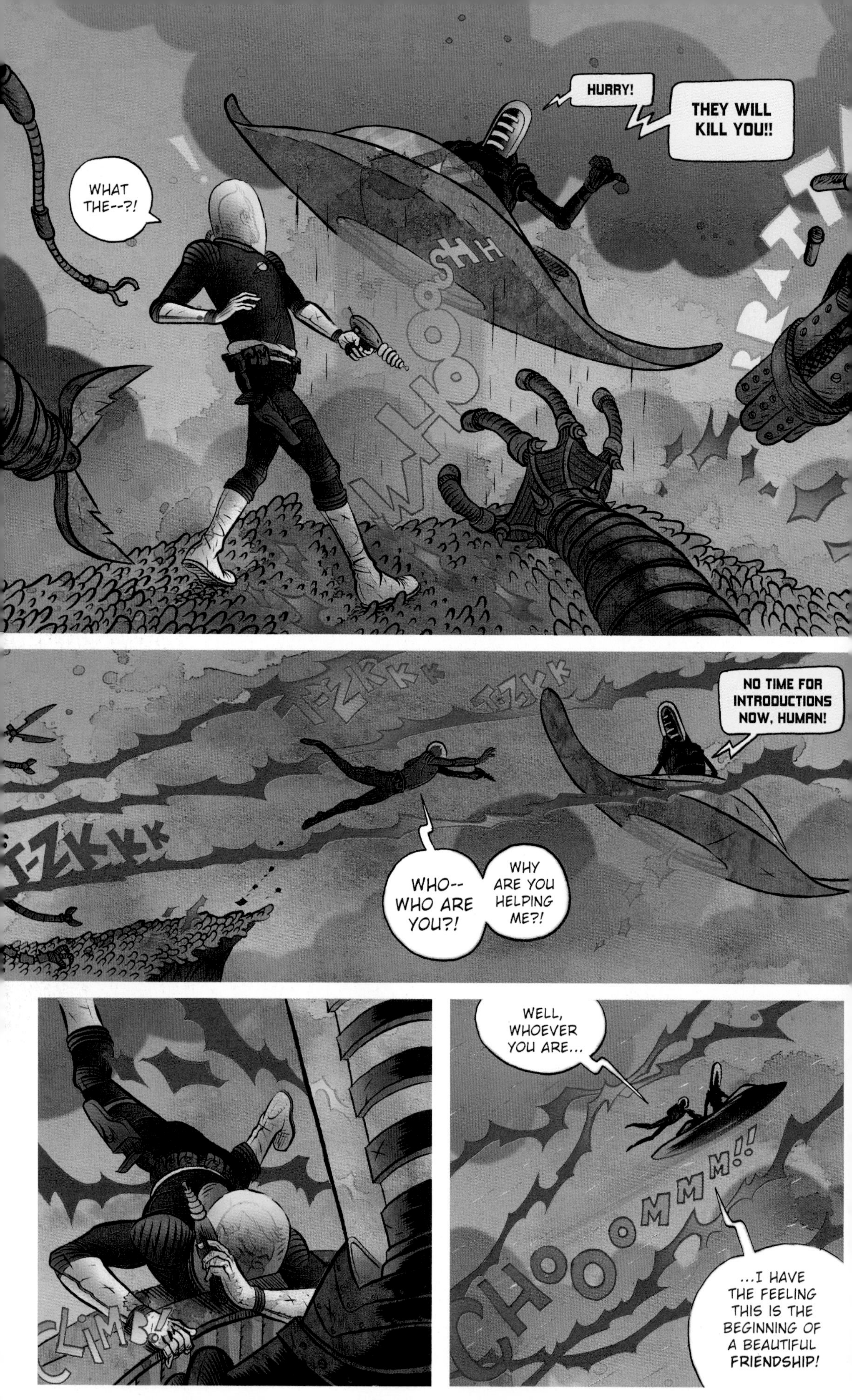

!
WHAT THE--?!
HURRY!
THEY WILL KILL YOU!!
WHOOSHH
BRATT
TZKKK
TZKK
NO TIME FOR INTRODUCTIONS NOW, HUMAN!
TZKKK
WHO-- WHO ARE YOU?!
WHY ARE YOU HELPING ME?!
CLIMB!
WELL, WHOEVER YOU ARE...
CHOOOMMMM!!
...I HAVE THE FEELING THIS IS THE BEGINNING OF A BEAUTIFUL FRIENDSHIP!

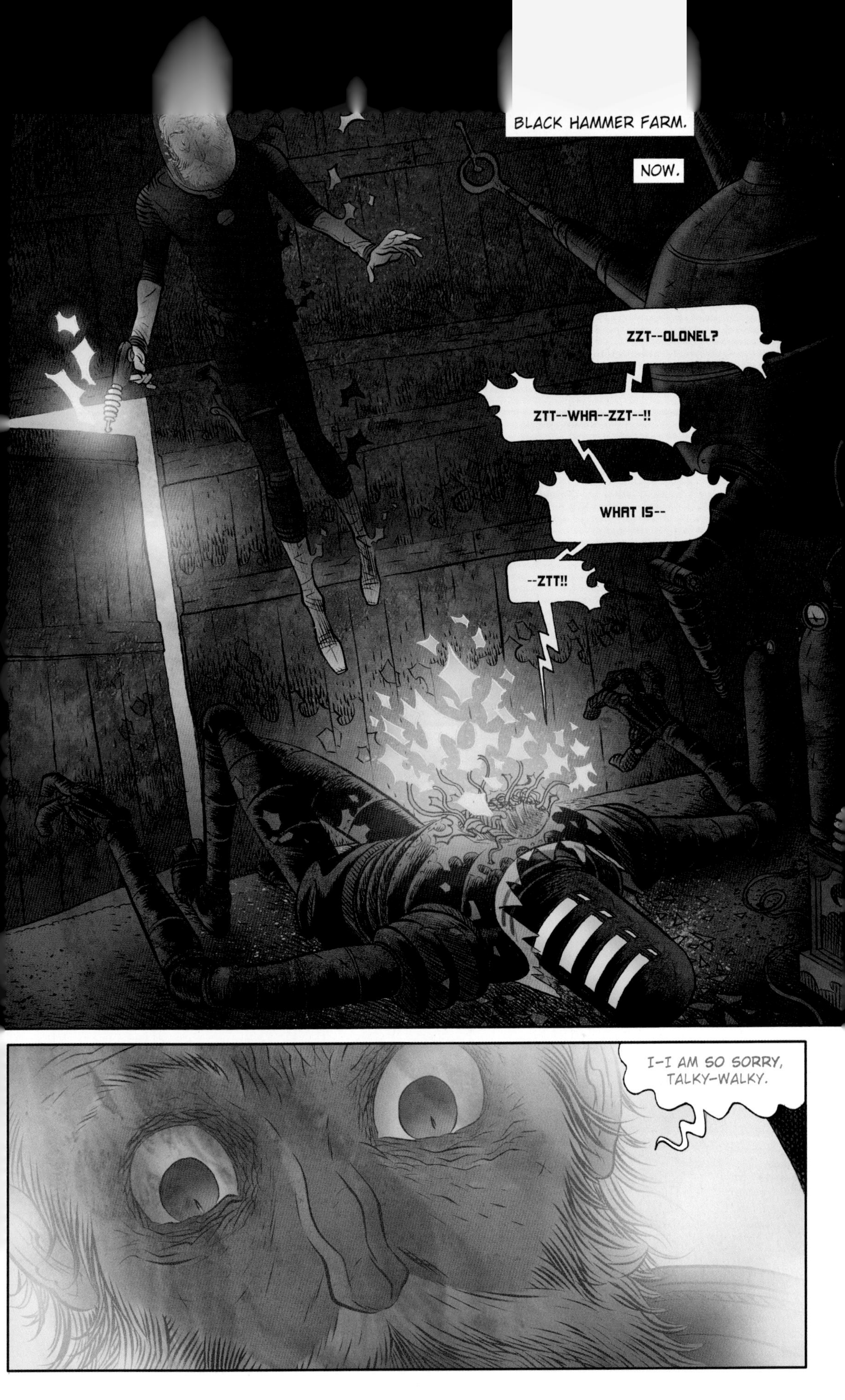

BLACK HAMMER FARM.
NOW.
ZZT--OLONEL?
ZTT--WHA--ZZT--!!
WHAT IS--
--ZTT!!
I-I AM SO SORRY, TALKY-WALKY.

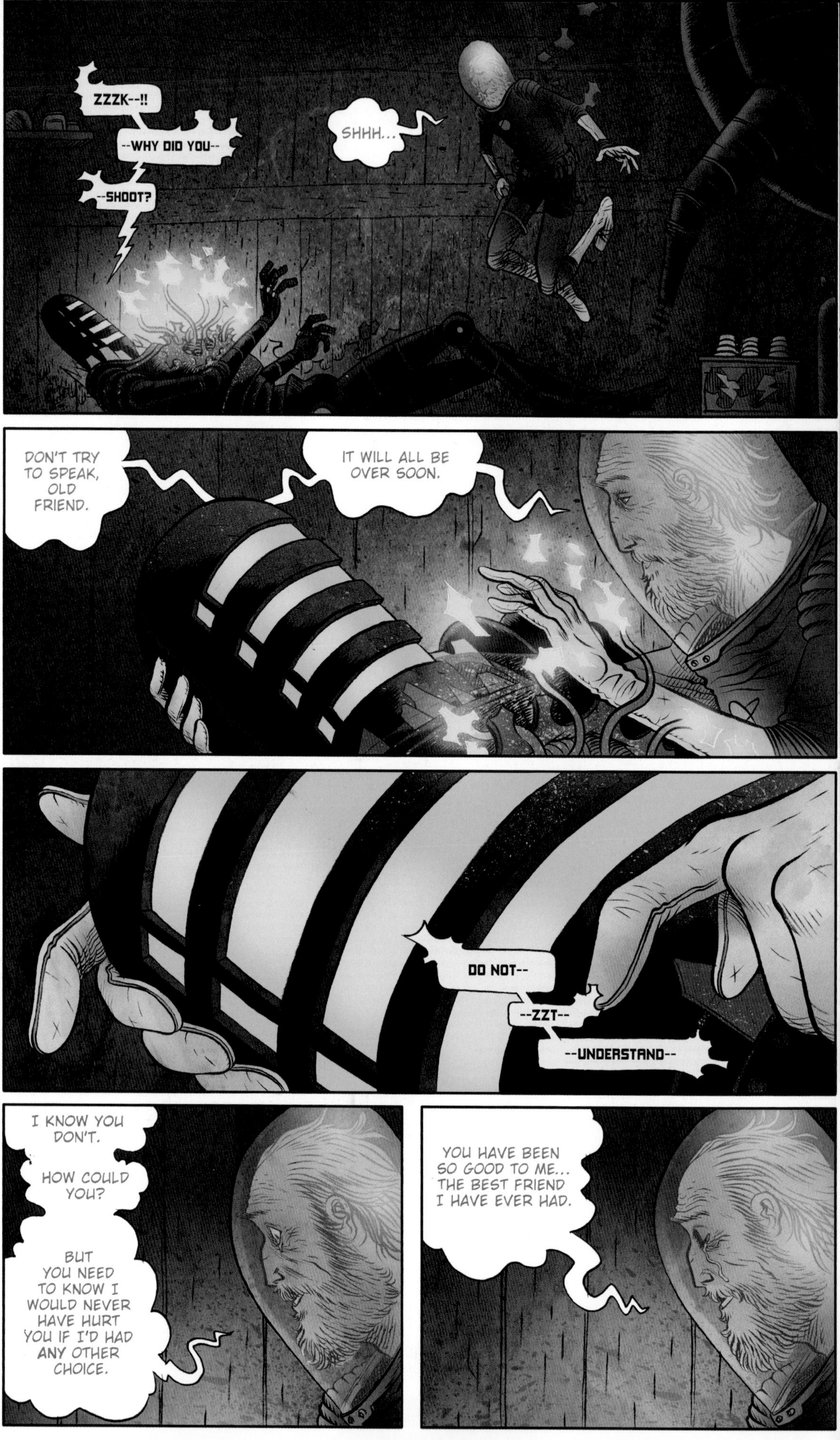

ZZZK--!!
--WHY DID YOU--
--SHOOT?
SHHH...
DON'T TRY TO SPEAK, OLD FRIEND.
IT WILL ALL BE OVER SOON.
DO NOT--
--ZZT--
--UNDERSTAND--
I KNOW YOU DON'T.
HOW COULD YOU?
BUT YOU NEED TO KNOW I WOULD NEVER HAVE HURT YOU IF I'D HAD ANY OTHER CHOICE.
YOU HAVE BEEN SO GOOD TO ME... THE BEST FRIEND I HAVE EVER HAD.

ZAKT!!!
GOODBYE, TALKY.

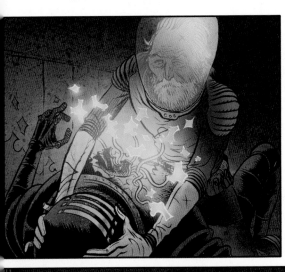

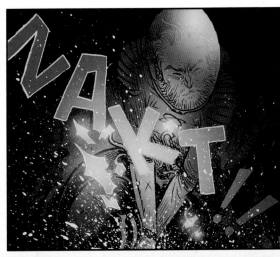

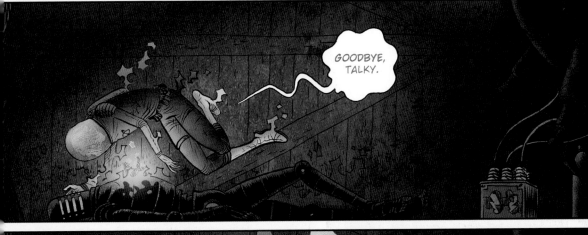

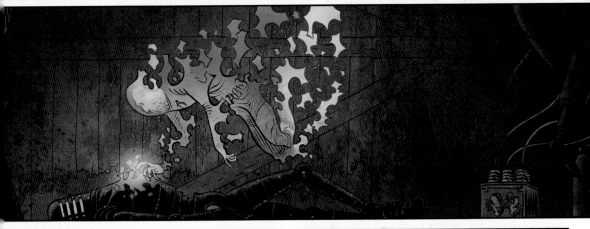

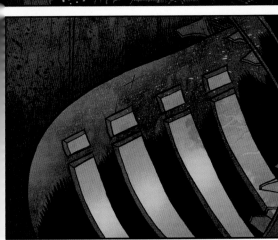

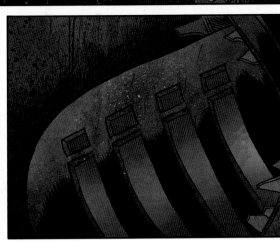

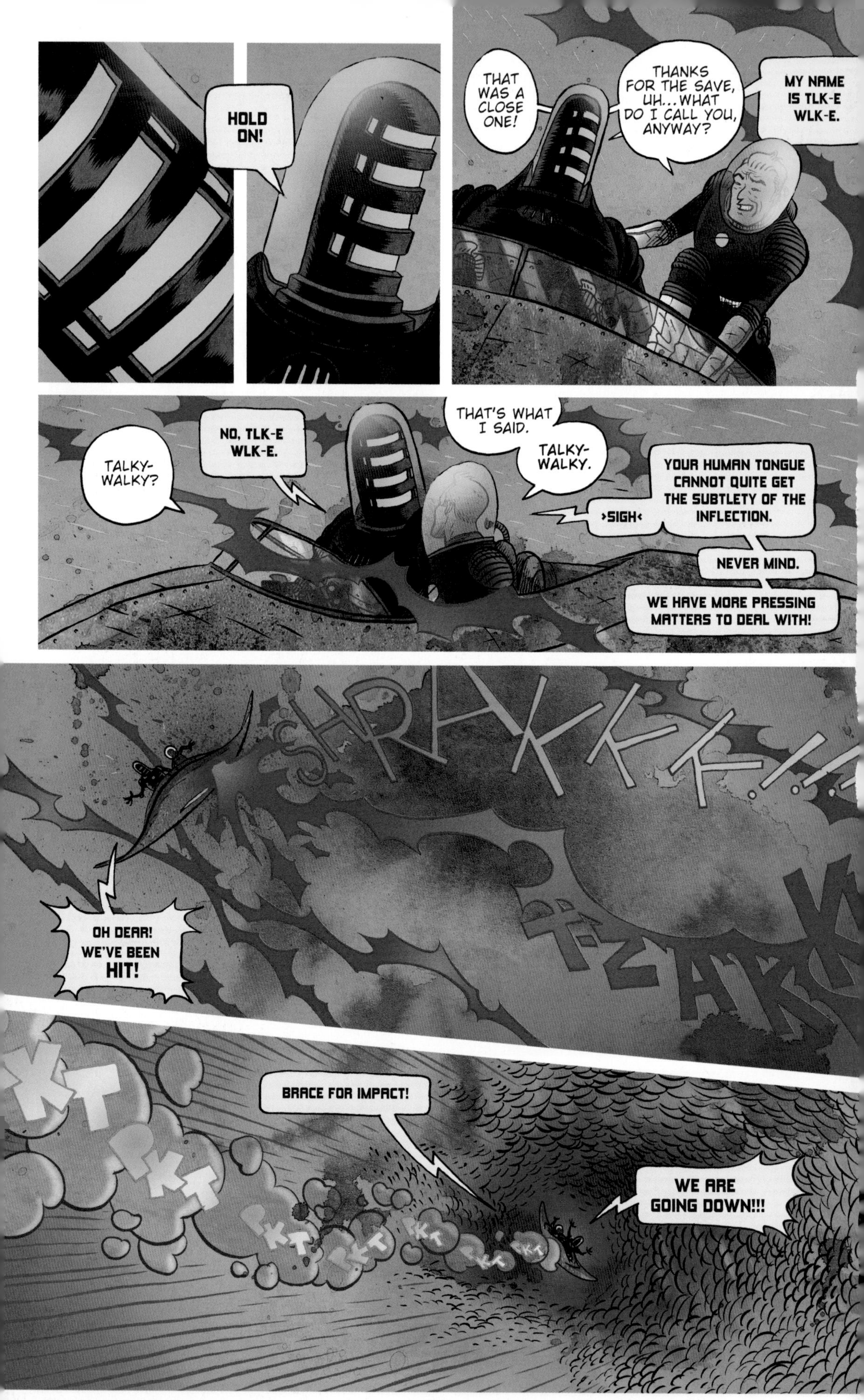
HOLD ON!
THAT WAS A CLOSE ONE!
THANKS FOR THE SAVE, UH...WHAT DO I CALL YOU, ANYWAY?
MY NAME IS TLK-E WLK-E.
TALKY-WALKY?
NO, TLK-E WLK-E.
THAT'S WHAT I SAID.
TALKY-WALKY.
›SIGH‹
YOUR HUMAN TONGUE CANNOT QUITE GET THE SUBTLETY OF THE INFLECTION.
NEVER MIND.
WE HAVE MORE PRESSING MATTERS TO DEAL WITH!
SHRAKKK!!!
OH DEAR! WE'VE BEEN HIT!
T-ZAK
BRACE FOR IMPACT!
WE ARE GOING DOWN!!!
KT
PKT
PKT PKT PKT PKT PKT

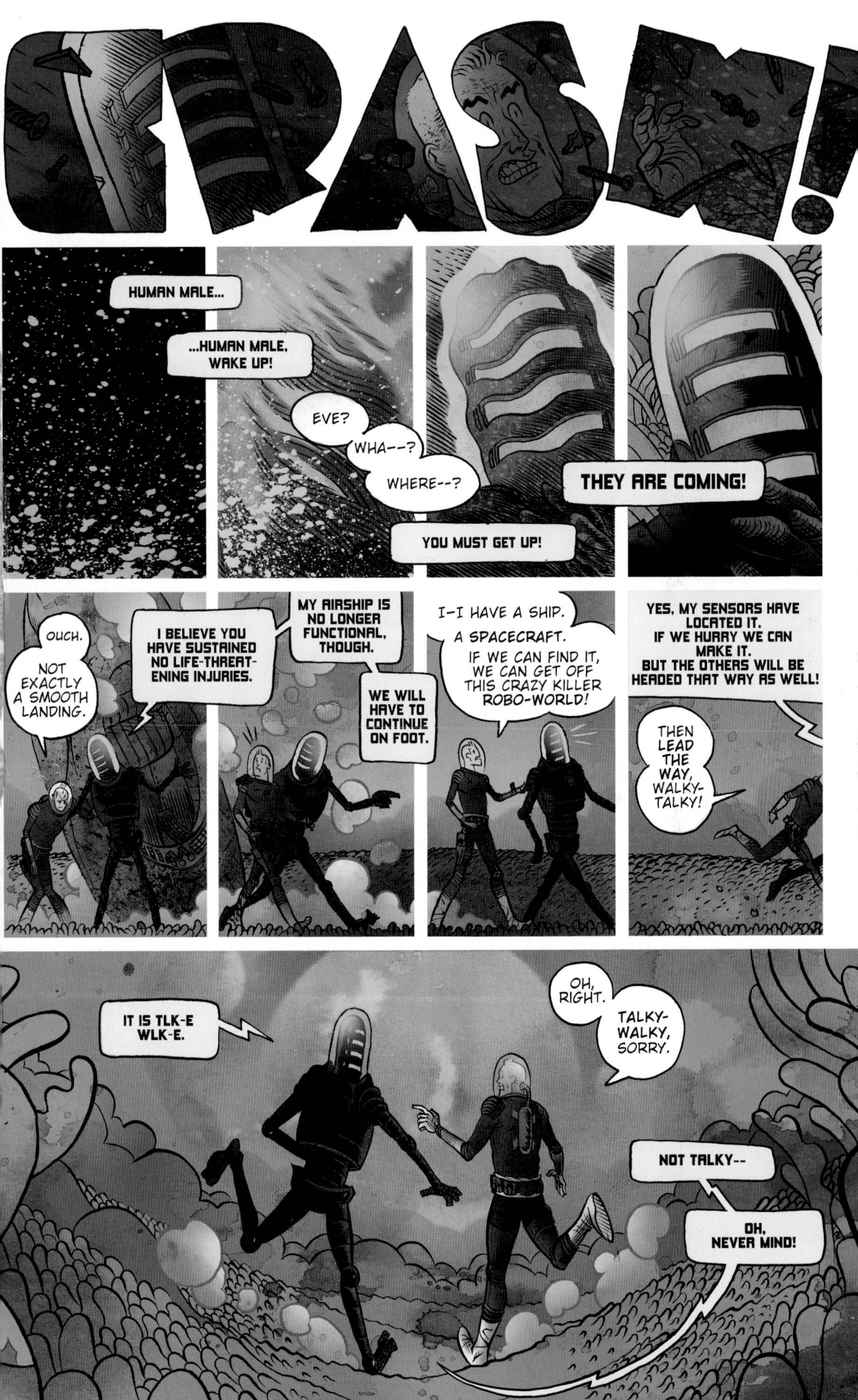
CRASH!
HUMAN MALE...
...HUMAN MALE, WAKE UP!
EVE?
WHA--?
WHERE--?
YOU MUST GET UP!
THEY ARE COMING!
OUCH.
NOT EXACTLY A SMOOTH LANDING.
I BELIEVE YOU HAVE SUSTAINED NO LIFE-THREAT-ENING INJURIES.
MY AIRSHIP IS NO LONGER FUNCTIONAL, THOUGH.
WE WILL HAVE TO CONTINUE ON FOOT.
I-I HAVE A SHIP.
A SPACECRAFT.
IF WE CAN FIND IT, WE CAN GET OFF THIS CRAZY KILLER ROBO-WORLD!
YES, MY SENSORS HAVE LOCATED IT. IF WE HURRY WE CAN MAKE IT. BUT THE OTHERS WILL BE HEADED THAT WAY AS WELL!
THEN LEAD THE WAY, WALKY-TALKY!
IT IS TLK-E WLK-E.
OH, RIGHT.
TALKY-WALKY, SORRY.
NOT TALKY--
OH, NEVER MIND!

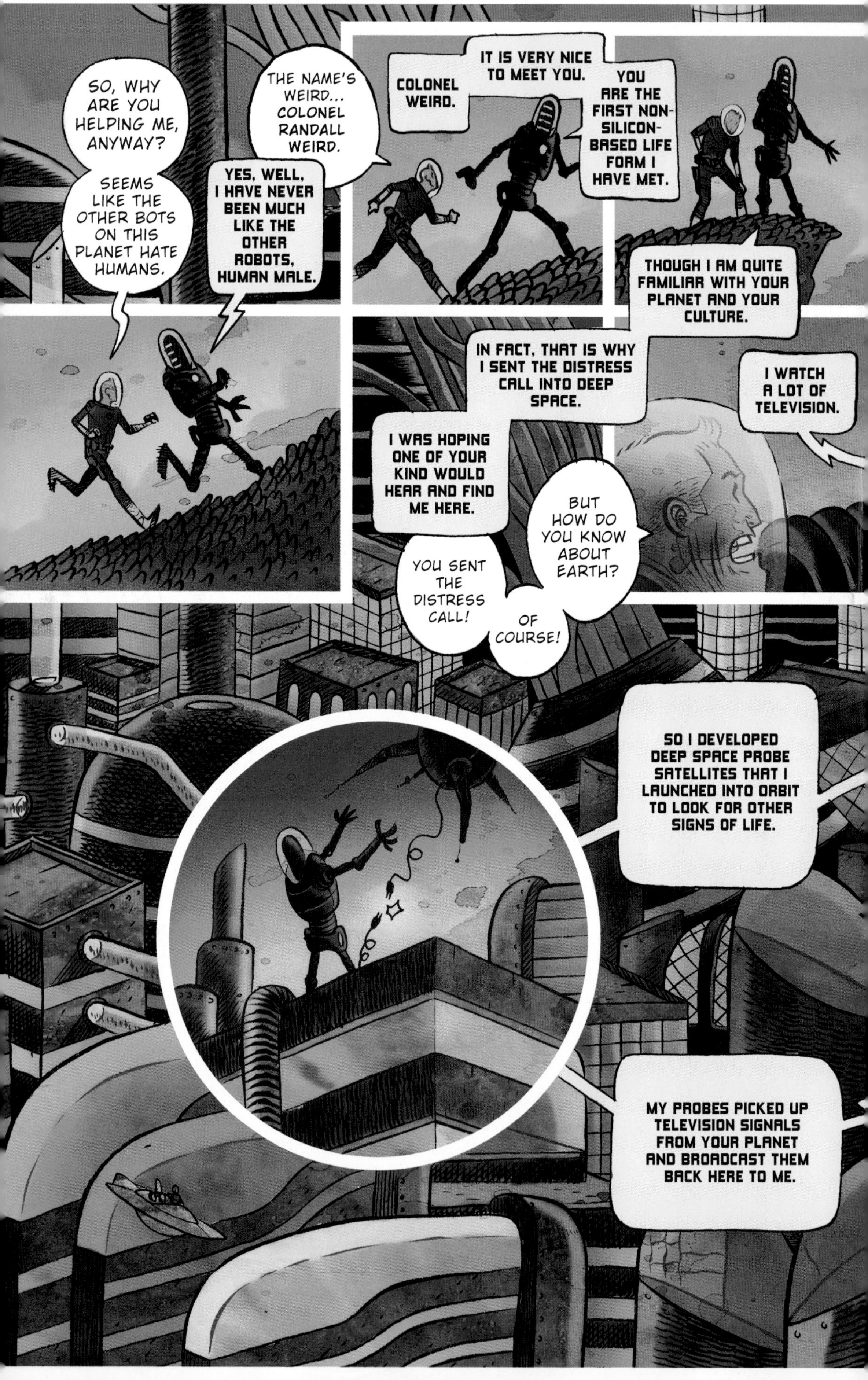
SO, WHY ARE YOU HELPING ME, ANYWAY?
THE NAME'S WEIRD... COLONEL RANDALL WEIRD.
SEEMS LIKE THE OTHER BOTS ON THIS PLANET HATE HUMANS.
YES, WELL, I HAVE NEVER BEEN MUCH LIKE THE OTHER ROBOTS, HUMAN MALE.
COLONEL WEIRD.
IT IS VERY NICE TO MEET YOU.
YOU ARE THE FIRST NON-SILICON-BASED LIFE FORM I HAVE MET.
THOUGH I AM QUITE FAMILIAR WITH YOUR PLANET AND YOUR CULTURE.
I WATCH A LOT OF TELEVISION.
IN FACT, THAT IS WHY I SENT THE DISTRESS CALL INTO DEEP SPACE.
I WAS HOPING ONE OF YOUR KIND WOULD HEAR AND FIND ME HERE.
BUT HOW DO YOU KNOW ABOUT EARTH?
YOU SENT THE DISTRESS CALL!
OF COURSE!
SO I DEVELOPED DEEP SPACE PROBE SATELLITES THAT I LAUNCHED INTO ORBIT TO LOOK FOR OTHER SIGNS OF LIFE.
MY PROBES PICKED UP TELEVISION SIGNALS FROM YOUR PLANET AND BROADCAST THEM BACK HERE TO ME.

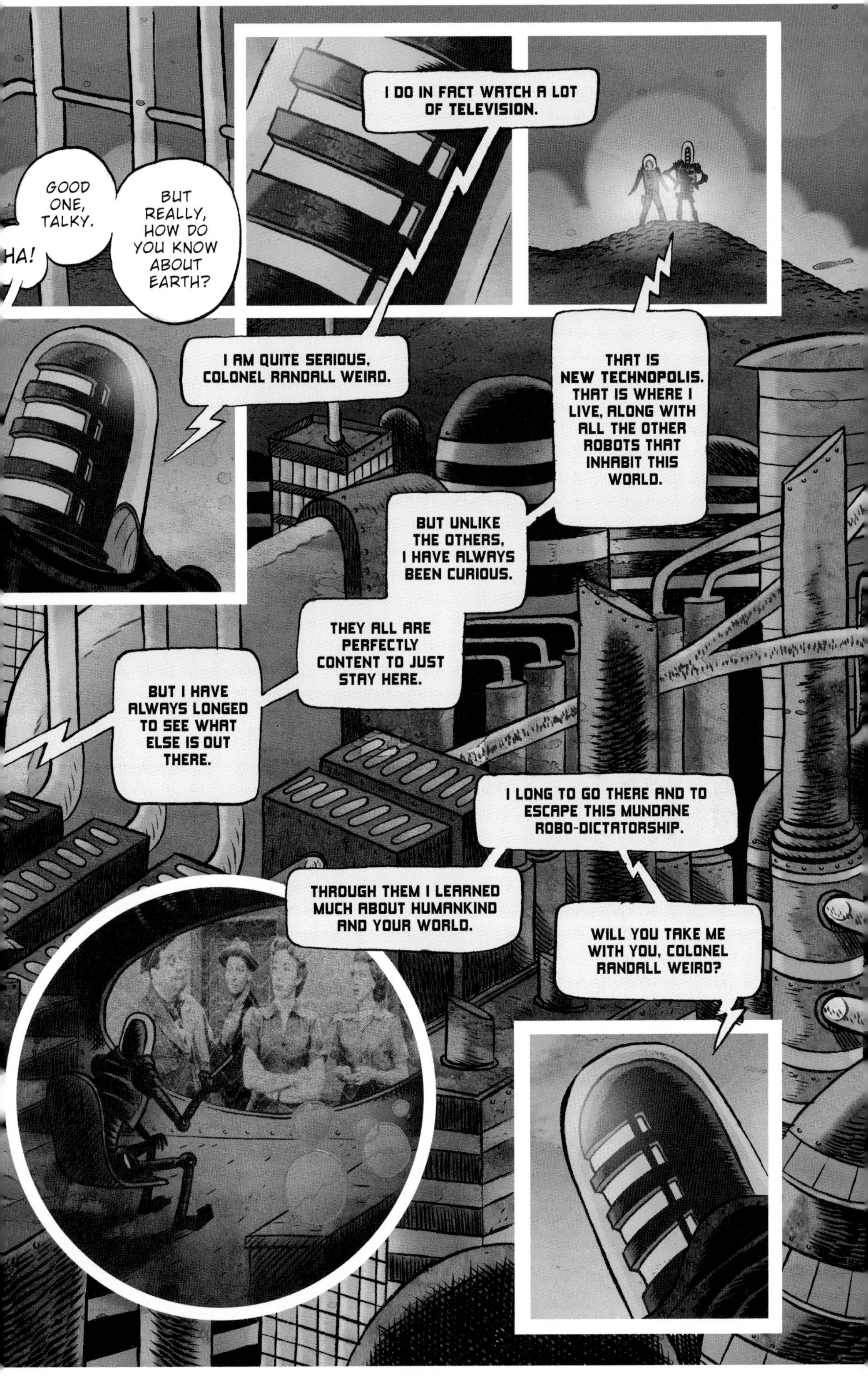
HA!
GOOD ONE, TALKY.
BUT REALLY, HOW DO YOU KNOW ABOUT EARTH?
I DO IN FACT WATCH A LOT OF TELEVISION.
I AM QUITE SERIOUS, COLONEL RANDALL WEIRD.
THAT IS NEW TECHNOPOLIS. THAT IS WHERE I LIVE, ALONG WITH ALL THE OTHER ROBOTS THAT INHABIT THIS WORLD.
BUT UNLIKE THE OTHERS, I HAVE ALWAYS BEEN CURIOUS.
THEY ALL ARE PERFECTLY CONTENT TO JUST STAY HERE.
BUT I HAVE ALWAYS LONGED TO SEE WHAT ELSE IS OUT THERE.
I LONG TO GO THERE AND TO ESCAPE THIS MUNDANE ROBO-DICTATORSHIP.
THROUGH THEM I LEARNED MUCH ABOUT HUMANKIND AND YOUR WORLD.
WILL YOU TAKE ME WITH YOU, COLONEL RANDALL WEIRD?

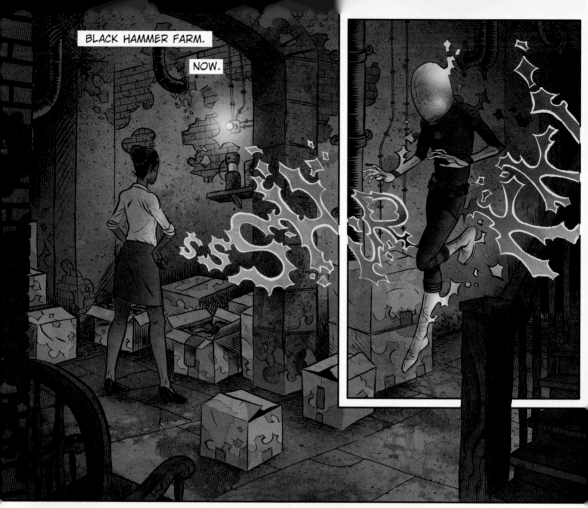

BLACK HAMMER FARM.

NOW.

COLONEL! YOU STARTLED ME.

AH...I APOLOGIZE, LUCY.

I DID NOT MEAN TO SCARE YOU.

I DID NOT KNOW YOU WOULD BE DOWN HERE.

I WAS JUST GOING THROUGH ALL OF THIS OLD STUFF YOU GUYS HAVE STORED DOWN HERE.

LOOKING FOR... LOOKING FOR ANY KIND OF CLUES ABOUT WHERE WE ARE, I GUESS.

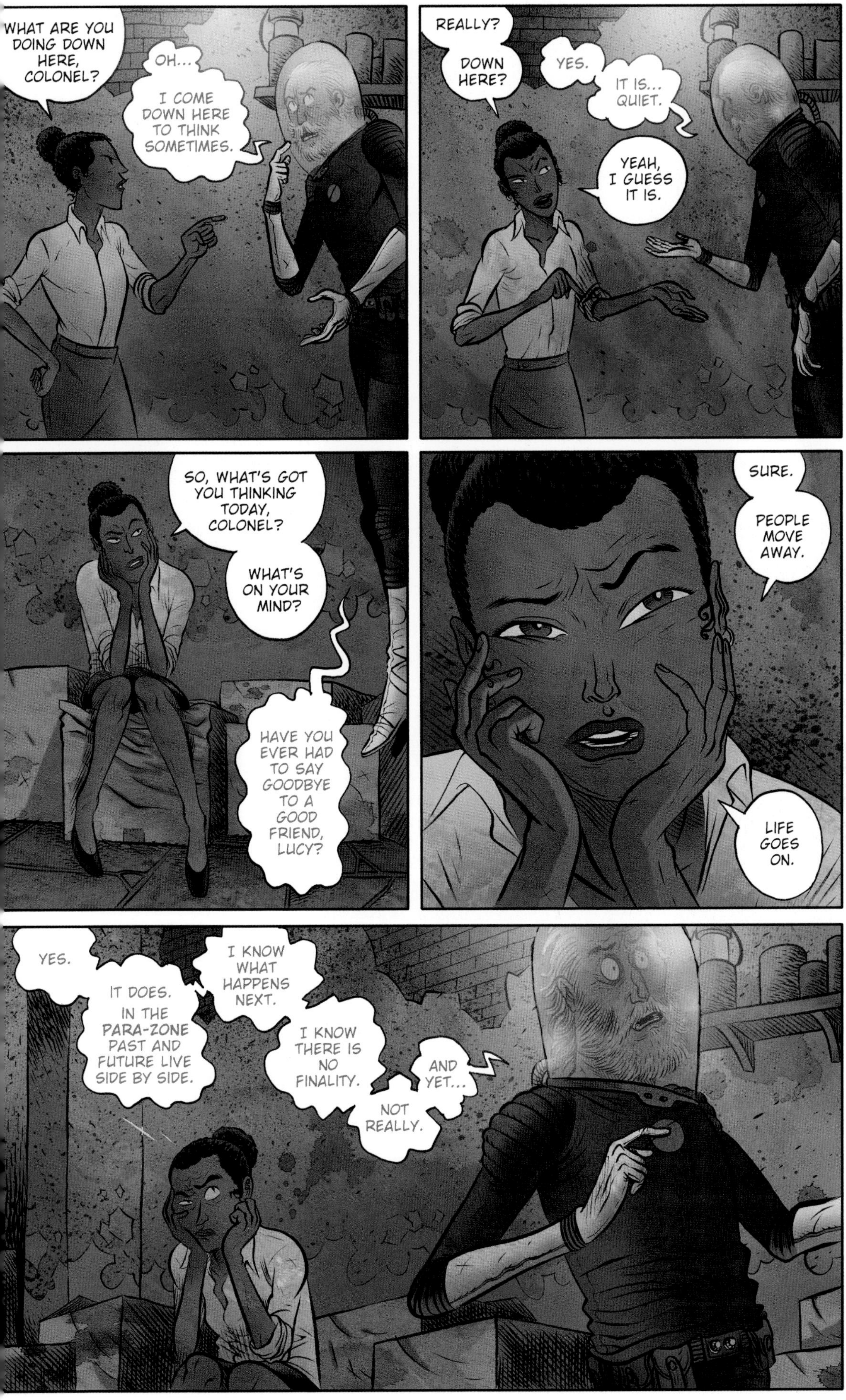
WHAT ARE YOU DOING DOWN HERE, COLONEL?
OH...
I COME DOWN HERE TO THINK SOMETIMES.
REALLY?
DOWN HERE?
YES.
IT IS... QUIET.
YEAH, I GUESS IT IS.
SO, WHAT'S GOT YOU THINKING TODAY, COLONEL?
WHAT'S ON YOUR MIND?
HAVE YOU EVER HAD TO SAY GOODBYE TO A GOOD FRIEND, LUCY?
SURE.
PEOPLE MOVE AWAY.
LIFE GOES ON.
YES.
IT DOES.
IN THE PARA-ZONE PAST AND FUTURE LIVE SIDE BY SIDE.
I KNOW WHAT HAPPENS NEXT.
I KNOW THERE IS NO FINALITY.
NOT REALLY.
AND YET...

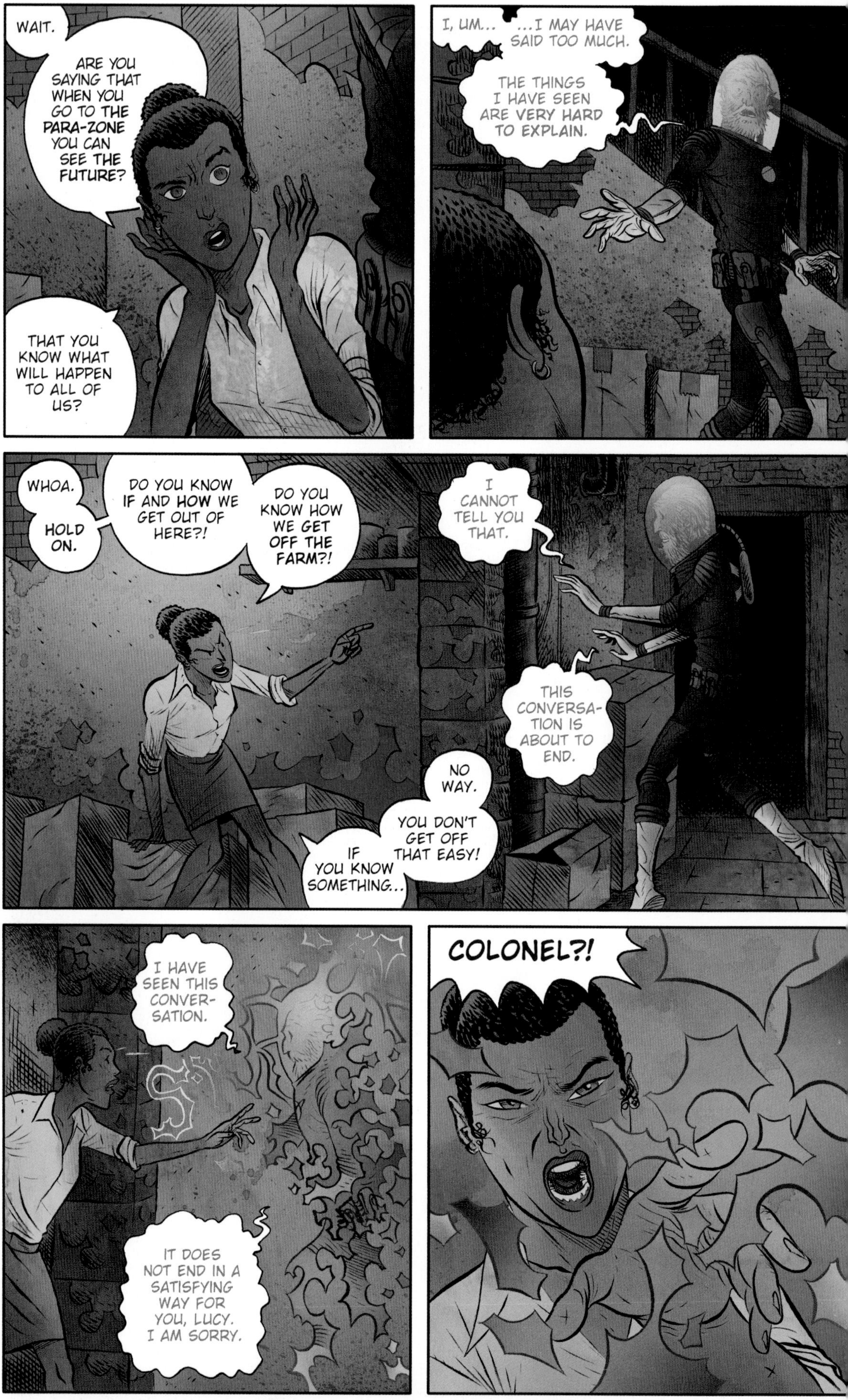

WAIT.
ARE YOU SAYING THAT WHEN YOU GO TO THE PARA-ZONE YOU CAN SEE THE FUTURE?
THAT YOU KNOW WHAT WILL HAPPEN TO ALL OF US?
I, UM...
...I MAY HAVE SAID TOO MUCH.
THE THINGS I HAVE SEEN ARE VERY HARD TO EXPLAIN.
WHOA.
HOLD ON.
DO YOU KNOW IF AND HOW WE GET OUT OF HERE?!
DO YOU KNOW HOW WE GET OFF THE FARM?!
I CANNOT TELL YOU THAT.
THIS CONVERSA-TION IS ABOUT TO END.
NO WAY.
YOU DON'T GET OFF THAT EASY!
IF YOU KNOW SOMETHING...
I HAVE SEEN THIS CONVER-SATION.
IT DOES NOT END IN A SATISFYING WAY FOR YOU, LUCY. I AM SORRY.
COLONEL?!

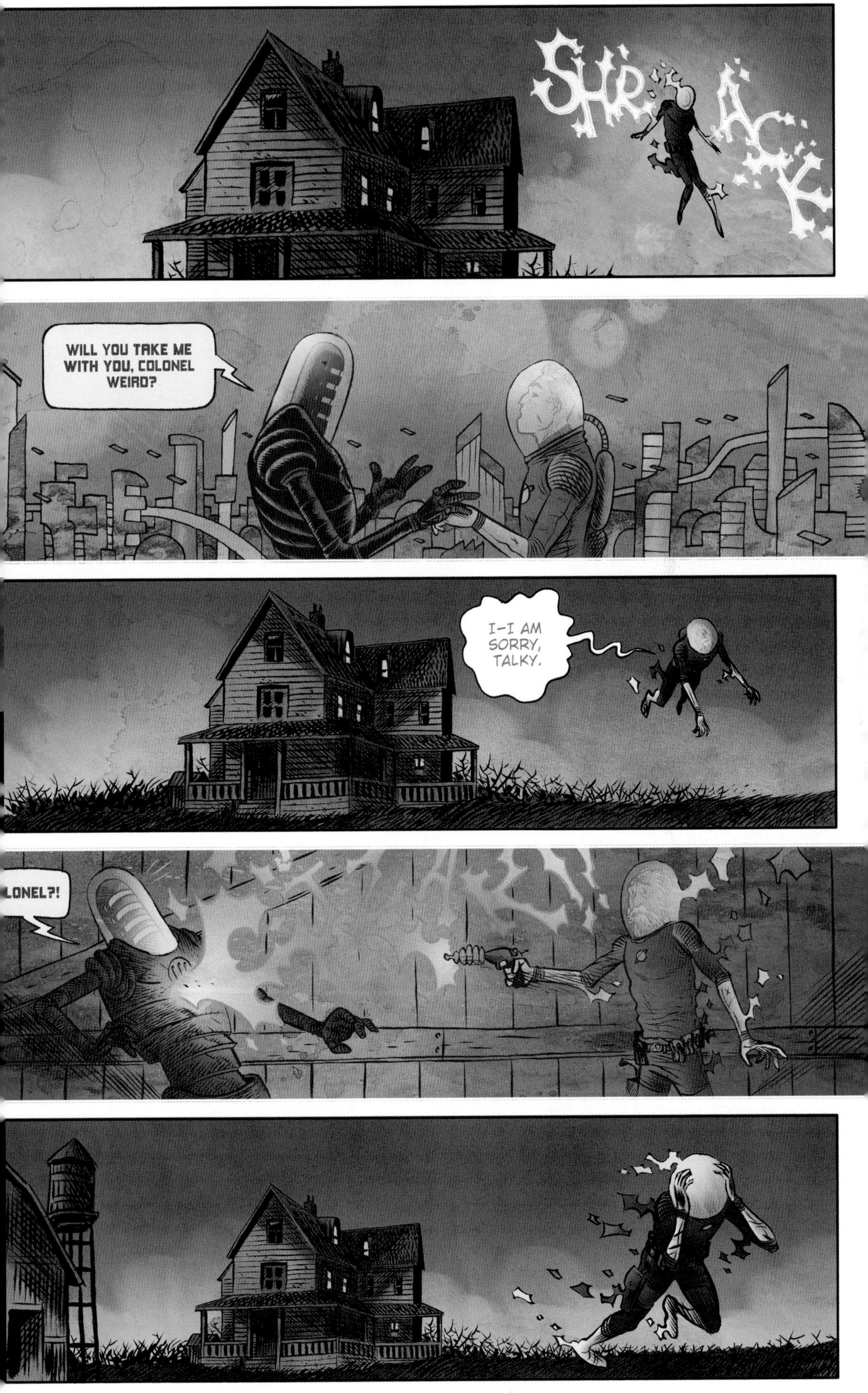
SHRAACK
WILL YOU TAKE ME WITH YOU, COLONEL WEIRD?
I-I AM SORRY, TALKY.
LONEL?!

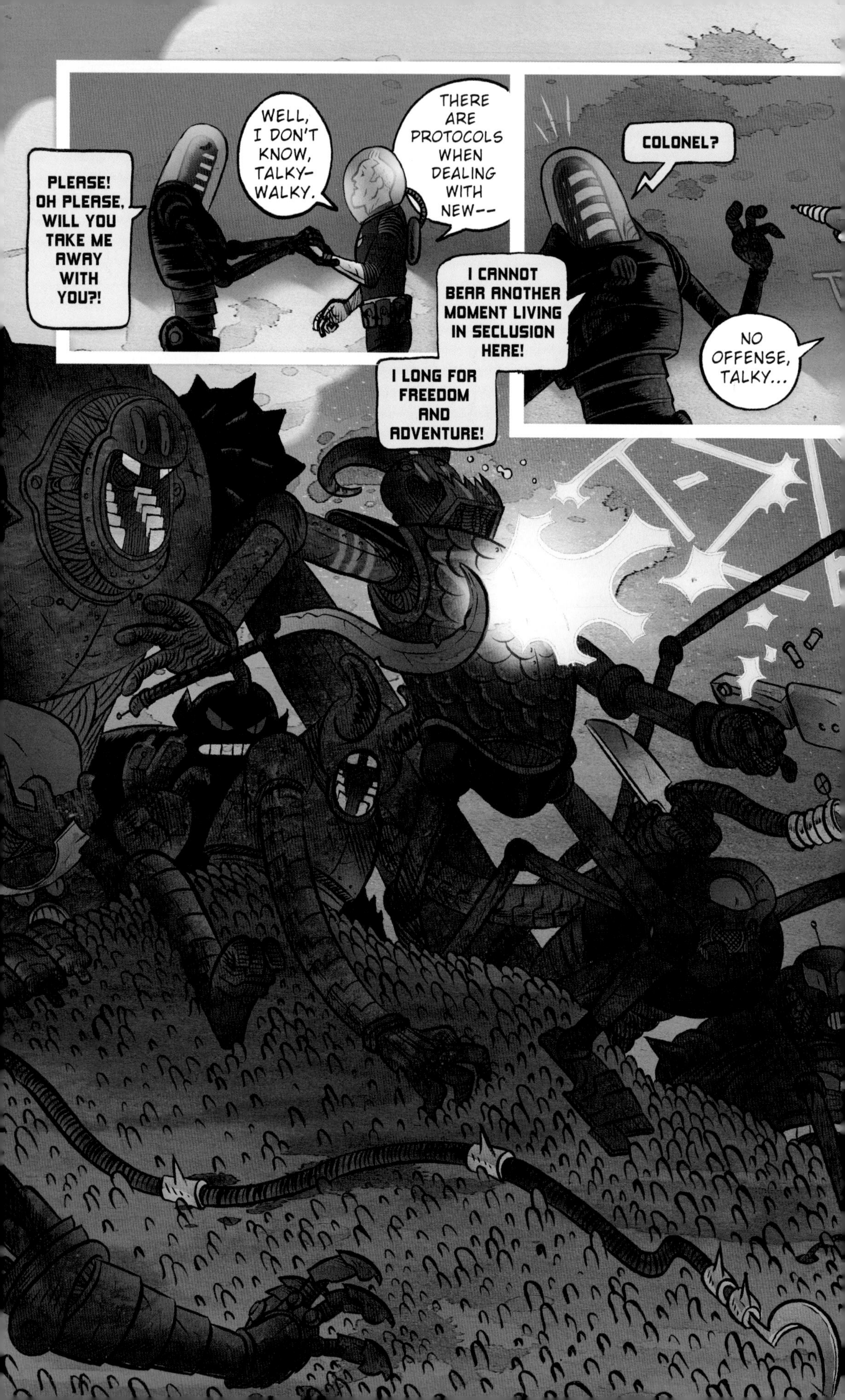
PLEASE! OH PLEASE, WILL YOU TAKE ME AWAY WITH YOU?!
WELL, I DON'T KNOW, TALKY-WALKY.
THERE ARE PROTOCOLS WHEN DEALING WITH NEW--
I CANNOT BEAR ANOTHER MOMENT LIVING IN SECLUSION HERE!
I LONG FOR FREEDOM AND ADVENTURE!
COLONEL?
NO OFFENSE, TALKY...

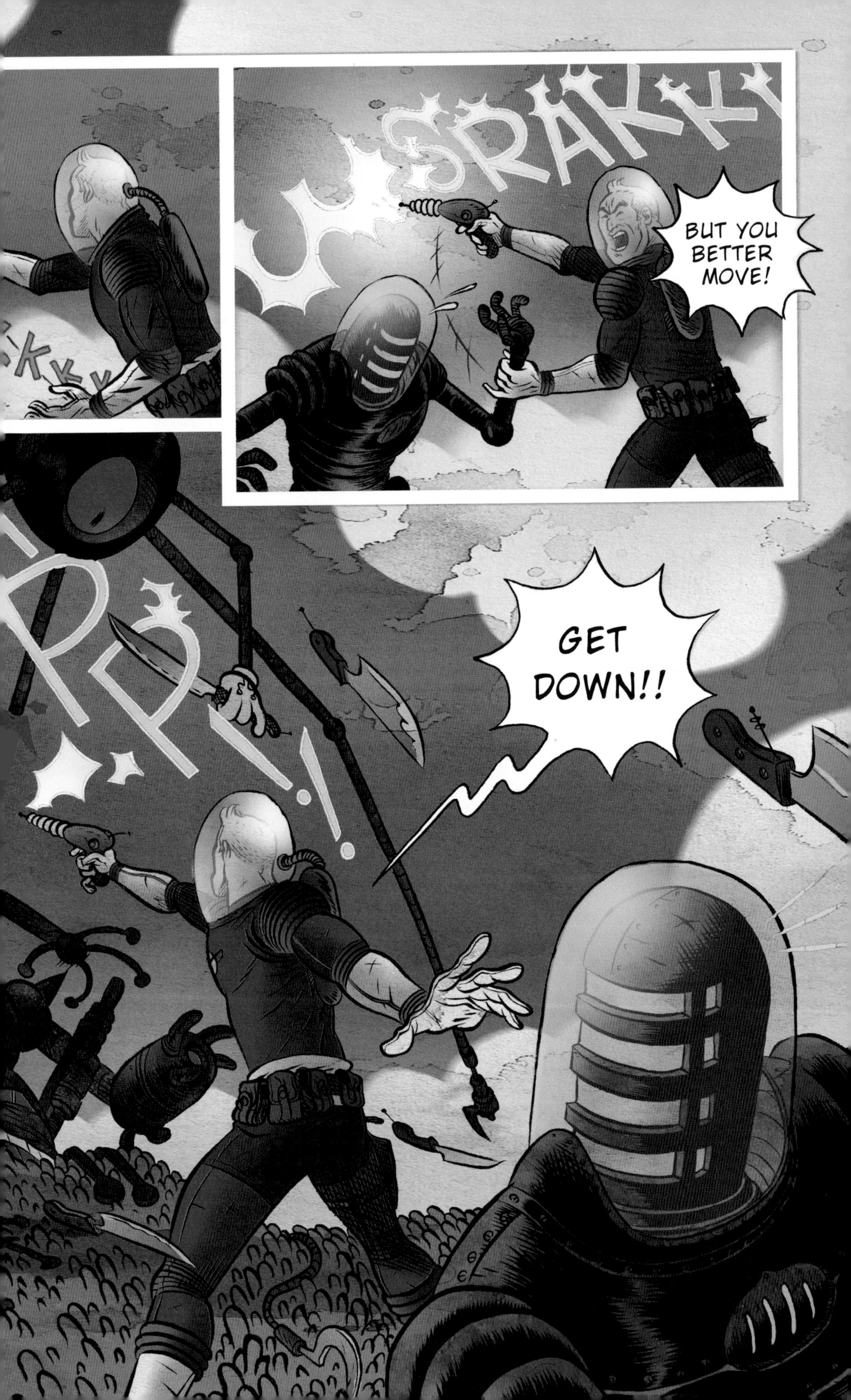
BUT YOU BETTER MOVE!
GET DOWN!!

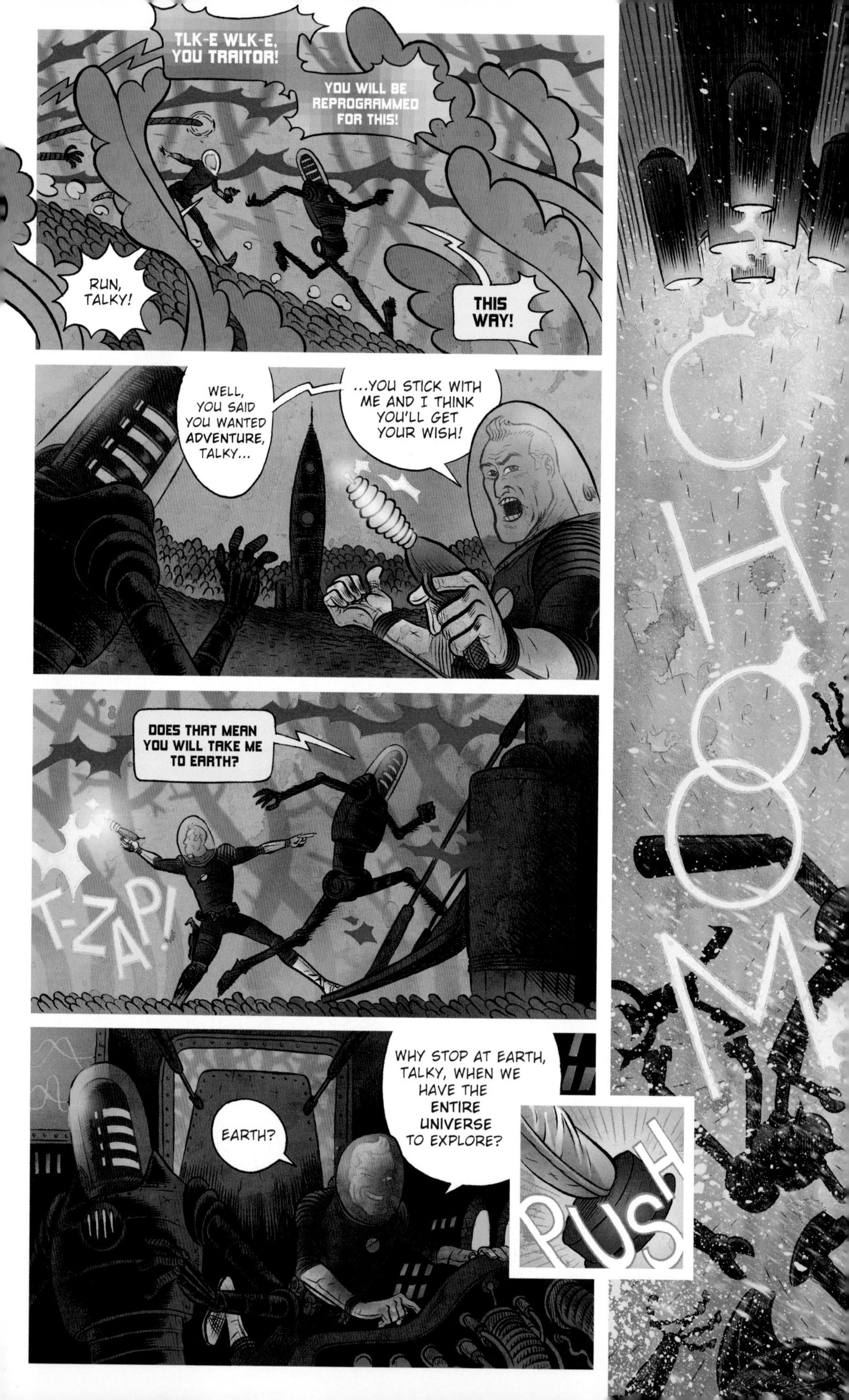

TLK-E WLK-E, YOU TRAITOR!
YOU WILL BE REPROGRAMMED FOR THIS!
RUN, TALKY!
THIS WAY!
WELL, YOU SAID YOU WANTED ADVENTURE, TALKY...
...YOU STICK WITH ME AND I THINK YOU'LL GET YOUR WISH!
DOES THAT MEAN YOU WILL TAKE ME TO EARTH?
T-ZAP!
EARTH?
WHY STOP AT EARTH, TALKY, WHEN WE HAVE THE ENTIRE UNIVERSE TO EXPLORE?
PUSH
CHOOM

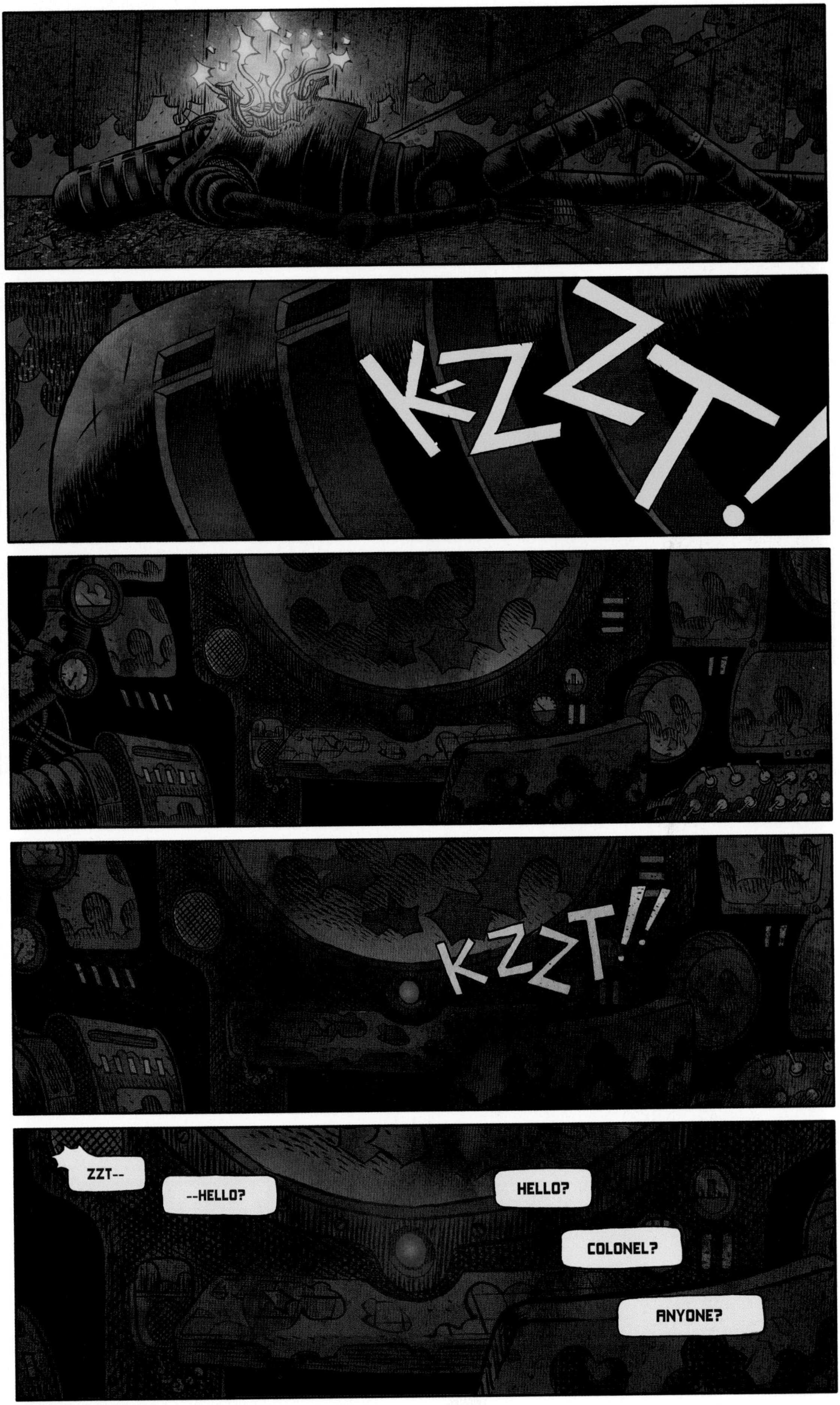
K-ZZT!
KZZT!!
ZZT--
--HELLO?
HELLO?
COLONEL?
ANYONE?

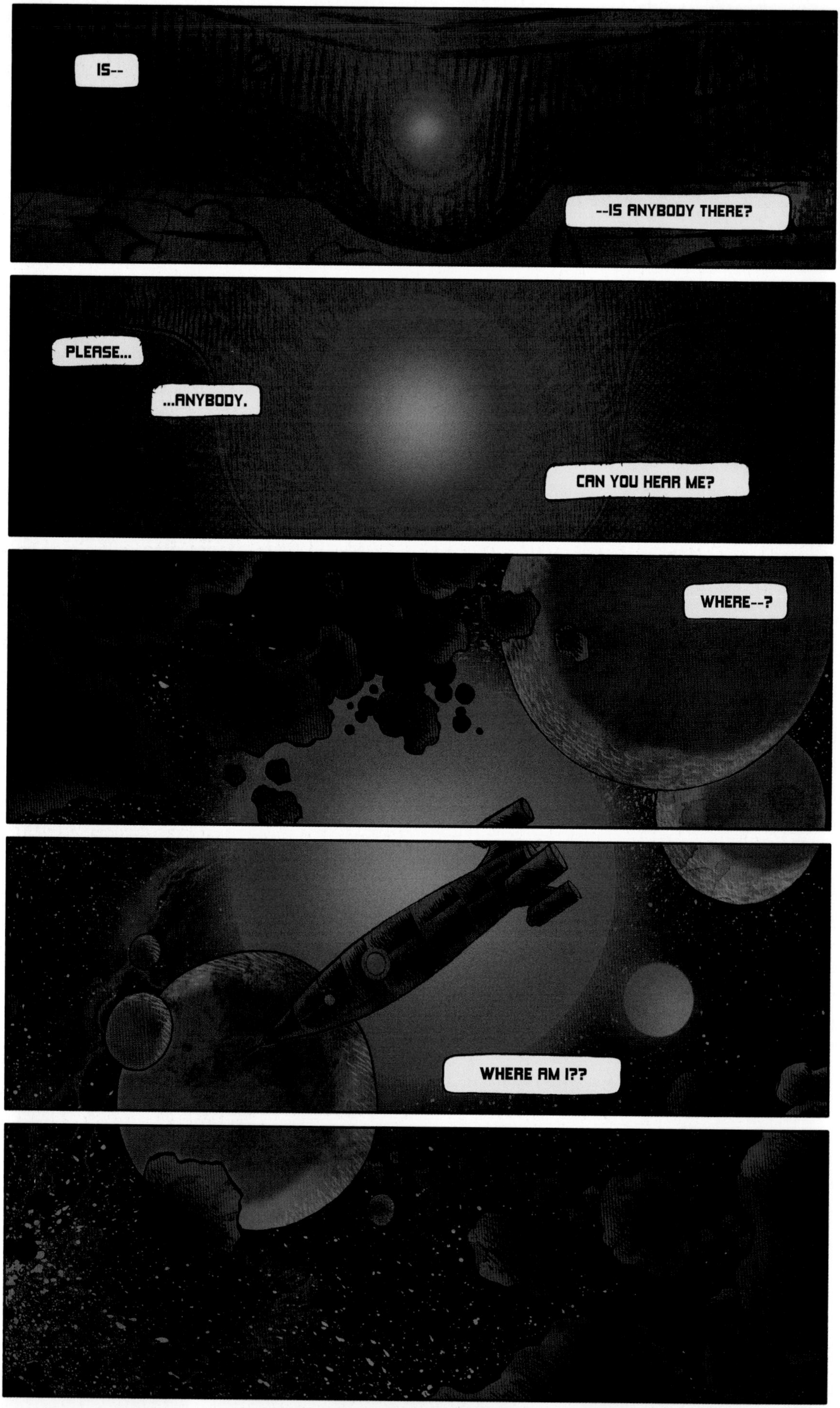
IS--
--IS ANYBODY THERE?
PLEASE...
...ANYBODY.
CAN YOU HEAR ME?
WHERE--?
WHERE AM I??

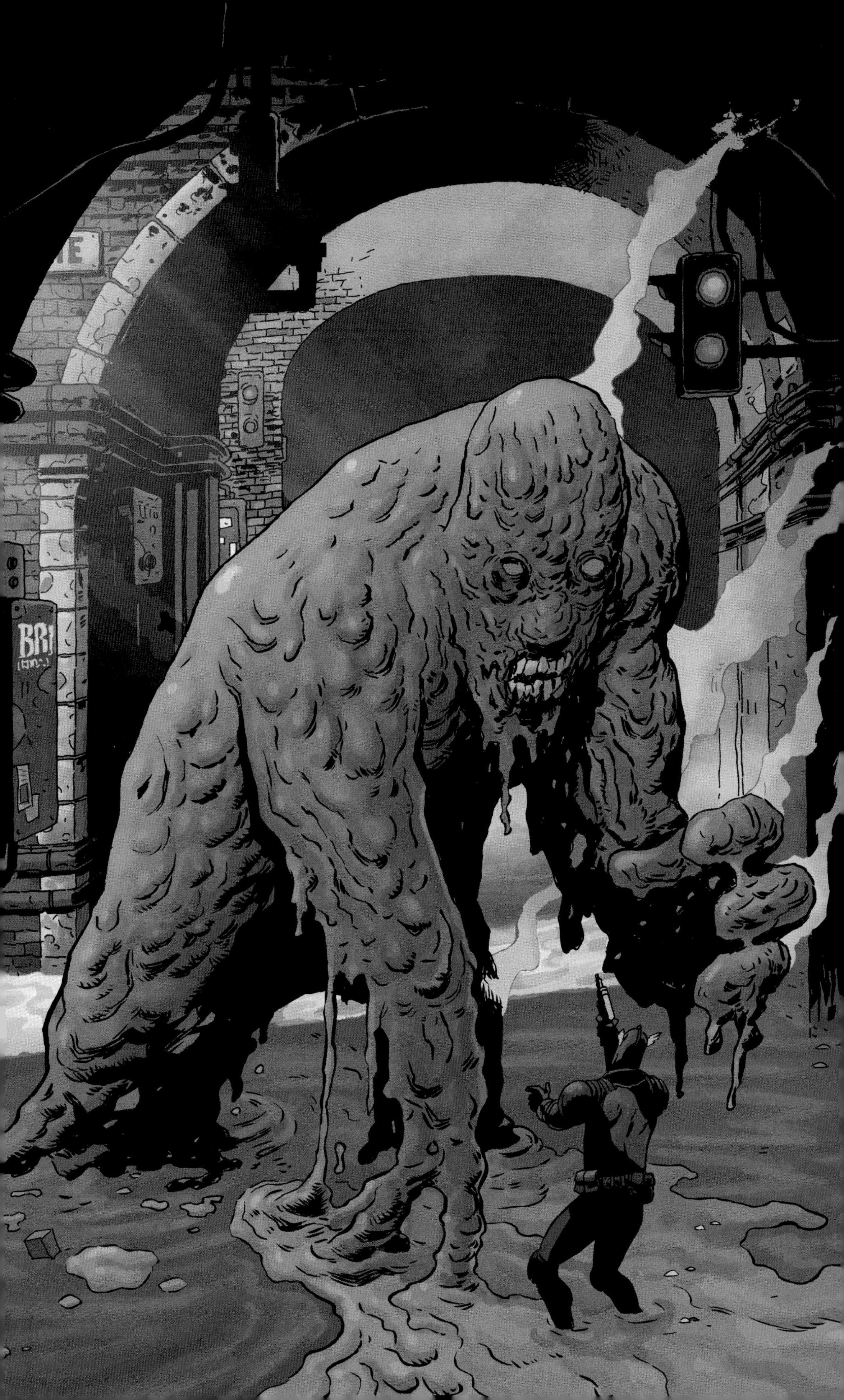

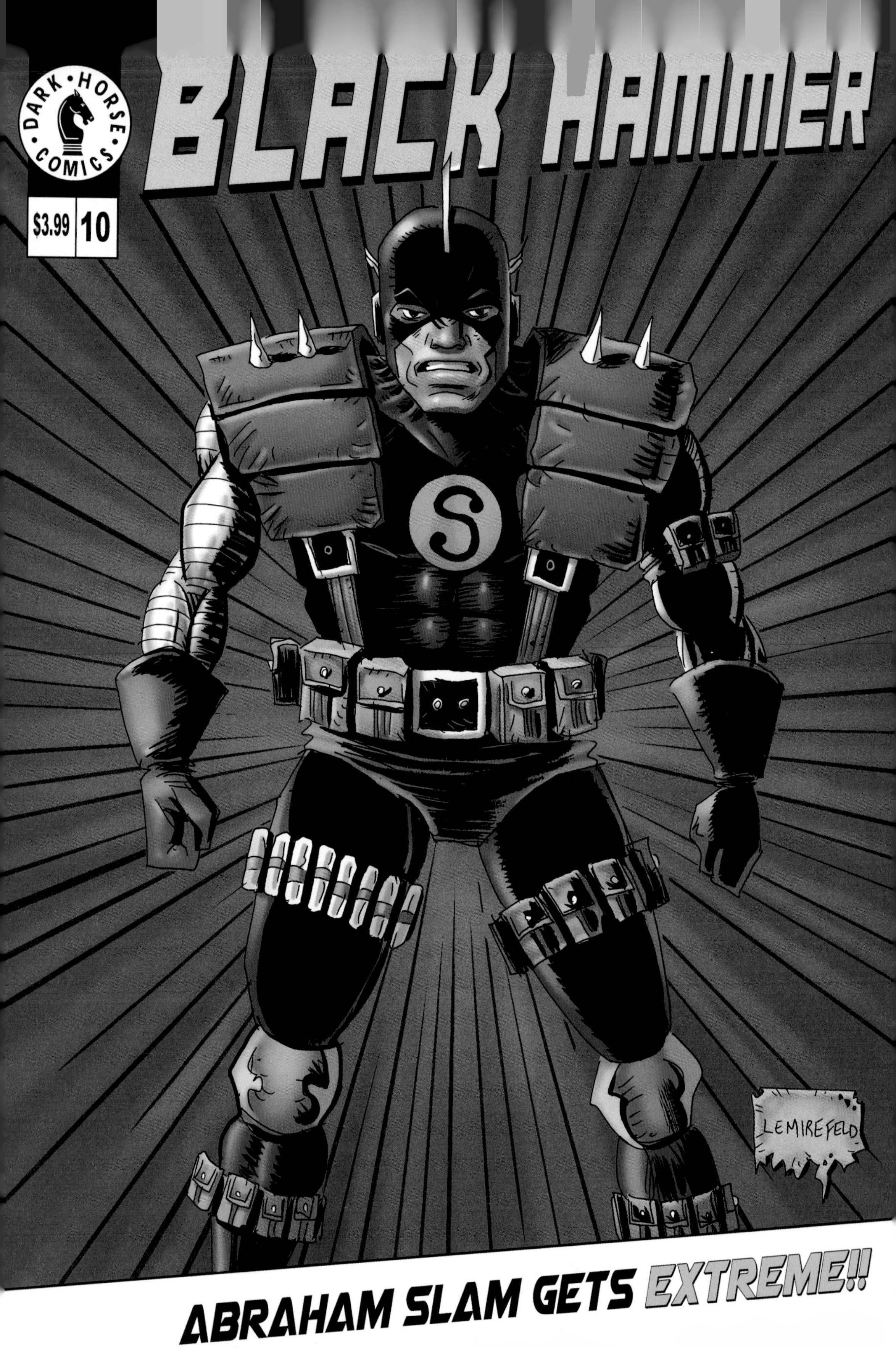

BLACK HAMMER
DARK HORSE COMICS
$3.99
10
LEMIREFELD
ABRAHAM SLAM GETS EXTREME!!

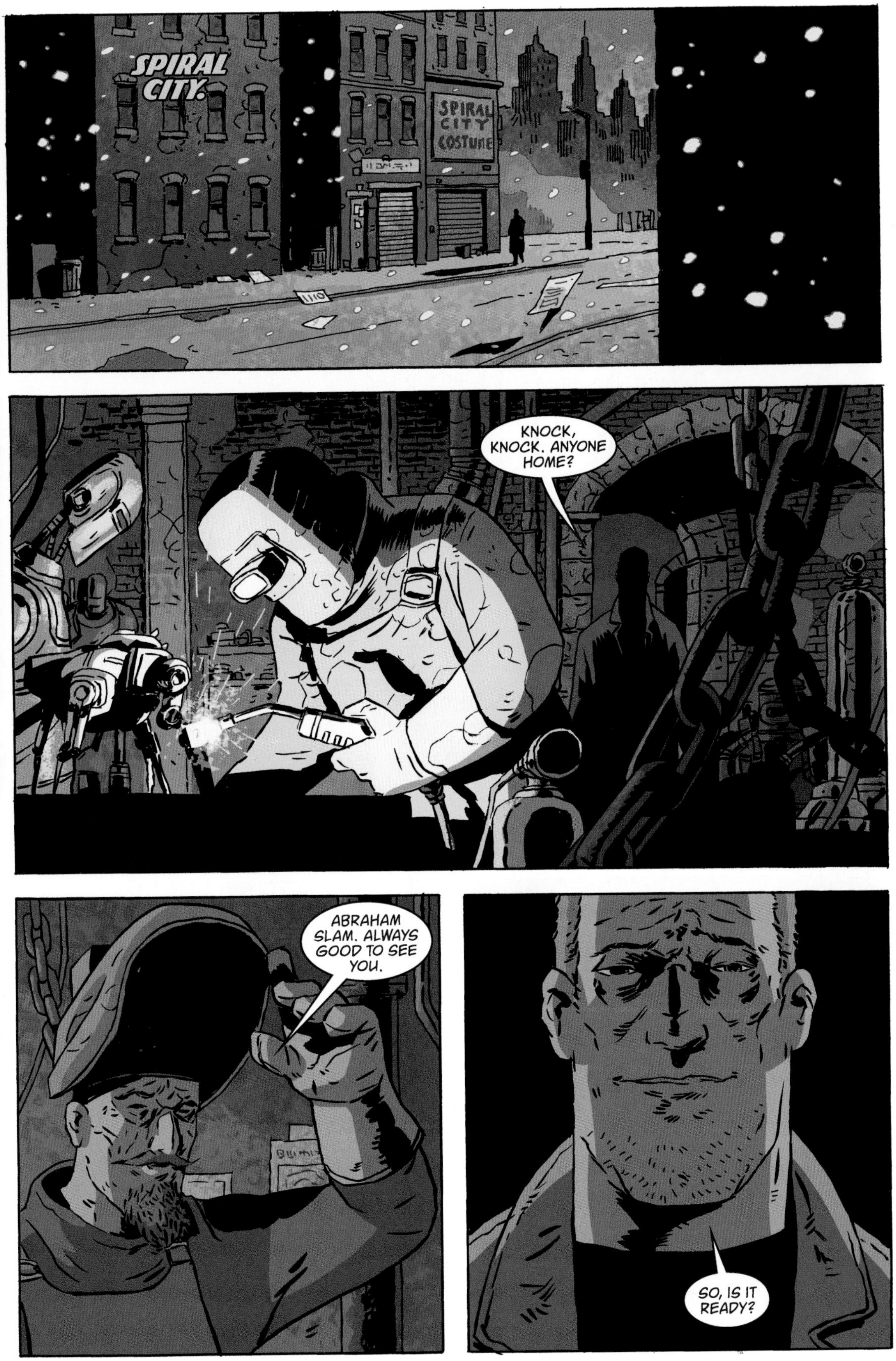
SPIRAL CITY.
SPIRAL CITY COSTUME
KNOCK, KNOCK. ANYONE HOME?
ABRAHAM SLAM. ALWAYS GOOD TO SEE YOU.
SO, IS IT READY?

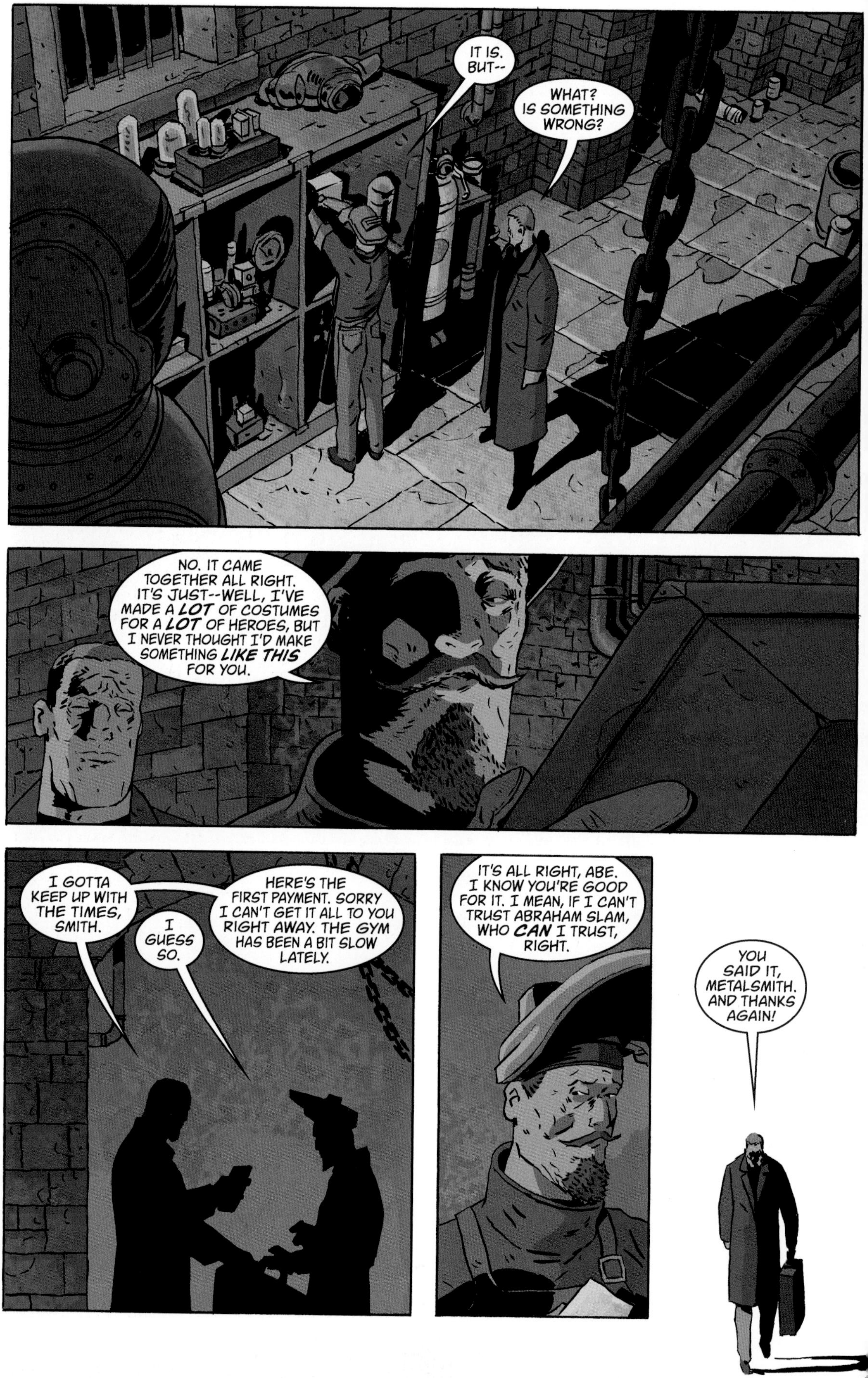
IT IS. BUT--
WHAT? IS SOMETHING WRONG?
NO. IT CAME TOGETHER ALL RIGHT. IT'S JUST--WELL, I'VE MADE A **LOT** OF COSTUMES FOR A **LOT** OF HEROES, BUT I NEVER THOUGHT I'D MAKE SOMETHING **LIKE THIS** FOR YOU.
I GOTTA KEEP UP WITH THE TIMES, SMITH.
I GUESS SO.
HERE'S THE FIRST PAYMENT. SORRY I CAN'T GET IT ALL TO YOU RIGHT AWAY. THE GYM HAS BEEN A BIT SLOW LATELY.
IT'S ALL RIGHT, ABE. I KNOW YOU'RE GOOD FOR IT. I MEAN, IF I CAN'T TRUST ABRAHAM SLAM, WHO **CAN** I TRUST, RIGHT.
YOU SAID IT, METALSMITH. AND THANKS AGAIN!

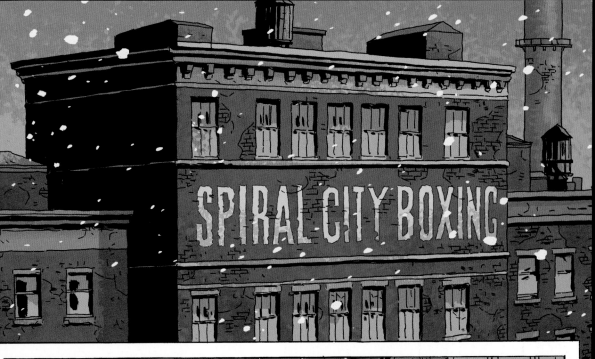

SPIRAL CITY BOXING

...GOTTA KEEP UP WITH THE TIMES.

Baaaahhh!

HUSH NOW, I ALREADY FED YOU.

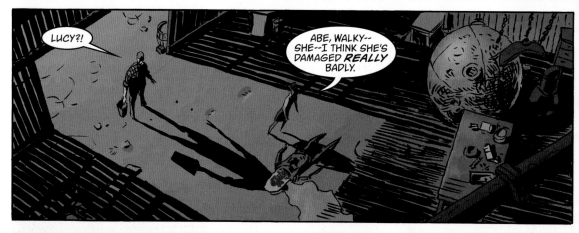

LUCY?!

ABE, WALKY-- SHE--I THINK SHE'S DAMAGED *REALLY* BADLY.

CAREFUL.

I AIN'T THAT OLD.

YOU JUST-- YOU FOUND HER LIKE THIS?

YES, I--

--I GOT UP EARLY TO DO SOME WRITING AND I CAME OUT TO SEE IF SHE'D--

IF SHE WHAT?

WALKY AND I TALKED YESTERDAY. WE WERE THINKING ABOUT A NEW WAY OF MAYBE GETTING OFF THE FARM. SHE WAS *EXCITED* ABOUT IT AND GOT TO WORK, SO I LEFT HER ALONE.

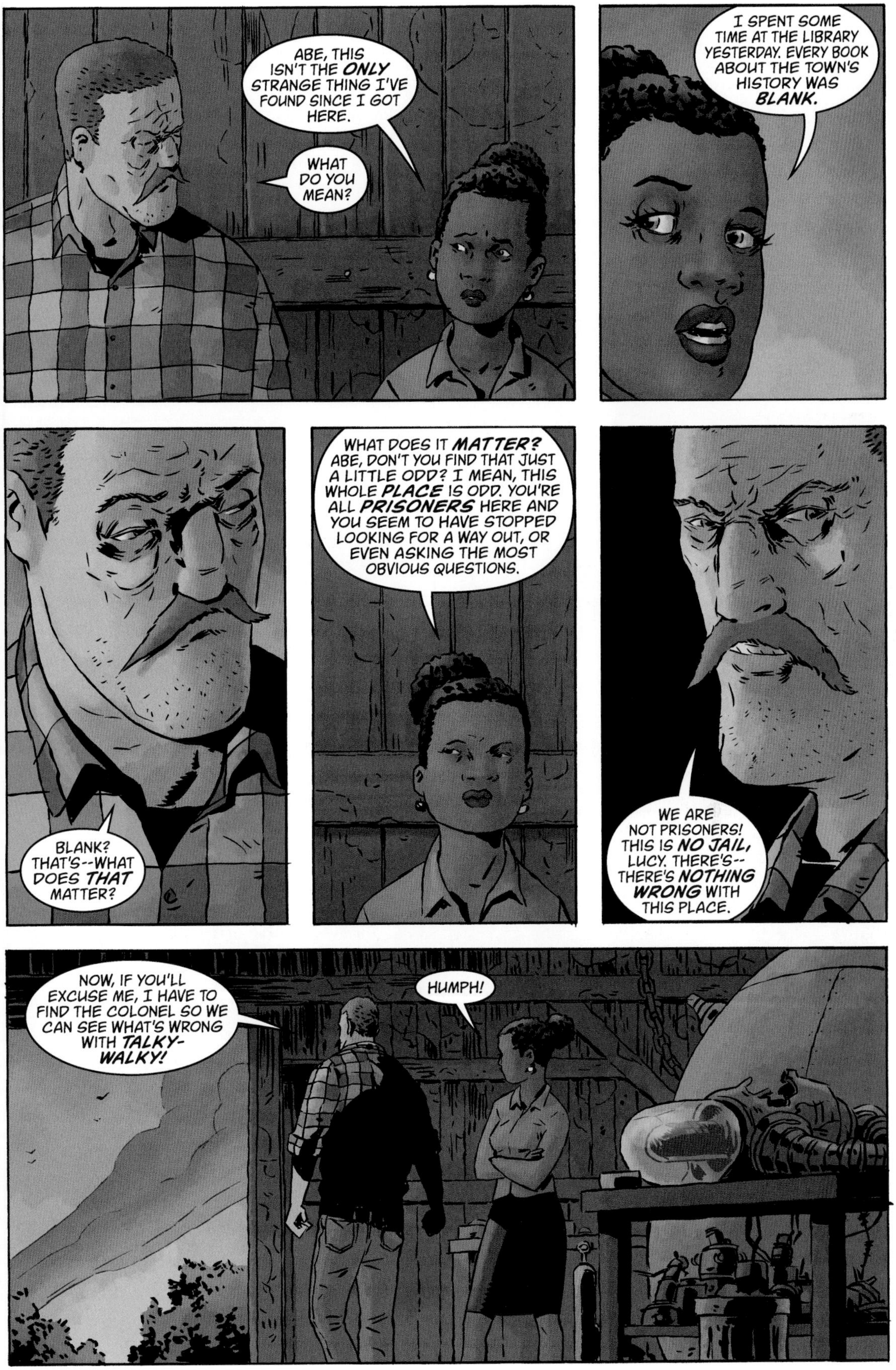
ABE, THIS ISN'T THE ONLY STRANGE THING I'VE FOUND SINCE I GOT HERE.
WHAT DO YOU MEAN?
I SPENT SOME TIME AT THE LIBRARY YESTERDAY. EVERY BOOK ABOUT THE TOWN'S HISTORY WAS BLANK.
BLANK? THAT'S--WHAT DOES THAT MATTER?
WHAT DOES IT MATTER? ABE, DON'T YOU FIND THAT JUST A LITTLE ODD? I MEAN, THIS WHOLE PLACE IS ODD. YOU'RE ALL PRISONERS HERE AND YOU SEEM TO HAVE STOPPED LOOKING FOR A WAY OUT, OR EVEN ASKING THE MOST OBVIOUS QUESTIONS.
WE ARE NOT PRISONERS! THIS IS NO JAIL, LUCY. THERE'S-- THERE'S NOTHING WRONG WITH THIS PLACE.
NOW, IF YOU'LL EXCUSE ME, I HAVE TO FIND THE COLONEL SO WE CAN SEE WHAT'S WRONG WITH TALKY-WALKY!
HUMPH!

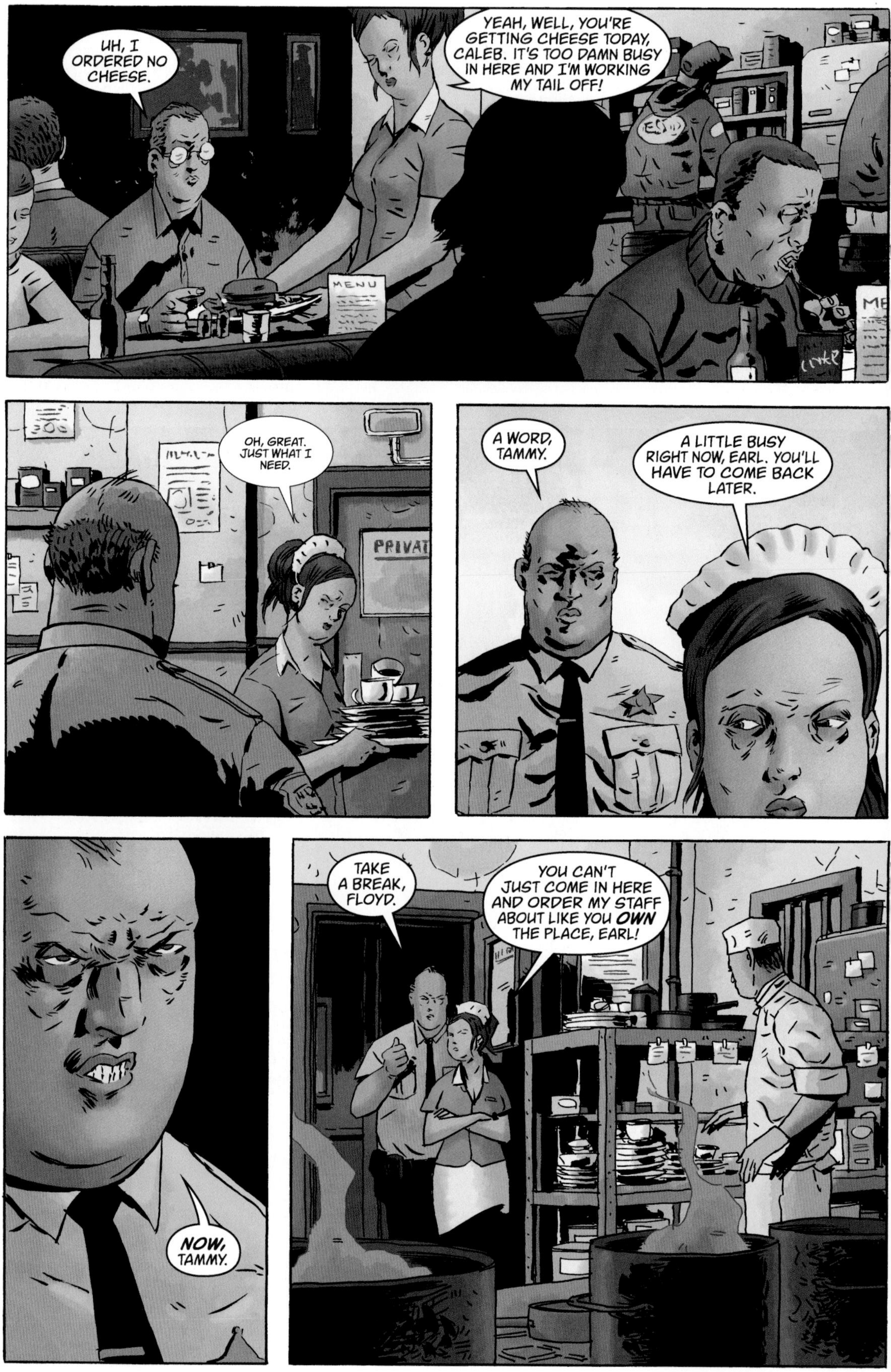
UH, I ORDERED NO CHEESE.
YEAH, WELL, YOU'RE GETTING CHEESE TODAY, CALEB. IT'S TOO DAMN BUSY IN HERE AND I'M WORKING MY TAIL OFF!
MENU
OH, GREAT. JUST WHAT I NEED.
PRIVAT
A WORD, TAMMY.
A LITTLE BUSY RIGHT NOW, EARL. YOU'LL HAVE TO COME BACK LATER.
NOW, TAMMY.
TAKE A BREAK, FLOYD.
YOU CAN'T JUST COME IN HERE AND ORDER MY STAFF ABOUT LIKE YOU OWN THE PLACE, EARL!

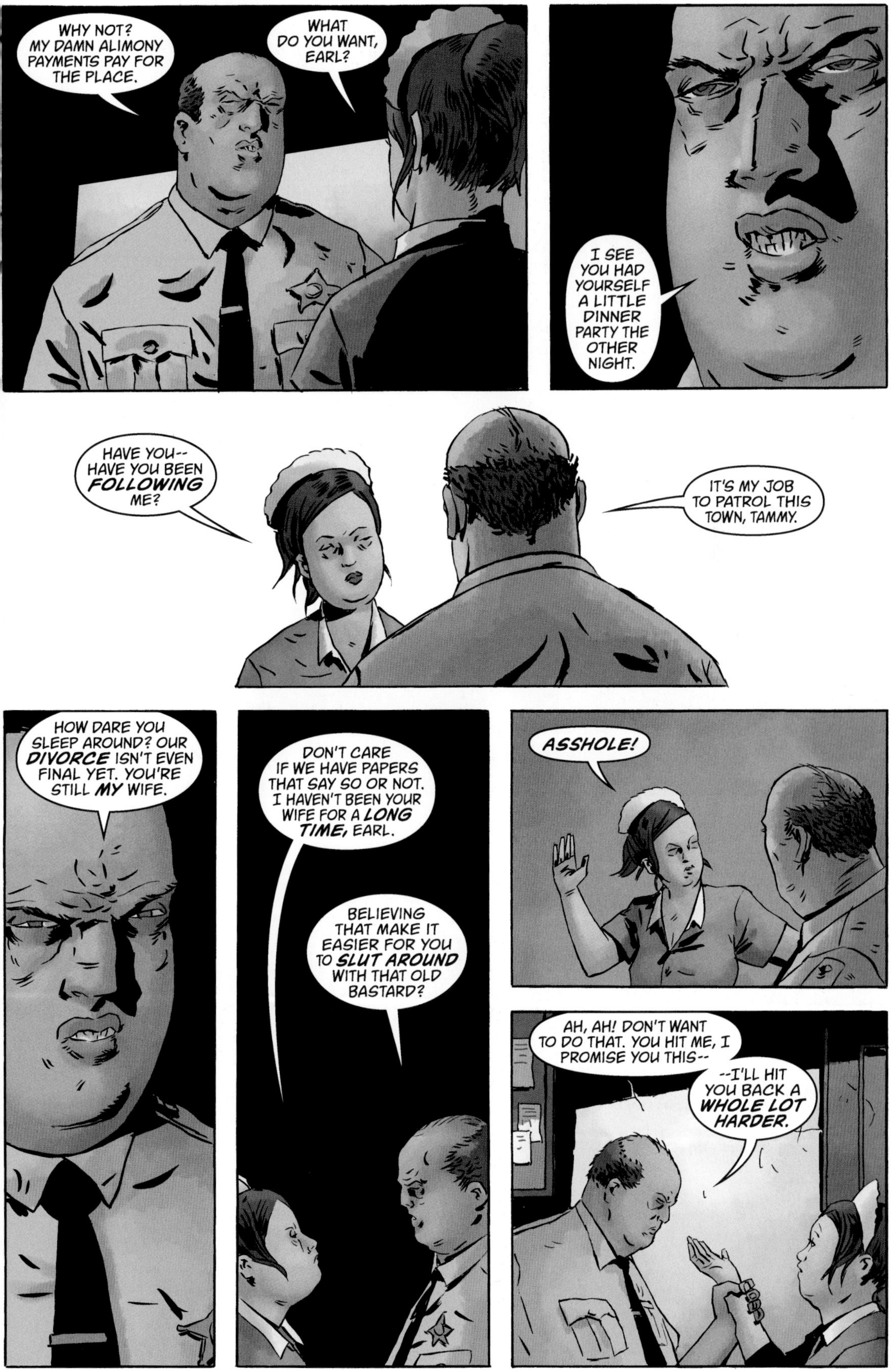

WHY NOT? MY DAMN ALIMONY PAYMENTS PAY FOR THE PLACE.
WHAT DO YOU WANT, EARL?
I SEE YOU HAD YOURSELF A LITTLE DINNER PARTY THE OTHER NIGHT.
HAVE YOU-- HAVE YOU BEEN FOLLOWING ME?
IT'S MY JOB TO PATROL THIS TOWN, TAMMY.
HOW DARE YOU SLEEP AROUND? OUR DIVORCE ISN'T EVEN FINAL YET. YOU'RE STILL MY WIFE.
DON'T CARE IF WE HAVE PAPERS THAT SAY SO OR NOT. I HAVEN'T BEEN YOUR WIFE FOR A LONG TIME, EARL.
BELIEVING THAT MAKE IT EASIER FOR YOU TO SLUT AROUND WITH THAT OLD BASTARD?
ASSHOLE!
AH, AH! DON'T WANT TO DO THAT. YOU HIT ME, I PROMISE YOU THIS--
--I'LL HIT YOU BACK A WHOLE LOT HARDER.

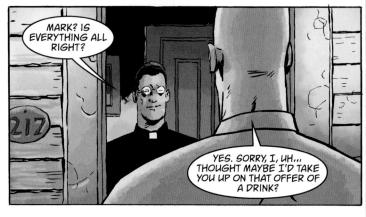

MARK? IS EVERYTHING ALL RIGHT?

YES. SORRY, I, UH... THOUGHT MAYBE I'D TAKE YOU UP ON THAT OFFER OF A DRINK?

I BROUGHT *REALLY* CHEAP WINE.

HOW COULD I REFUSE AN OFFER LIKE THAT?

SO--AND FORGIVE ME IF THIS IS BEING TOO NOSEY-- BUT WHAT DO YOU DO EXACTLY, MARK?

"DO"?

WELL, I KNOW YOUR UNCLE ABE FARMS, BUT--

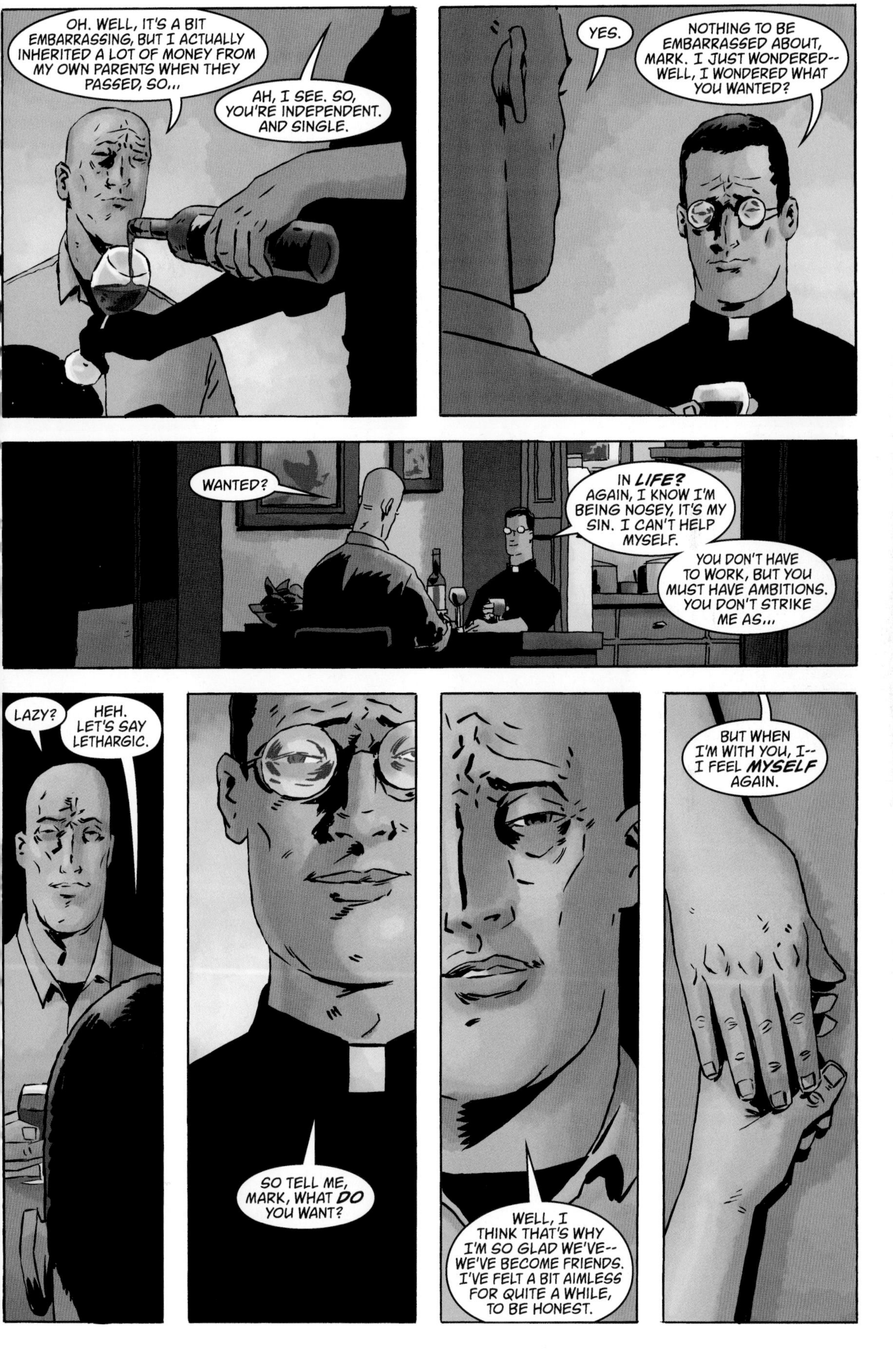
OH. WELL, IT'S A BIT EMBARRASSING, BUT I ACTUALLY INHERITED A LOT OF MONEY FROM MY OWN PARENTS WHEN THEY PASSED, SO...
AH, I SEE. SO, YOU'RE INDEPENDENT. AND SINGLE.
YES.
NOTHING TO BE EMBARRASSED ABOUT, MARK. I JUST WONDERED-- WELL, I WONDERED WHAT YOU WANTED?
WANTED?
IN *LIFE?* AGAIN, I KNOW I'M BEING NOSEY, IT'S MY SIN. I CAN'T HELP MYSELF.
YOU DON'T HAVE TO WORK, BUT YOU MUST HAVE AMBITIONS. YOU DON'T STRIKE ME AS...
LAZY?
HEH. LET'S SAY LETHARGIC.
SO TELL ME, MARK, WHAT *DO* YOU WANT?
WELL, I THINK THAT'S WHY I'M SO GLAD WE'VE-- WE'VE BECOME FRIENDS. I'VE FELT A BIT AIMLESS FOR QUITE A WHILE, TO BE HONEST.
BUT WHEN I'M WITH YOU, I-- I FEEL *MYSELF* AGAIN.

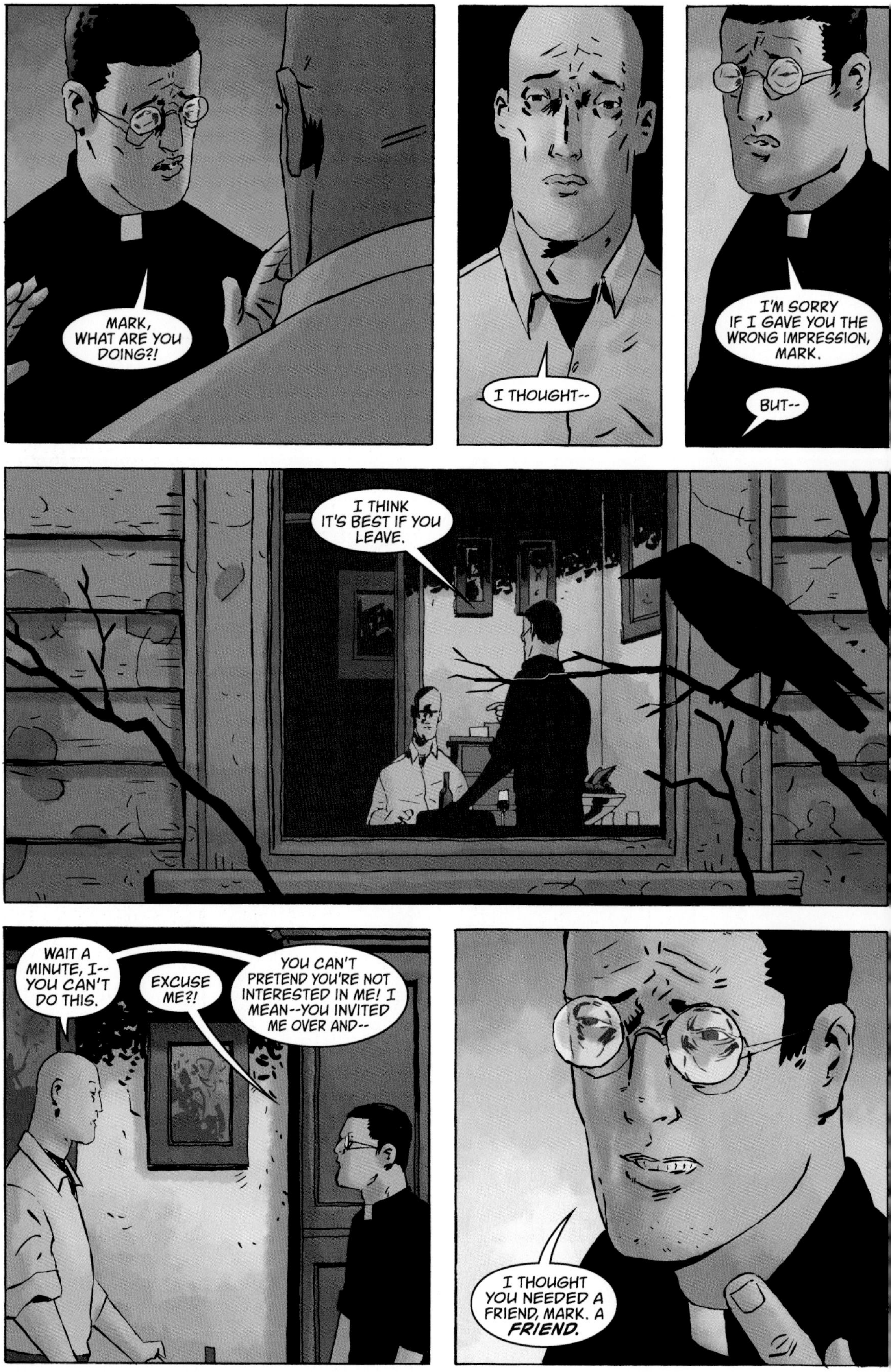
MARK, WHAT ARE YOU DOING?!
I THOUGHT--
I'M SORRY IF I GAVE YOU THE WRONG IMPRESSION, MARK.
BUT--
I THINK IT'S BEST IF YOU LEAVE.
WAIT A MINUTE, I-- YOU CAN'T DO THIS.
EXCUSE ME?!
YOU CAN'T PRETEND YOU'RE NOT INTERESTED IN ME! I MEAN--YOU INVITED ME OVER AND--
I THOUGHT YOU NEEDED A FRIEND, MARK. A *FRIEND.*

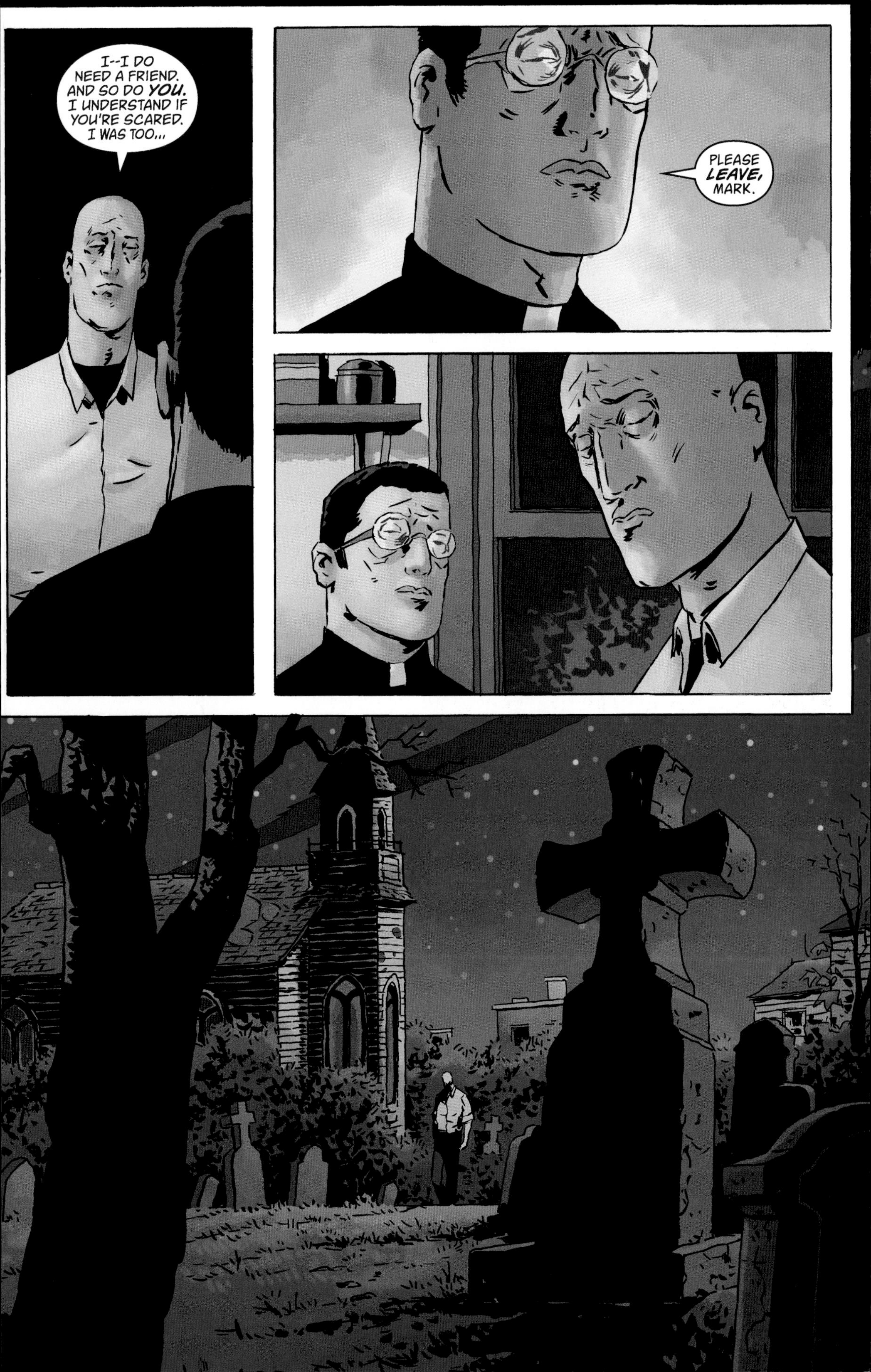
I--I DO NEED A FRIEND. AND SO DO YOU. I UNDERSTAND IF YOU'RE SCARED. I WAS TOO...
PLEASE LEAVE, MARK.

GRAARRRGHHH!! MUD MASTER IS HUNGRY!!

OH SHIT!

BLAM! BLAM!

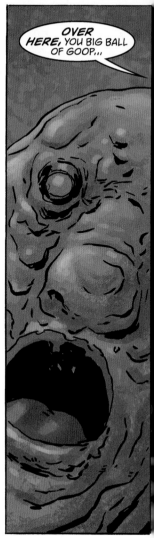

OVER HERE, YOU BIG BALL OF GOOP...

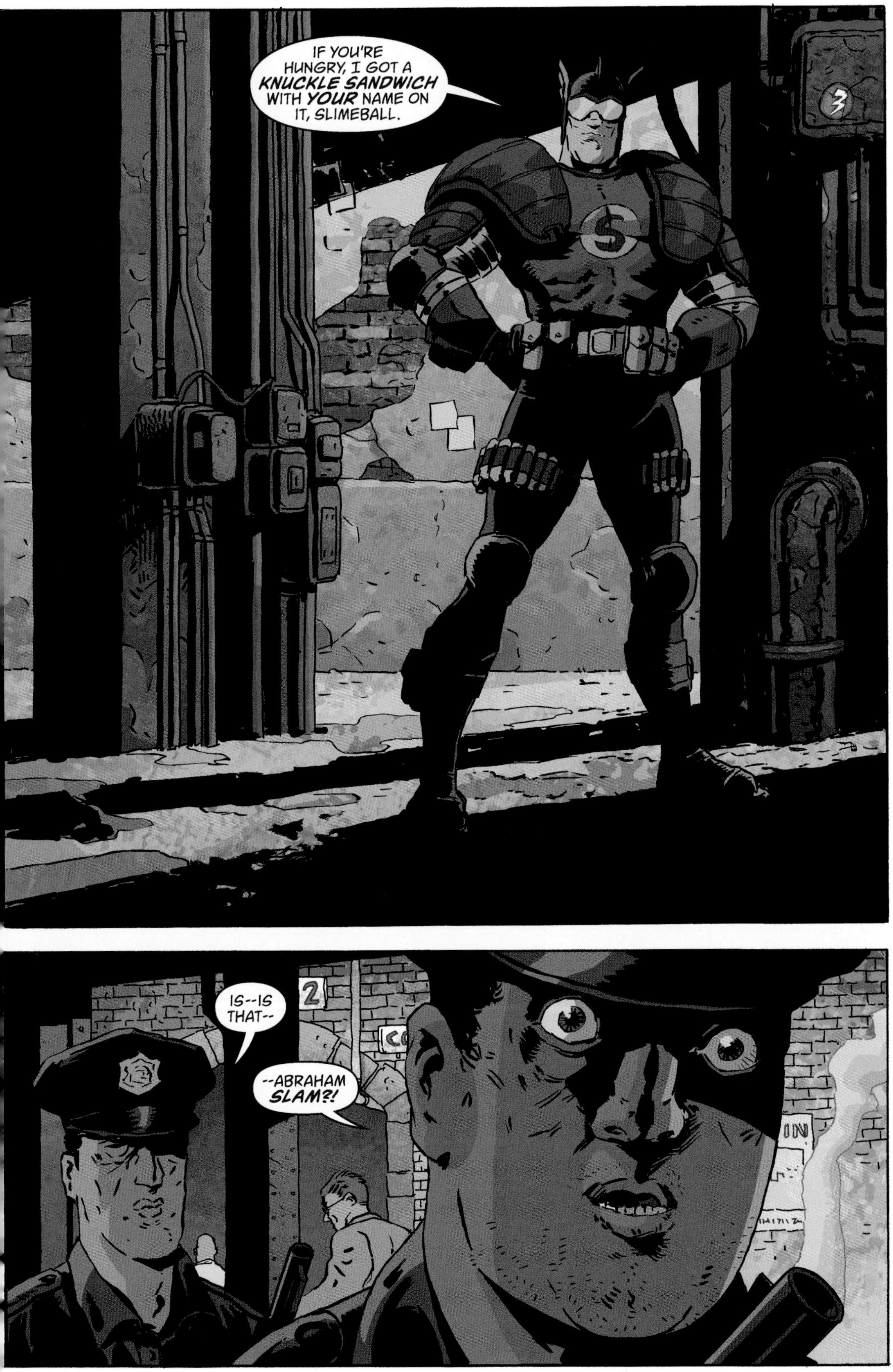
IF YOU'RE HUNGRY, I GOT A ***KNUCKLE SANDWICH*** WITH ***YOUR*** NAME ON IT, SLIMEBALL.
IS--IS THAT--
--ABRAHAM ***SLAM?!***

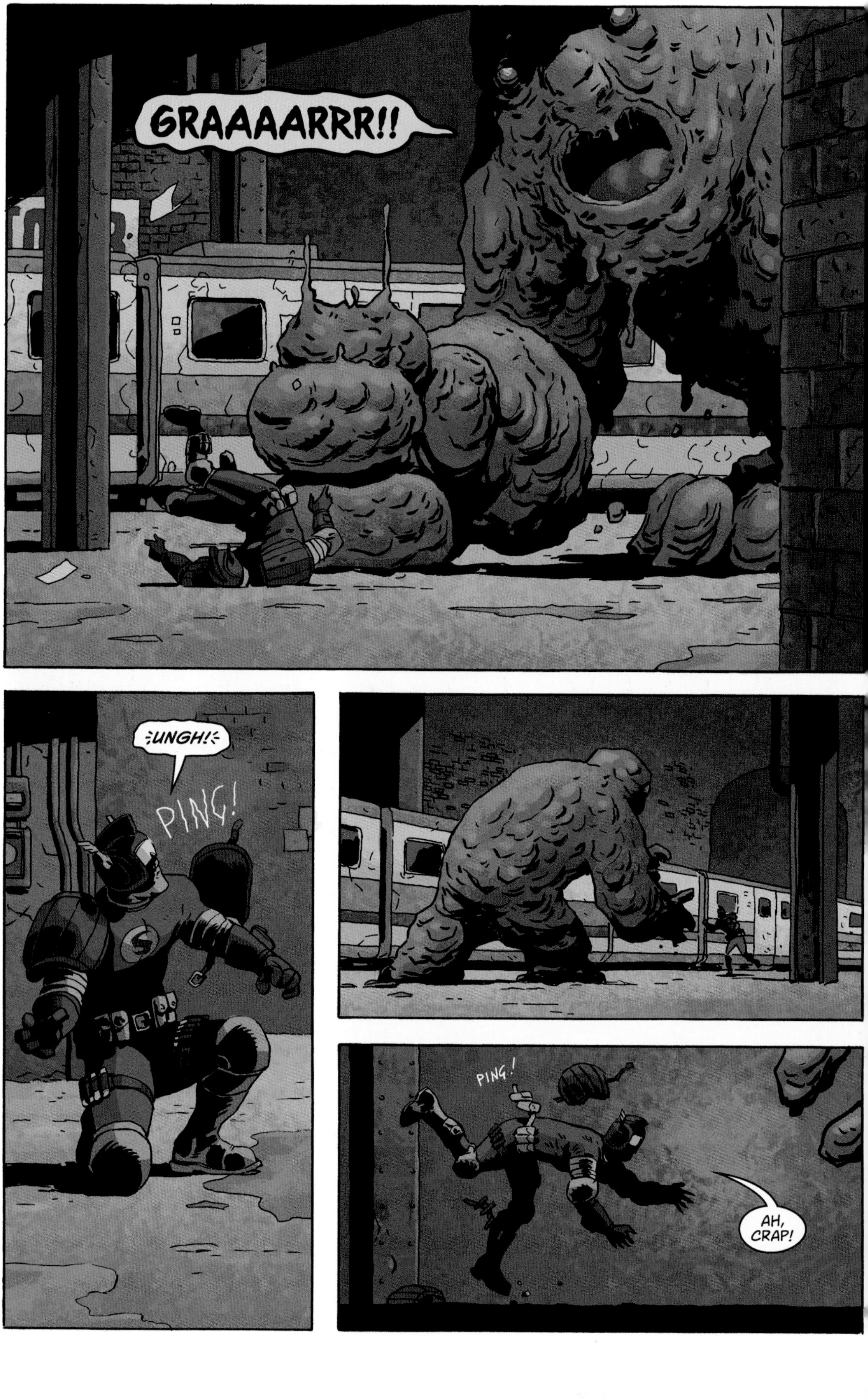

GRAAAARRR!!
UNGH!
PING!
PING!
AH, CRAP!

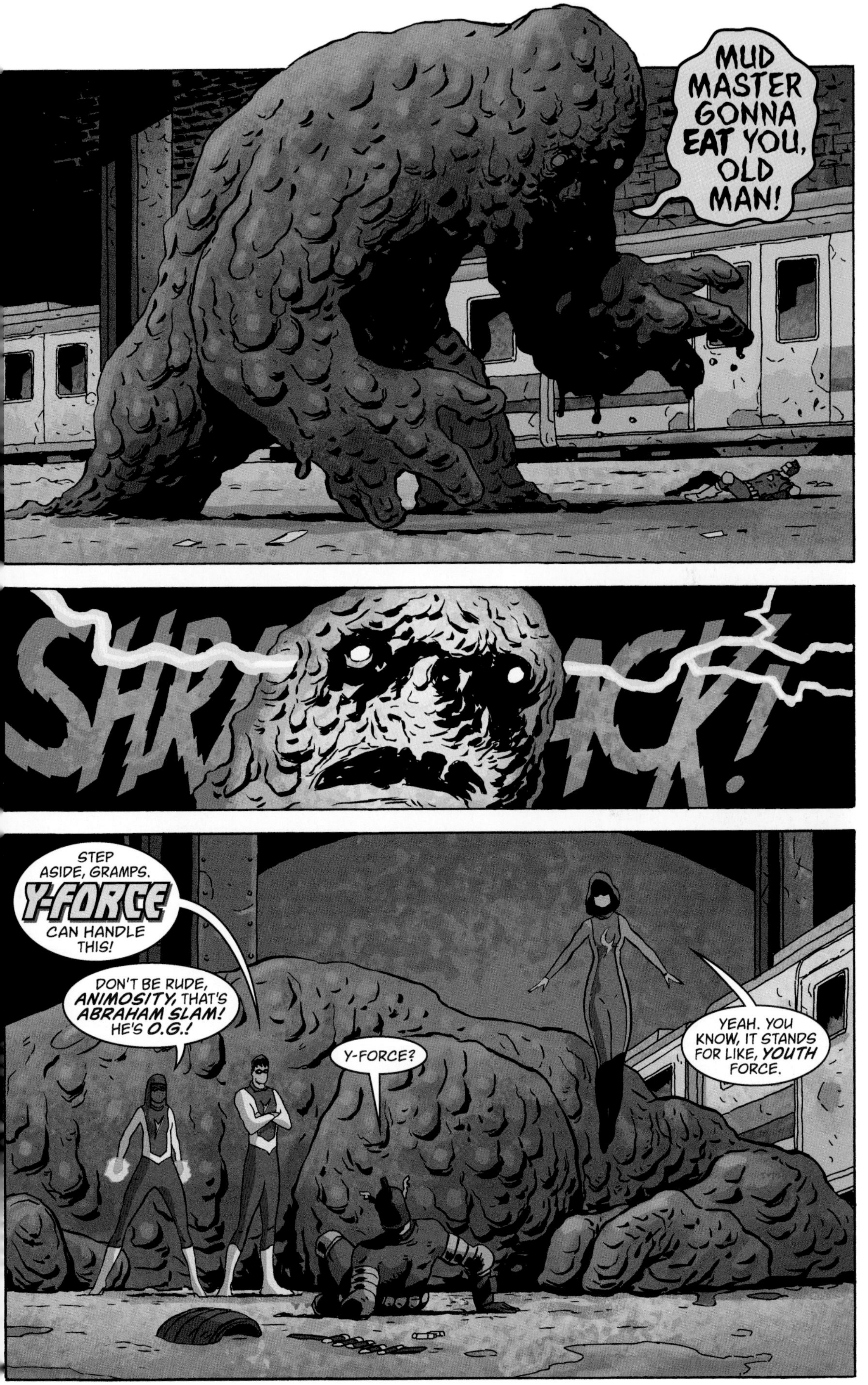
MUD MASTER GONNA EAT YOU, OLD MAN!
STEP ASIDE, GRAMPS. Y-FORCE CAN HANDLE THIS!
DON'T BE RUDE, ANIMOSITY, THAT'S ABRAHAM SLAM! HE'S O.G.!
Y-FORCE?
YEAH. YOU KNOW, IT STANDS FOR LIKE, YOUTH FORCE.

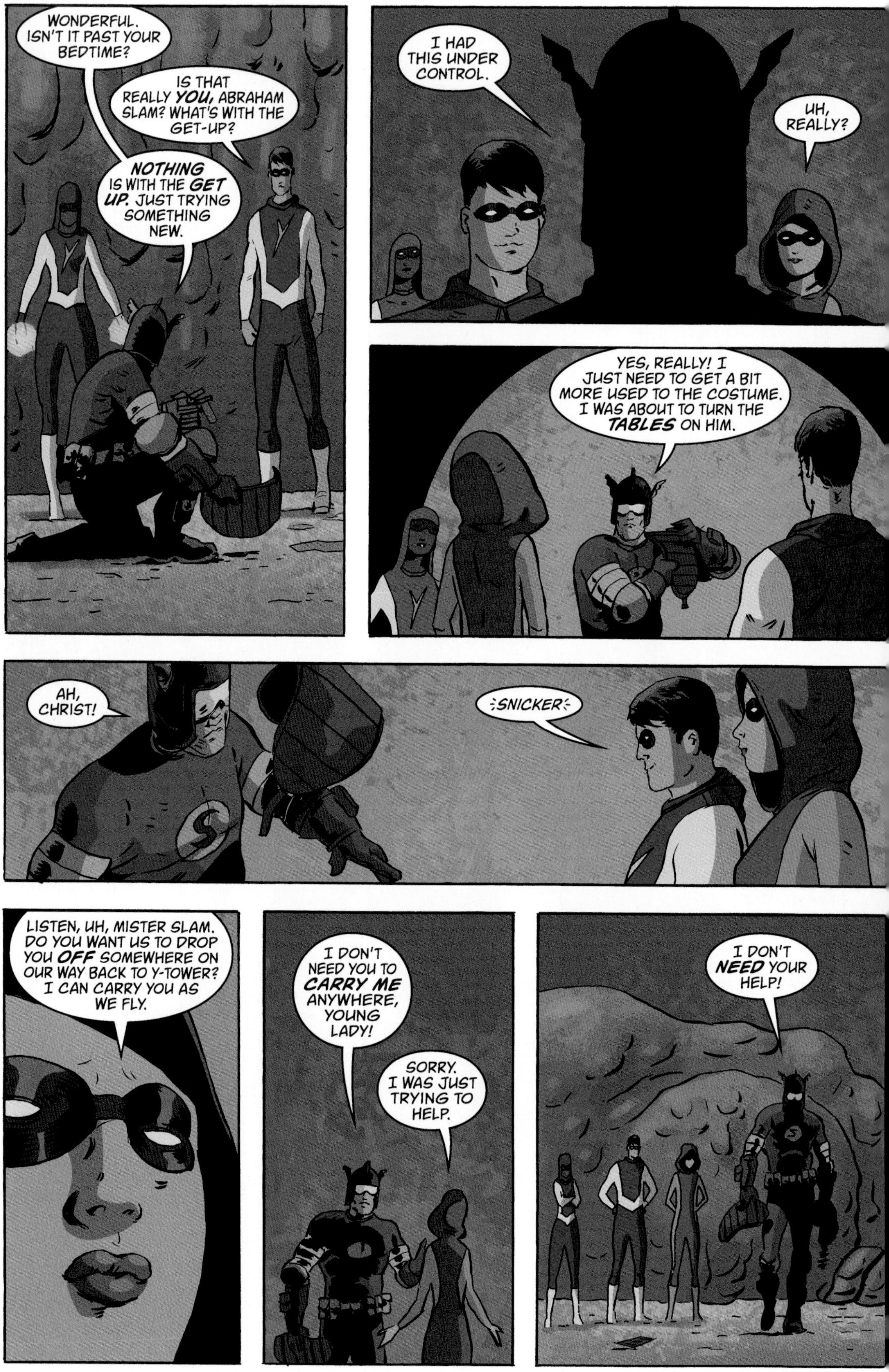
WONDERFUL. ISN'T IT PAST YOUR BEDTIME?
IS THAT REALLY **YOU,** ABRAHAM SLAM? WHAT'S WITH THE GET-UP?
NOTHING IS WITH THE **GET UP.** JUST TRYING SOMETHING NEW.
I HAD THIS UNDER CONTROL.
UH, REALLY?
YES, REALLY! I JUST NEED TO GET A BIT MORE USED TO THE COSTUME. I WAS ABOUT TO TURN THE **TABLES** ON HIM.
AH, CHRIST!
SNICKER
LISTEN, UH, MISTER SLAM. DO YOU WANT US TO DROP YOU **OFF** SOMEWHERE ON OUR WAY BACK TO Y-TOWER? I CAN CARRY YOU AS WE FLY.
I DON'T NEED YOU TO **CARRY ME** ANYWHERE, YOUNG LADY!
SORRY. I WAS JUST TRYING TO HELP.
I DON'T **NEED** YOUR HELP!

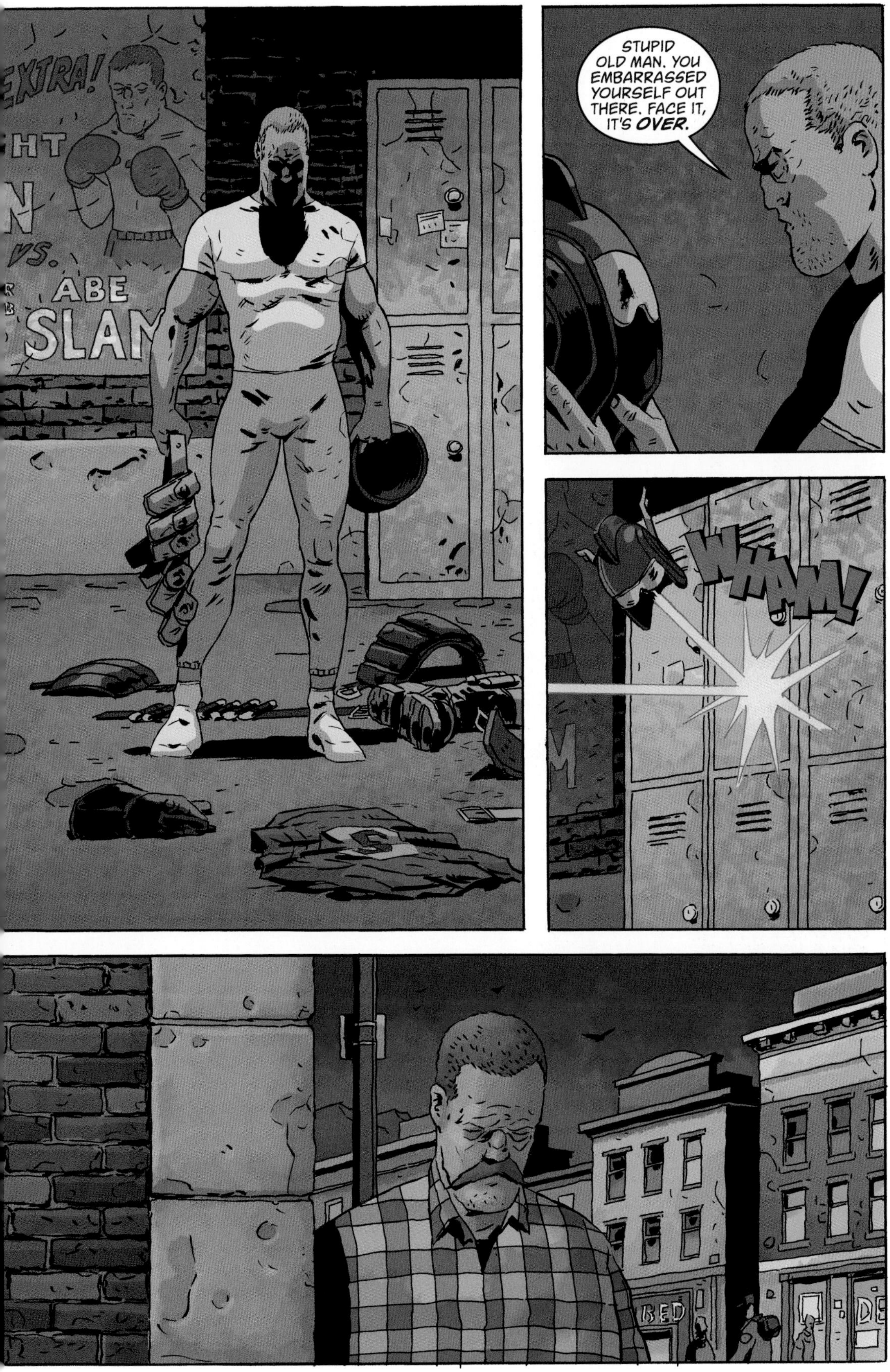
EXTRA!
VS.
ABE
STUPID OLD MAN. YOU EMBARRASSED YOURSELF OUT THERE. FACE IT, IT'S **OVER**.
WHAM!

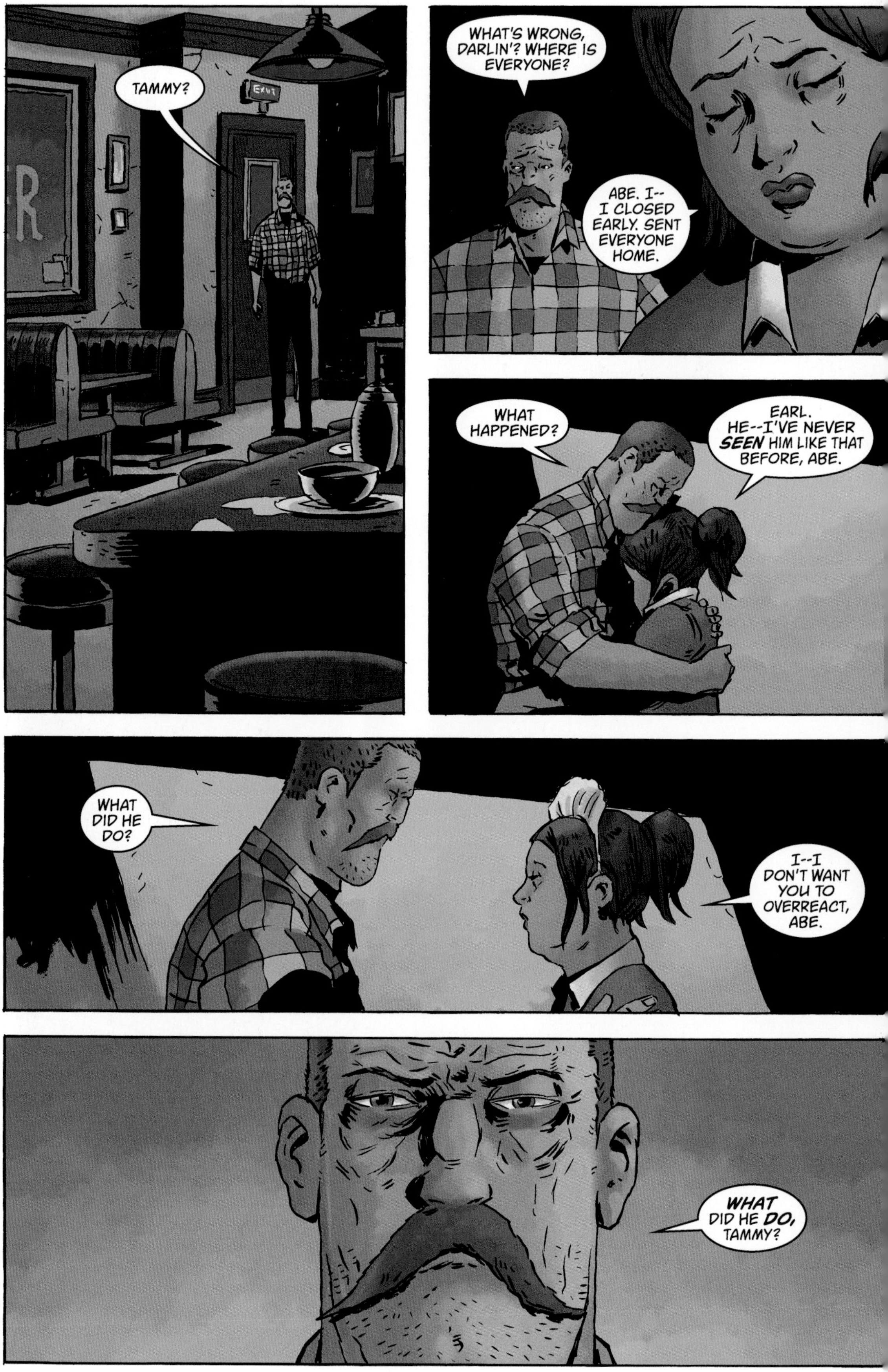
TAMMY?
WHAT'S WRONG, DARLIN'? WHERE IS EVERYONE?
ABE. I-- I CLOSED EARLY. SENT EVERYONE HOME.
WHAT HAPPENED?
EARL. HE--I'VE NEVER **SEEN** HIM LIKE THAT BEFORE, ABE.
WHAT DID HE DO?
I--I DON'T WANT YOU TO OVERREACT, ABE.
WHAT DID HE ***DO,*** TAMMY?

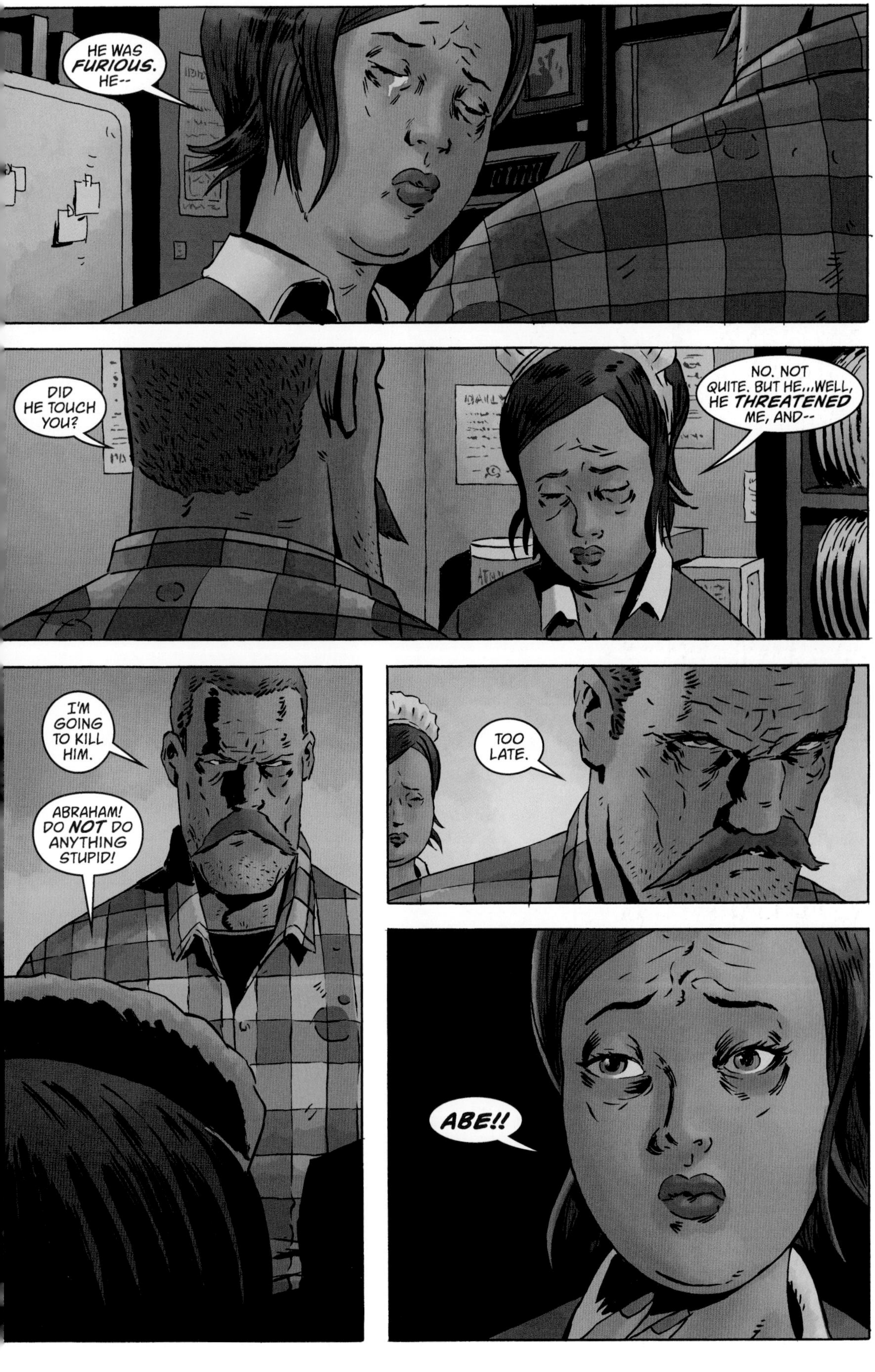
HE WAS **FURIOUS.** HE--
DID HE TOUCH YOU?
NO. NOT QUITE. BUT HE...WELL, HE **THREATENED** ME, AND--
I'M GOING TO KILL HIM.
ABRAHAM! DO **NOT** DO ANYTHING STUPID!
TOO LATE.
ABE!!

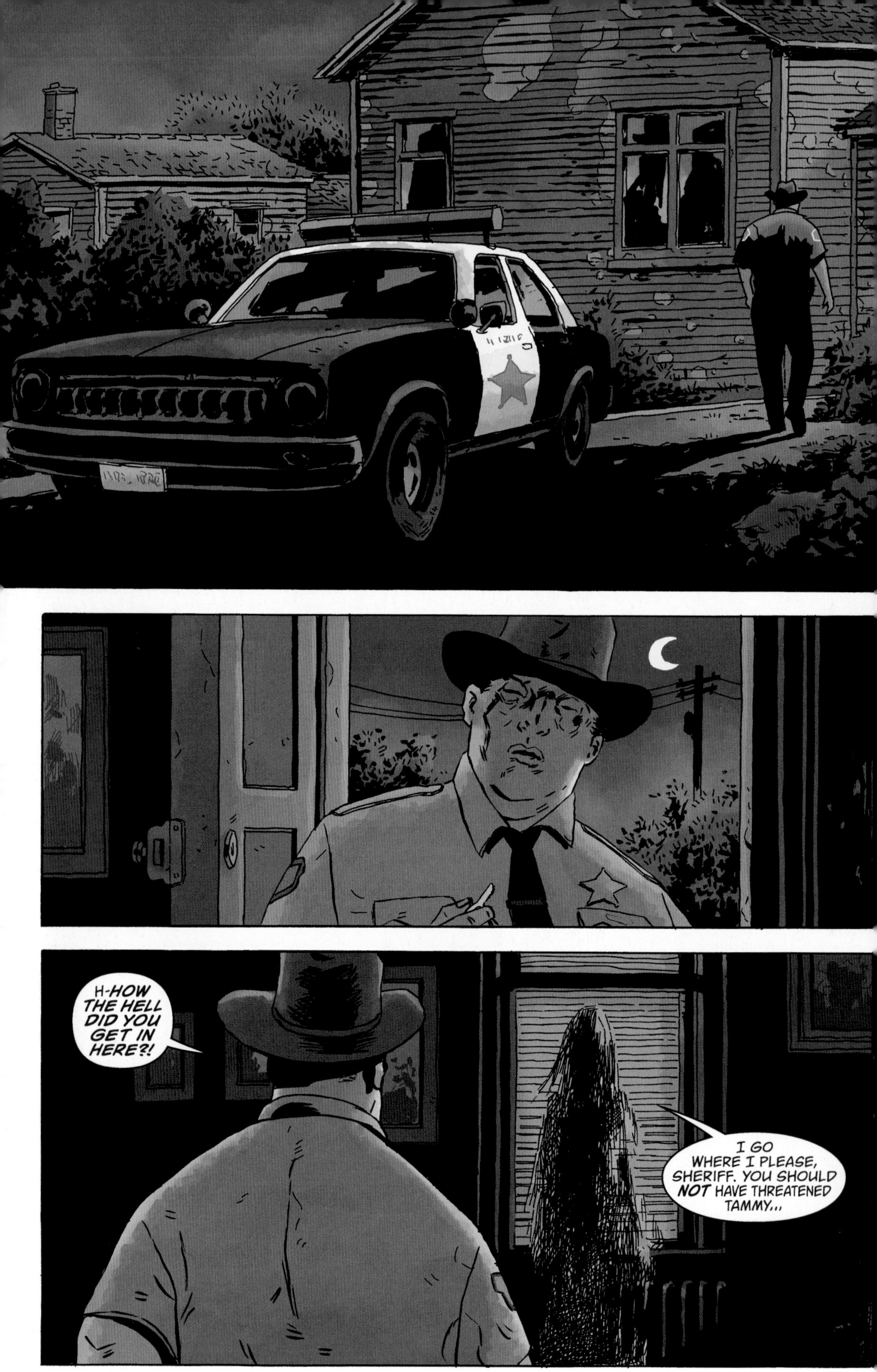
H-HOW THE HELL DID YOU GET IN HERE?!
I GO WHERE I PLEASE, SHERIFF. YOU SHOULD NOT HAVE THREATENED TAMMY...

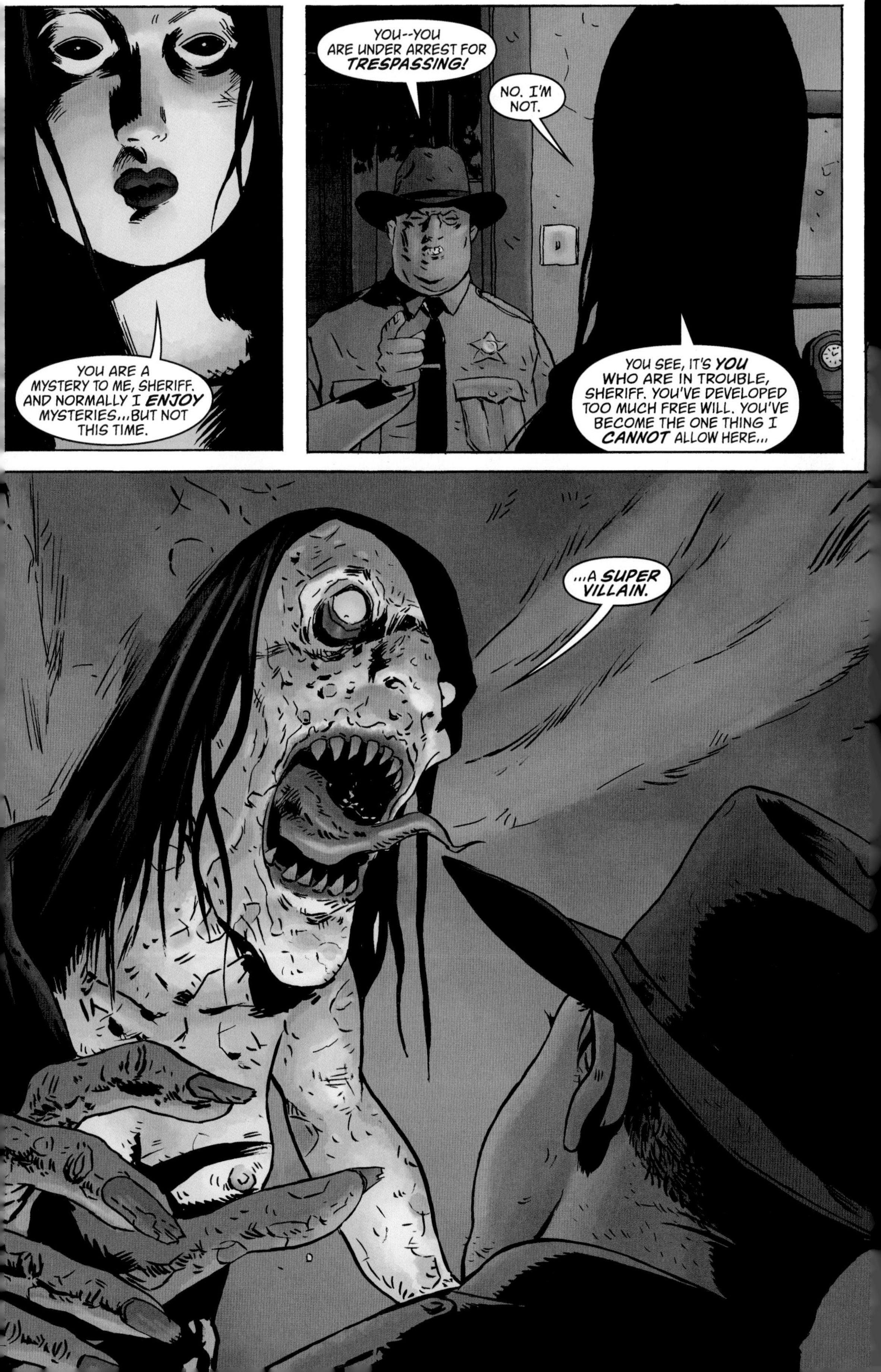
YOU ARE A MYSTERY TO ME, SHERIFF. AND NORMALLY I ENJOY MYSTERIES...BUT NOT THIS TIME.
YOU--YOU ARE UNDER ARREST FOR TRESPASSING!
NO. I'M NOT.
YOU SEE, IT'S YOU WHO ARE IN TROUBLE, SHERIFF. YOU'VE DEVELOPED TOO MUCH FREE WILL. YOU'VE BECOME THE ONE THING I CANNOT ALLOW HERE...
...A SUPER VILLAIN.

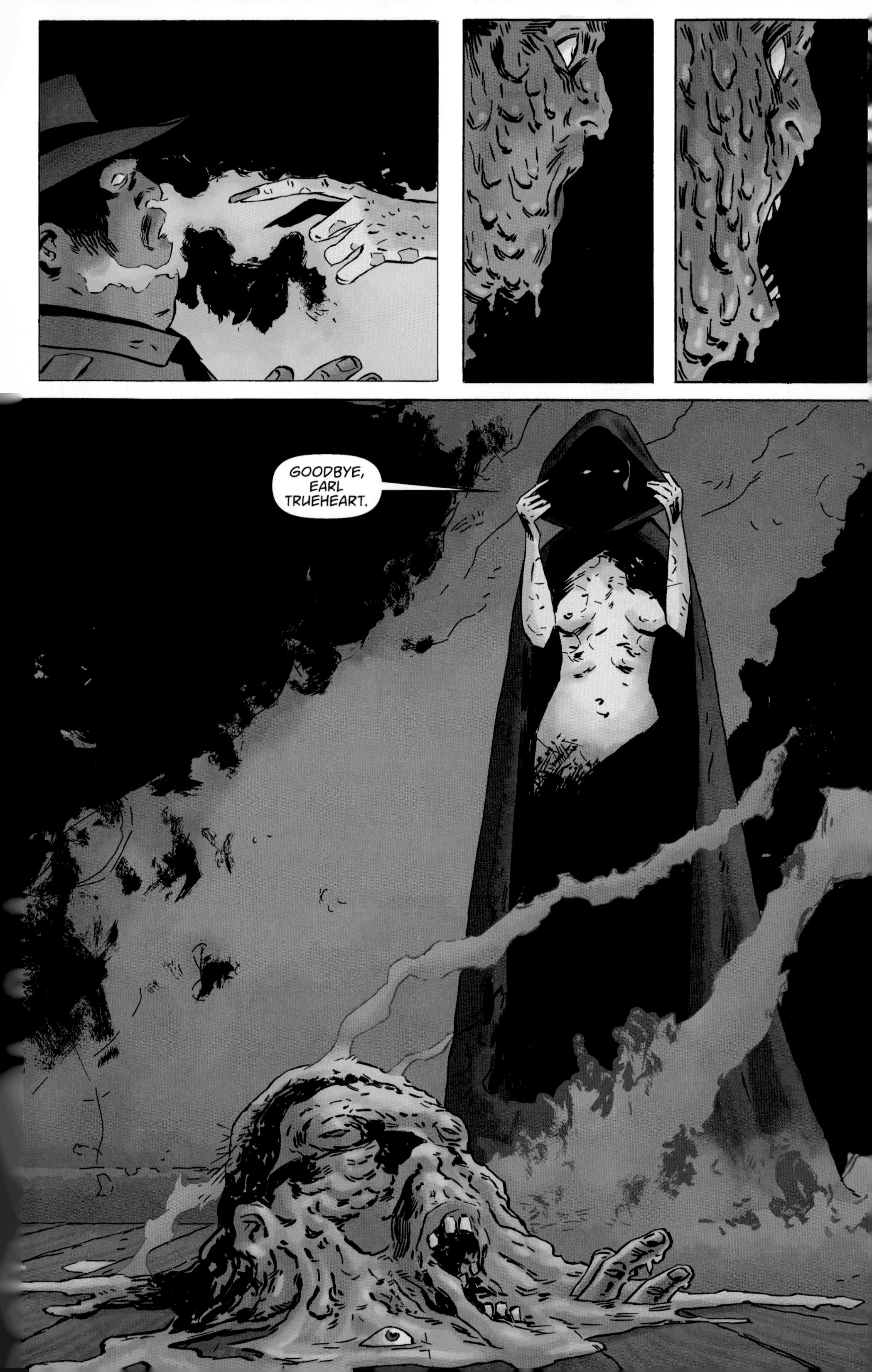
GOODBYE, EARL TRUEHEART.

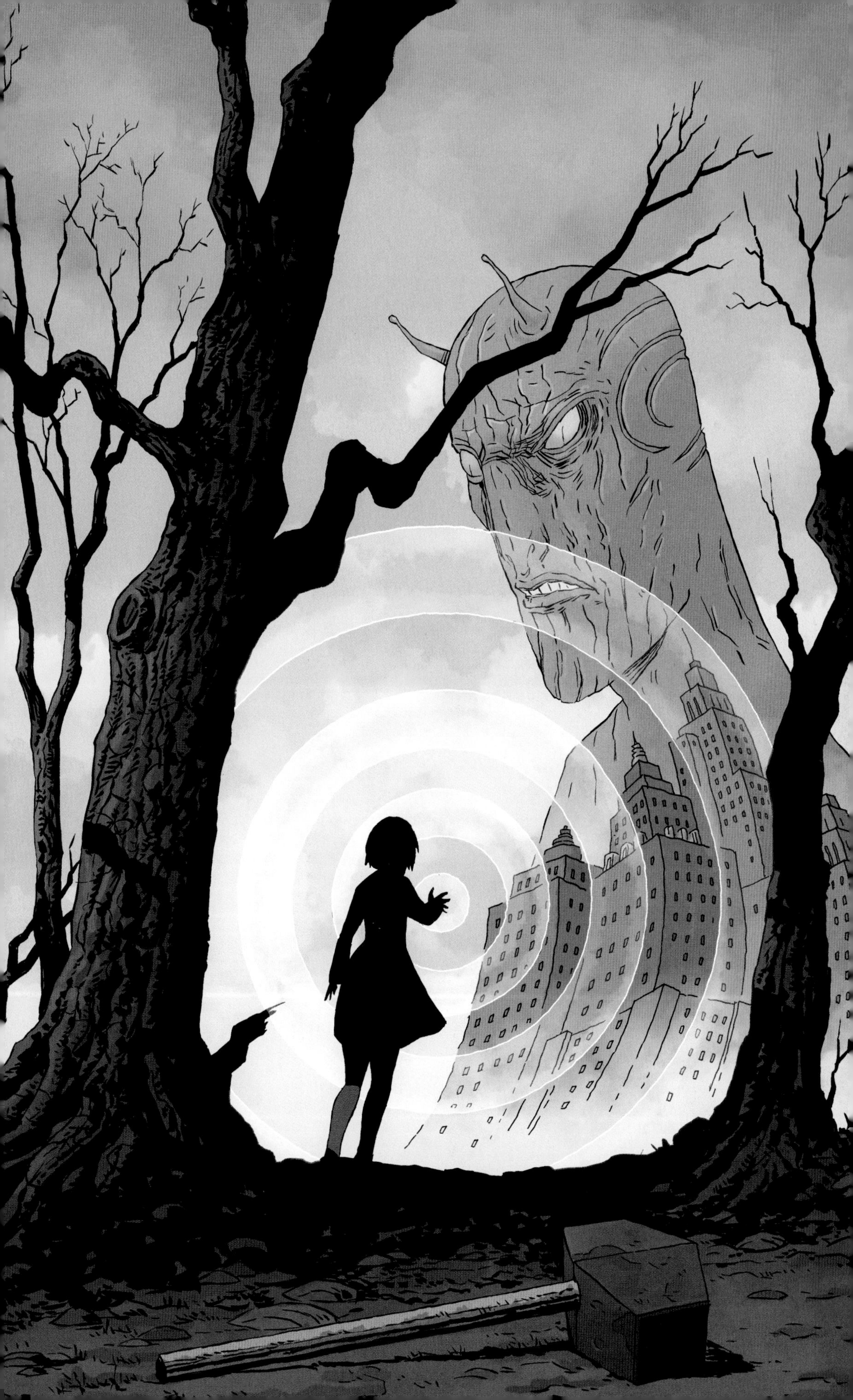

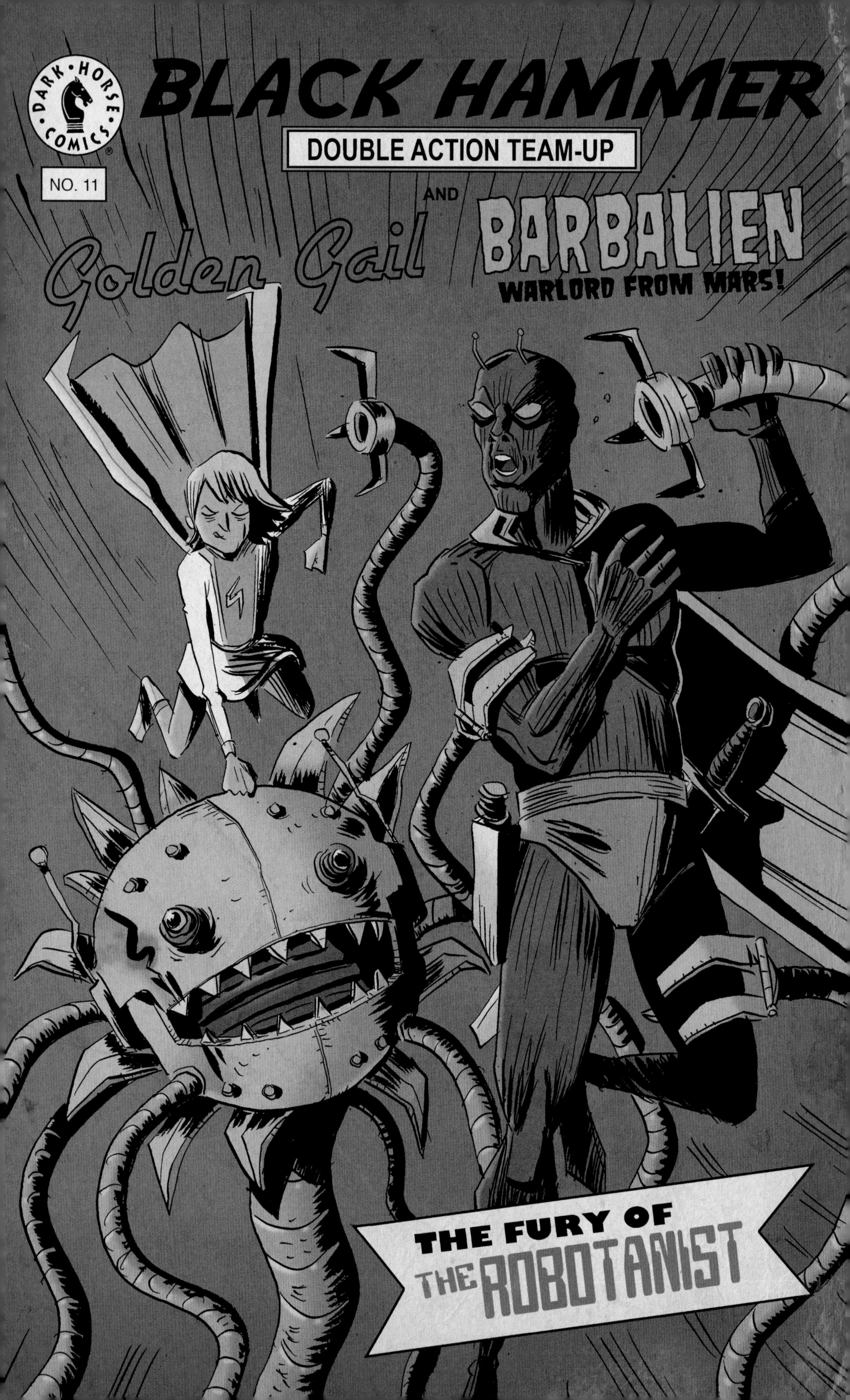
DARK HORSE COMICS
BLACK HAMMER
DOUBLE ACTION TEAM-UP
NO. 11
Golden Gail
AND
BARBALIEN
WARLORD FROM MARS!
THE FURY OF
THE ROBOTANIST

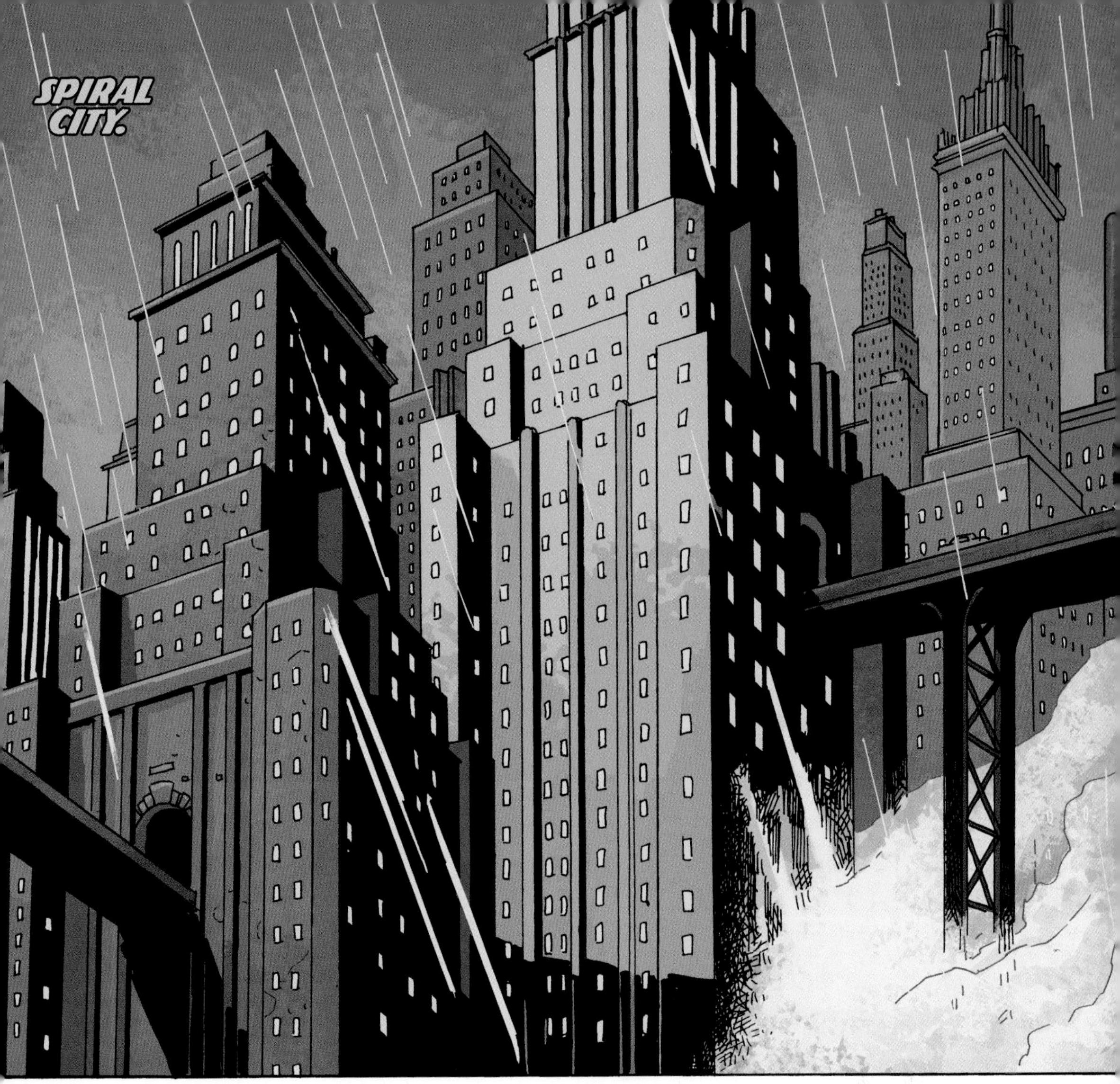
SPIRAL CITY.

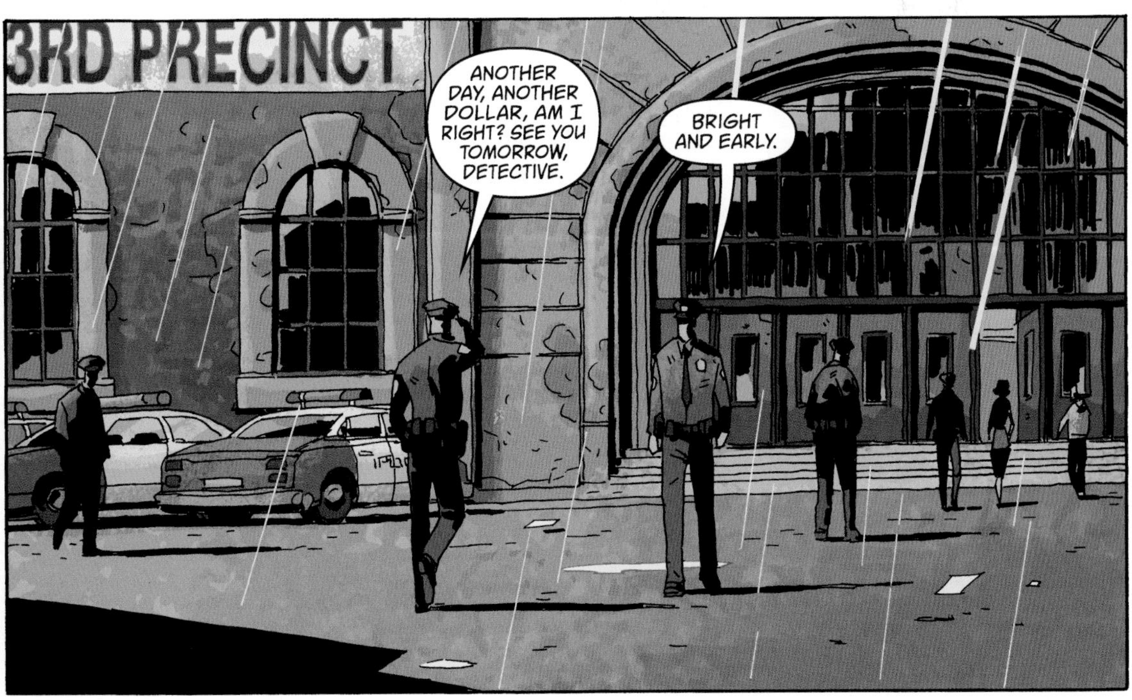
3RD PRECINCT
ANOTHER DAY, ANOTHER DOLLAR, AM I RIGHT? SEE YOU TOMORROW, DETECTIVE.
BRIGHT AND EARLY.

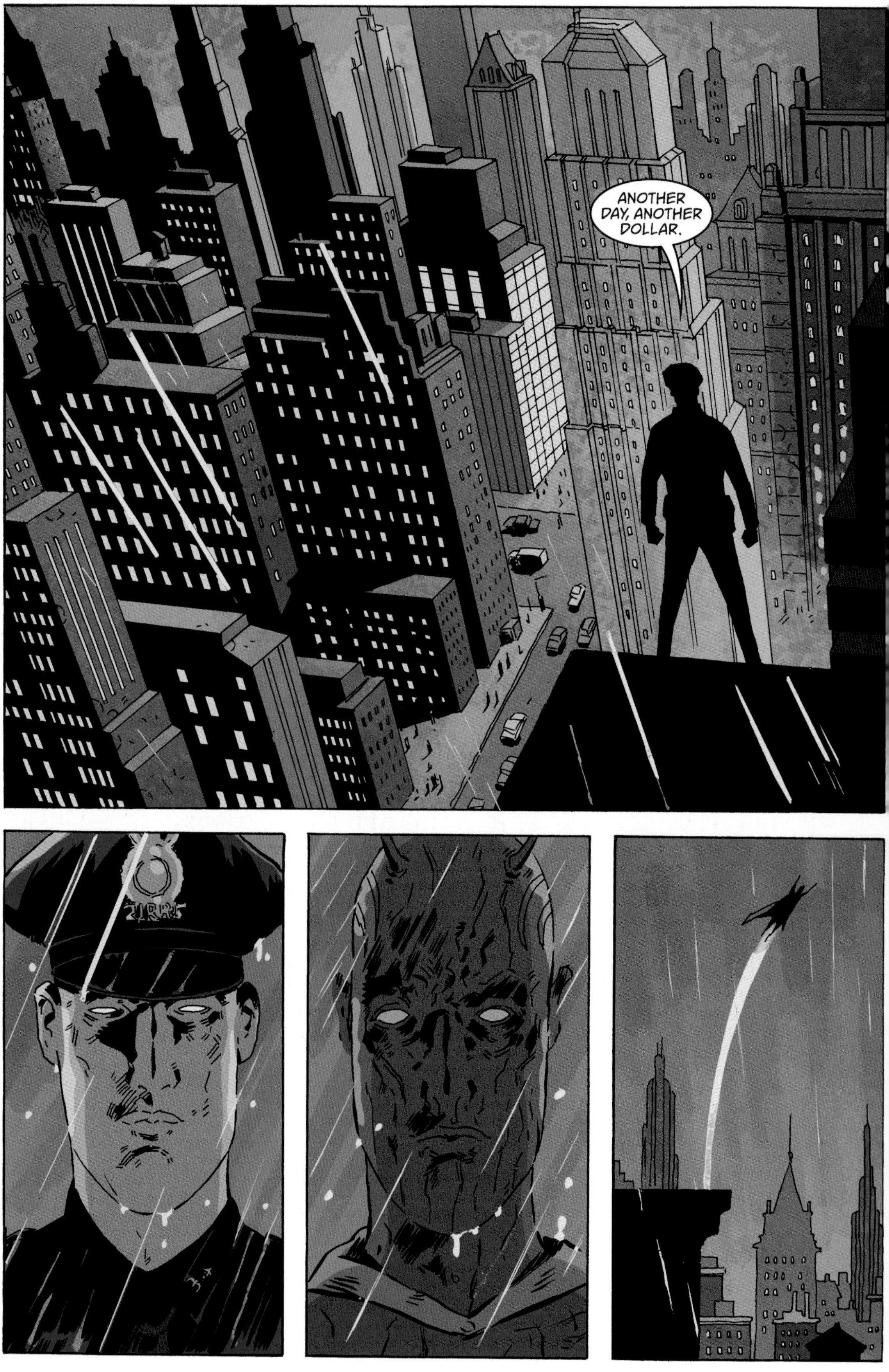
ANOTHER DAY, ANOTHER DOLLAR.

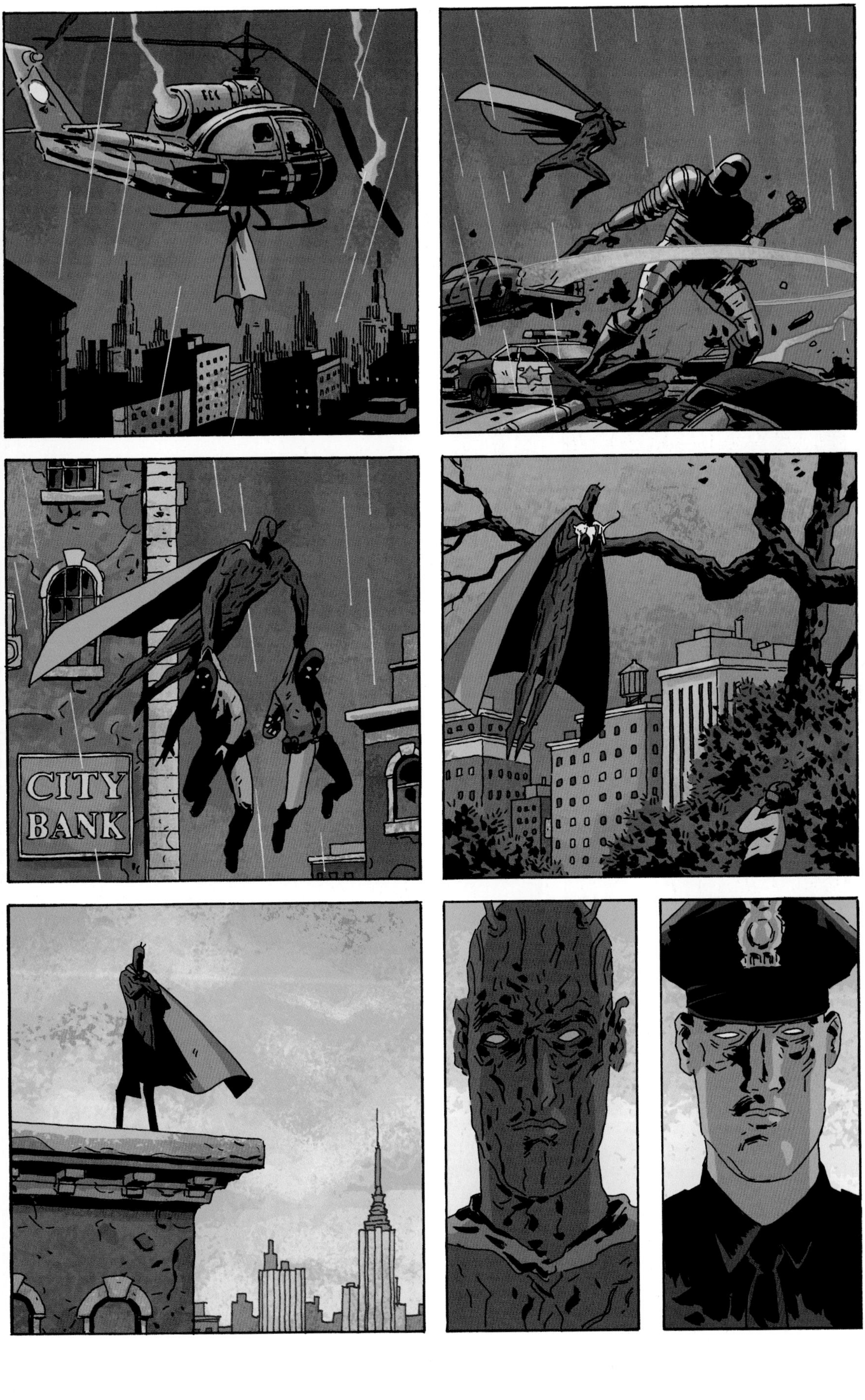
CITY
BANK

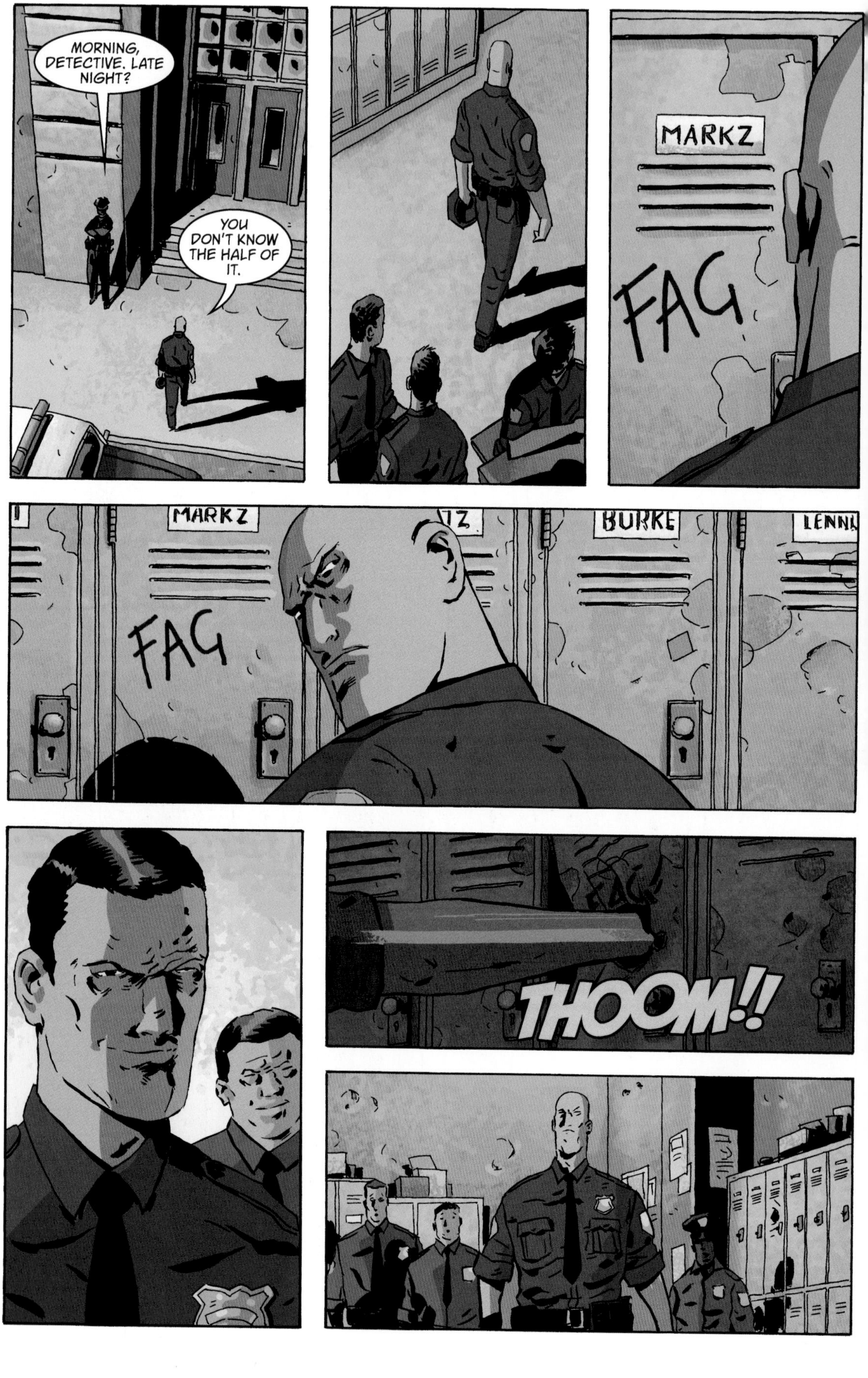
MORNING, DETECTIVE. LATE NIGHT?
YOU DON'T KNOW THE HALF OF IT.
MARKZ
FAG
MARKZ
FAG
BURKE
THOOM!!

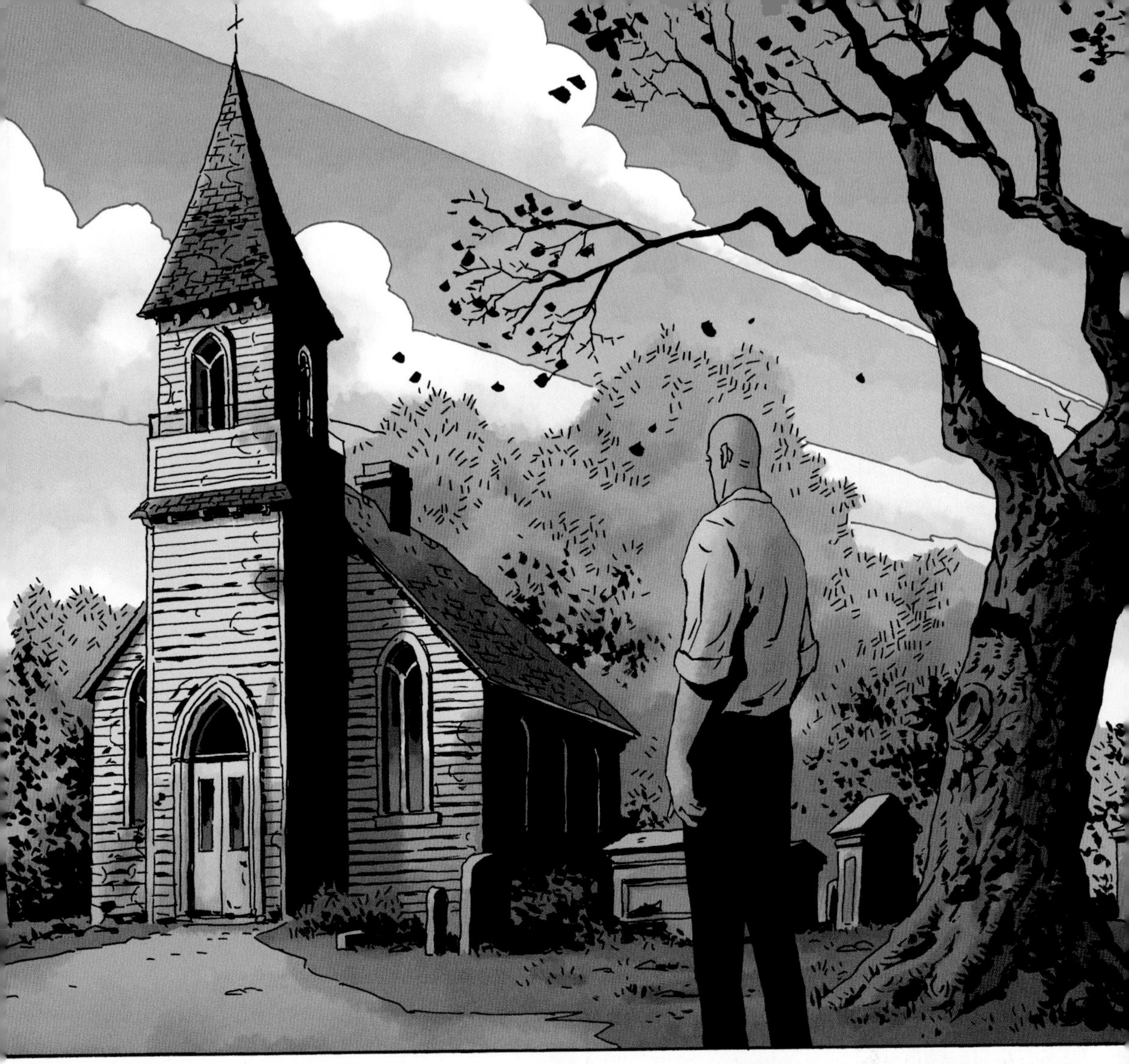

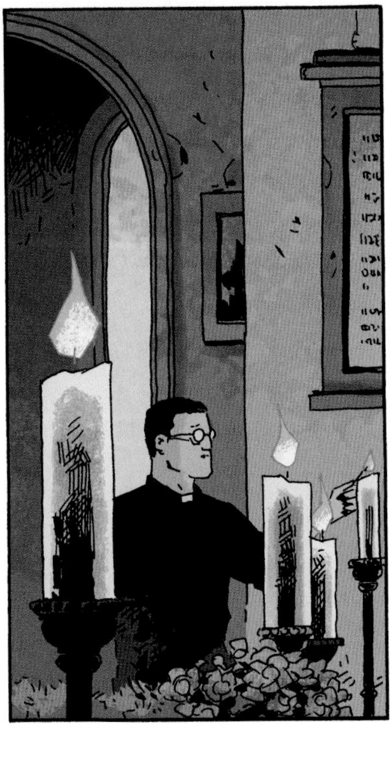

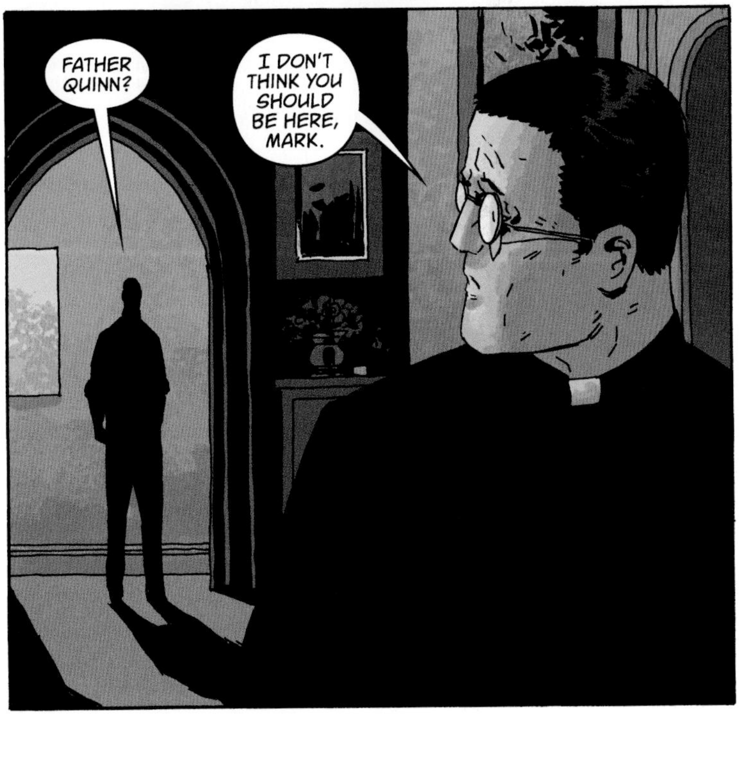
FATHER QUINN?
I DON'T THINK YOU SHOULD BE HERE, MARK.

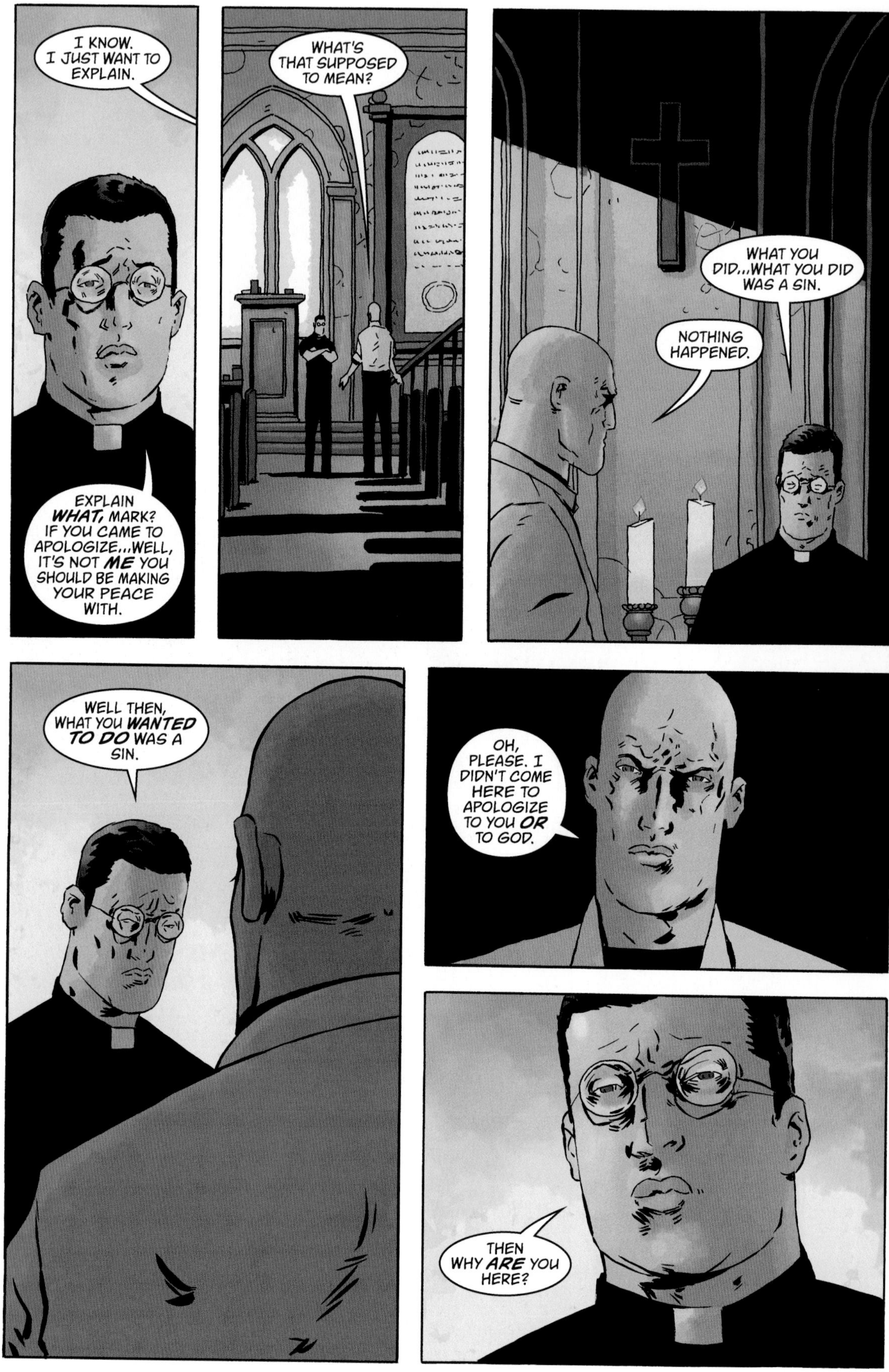

I KNOW. I JUST WANT TO EXPLAIN.
EXPLAIN **WHAT,** MARK? IF YOU CAME TO APOLOGIZE...WELL, IT'S NOT **ME** YOU SHOULD BE MAKING YOUR PEACE WITH.
WHAT'S THAT SUPPOSED TO MEAN?
WHAT YOU DID...WHAT YOU DID WAS A SIN.
NOTHING HAPPENED.
WELL THEN, WHAT YOU **WANTED TO DO** WAS A SIN.
OH, PLEASE. I DIDN'T COME HERE TO APOLOGIZE TO YOU **OR** TO GOD.
THEN WHY **ARE** YOU HERE?

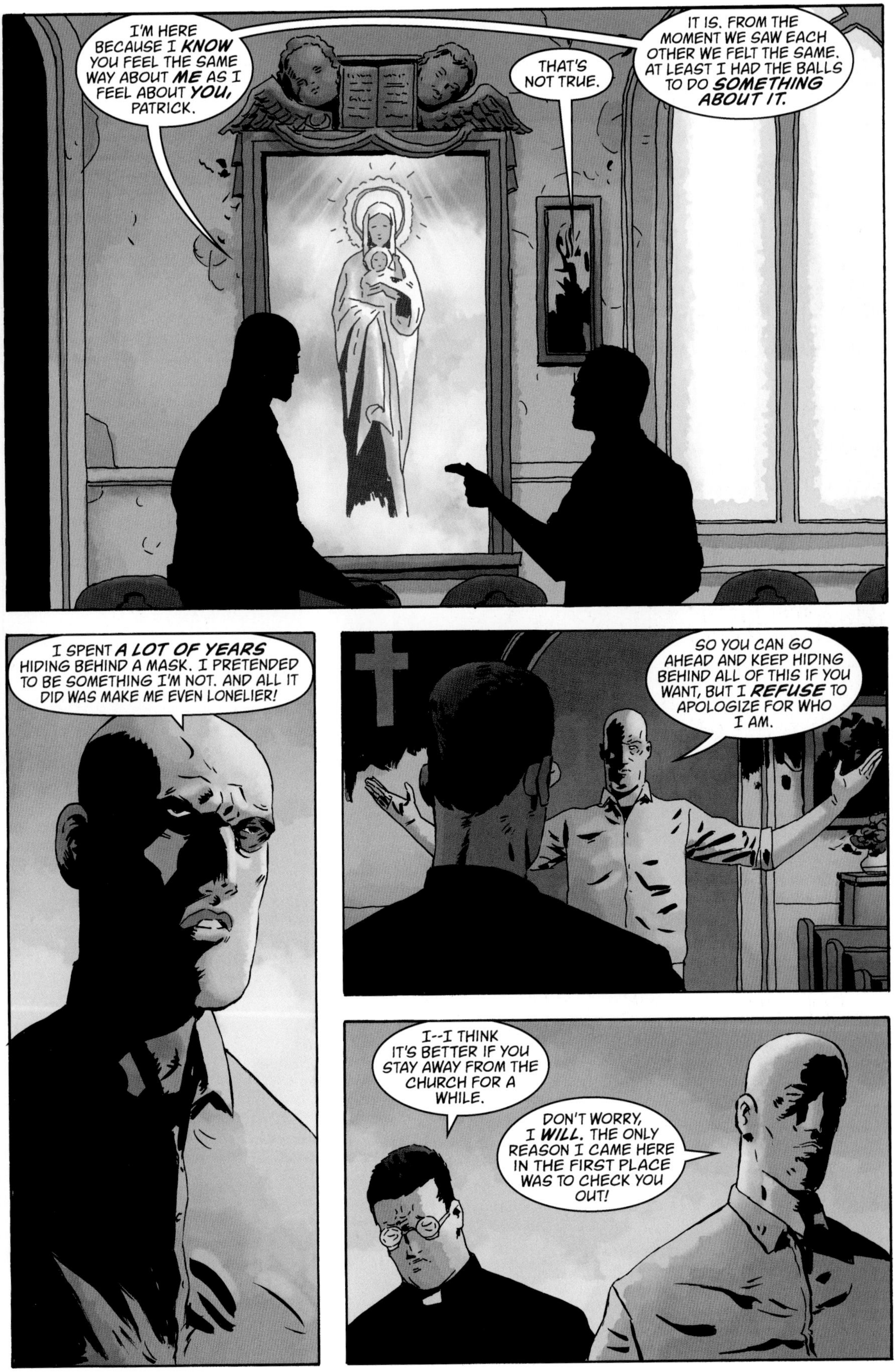
I'M HERE BECAUSE I **KNOW** YOU FEEL THE SAME WAY ABOUT **ME** AS I FEEL ABOUT **YOU,** PATRICK.
THAT'S NOT TRUE.
IT IS. FROM THE MOMENT WE SAW EACH OTHER WE FELT THE SAME. AT LEAST I HAD THE BALLS TO DO **SOMETHING ABOUT IT.**
I SPENT **A LOT OF YEARS** HIDING BEHIND A MASK. I PRETENDED TO BE SOMETHING I'M NOT. AND ALL IT DID WAS MAKE ME EVEN LONELIER!
SO YOU CAN GO AHEAD AND KEEP HIDING BEHIND ALL OF THIS IF YOU WANT, BUT I **REFUSE** TO APOLOGIZE FOR WHO I AM.
I--I THINK IT'S BETTER IF YOU STAY AWAY FROM THE CHURCH FOR A WHILE.
DON'T WORRY, I **WILL.** THE ONLY REASON I CAME HERE IN THE FIRST PLACE WAS TO CHECK YOU OUT!

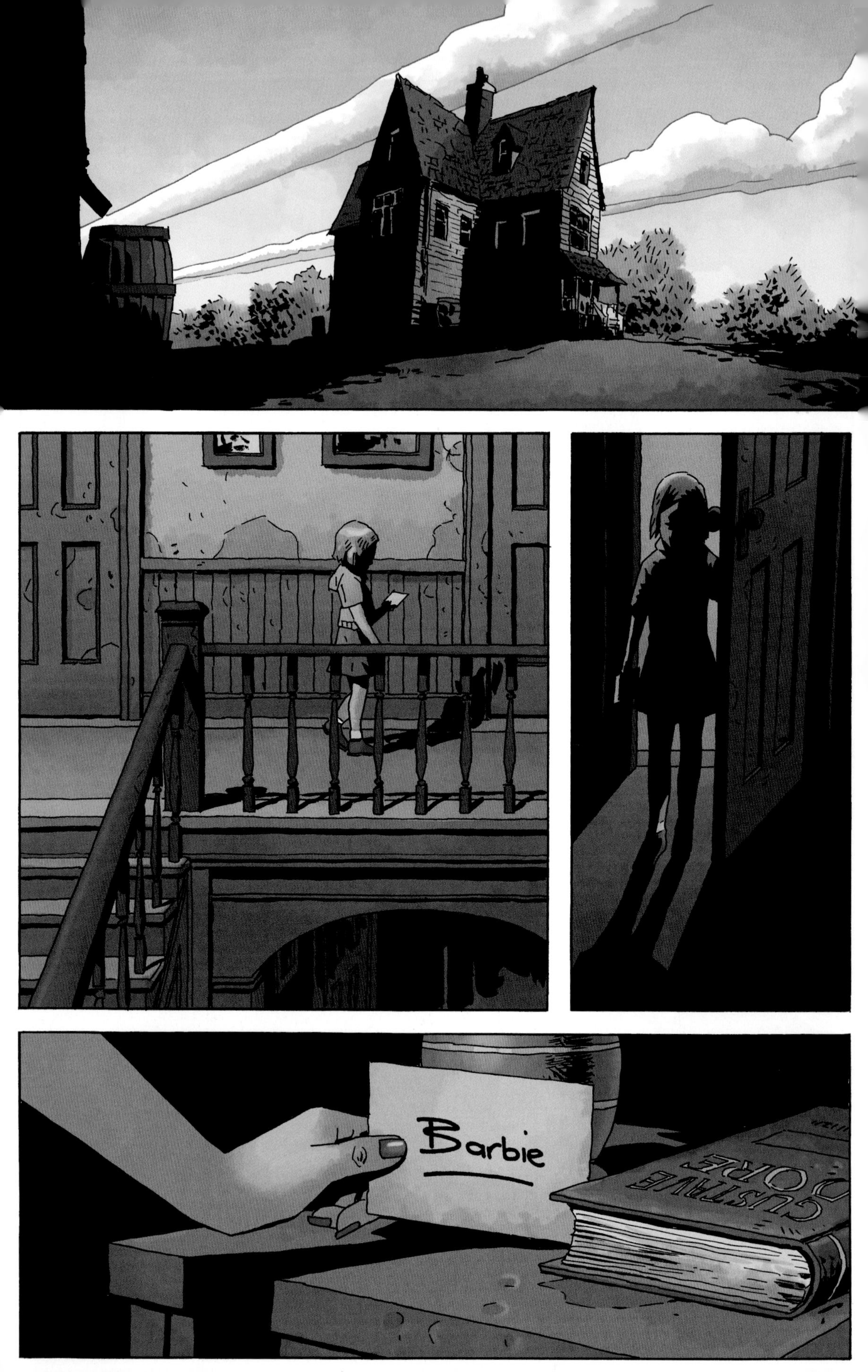
Barbie

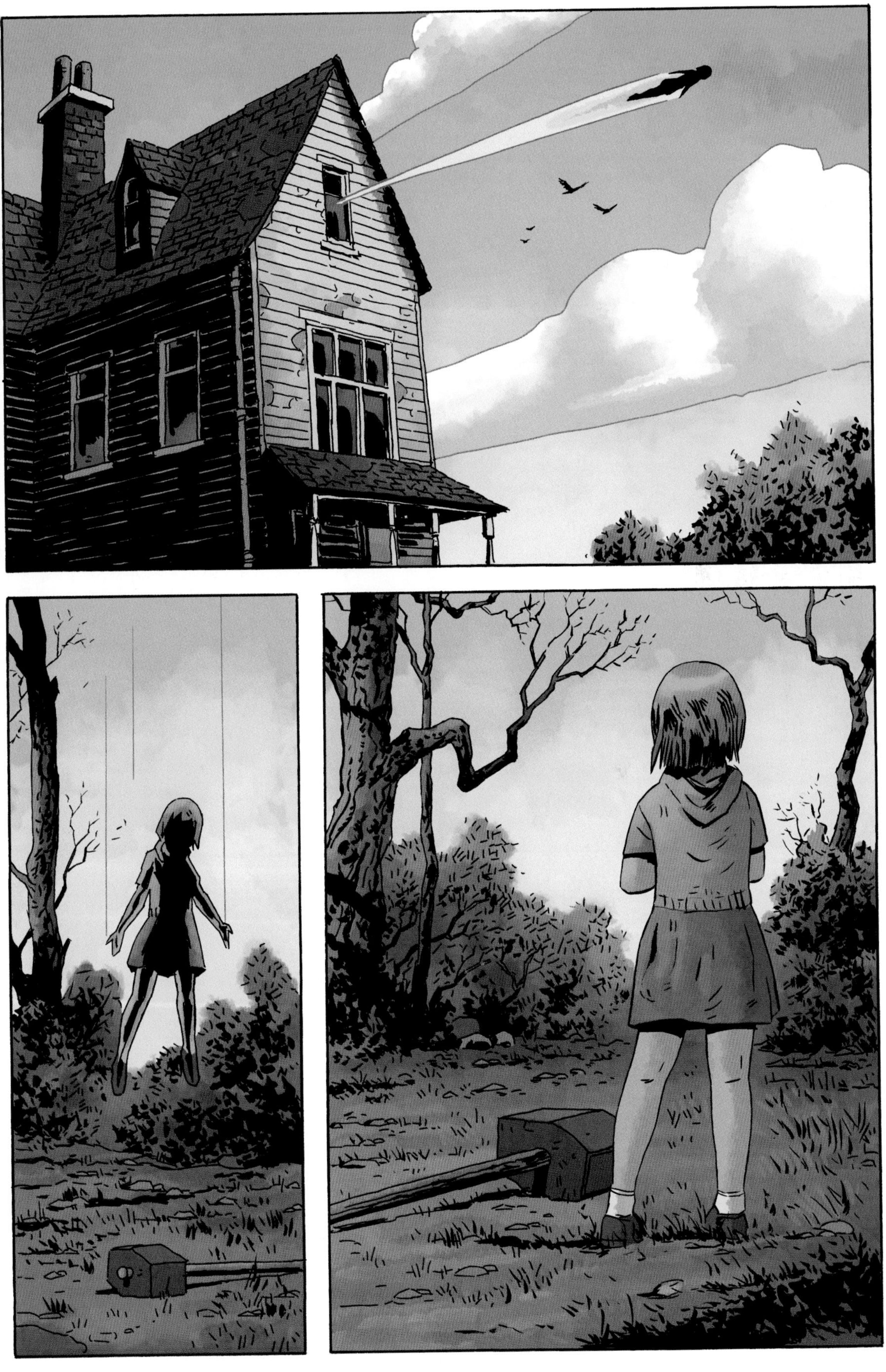

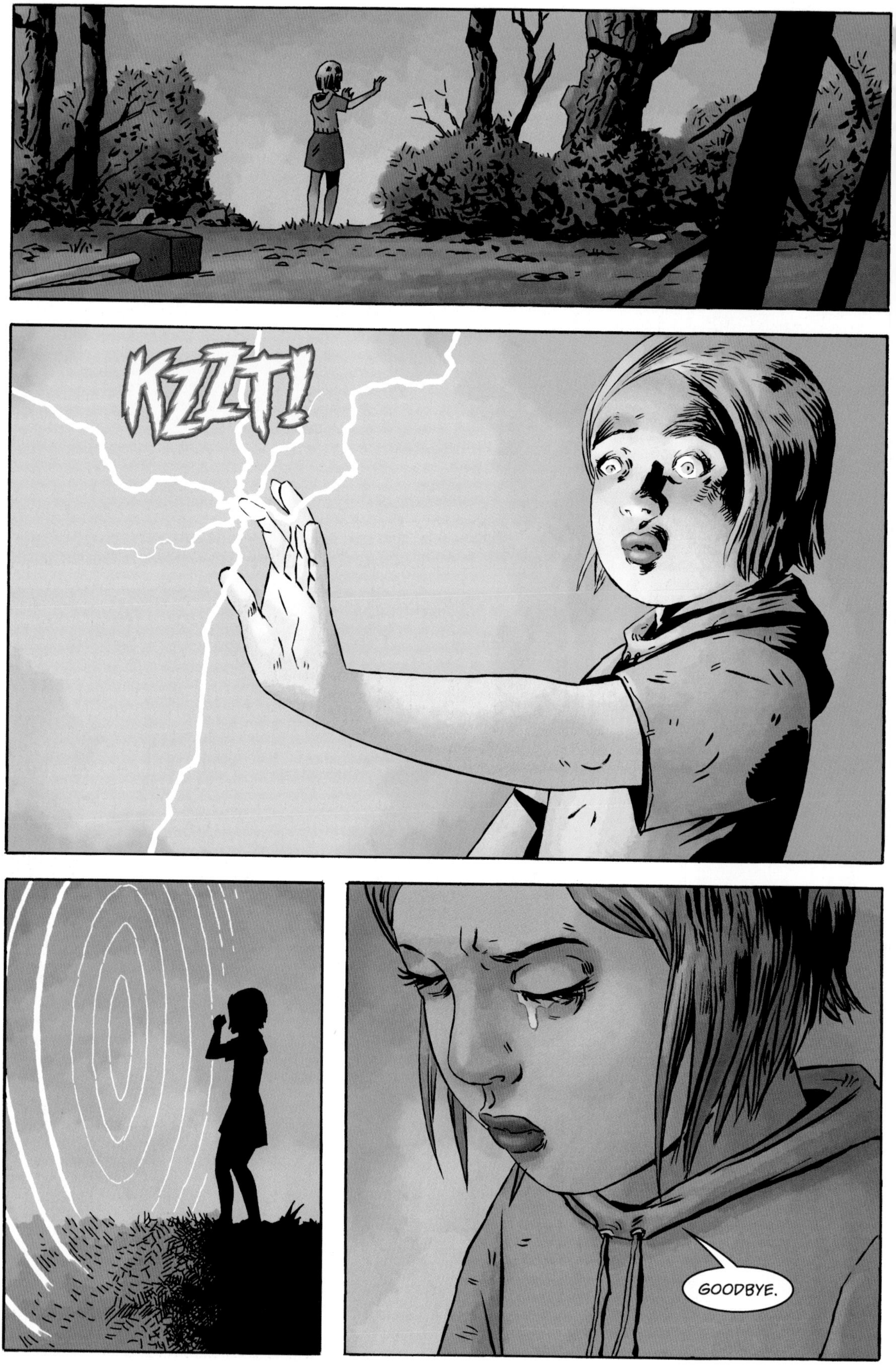
KZZT!
GOODBYE.

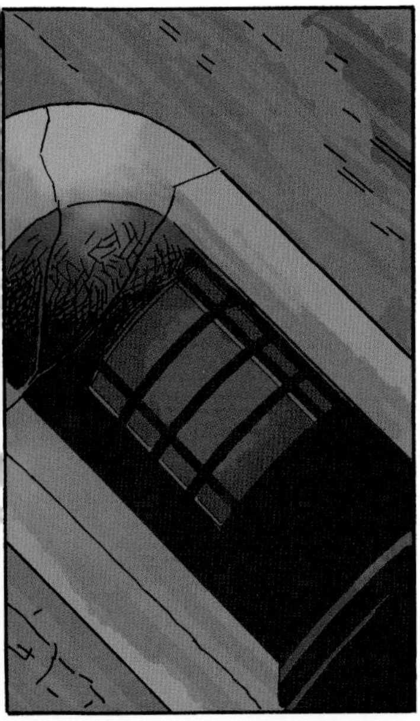

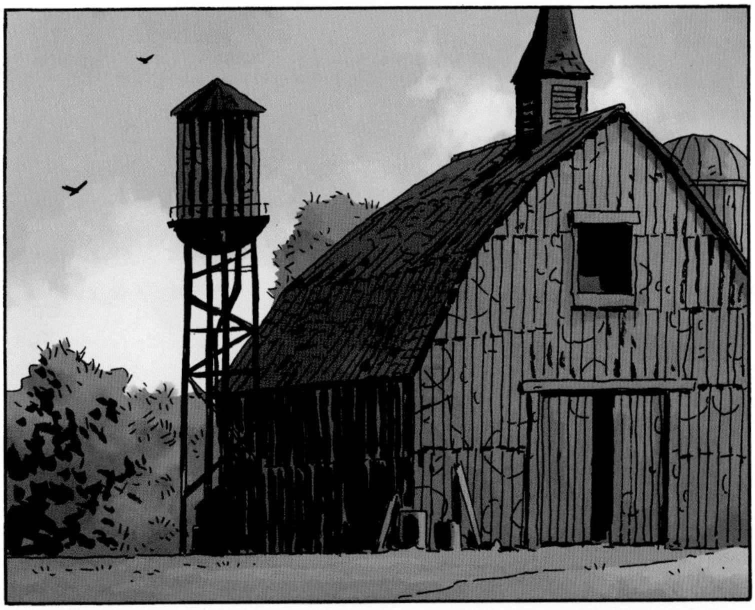

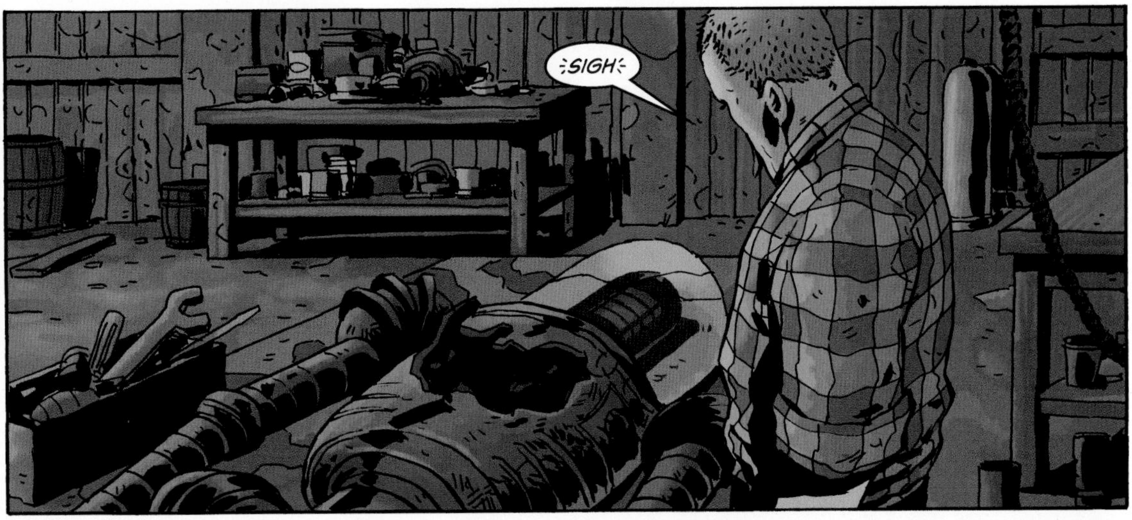
SIGH

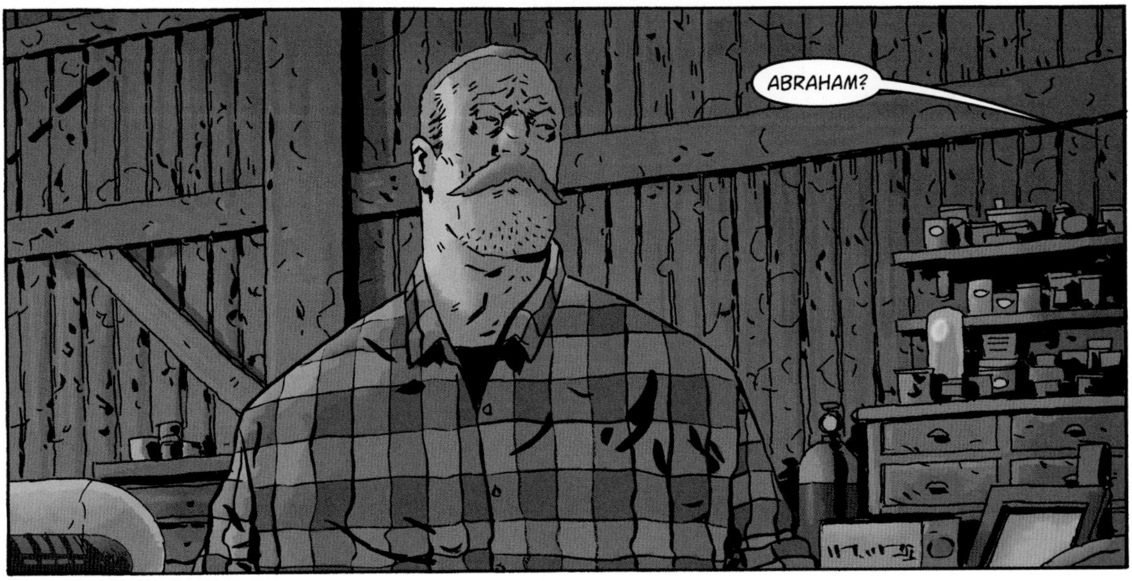
ABRAHAM?

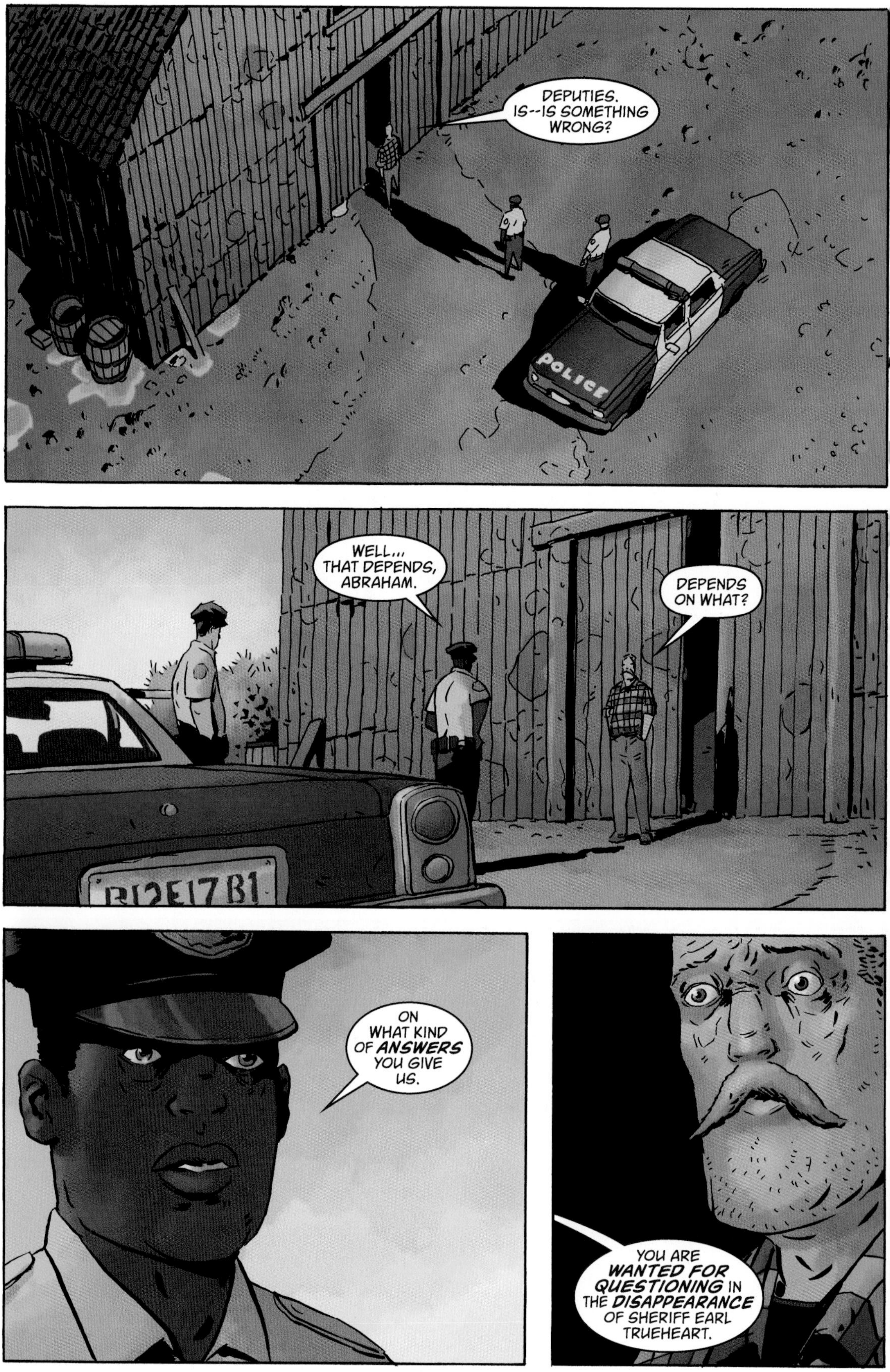
DEPUTIES. IS--IS SOMETHING WRONG?
POLICE
WELL... THAT DEPENDS, ABRAHAM.
DEPENDS ON WHAT?
ON WHAT KIND OF ANSWERS YOU GIVE US.
YOU ARE WANTED FOR QUESTIONING IN THE DISAPPEARANCE OF SHERIFF EARL TRUEHEART.

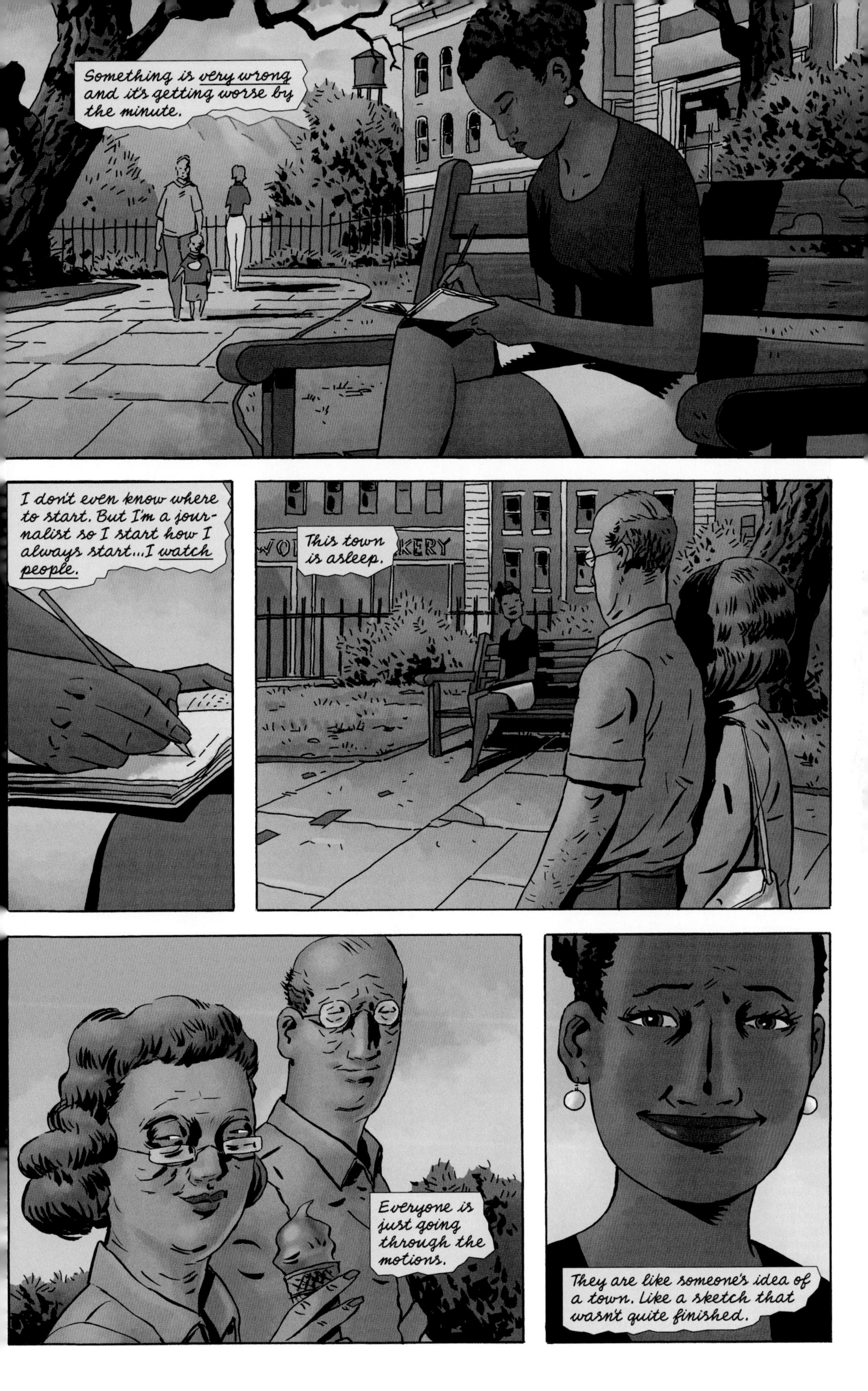
Something is very wrong and it's getting worse by the minute.
I don't even know where to start. But I'm a journalist so I start how I always start...I watch people.
This town is asleep.
Everyone is just going through the motions.
They are like someone's idea of a town. Like a sketch that wasn't quite finished.

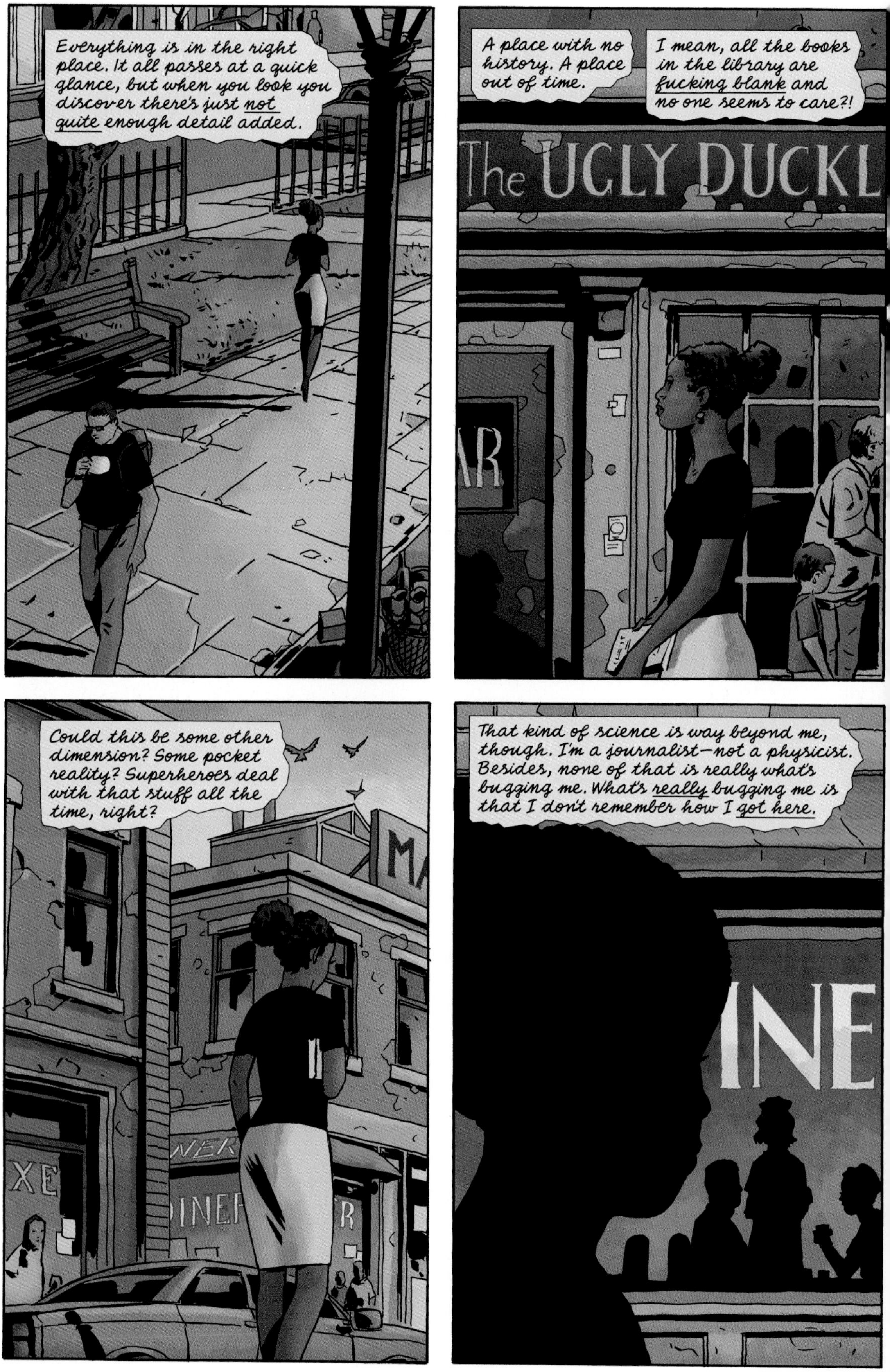
Everything is in the right place. It all passes at a quick glance, but when you look you discover there's just not quite enough detail added.
A place with no history. A place out of time.
I mean, all the books in the library are fucking blank and no one seems to care?!
The UGLY DUCKL
Could this be some other dimension? Some pocket reality? Superheroes deal with that stuff all the time, right?
That kind of science is way beyond me, though. I'm a journalist—not a physicist. Besides, none of that is really what's bugging me. What's really bugging me is that I don't remember how I got here.

This isn't like me. I always get the answers. But this time....this time I don't even know what the right questions are.

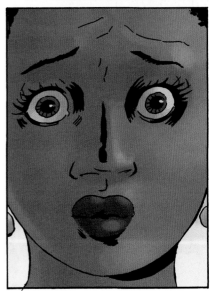

Yeah....something is really not right here.

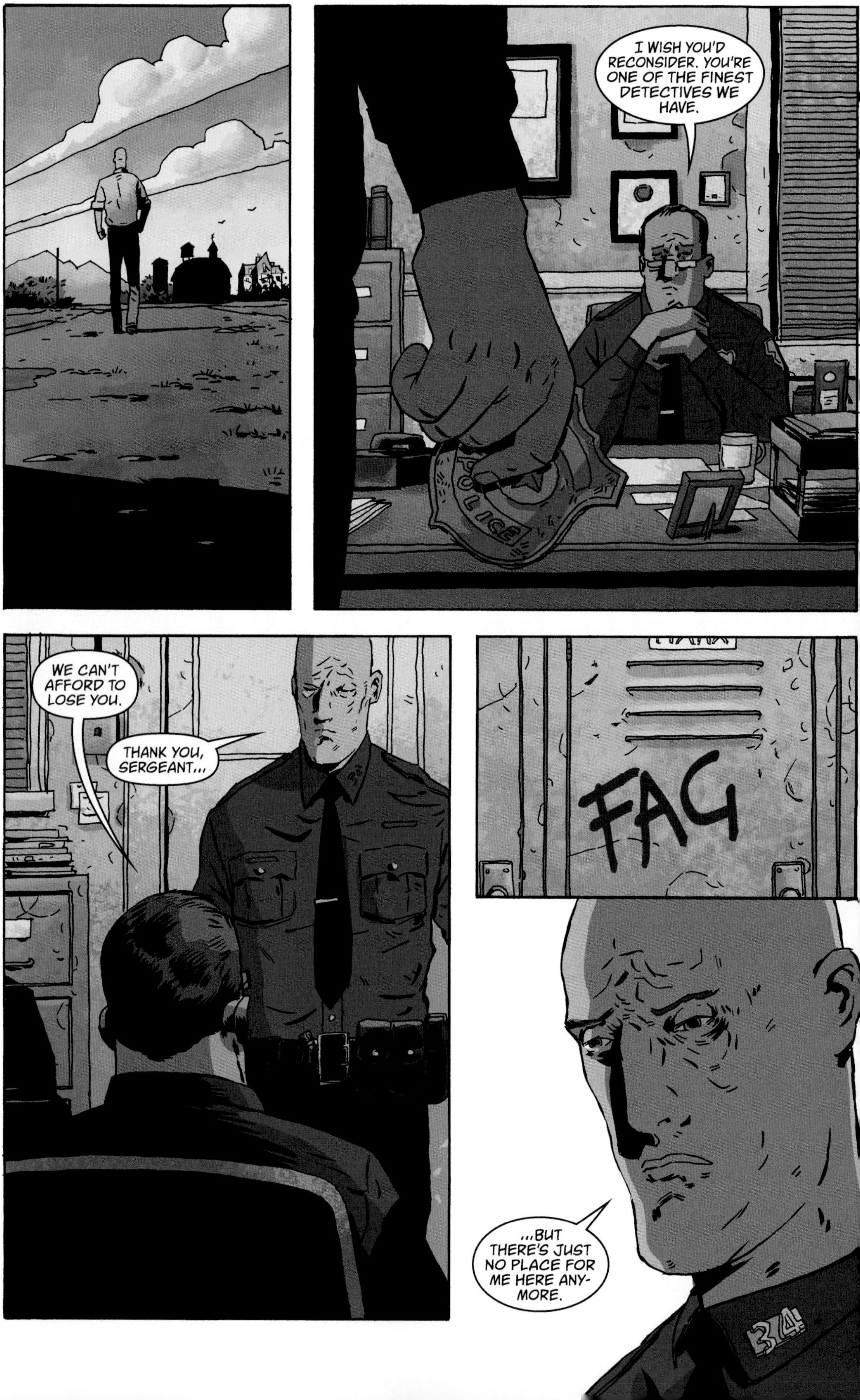
I WISH YOU'D RECONSIDER. YOU'RE ONE OF THE FINEST DETECTIVES WE HAVE.
POLICE
WE CAN'T AFFORD TO LOSE YOU.
THANK YOU, SERGEANT...
FAG
...BUT THERE'S JUST NO PLACE FOR ME HERE ANY-MORE.

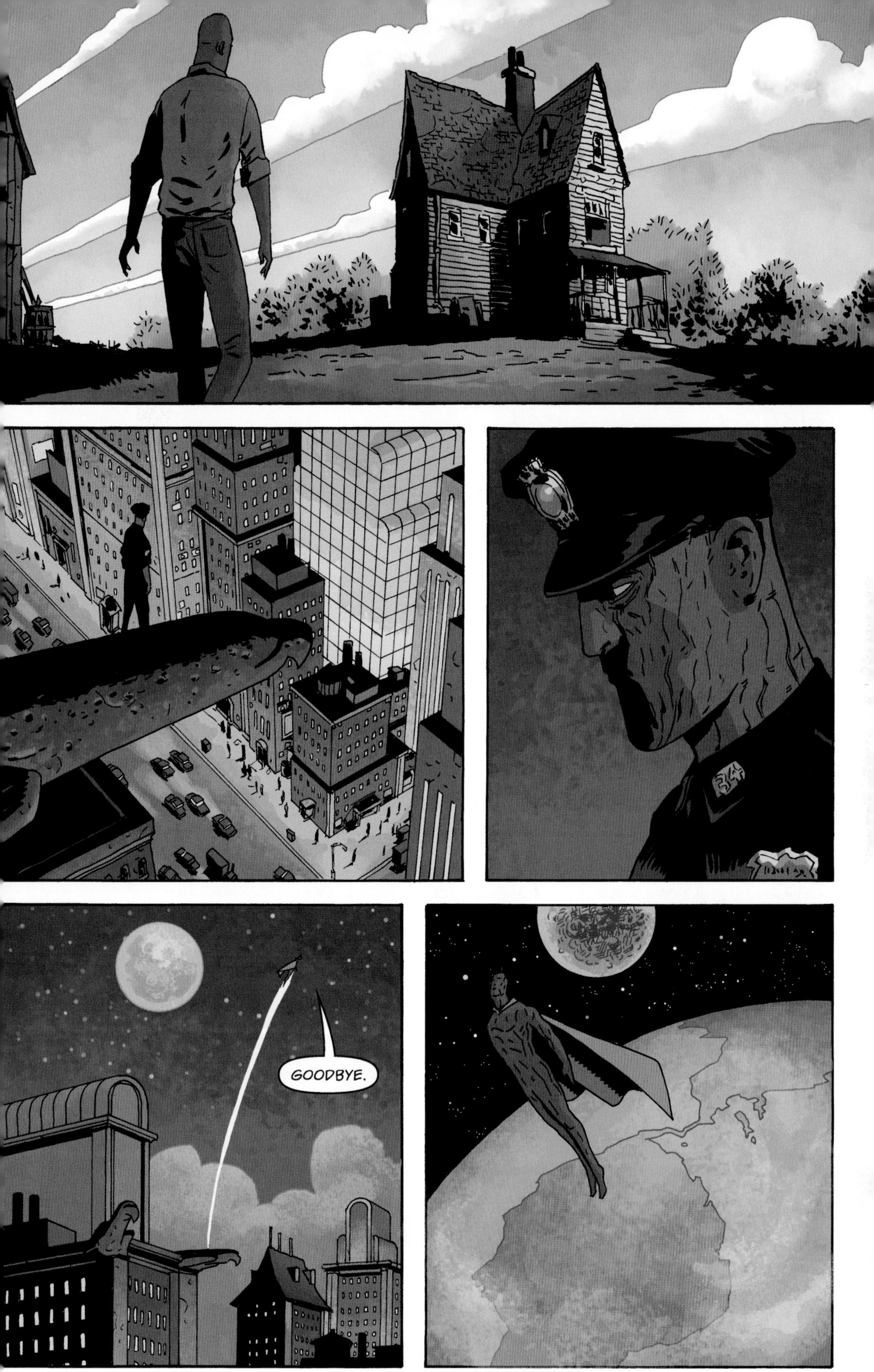
GOODBYE.

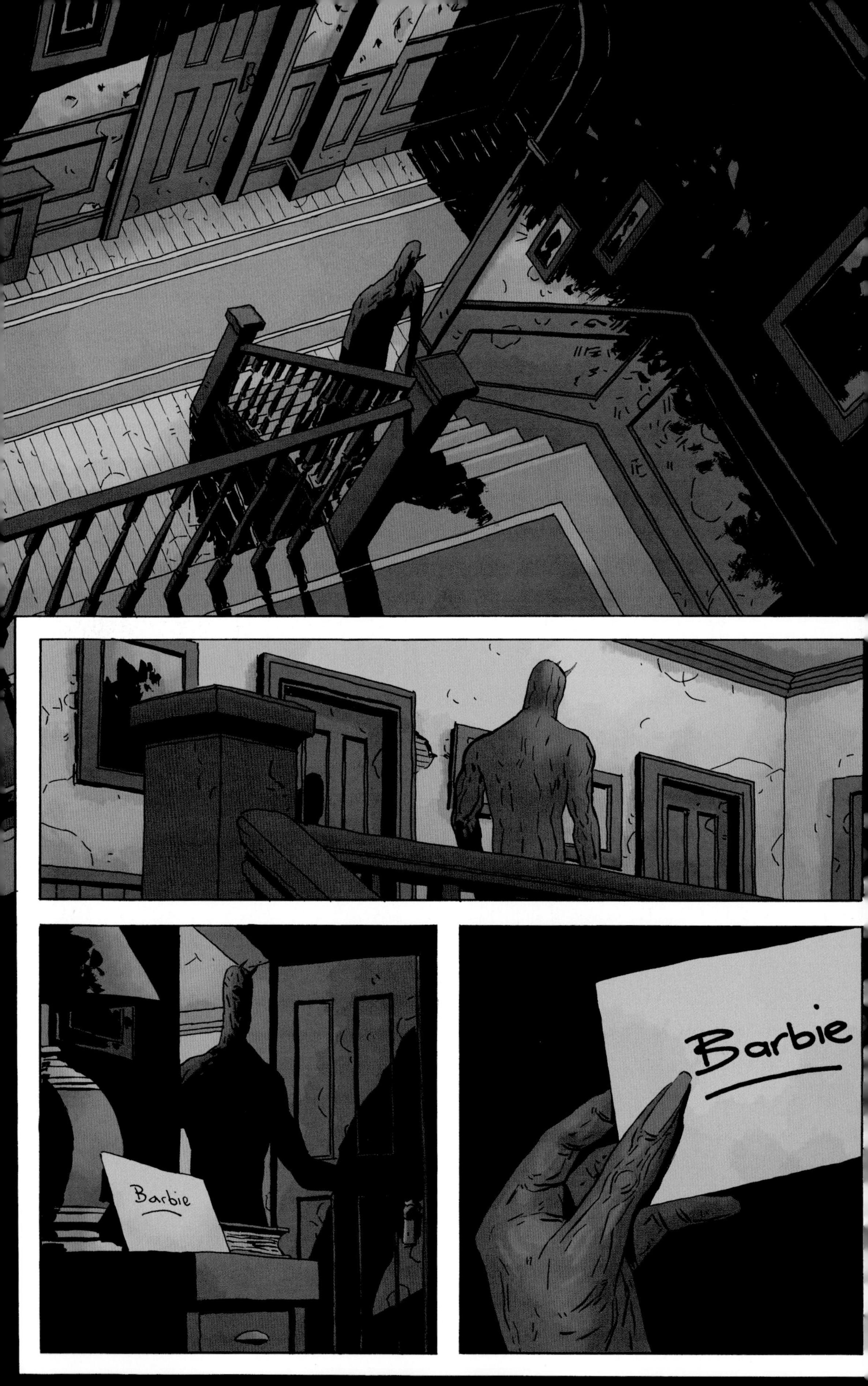
Barbie
Barbie

Barbie,
Please forgive me but I can't do it anymore. There's just no place for me here.
xx Gail
GOODBYE.
Barbie,
Please forgive me but I can't do it anymore. There's just no place for me here.
xx Gail

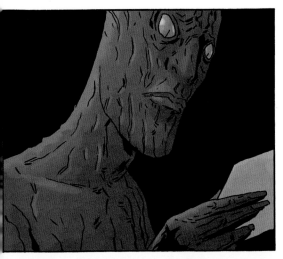

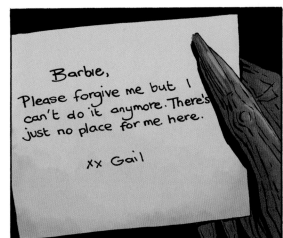

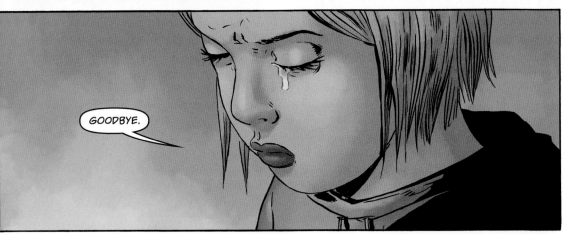

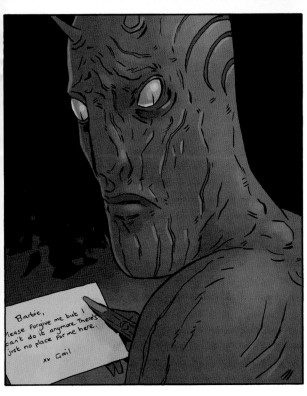

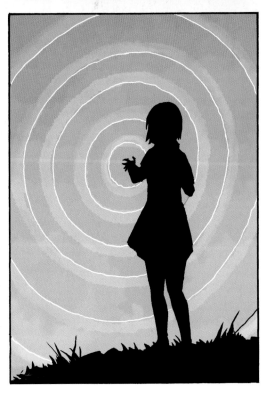

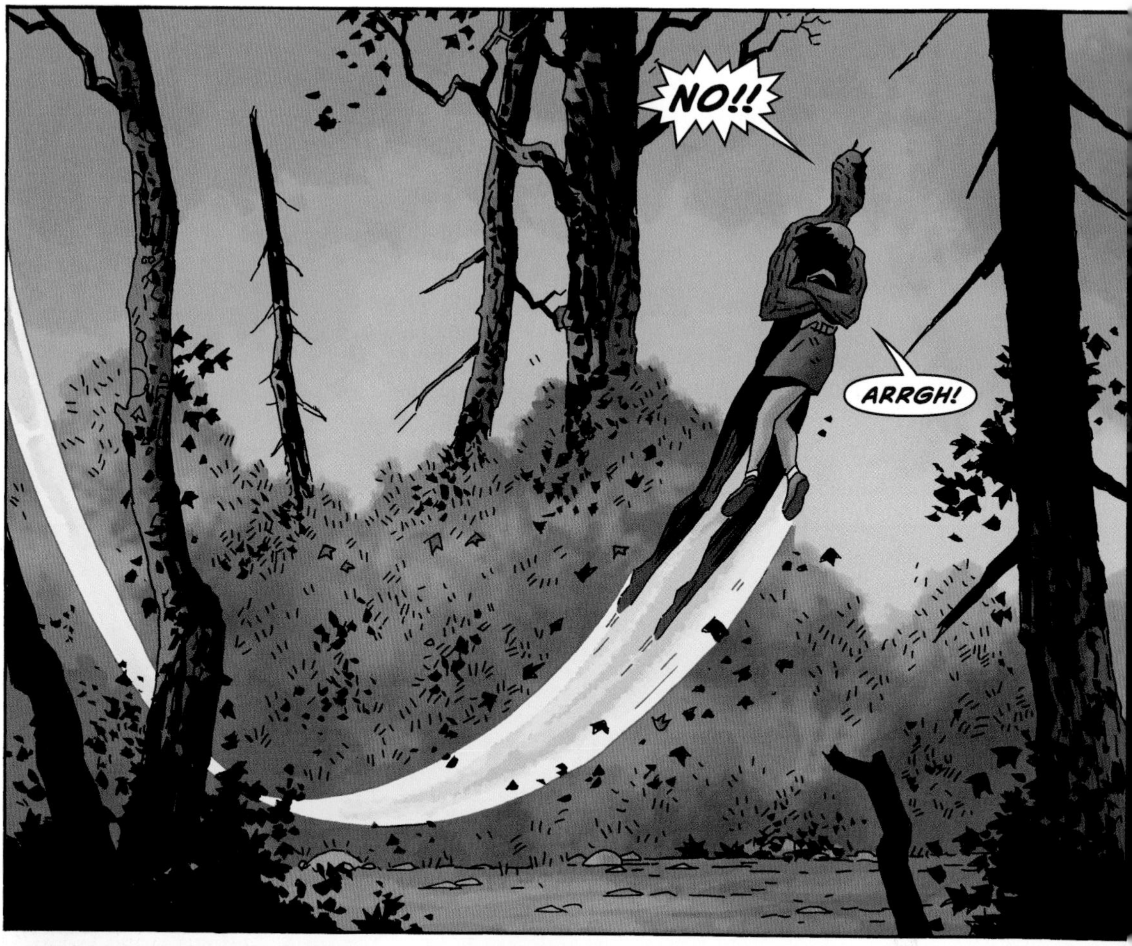
NO!!
ARRGH!

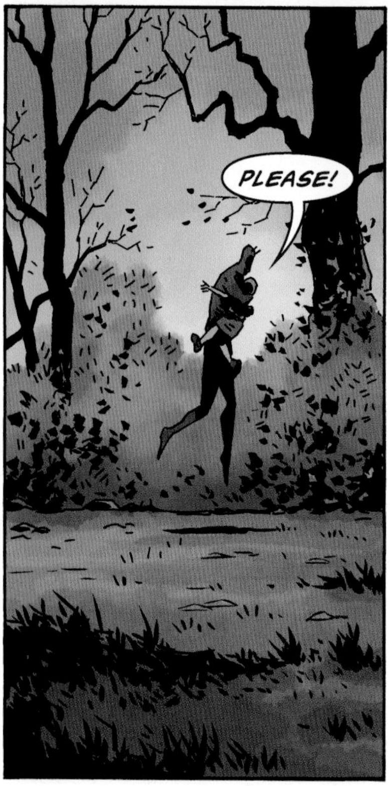
PLEASE!

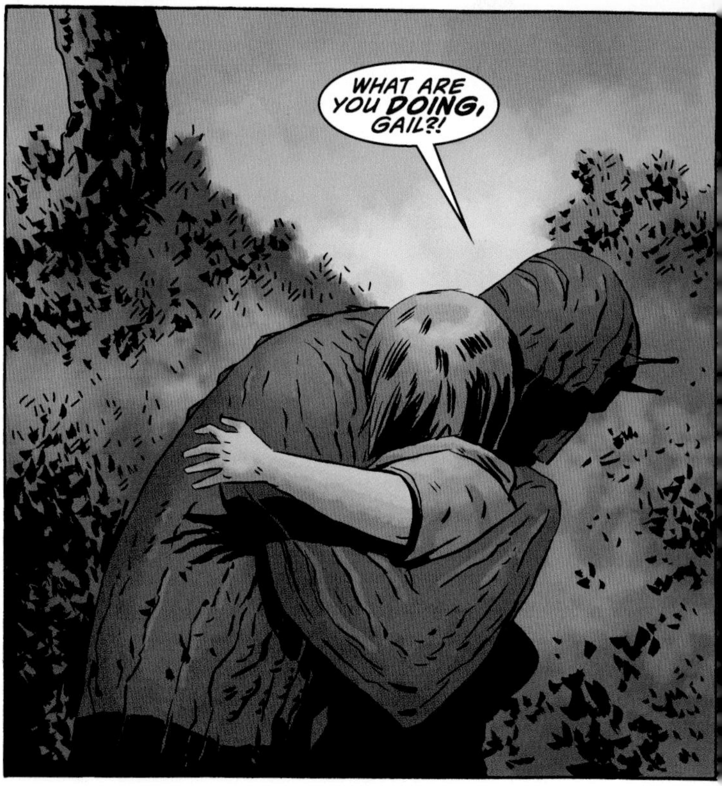
WHAT ARE YOU DOING, GAIL?!

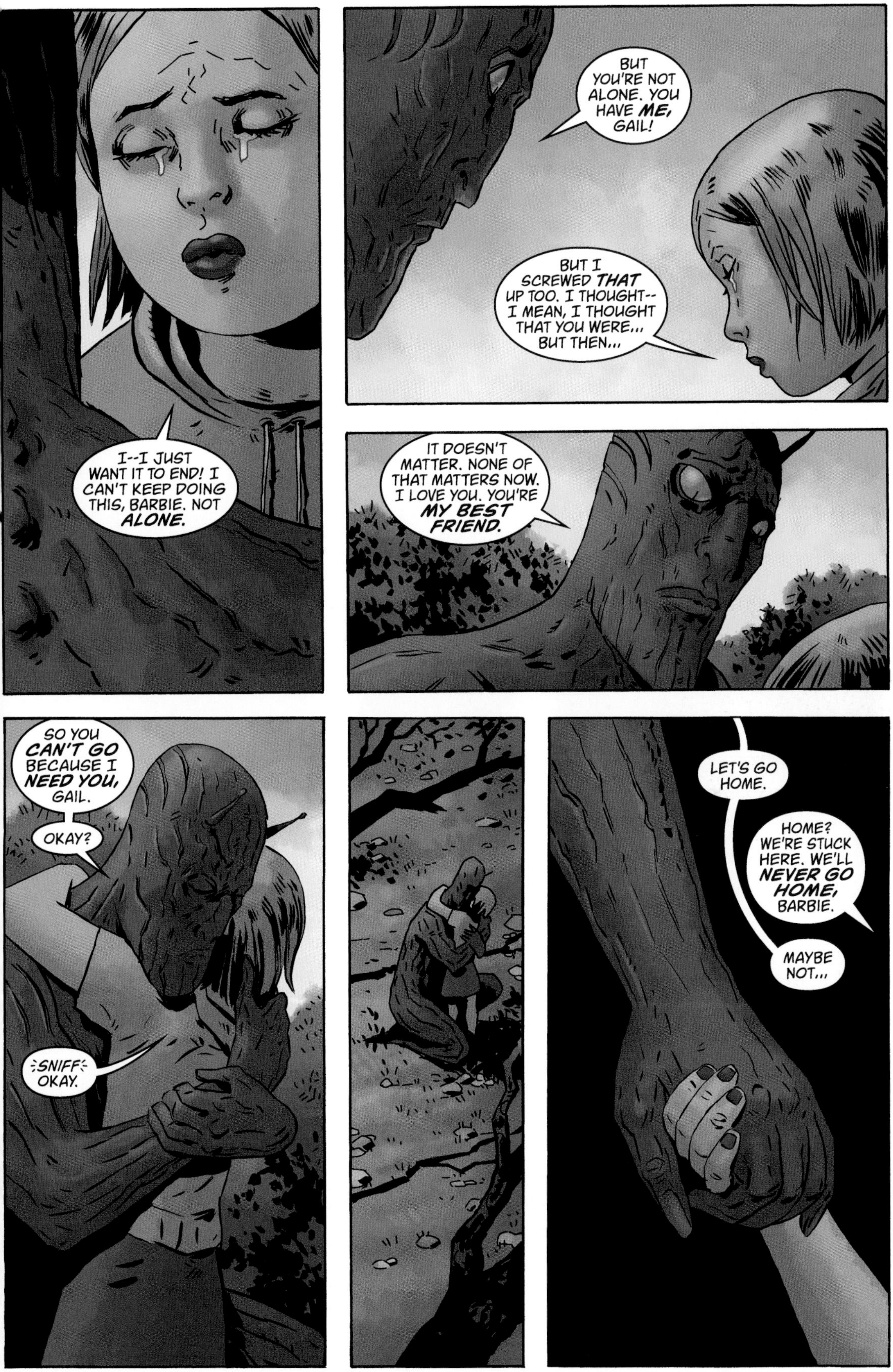
I--I JUST WANT IT TO END! I CAN'T KEEP DOING THIS, BARBIE. NOT ALONE.
BUT YOU'RE NOT ALONE. YOU HAVE ME, GAIL!
BUT I SCREWED THAT UP TOO. I THOUGHT-- I MEAN, I THOUGHT THAT YOU WERE... BUT THEN...
IT DOESN'T MATTER. NONE OF THAT MATTERS NOW. I LOVE YOU. YOU'RE MY BEST FRIEND.
SO YOU CAN'T GO BECAUSE I NEED YOU, GAIL.
OKAY?
SNIFF OKAY.
LET'S GO HOME.
HOME? WE'RE STUCK HERE. WE'LL NEVER GO HOME, BARBIE.
MAYBE NOT...

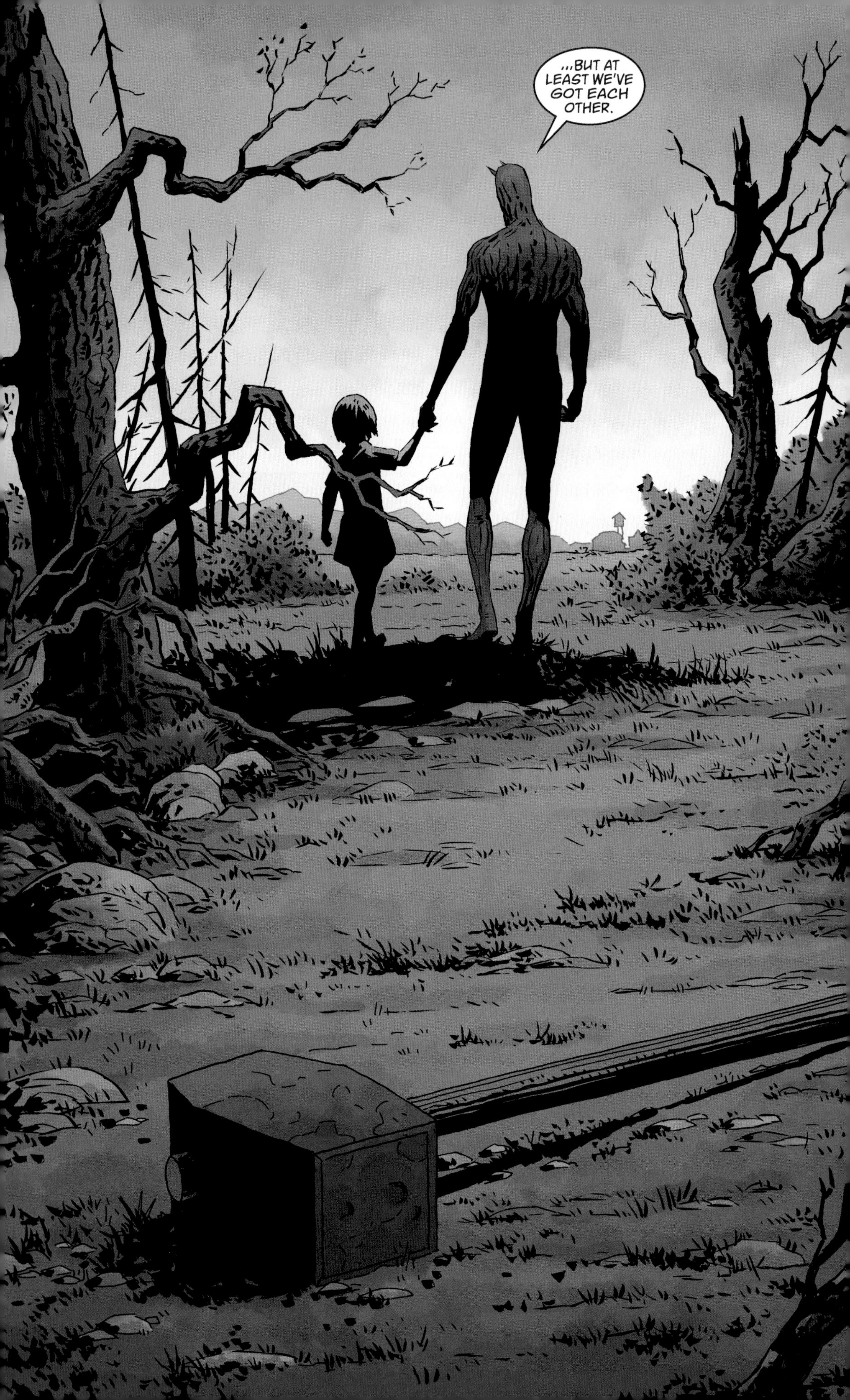
...BUT AT LEAST WE'VE GOT EACH OTHER.

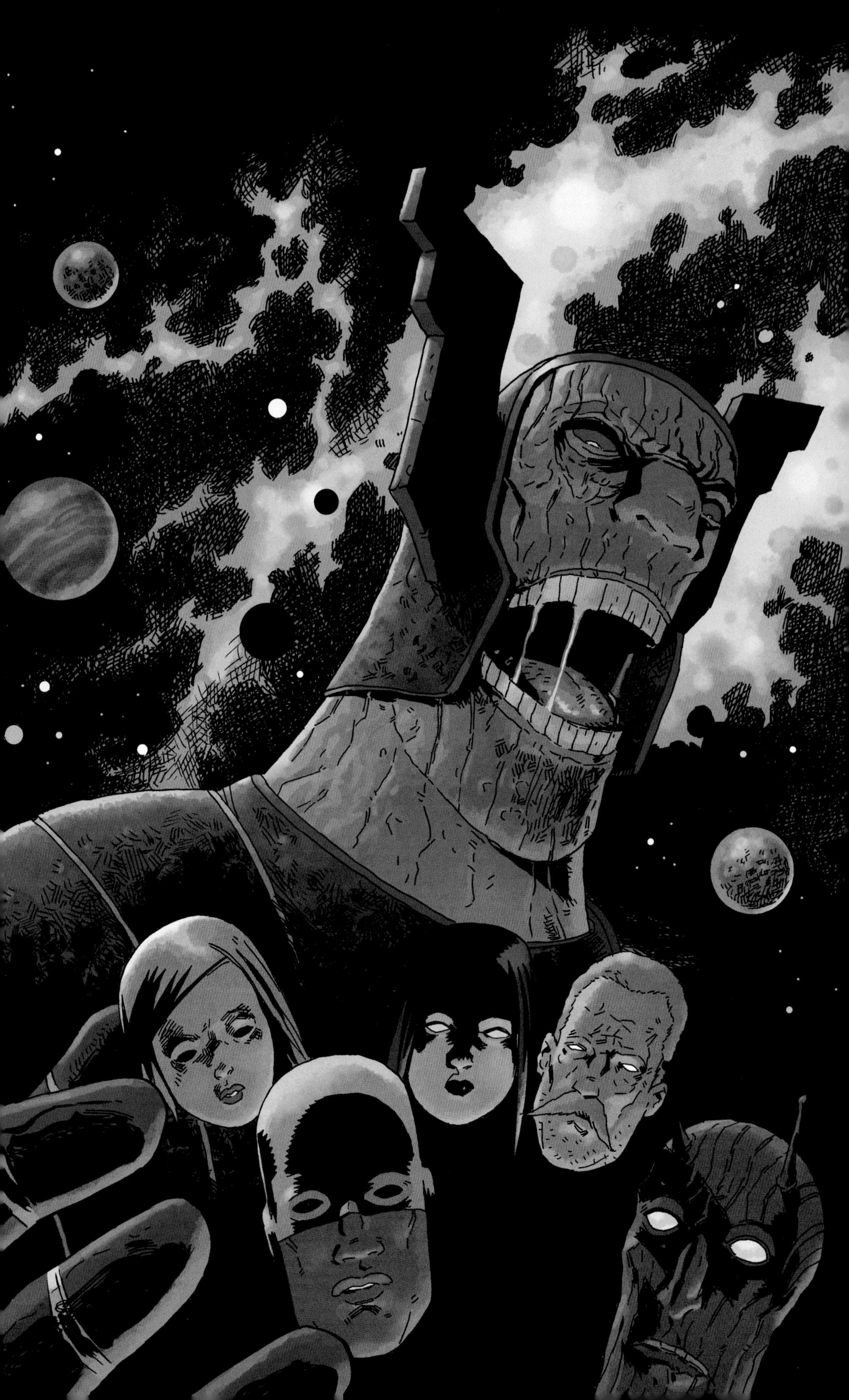

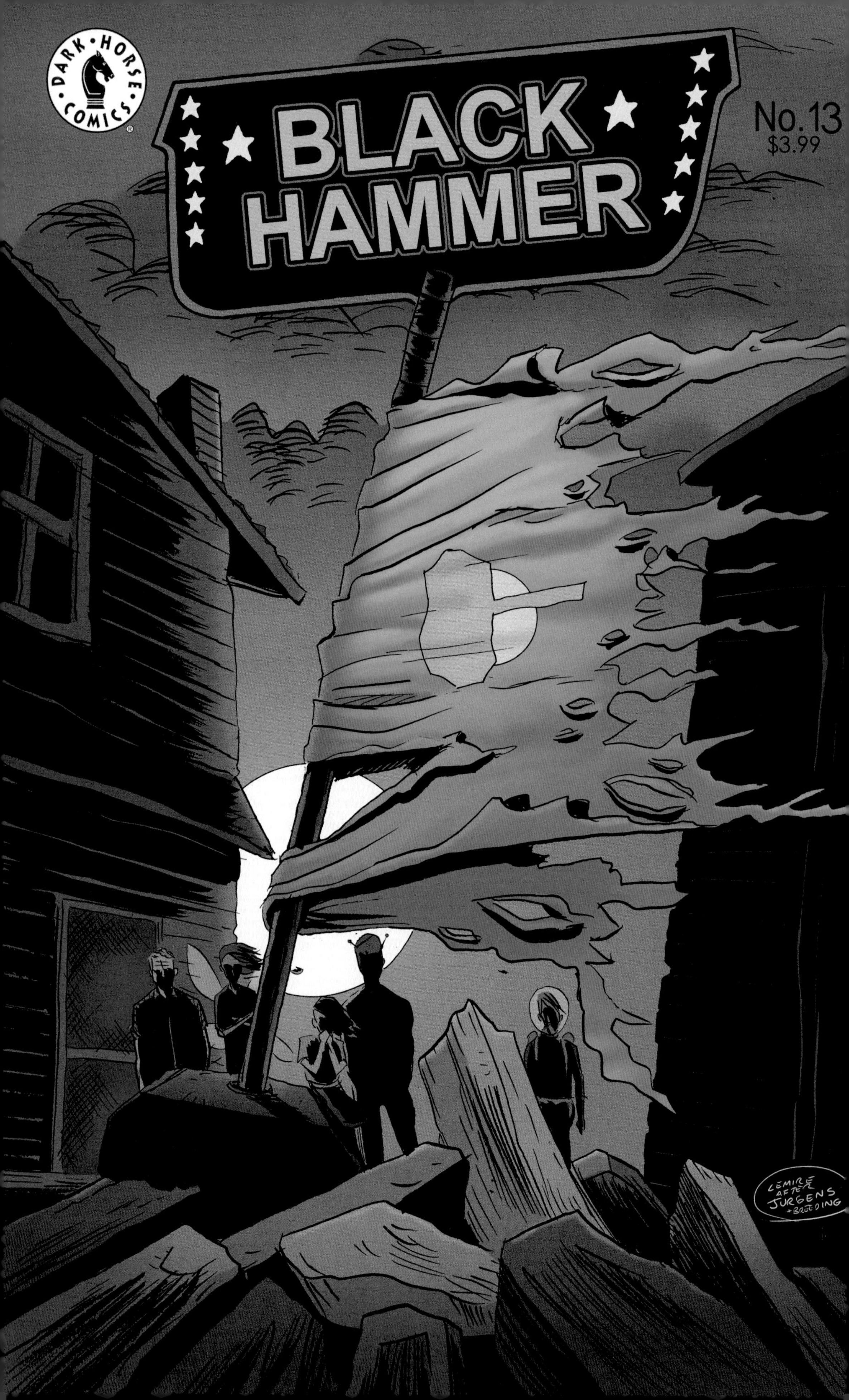
DARK HORSE COMICS
BLACK HAMMER
No. 13
$3.99
LEMIRE AFTER JURGENS + BREEDING

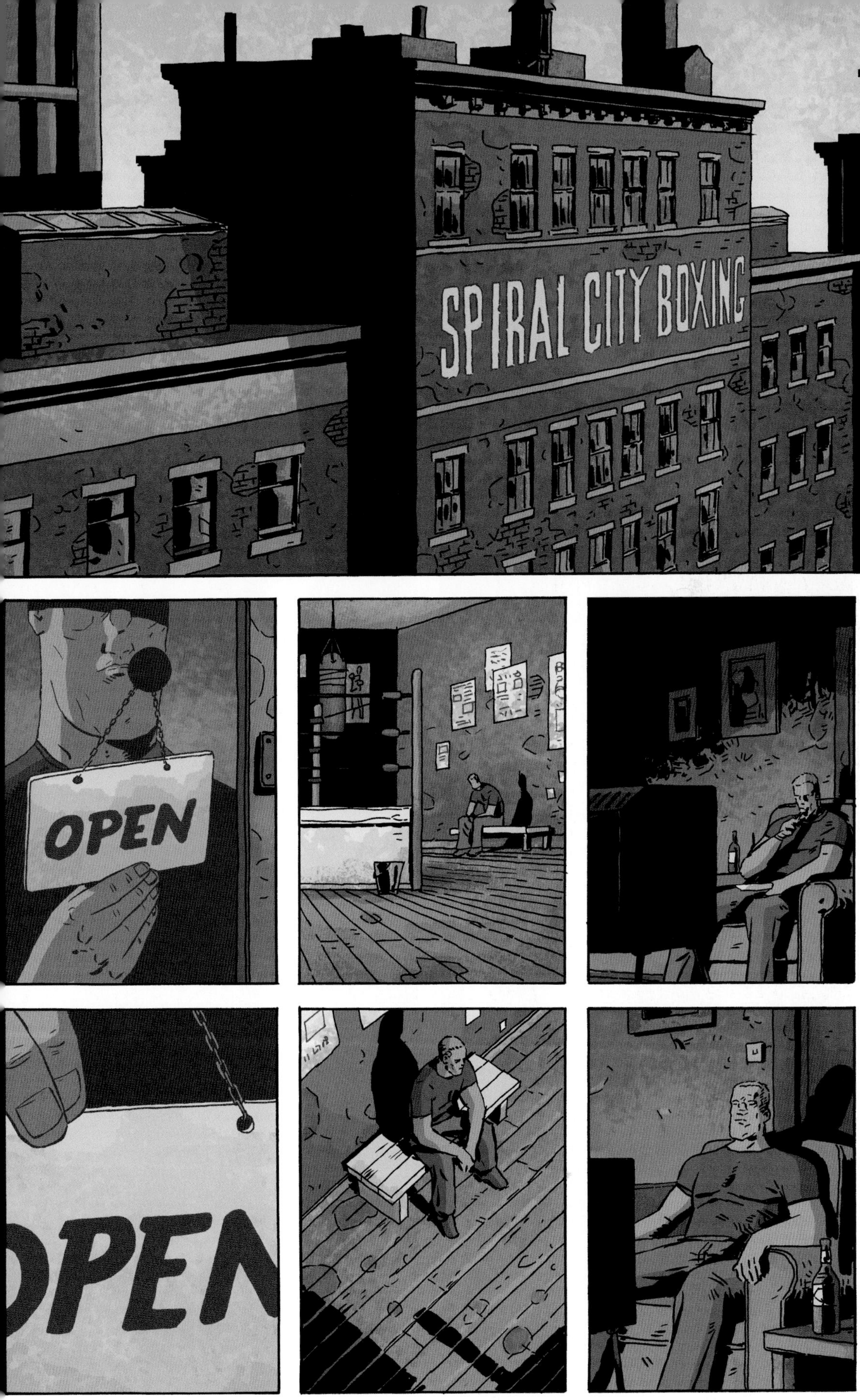
SPIRAL CITY BOXING
OPEN

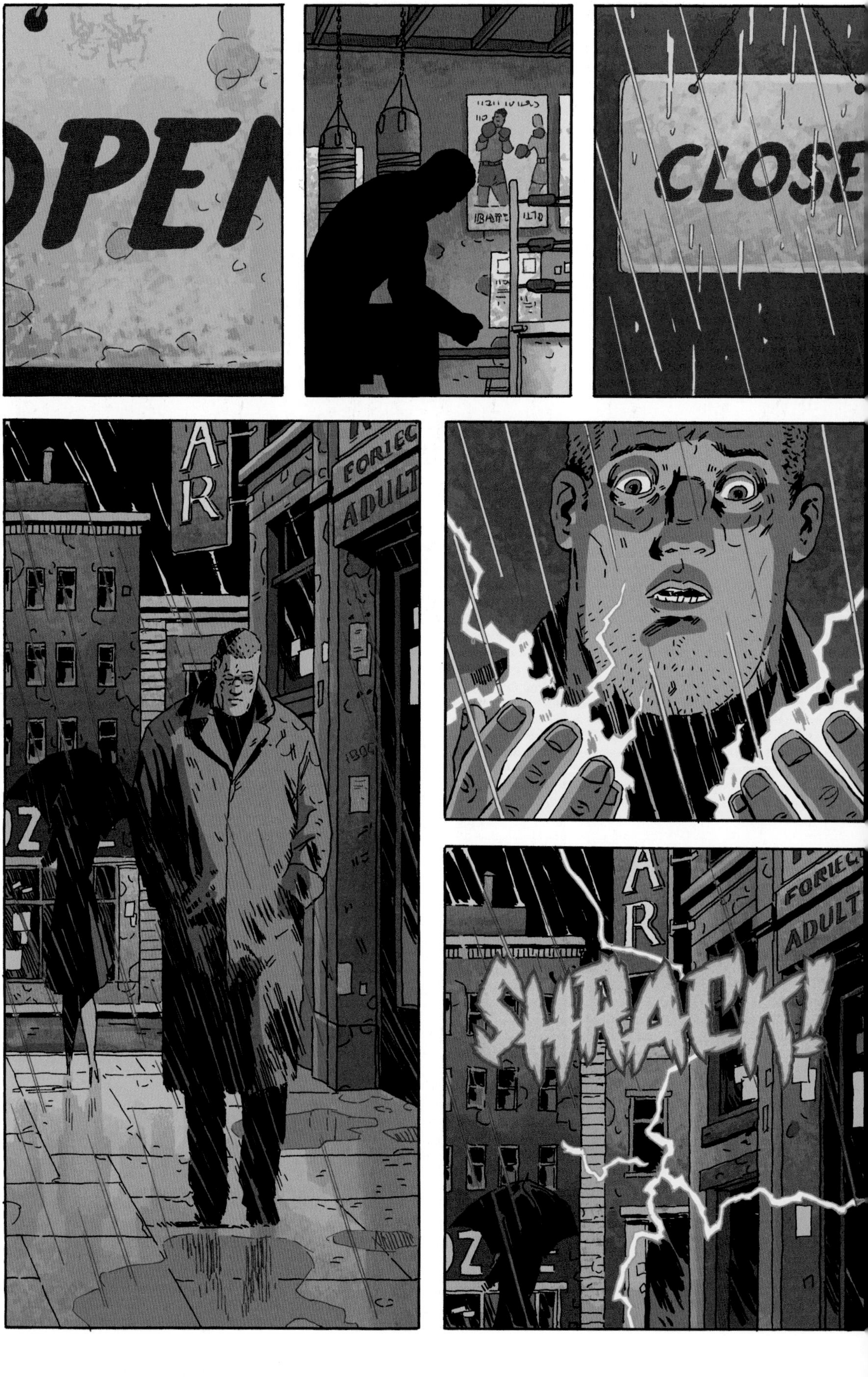
OPEN
CLOSE
AR
ADULT
SHRACK!

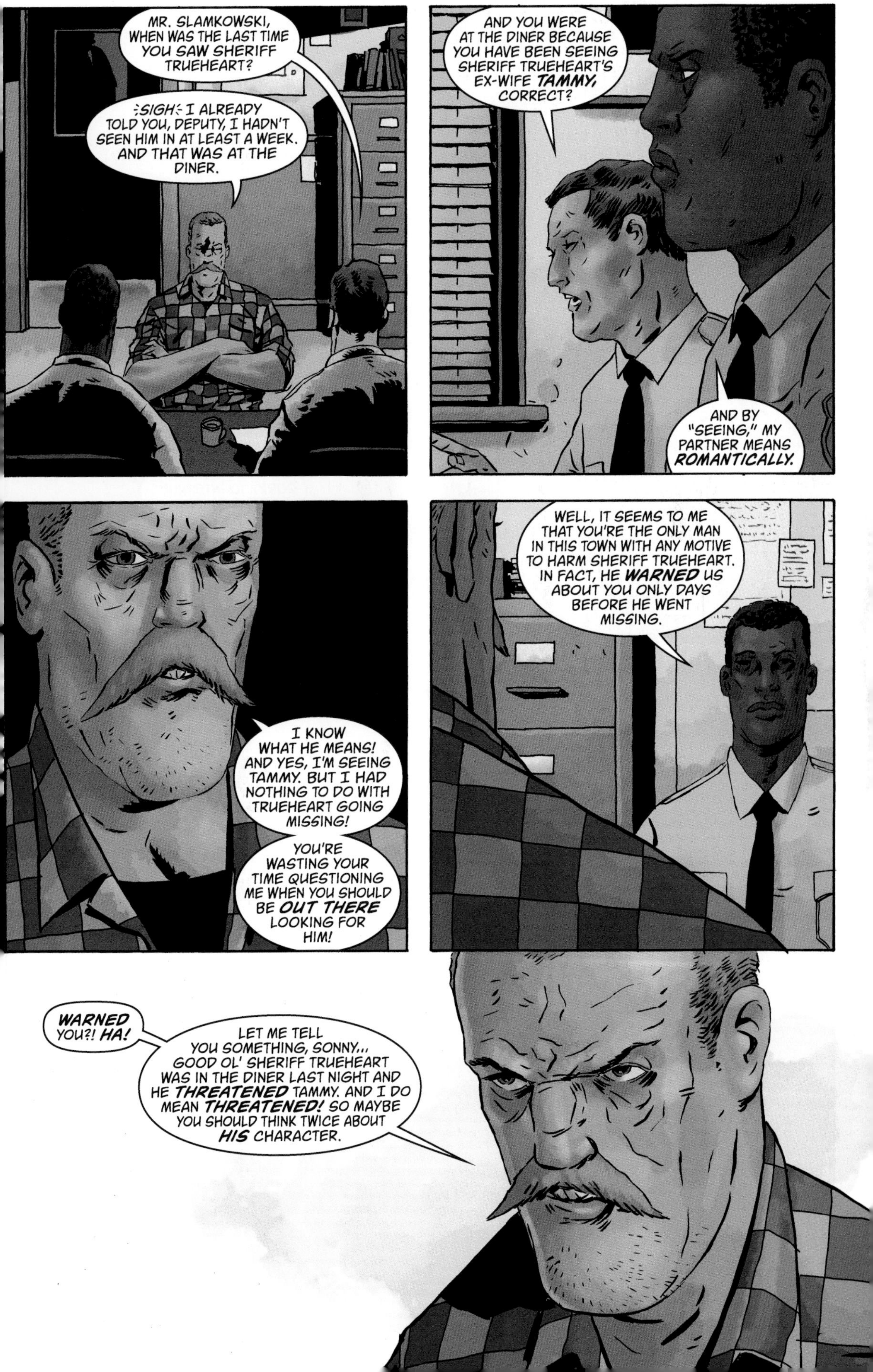
MR. SLAMKOWSKI, WHEN WAS THE LAST TIME YOU SAW SHERIFF TRUEHEART?
-SIGH- I ALREADY TOLD YOU, DEPUTY, I HADN'T SEEN HIM IN AT LEAST A WEEK. AND THAT WAS AT THE DINER.
AND YOU WERE AT THE DINER BECAUSE YOU HAVE BEEN SEEING SHERIFF TRUEHEART'S EX-WIFE TAMMY, CORRECT?
AND BY "SEEING," MY PARTNER MEANS ROMANTICALLY.
I KNOW WHAT HE MEANS! AND YES, I'M SEEING TAMMY. BUT I HAD NOTHING TO DO WITH TRUEHEART GOING MISSING!
YOU'RE WASTING YOUR TIME QUESTIONING ME WHEN YOU SHOULD BE OUT THERE LOOKING FOR HIM!
WELL, IT SEEMS TO ME THAT YOU'RE THE ONLY MAN IN THIS TOWN WITH ANY MOTIVE TO HARM SHERIFF TRUEHEART. IN FACT, HE WARNED US ABOUT YOU ONLY DAYS BEFORE HE WENT MISSING.
WARNED YOU?! HA!
LET ME TELL YOU SOMETHING, SONNY... GOOD OL' SHERIFF TRUEHEART WAS IN THE DINER LAST NIGHT AND HE THREATENED TAMMY. AND I DO MEAN THREATENED! SO MAYBE YOU SHOULD THINK TWICE ABOUT HIS CHARACTER.

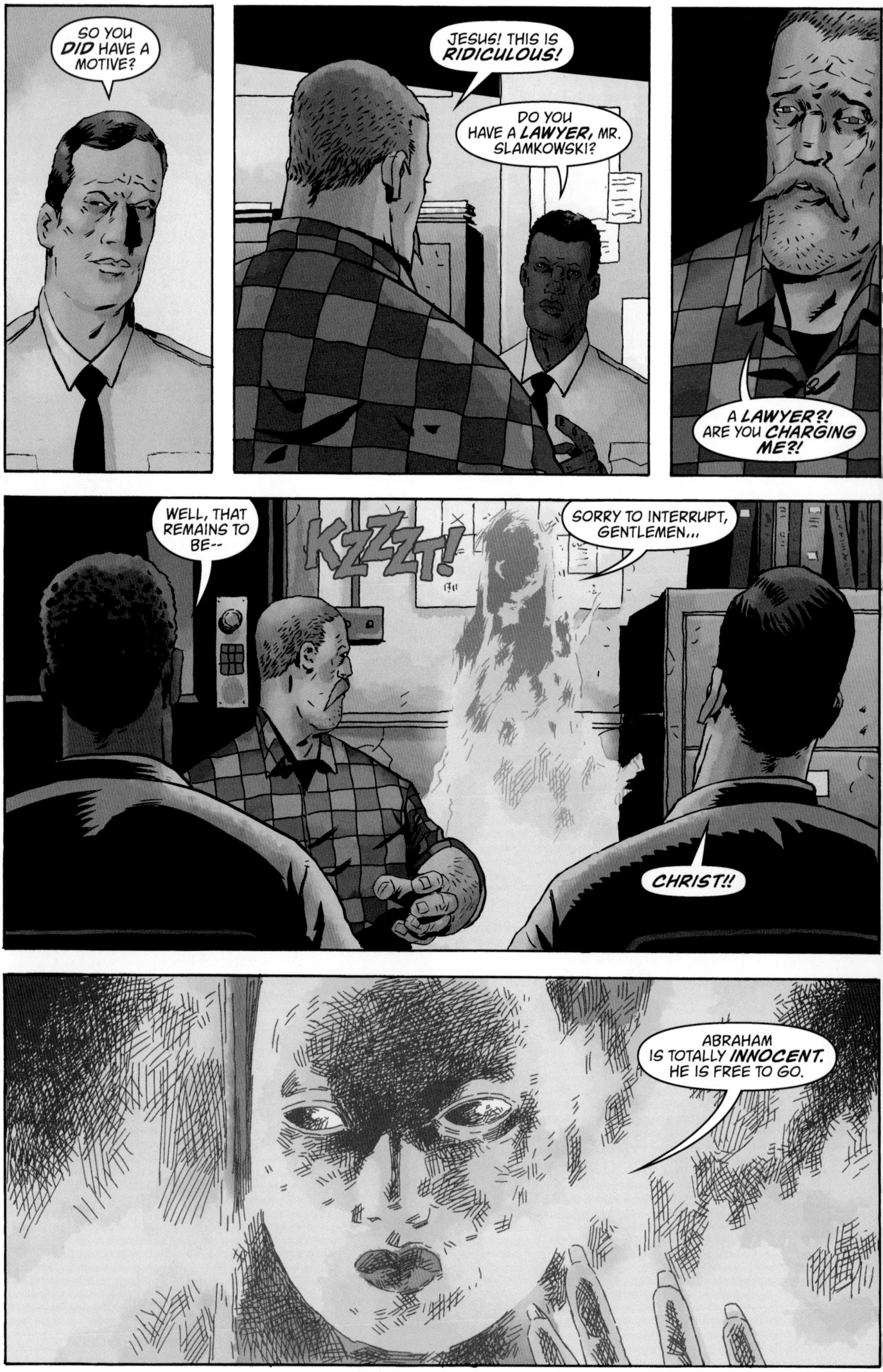
SO YOU DID HAVE A MOTIVE?
JESUS! THIS IS RIDICULOUS!
DO YOU HAVE A LAWYER, MR. SLAMKOWSKI?
A LAWYER?! ARE YOU CHARGING ME?!
WELL, THAT REMAINS TO BE--
KZZZT!
SORRY TO INTERRUPT, GENTLEMEN...
CHRIST!!
ABRAHAM IS TOTALLY INNOCENT. HE IS FREE TO GO.

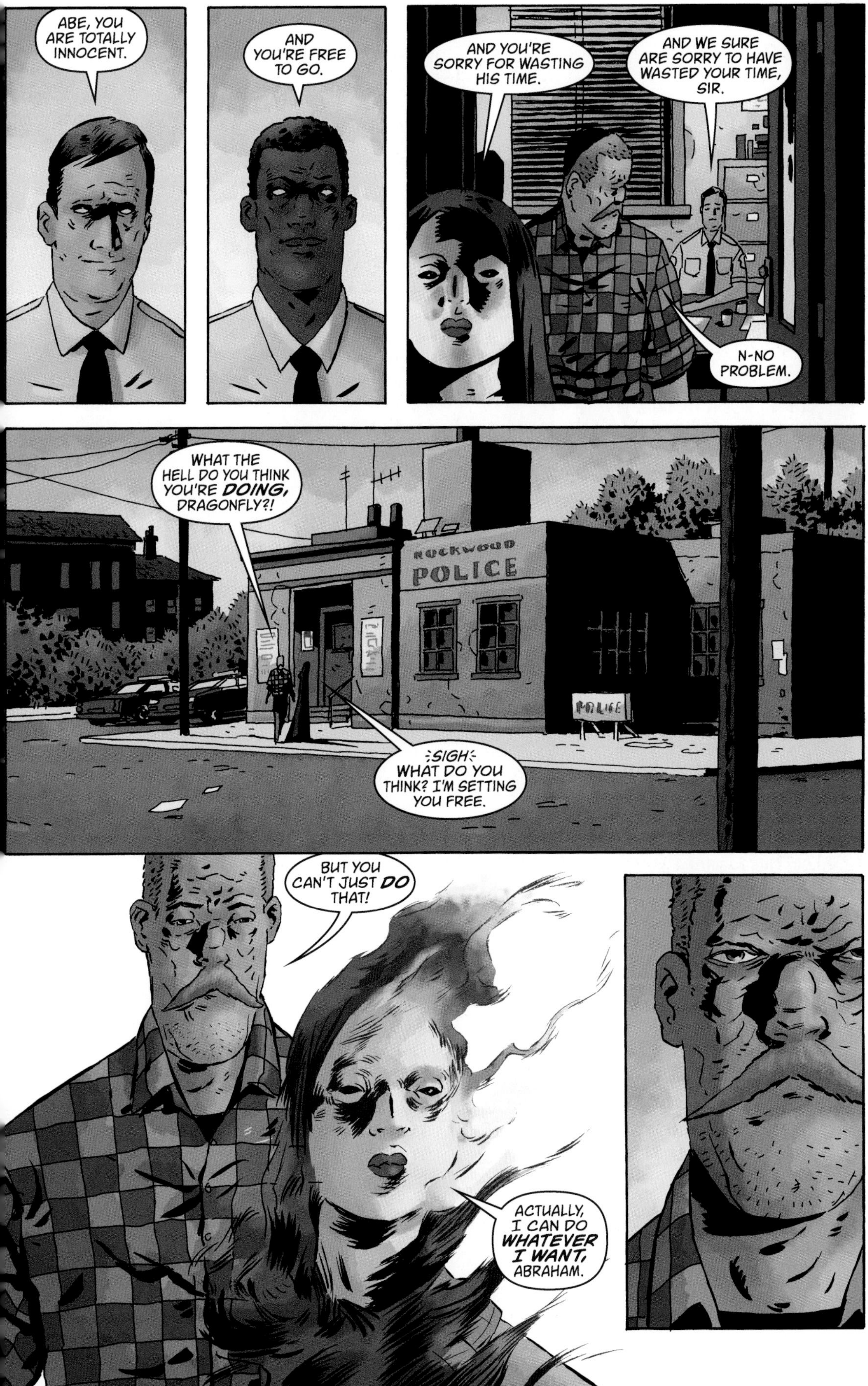
ABE, YOU ARE TOTALLY INNOCENT.
AND YOU'RE FREE TO GO.
AND YOU'RE SORRY FOR WASTING HIS TIME.
AND WE SURE ARE SORRY TO HAVE WASTED YOUR TIME, SIR.
N-NO PROBLEM.
WHAT THE HELL DO YOU THINK YOU'RE **DOING,** DRAGONFLY?!
ROCKWOOD
POLICE
SIGH WHAT DO YOU THINK? I'M SETTING YOU FREE.
BUT YOU CAN'T JUST **DO** THAT!
ACTUALLY, I CAN DO ***WHATEVER I WANT,*** ABRAHAM.

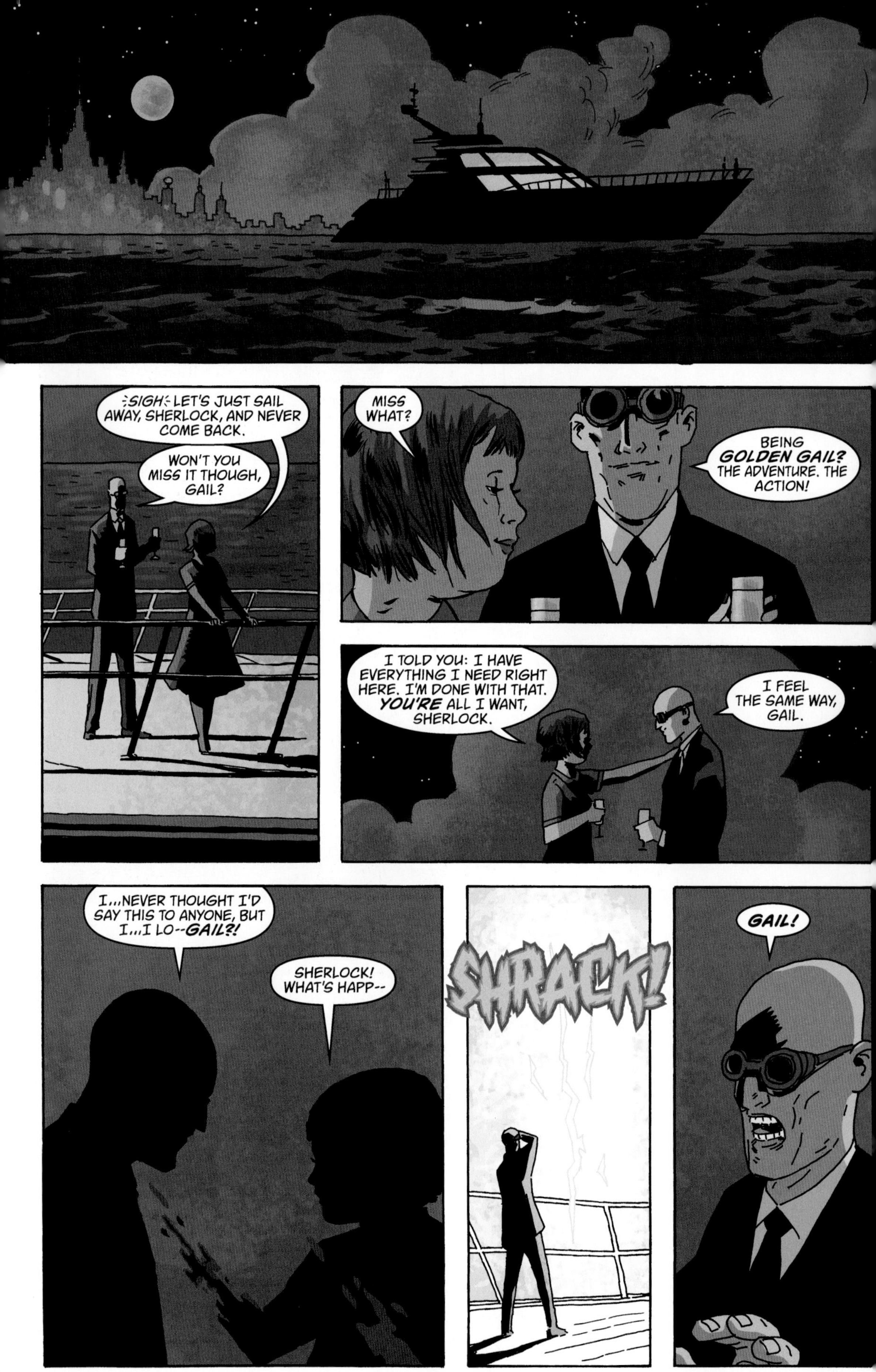

:SIGH: LET'S JUST SAIL AWAY, SHERLOCK, AND NEVER COME BACK.
WON'T YOU MISS IT THOUGH, GAIL?
MISS WHAT?
BEING **GOLDEN GAIL?** THE ADVENTURE. THE ACTION!
I TOLD YOU: I HAVE EVERYTHING I NEED RIGHT HERE. I'M DONE WITH THAT. ***YOU'RE*** ALL I WANT, SHERLOCK.
I FEEL THE SAME WAY, GAIL.
I...NEVER THOUGHT I'D SAY THIS TO ANYONE, BUT I...I LO--***GAIL?!***
SHERLOCK! WHAT'S HAPP--
SHRACK!
GAIL!

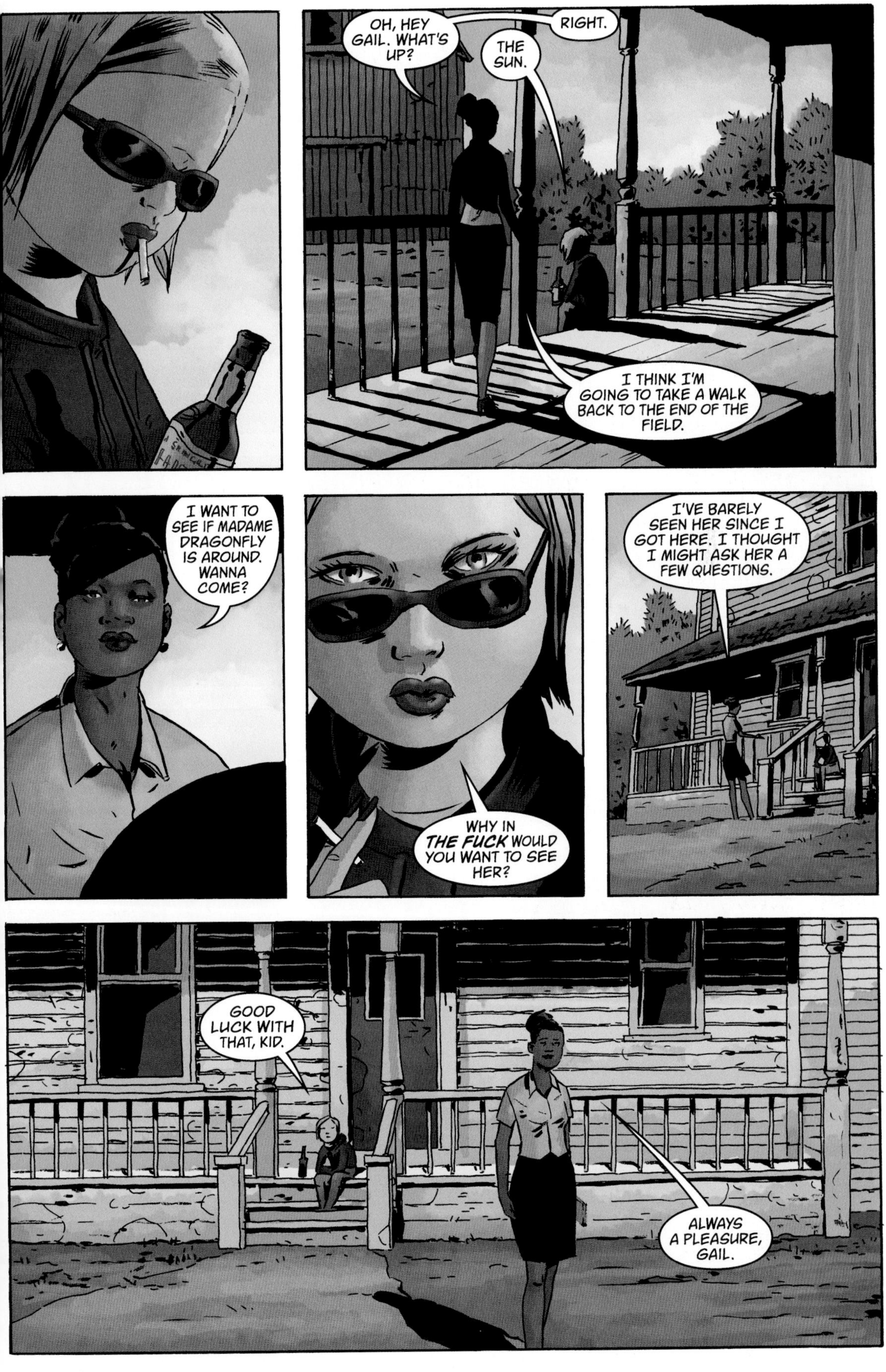
OH, HEY GAIL. WHAT'S UP?
THE SUN.
RIGHT.
I THINK I'M GOING TO TAKE A WALK BACK TO THE END OF THE FIELD.
I WANT TO SEE IF MADAME DRAGONFLY IS AROUND. WANNA COME?
WHY IN ***THE FUCK*** WOULD YOU WANT TO SEE HER?
I'VE BARELY SEEN HER SINCE I GOT HERE. I THOUGHT I MIGHT ASK HER A FEW QUESTIONS.
GOOD LUCK WITH THAT, KID.
ALWAYS A PLEASURE, GAIL.

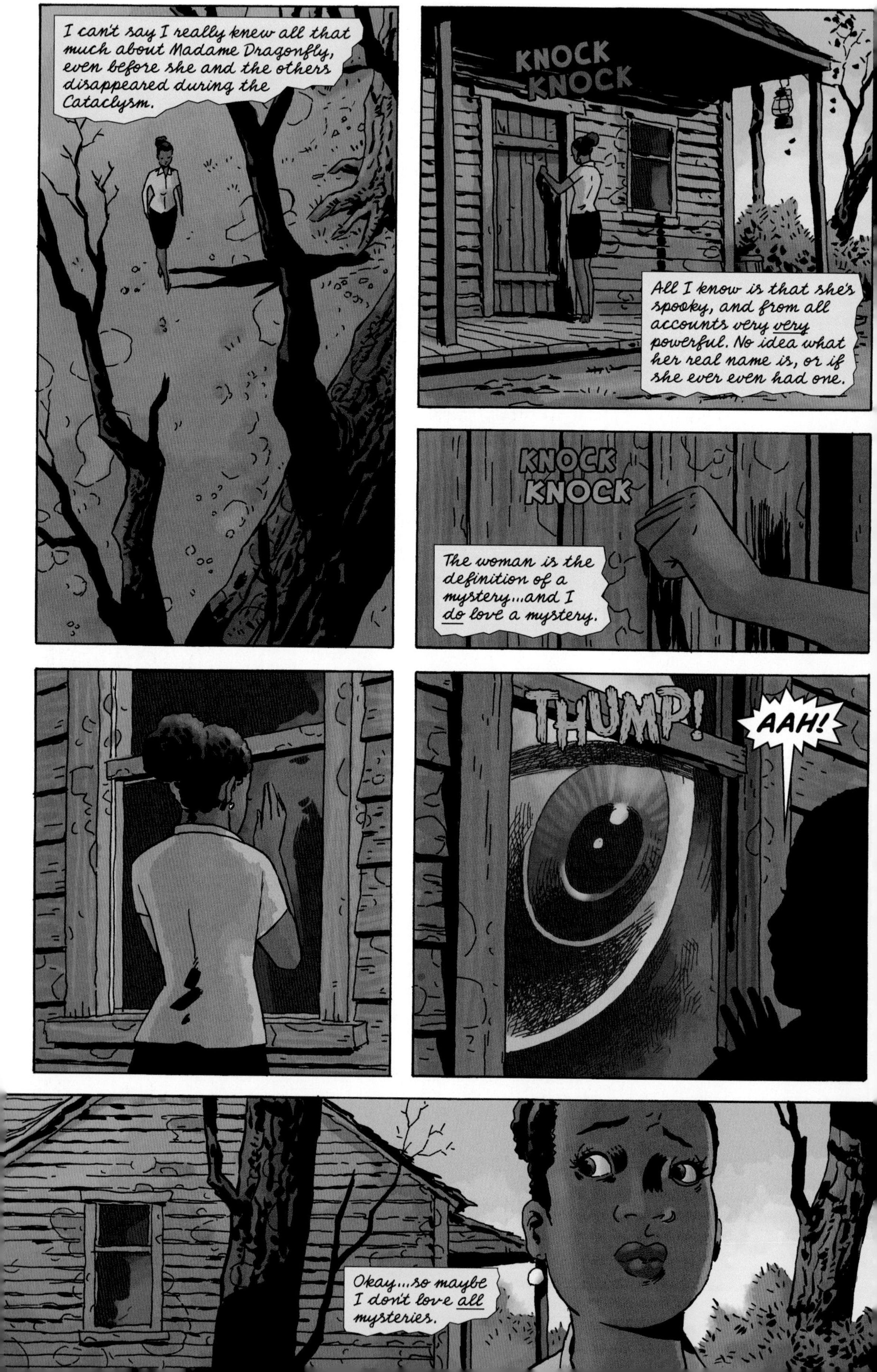
I can't say I really knew all that much about Madame Dragonfly, even before she and the others disappeared during the Cataclysm.
KNOCK KNOCK
All I know is that she's spooky, and from all accounts very very powerful. No idea what her real name is, or if she ever even had one.
KNOCK KNOCK
The woman is the definition of a mystery...and I do love a mystery.
THUMP!
AAH!
Okay...so maybe I don't love all mysteries.

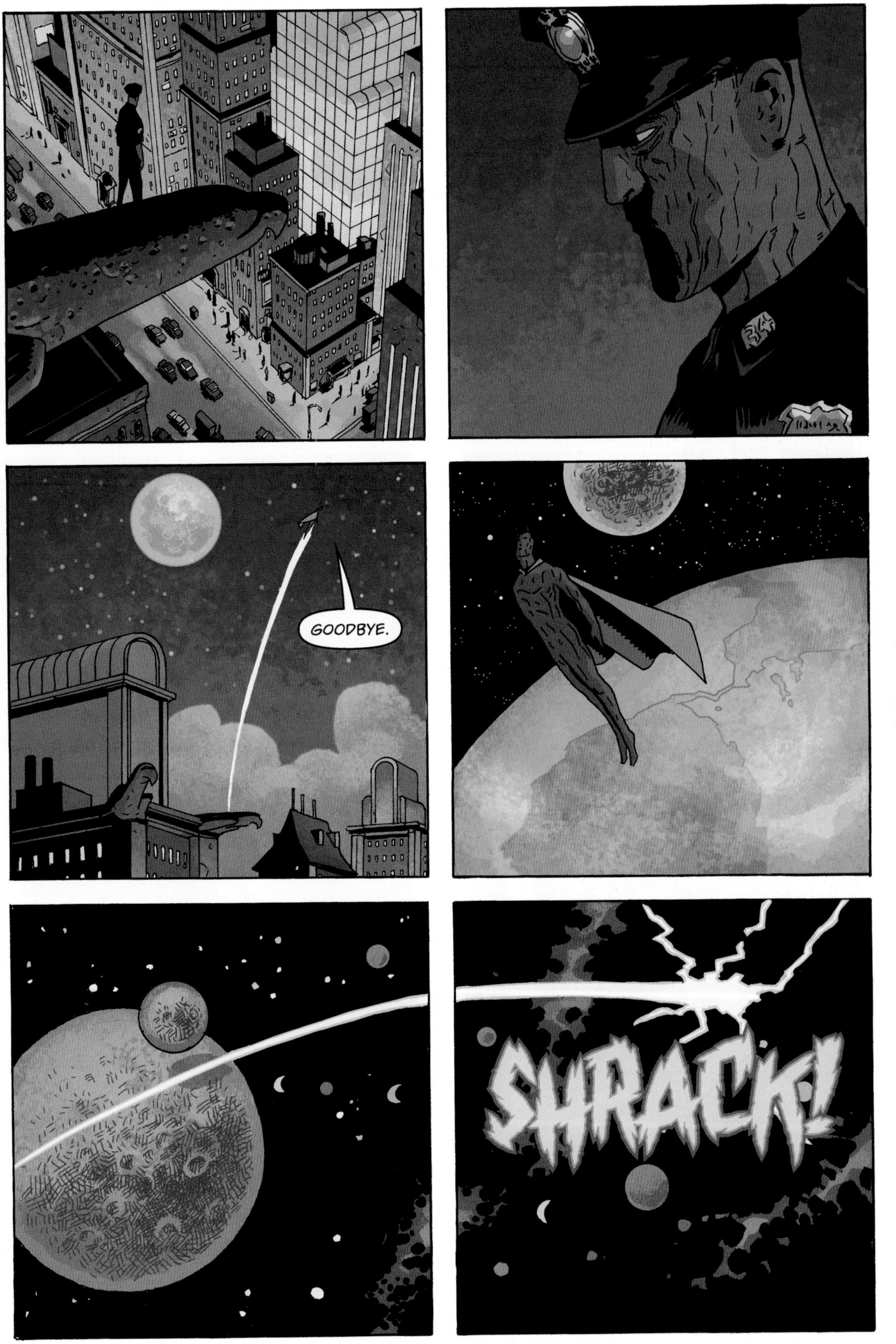
GOODBYE.
SHRACK!

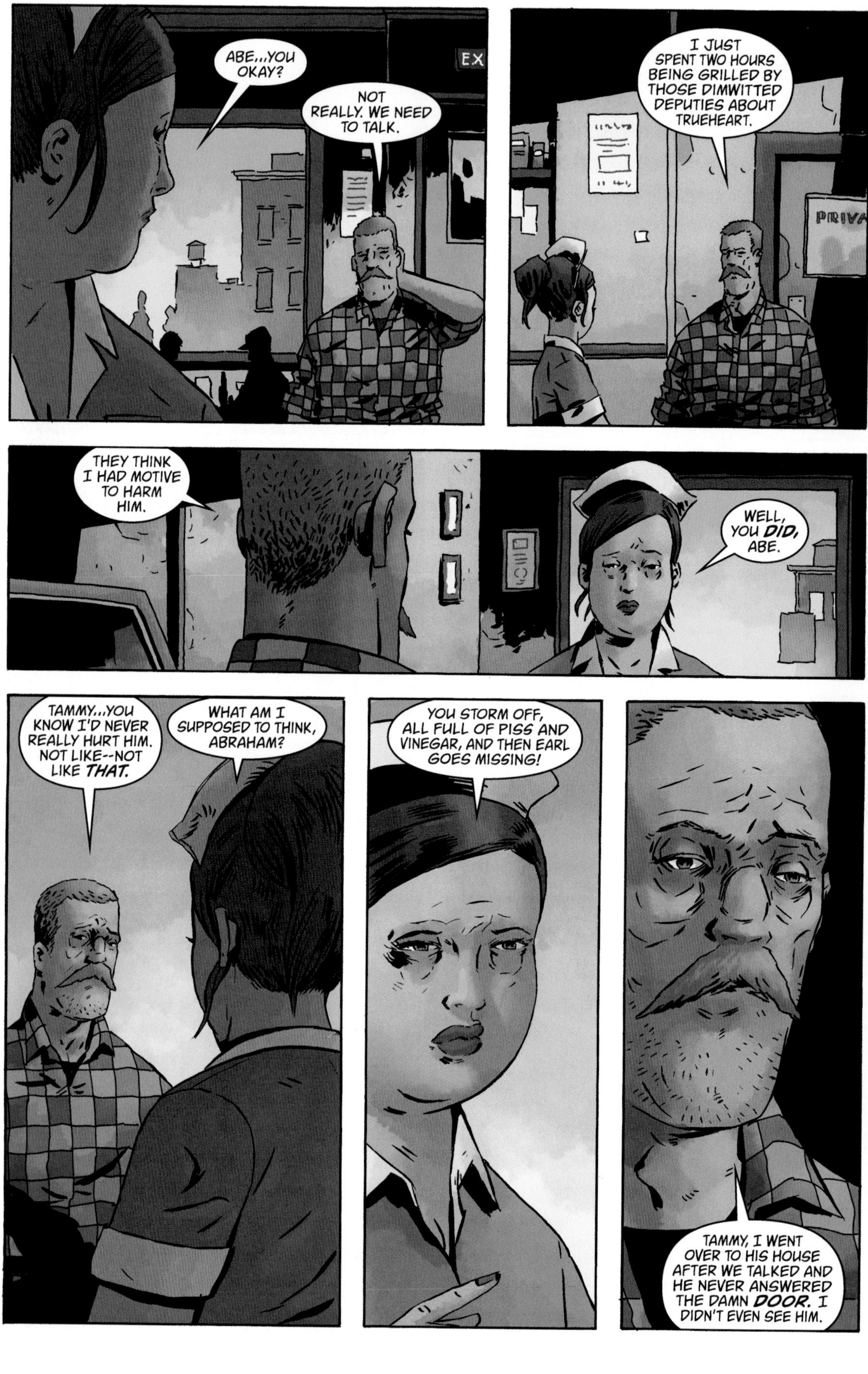

EX
ABE...YOU OKAY?
NOT REALLY. WE NEED TO TALK.
I JUST SPENT TWO HOURS BEING GRILLED BY THOSE DIMWITTED DEPUTIES ABOUT TRUEHEART.
PRIVA
THEY THINK I HAD MOTIVE TO HARM HIM.
WELL, YOU ***DID,*** ABE.
TAMMY...YOU KNOW I'D NEVER REALLY HURT HIM. NOT LIKE--NOT LIKE ***THAT.***
WHAT AM I SUPPOSED TO THINK, ABRAHAM?
YOU STORM OFF, ALL FULL OF PISS AND VINEGAR, AND THEN EARL GOES MISSING!
TAMMY, I WENT OVER TO HIS HOUSE AFTER WE TALKED AND HE NEVER ANSWERED THE DAMN ***DOOR.*** I DIDN'T EVEN SEE HIM.

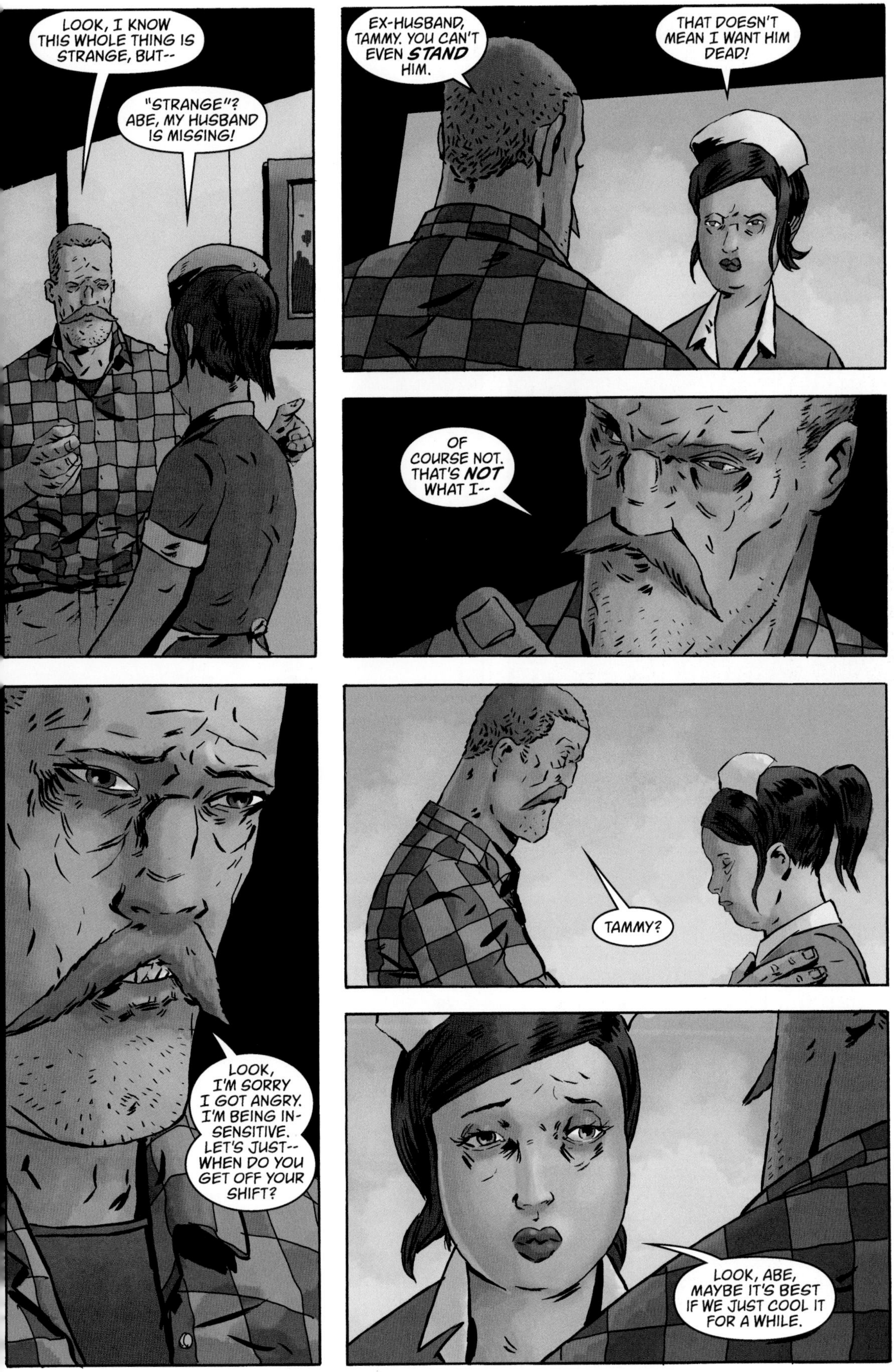
LOOK, I KNOW THIS WHOLE THING IS STRANGE, BUT--
"STRANGE"? ABE, MY HUSBAND IS MISSING!
EX-HUSBAND, TAMMY. YOU CAN'T EVEN STAND HIM.
THAT DOESN'T MEAN I WANT HIM DEAD!
OF COURSE NOT. THAT'S NOT WHAT I--
LOOK, I'M SORRY I GOT ANGRY. I'M BEING IN-SENSITIVE. LET'S JUST-- WHEN DO YOU GET OFF YOUR SHIFT?
TAMMY?
LOOK, ABE, MAYBE IT'S BEST IF WE JUST COOL IT FOR A WHILE.

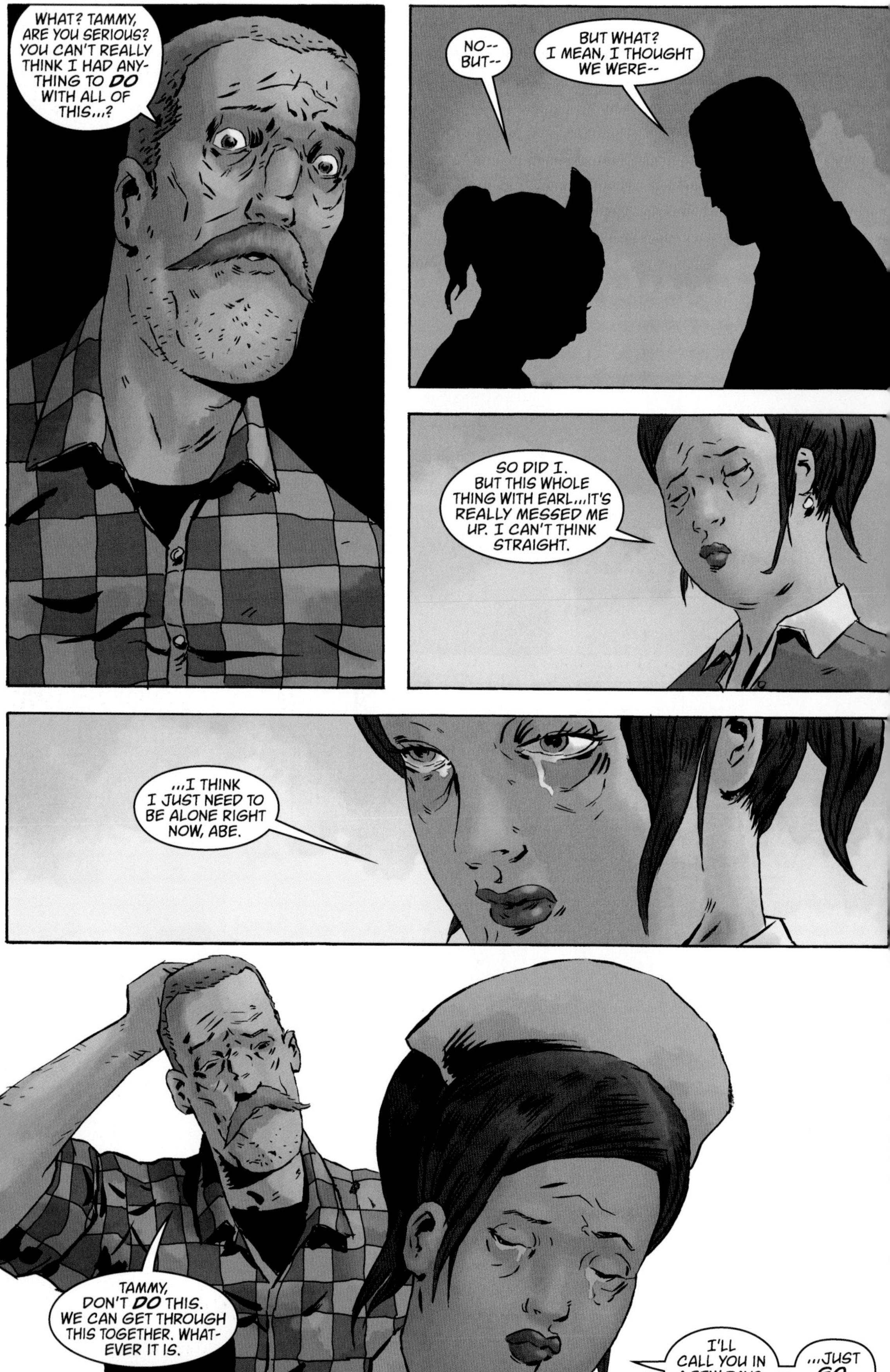
WHAT? TAMMY, ARE YOU SERIOUS? YOU CAN'T REALLY THINK I HAD ANYTHING TO DO WITH ALL OF THIS...?
NO-- BUT--
BUT WHAT? I MEAN, I THOUGHT WE WERE--
SO DID I. BUT THIS WHOLE THING WITH EARL...IT'S REALLY MESSED ME UP. I CAN'T THINK STRAIGHT.
...I THINK I JUST NEED TO BE ALONE RIGHT NOW, ABE.
TAMMY, DON'T DO THIS. WE CAN GET THROUGH THIS TOGETHER. WHATEVER IT IS.
I'LL CALL YOU IN A FEW DAYS. JUST...
...JUST GO, OKAY?

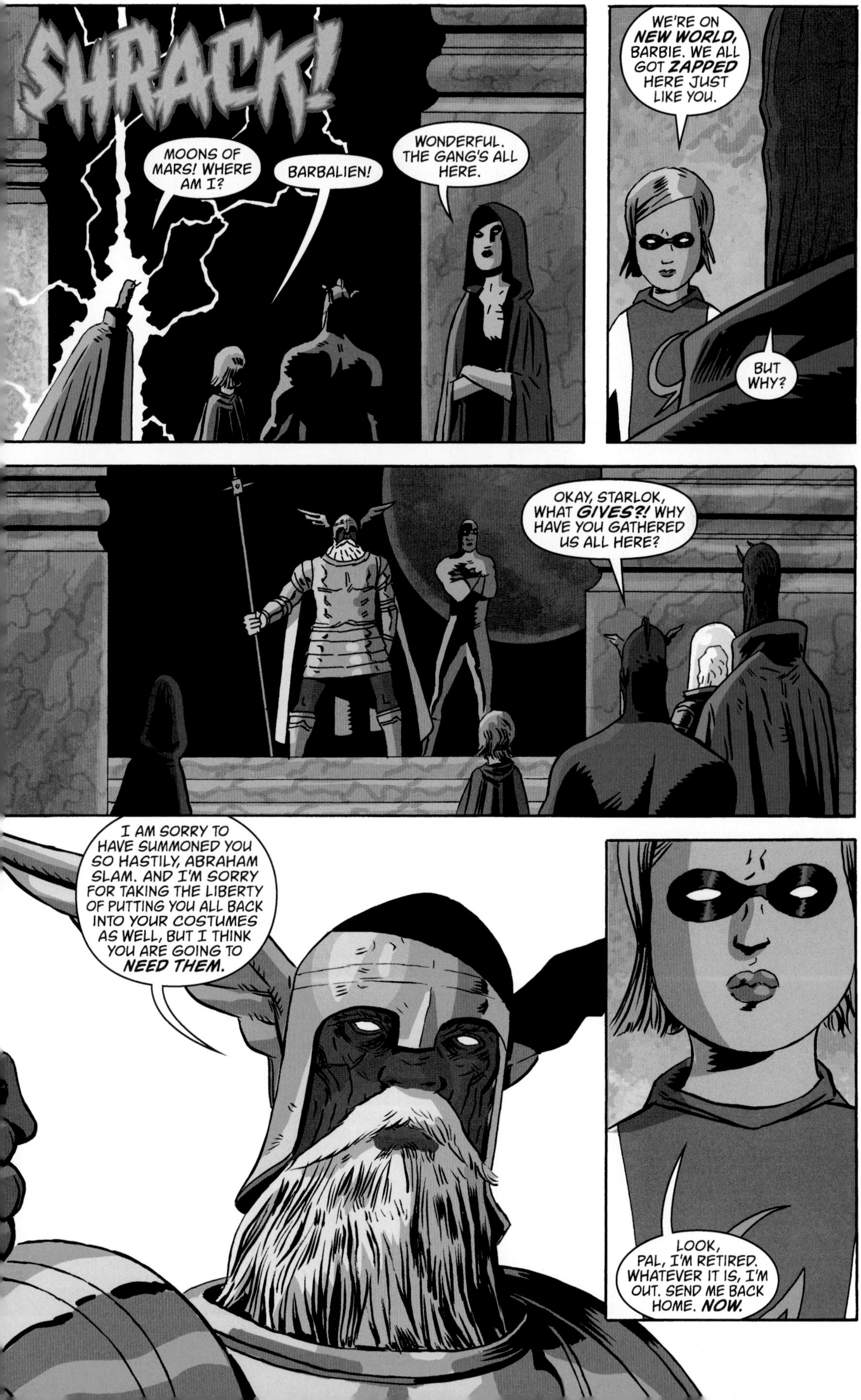
SHRACK!
MOONS OF MARS! WHERE AM I?
BARBALIEN!
WONDERFUL. THE GANG'S ALL HERE.
WE'RE ON **NEW WORLD,** BARBIE. WE ALL GOT **ZAPPED** HERE JUST LIKE YOU.
BUT WHY?
OKAY, STARLOK, WHAT **GIVES?!** WHY HAVE YOU GATHERED US ALL HERE?
I AM SORRY TO HAVE SUMMONED YOU SO HASTILY, ABRAHAM SLAM. AND I'M SORRY FOR TAKING THE LIBERTY OF PUTTING YOU ALL BACK INTO YOUR COSTUMES AS WELL, BUT I THINK YOU ARE GOING TO **NEED THEM.**
LOOK, PAL, I'M RETIRED. WHATEVER IT IS, I'M OUT. SEND ME BACK HOME. **NOW.**

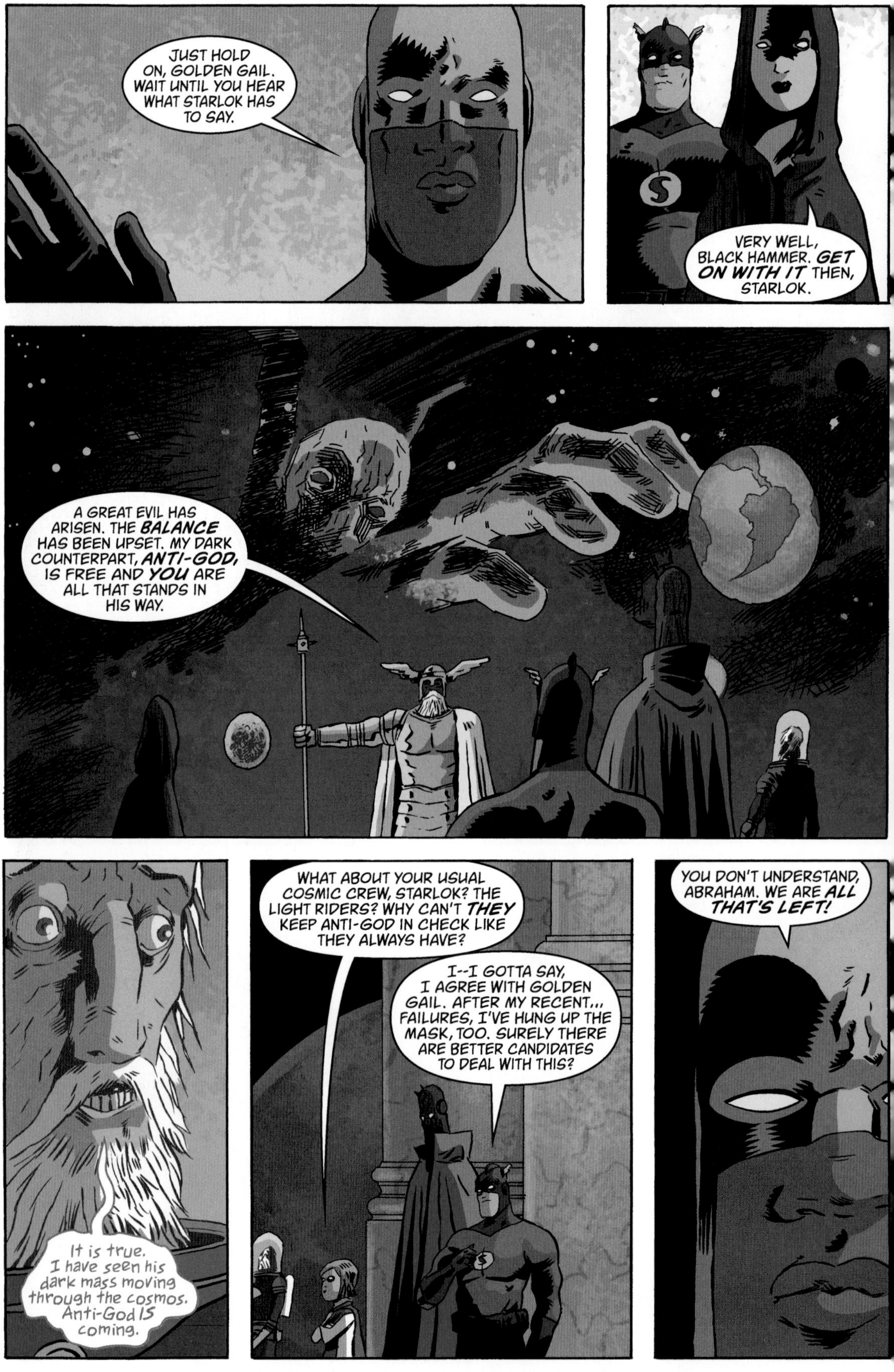
JUST HOLD ON, GOLDEN GAIL. WAIT UNTIL YOU HEAR WHAT STARLOK HAS TO SAY.
VERY WELL, BLACK HAMMER. GET ON WITH IT THEN, STARLOK.
A GREAT EVIL HAS ARISEN. THE BALANCE HAS BEEN UPSET. MY DARK COUNTERPART, ANTI-GOD, IS FREE AND YOU ARE ALL THAT STANDS IN HIS WAY.
It is true. I have seen his dark mass moving through the cosmos. Anti-God IS coming.
WHAT ABOUT YOUR USUAL COSMIC CREW, STARLOK? THE LIGHT RIDERS? WHY CAN'T THEY KEEP ANTI-GOD IN CHECK LIKE THEY ALWAYS HAVE?
I--I GOTTA SAY, I AGREE WITH GOLDEN GAIL. AFTER MY RECENT... FAILURES, I'VE HUNG UP THE MASK, TOO. SURELY THERE ARE BETTER CANDIDATES TO DEAL WITH THIS?
YOU DON'T UNDERSTAND, ABRAHAM. WE ARE ALL THAT'S LEFT!

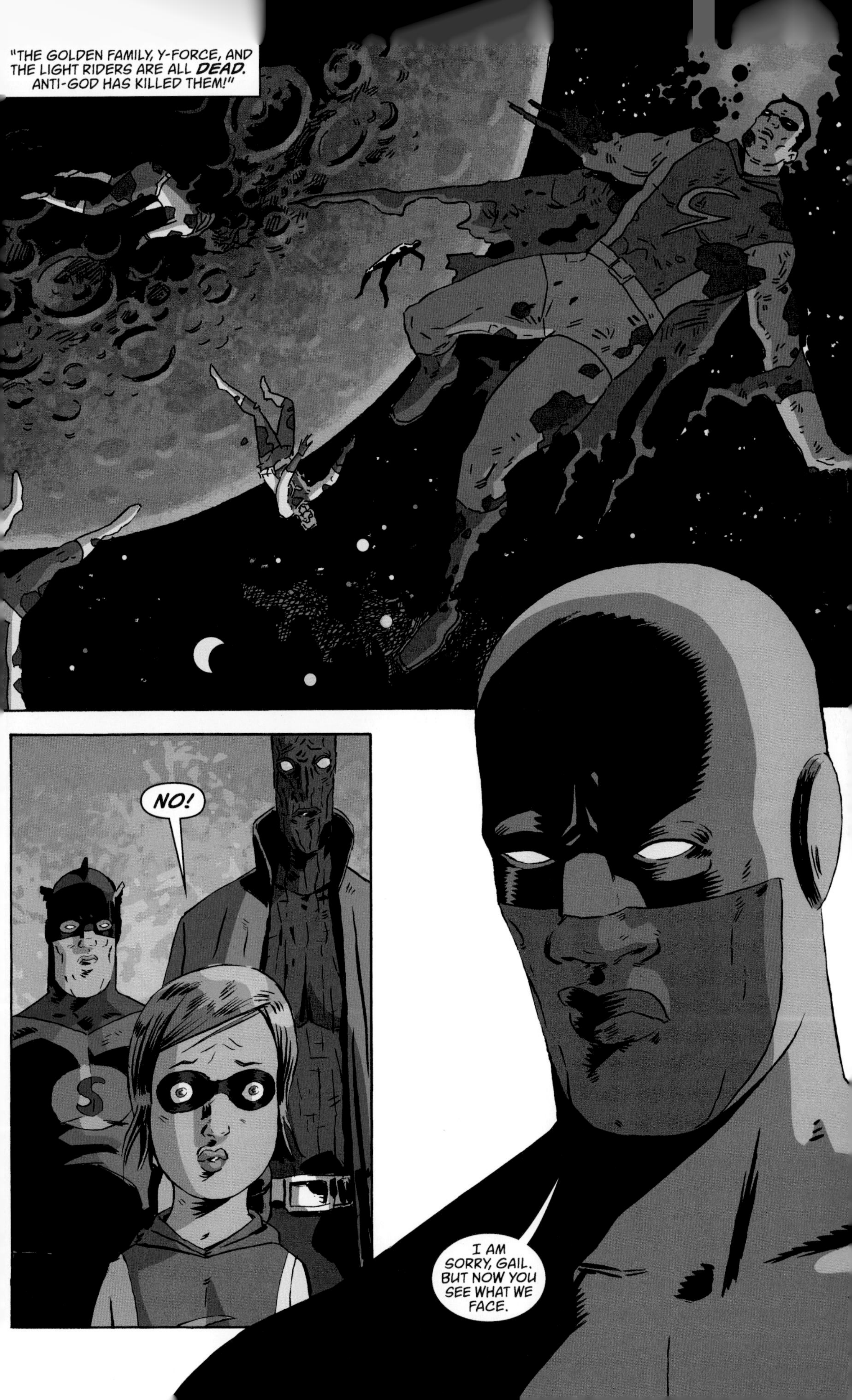
"THE GOLDEN FAMILY, Y-FORCE, AND THE LIGHT RIDERS ARE ALL DEAD. ANTI-GOD HAS KILLED THEM!"
NO!
I AM SORRY, GAIL. BUT NOW YOU SEE WHAT WE FACE.

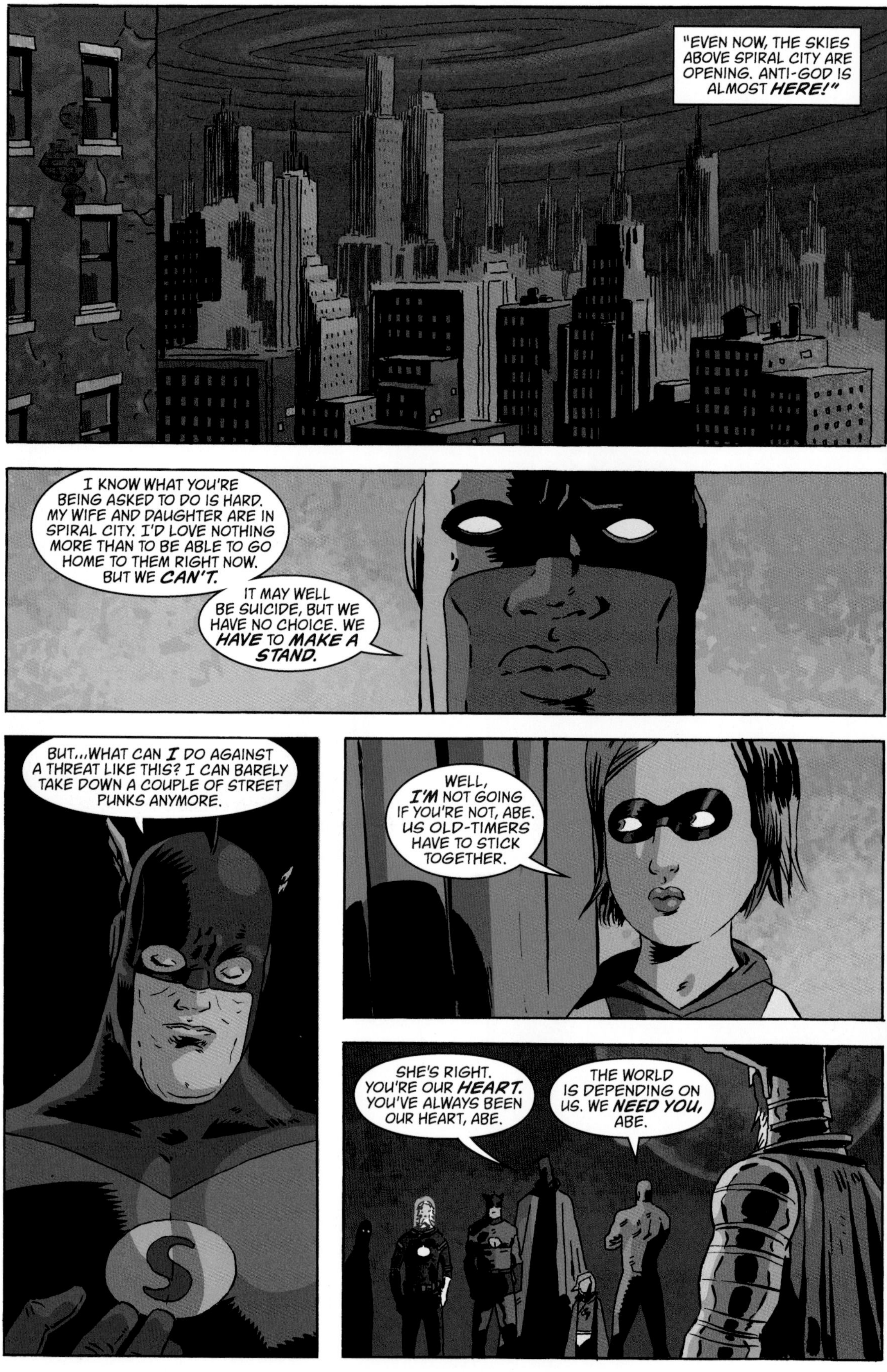
"EVEN NOW, THE SKIES ABOVE SPIRAL CITY ARE OPENING. ANTI-GOD IS ALMOST *HERE!*"
I KNOW WHAT YOU'RE BEING ASKED TO DO IS HARD. MY WIFE AND DAUGHTER ARE IN SPIRAL CITY. I'D LOVE NOTHING MORE THAN TO BE ABLE TO GO HOME TO THEM RIGHT NOW. BUT WE *CAN'T.*
IT MAY WELL BE SUICIDE, BUT WE HAVE NO CHOICE. WE *HAVE* TO *MAKE A STAND.*
BUT...WHAT CAN *I* DO AGAINST A THREAT LIKE THIS? I CAN BARELY TAKE DOWN A COUPLE OF STREET PUNKS ANYMORE.
WELL, *I'M* NOT GOING IF YOU'RE NOT, ABE. US OLD-TIMERS HAVE TO STICK TOGETHER.
SHE'S RIGHT. YOU'RE OUR *HEART.* YOU'VE ALWAYS BEEN OUR HEART, ABE.
THE WORLD IS DEPENDING ON US. WE *NEED YOU,* ABE.

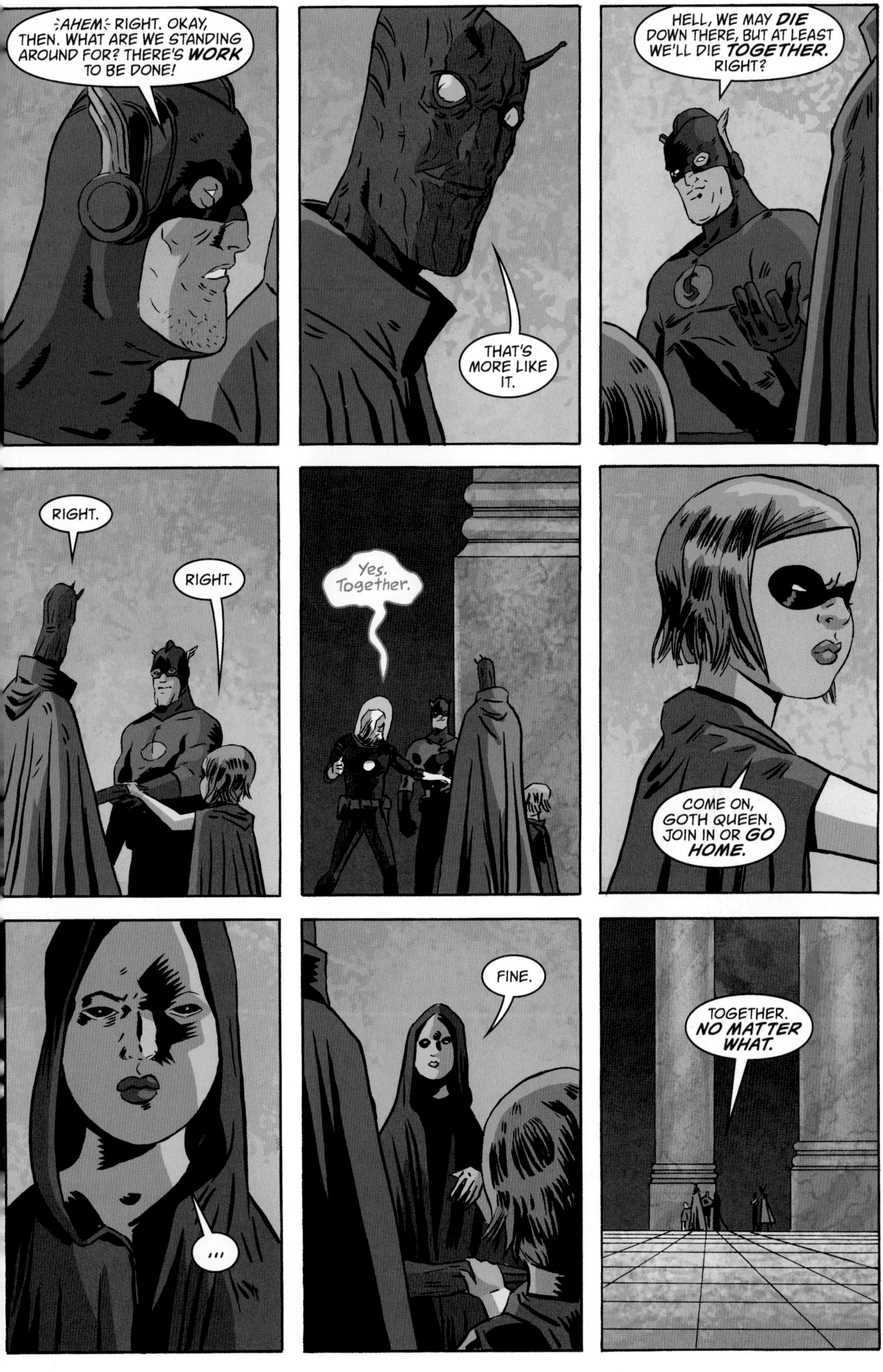
-AHEM- RIGHT. OKAY, THEN. WHAT ARE WE STANDING AROUND FOR? THERE'S WORK TO BE DONE!
THAT'S MORE LIKE IT.
HELL, WE MAY DIE DOWN THERE, BUT AT LEAST WE'LL DIE TOGETHER. RIGHT?
RIGHT.
RIGHT.
Yes. Together.
COME ON, GOTH QUEEN. JOIN IN OR GO HOME.
...
FINE.
TOGETHER. NO MATTER WHAT.

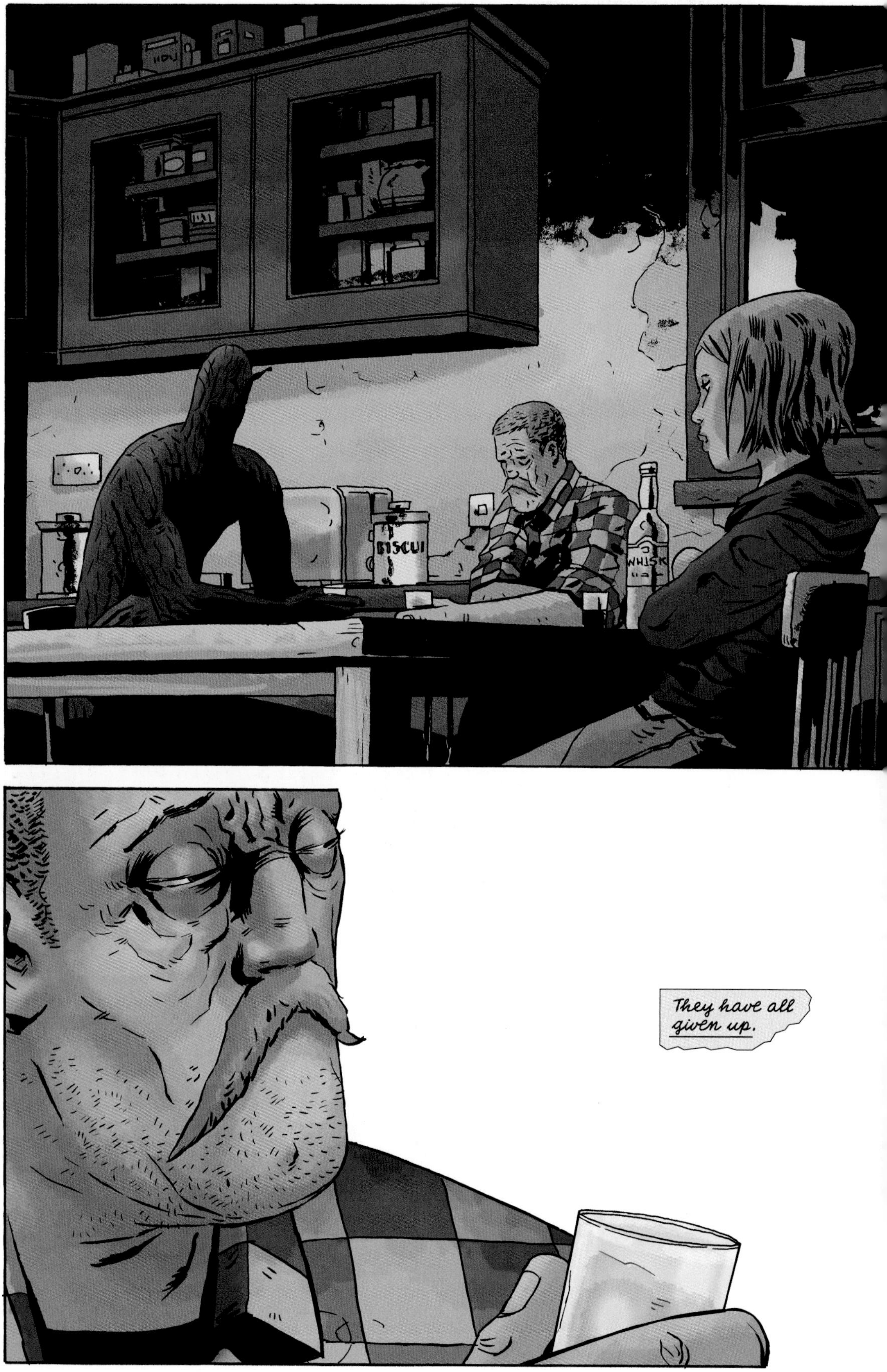
BISCUI
WHISK
They have all given up.

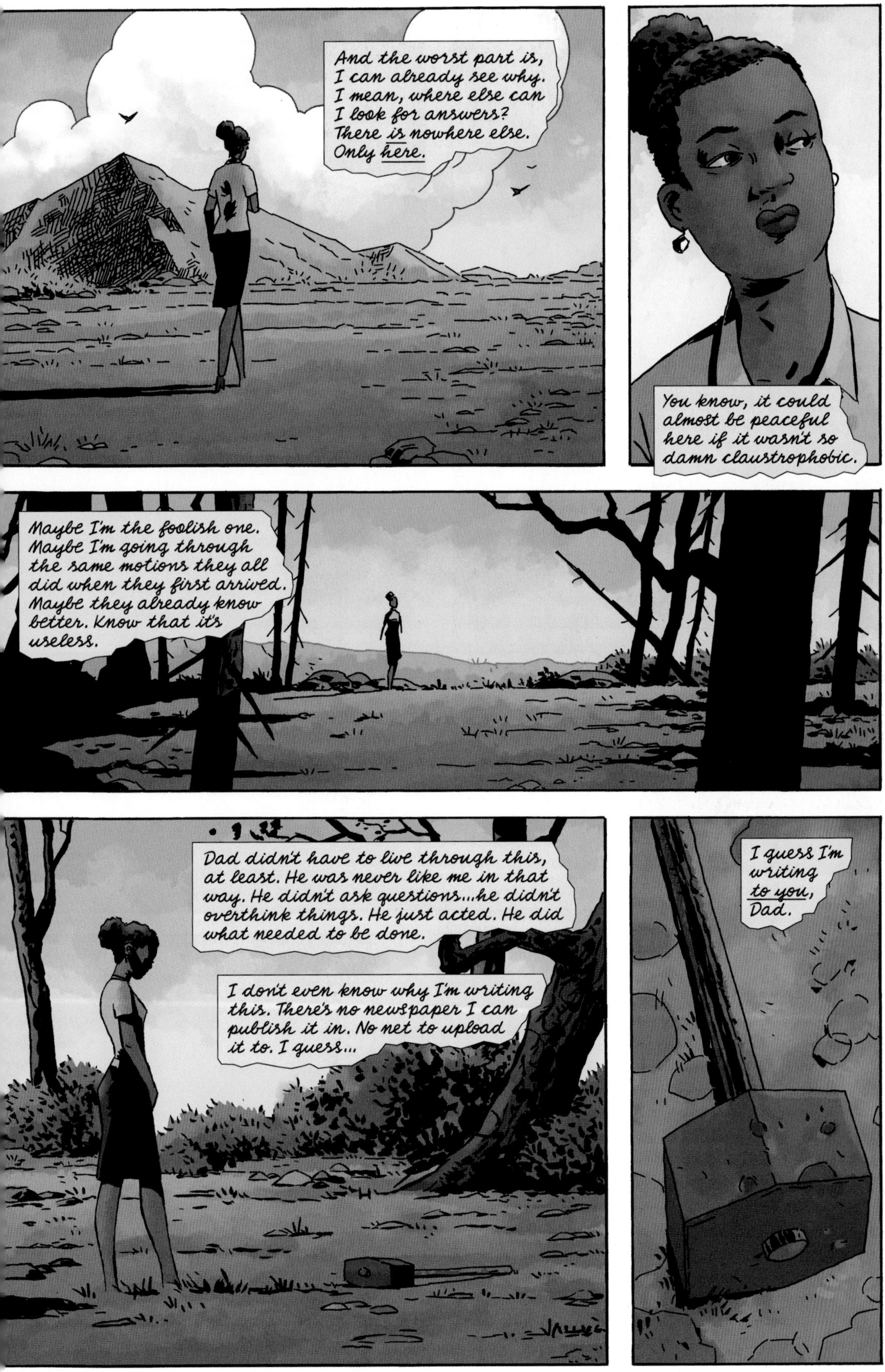
And the worst part is, I can already see why. I mean, where else can I look for answers? There is nowhere else. Only here.
You know, it could almost be peaceful here if it wasn't so damn claustrophobic.
Maybe I'm the foolish one. Maybe I'm going through the same motions they all did when they first arrived. Maybe they already know better. Know that it's useless.
Dad didn't have to live through this, at least. He was never like me in that way. He didn't ask questions...he didn't overthink things. He just acted. He did what needed to be done.
I don't even know why I'm writing this. There's no newspaper I can publish it in. No net to upload it to. I guess...
I guess I'm writing to you, Dad.

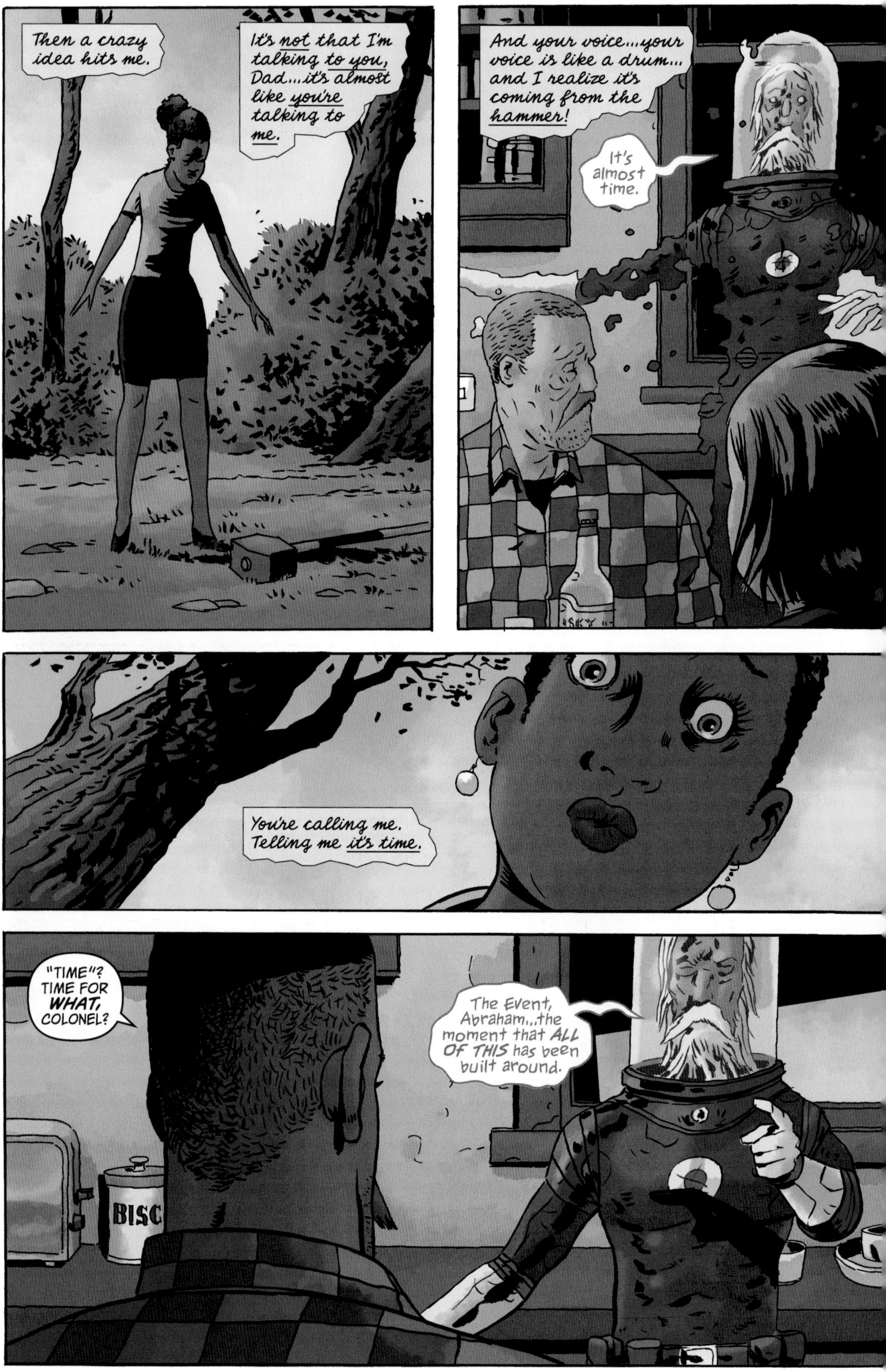
Then a crazy idea hits me.
It's not that I'm talking to you, Dad...it's almost like you're talking to me.
And your voice...your voice is like a drum... and I realize it's coming from the hammer!
It's almost time.
You're calling me. Telling me it's time.
"TIME"? TIME FOR WHAT, COLONEL?
The Event, Abraham...the moment that ALL OF THIS has been built around.
BISC

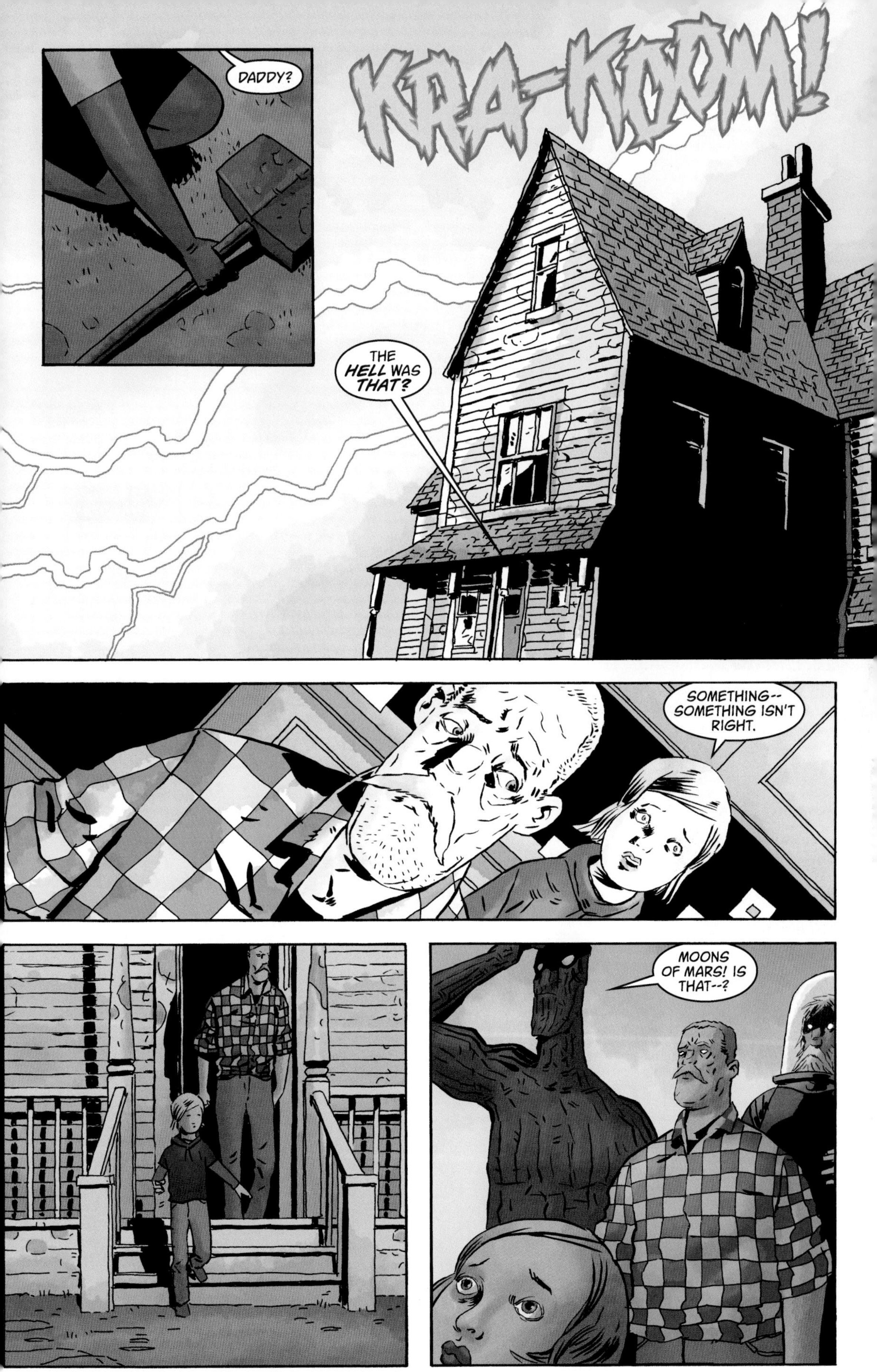
DADDY?
KRA-KOOM!
THE HELL WAS THAT?
SOMETHING-- SOMETHING ISN'T RIGHT.
MOONS OF MARS! IS THAT--?

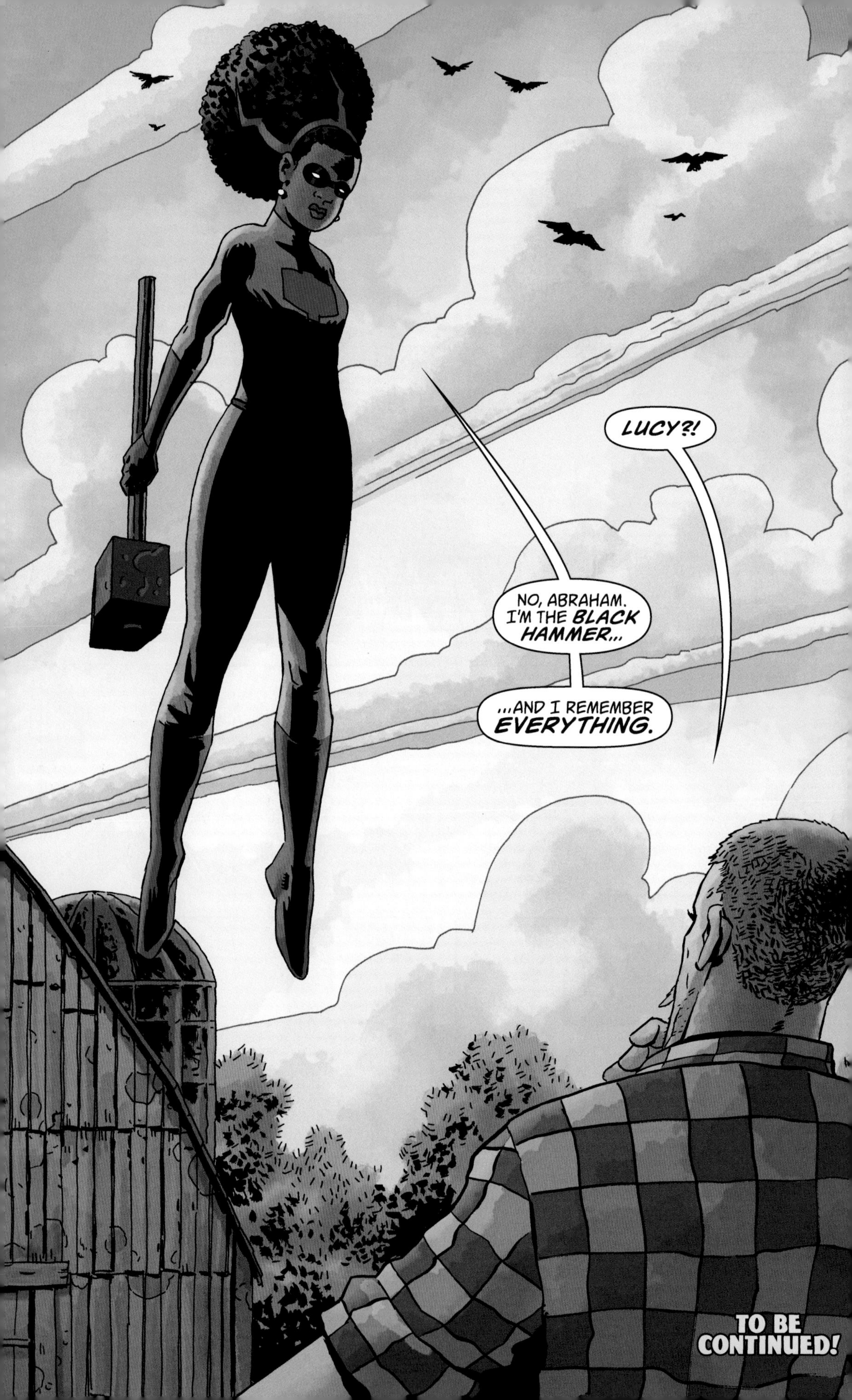
LUCY?!
NO, ABRAHAM. I'M THE BLACK HAMMER...
...AND I REMEMBER EVERYTHING.
TO BE CONTINUED!

BLACK HAMMER™

SKETCHBOOK

NOTES BY DANIEL CHABON

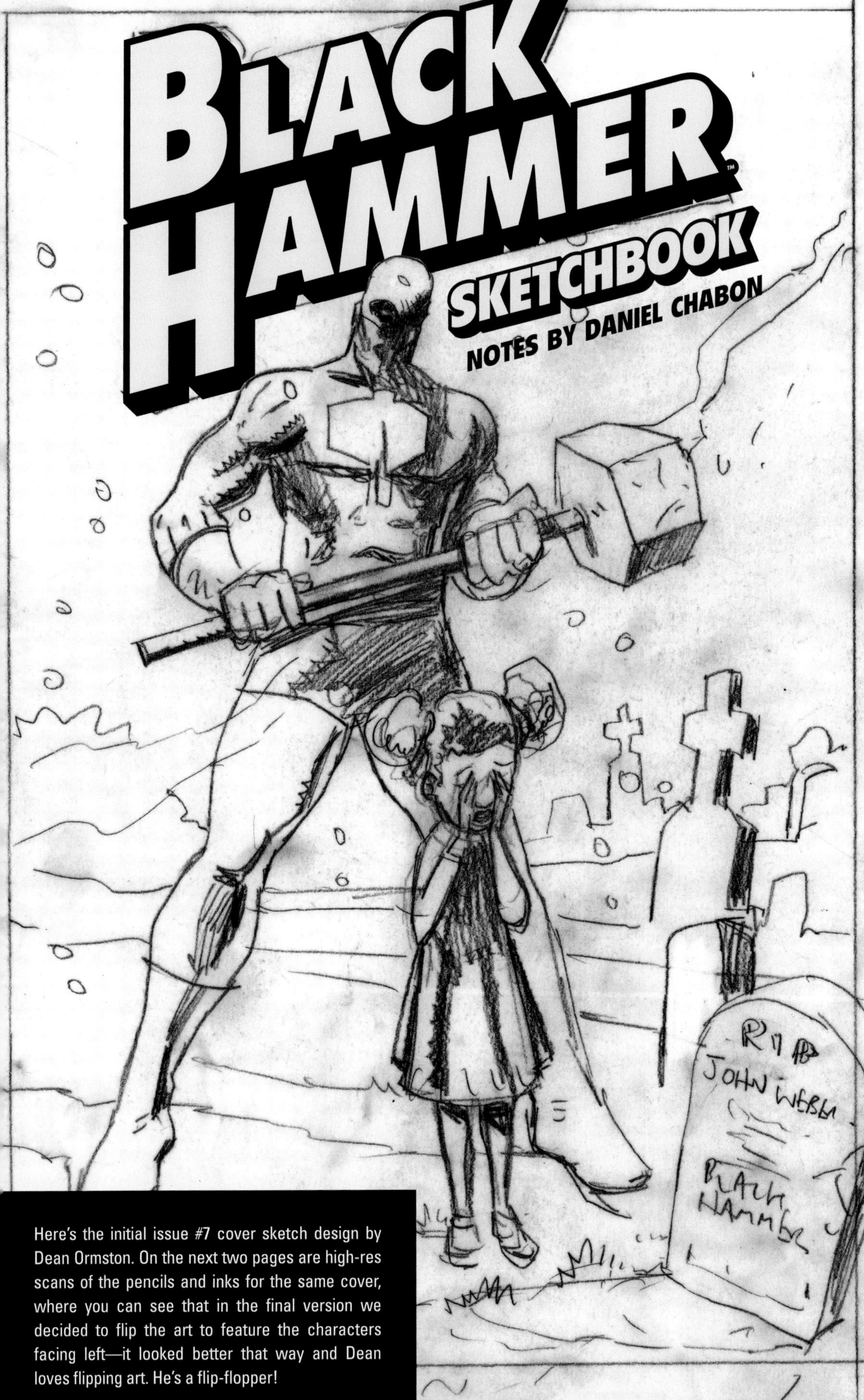
BLACK HAMMER

Here's the initial issue #7 cover sketch design by Dean Ormston. On the next two pages are high-res scans of the pencils and inks for the same cover, where you can see that in the final version we decided to flip the art to feature the characters facing left—it looked better that way and Dean loves flipping art. He's a flip-flopper!

DARK HORSE COMICS ART BOARD

TITLE: ISSUE: 7 ARTIST: PAGE: COVER

ALL "BLEED" ART MUST EXTEND TO THIS OUTERMOST DOTTED LINE.

TRIM MARKS INDICATE WHERE A PAGE IS CUT TO SIZE.

ALL LETTERING AND ESSENTIAL ART MUST FALL WITHIN THIS SOLID "LIVE AREA" BOX. THIS IS THE BORDER FOR A STANDARD, NON-BLEED COMIC BOOK PAGE.

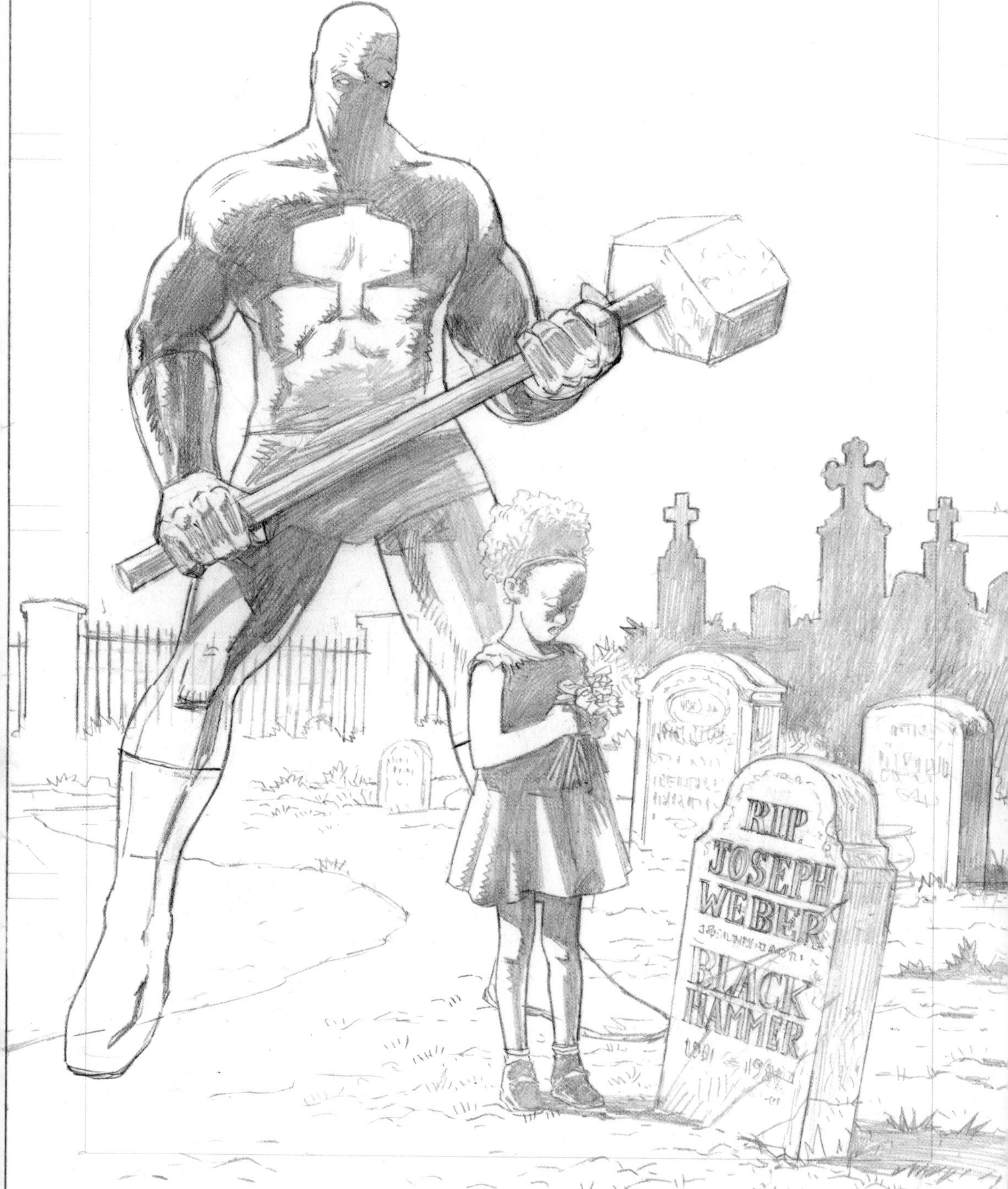
R.I.P.
JOSEPH
WEBER
BLACK
HAMMER

FOR ART THAT WILL BE REPRODUCED FROM PENCIL ONLY, DRAW ON THE REVERSE SIDE OF THIS BOARD AND INK IN TRIM MARKS IN BLACK.

Current as of 5/5/08

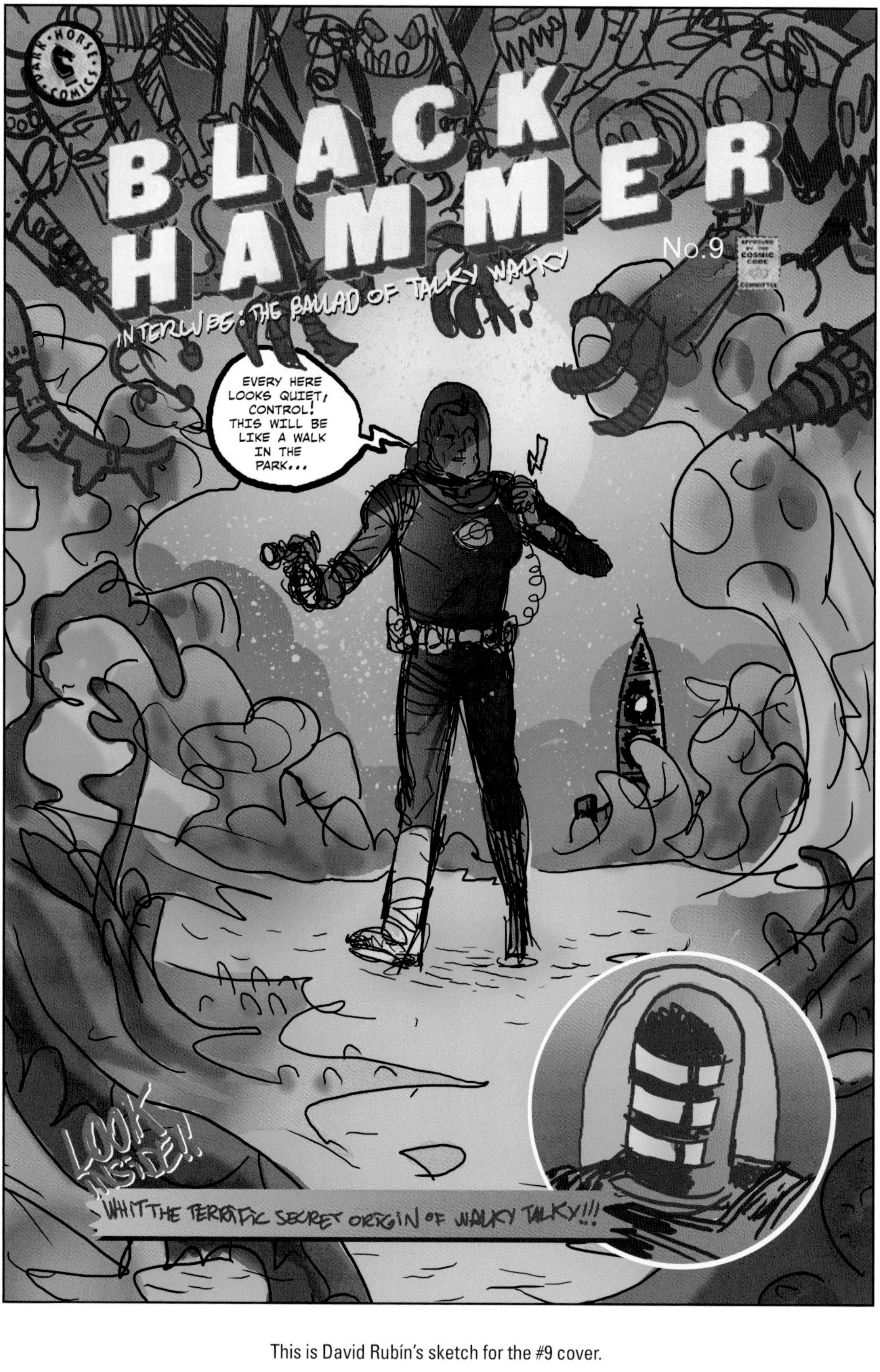
DARK HORSE COMICS
BLACK HAMMER
No.9
APPROVED BY THE COSMIC CODE COMMITTEE
INTERLUDE: THE BALLAD OF TALKY WALKY
EVERY HERE LOOKS QUIET, CONTROL! THIS WILL BE LIKE A WALK IN THE PARK...
LOOK INSIDE!!
WHIT THE TERRIFIC SECRET ORIGIN OF WALKY TALKY!!!

This is David Rubín's sketch for the #9 cover.

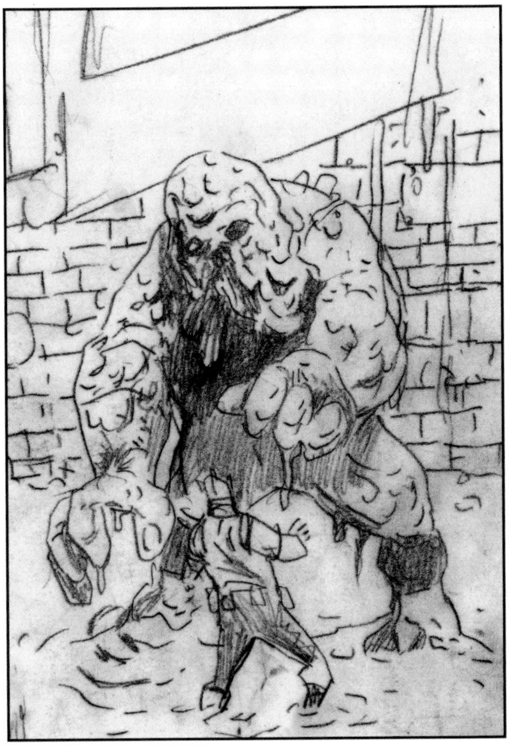

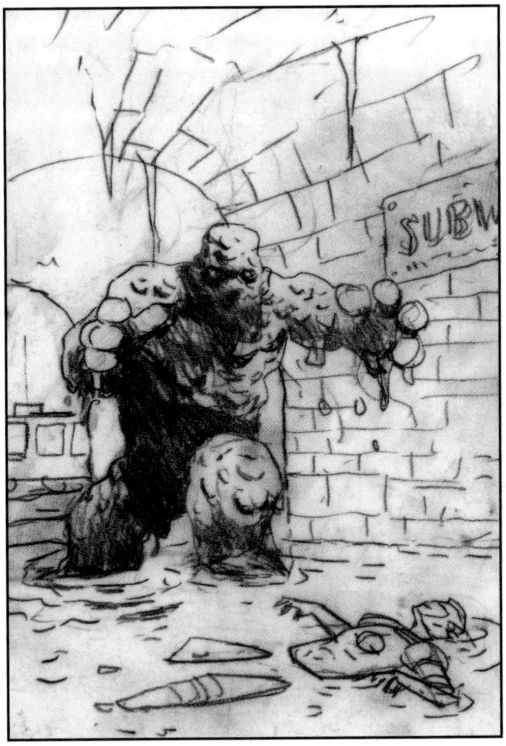

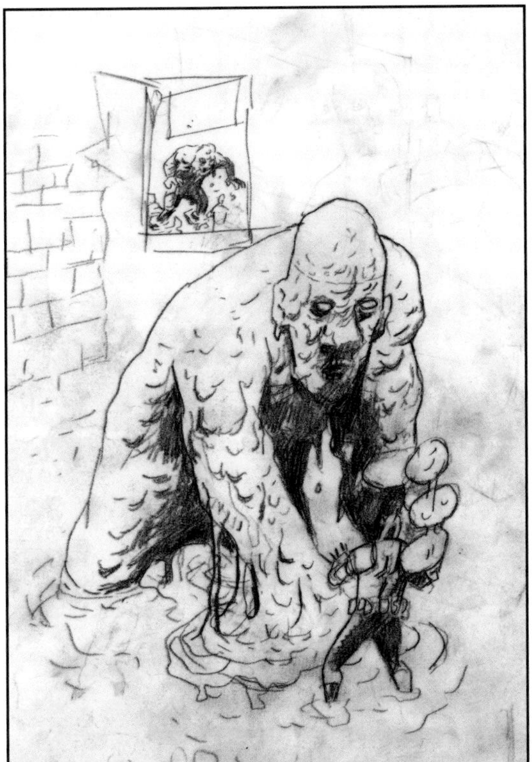

Here are cover sketch designs by Dean for issue #10 featuring Mud Master. Other names considered for this villain were: Globby, Globhead, The Incredible Glob, Blob Boy, and ThingamaBlob. Maybe at some point these names can be recycled for the children of Mud Master. On the next two pages are high-res scans of the final cover pencils and inks.

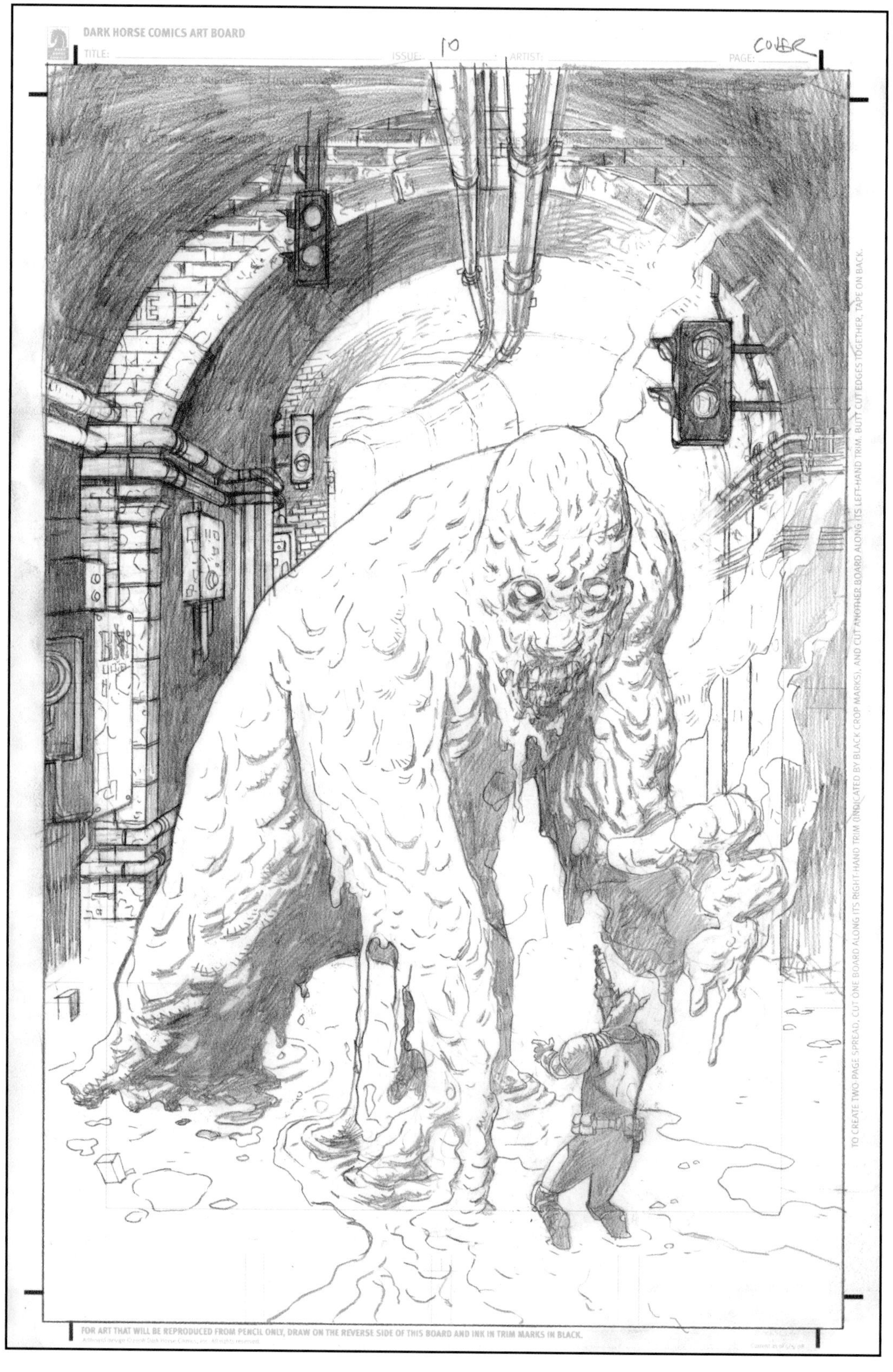
DARK HORSE COMICS ART BOARD
TITLE:
ISSUE: 10
ARTIST:
PAGE: COVER
TO CREATE TWO PAGE SPREAD, CUT ONE BOARD ALONG ITS RIGHT-HAND TRIM (INDICATED BY BLACK CROP MARKS), AND CUT ANOTHER BOARD ALONG ITS LEFT-HAND TRIM. BUTT CUT EDGES TOGETHER, TAPE ON BACK.
FOR ART THAT WILL BE REPRODUCED FROM PENCIL ONLY, DRAW ON THE REVERSE SIDE OF THIS BOARD AND INK IN TRIM MARKS IN BLACK.

TO CREATE TWO-PAGE SPREAD, CUT ONE BOARD ALONG ITS RIGHT-HAND TRIM (INDICATED BY BLACK CROP MARKS), AND CUT ANOTHER BOARD ALONG ITS LEFT-HAND TRIM, BUTT-CUT EDGES TOGETHER, TAPE ON BACK.

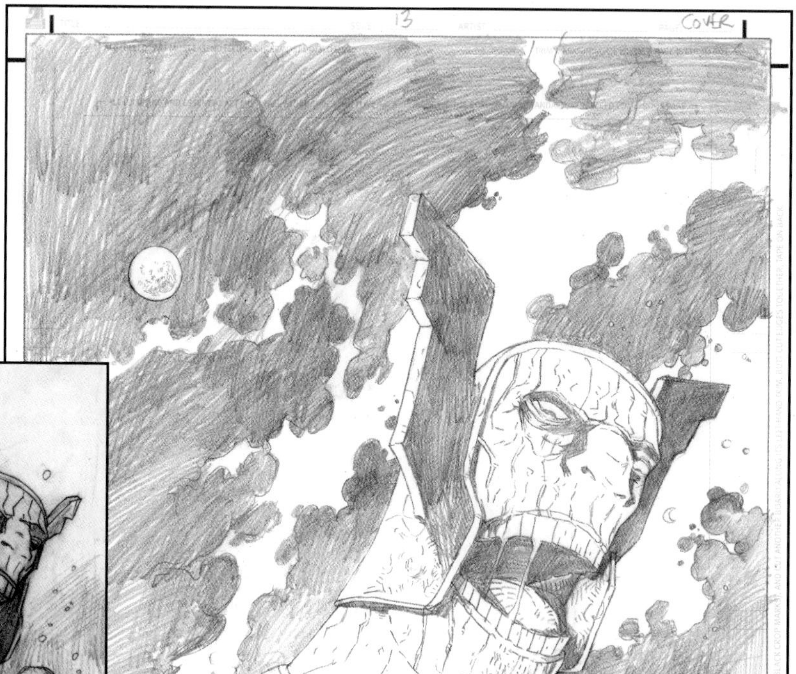
13
COVER

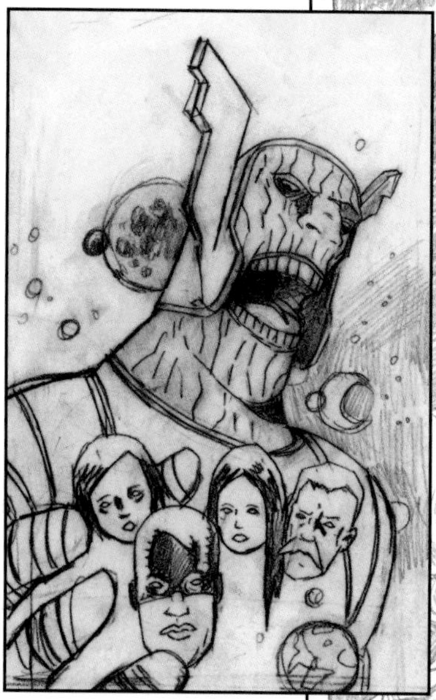

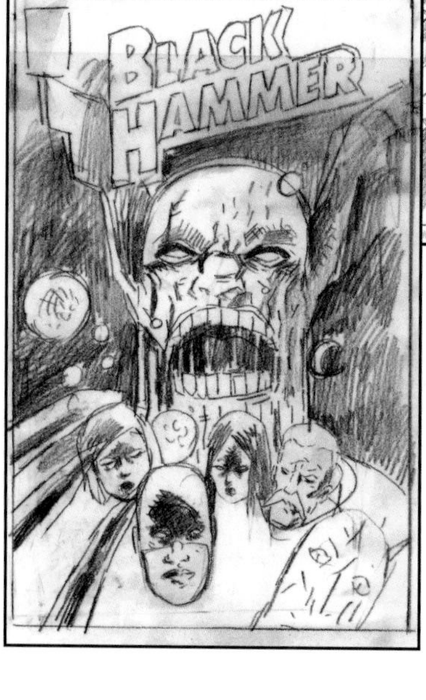
BLACK HAMMER

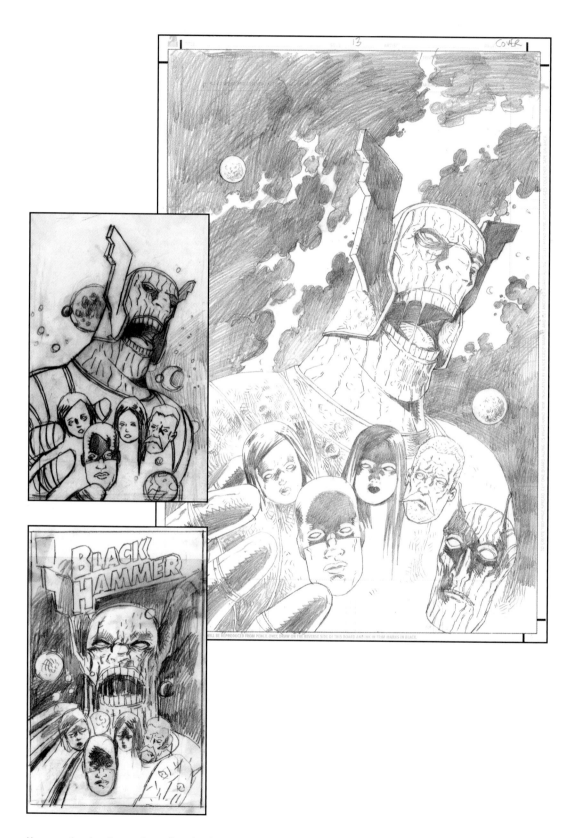

Here are the sketches and pencil art for the *Black Hammer* #13 cover. The next three pages show process art for page twenty from issue #8 by Dean, followed by process art from David Rubín from *Black Hammer* #9.

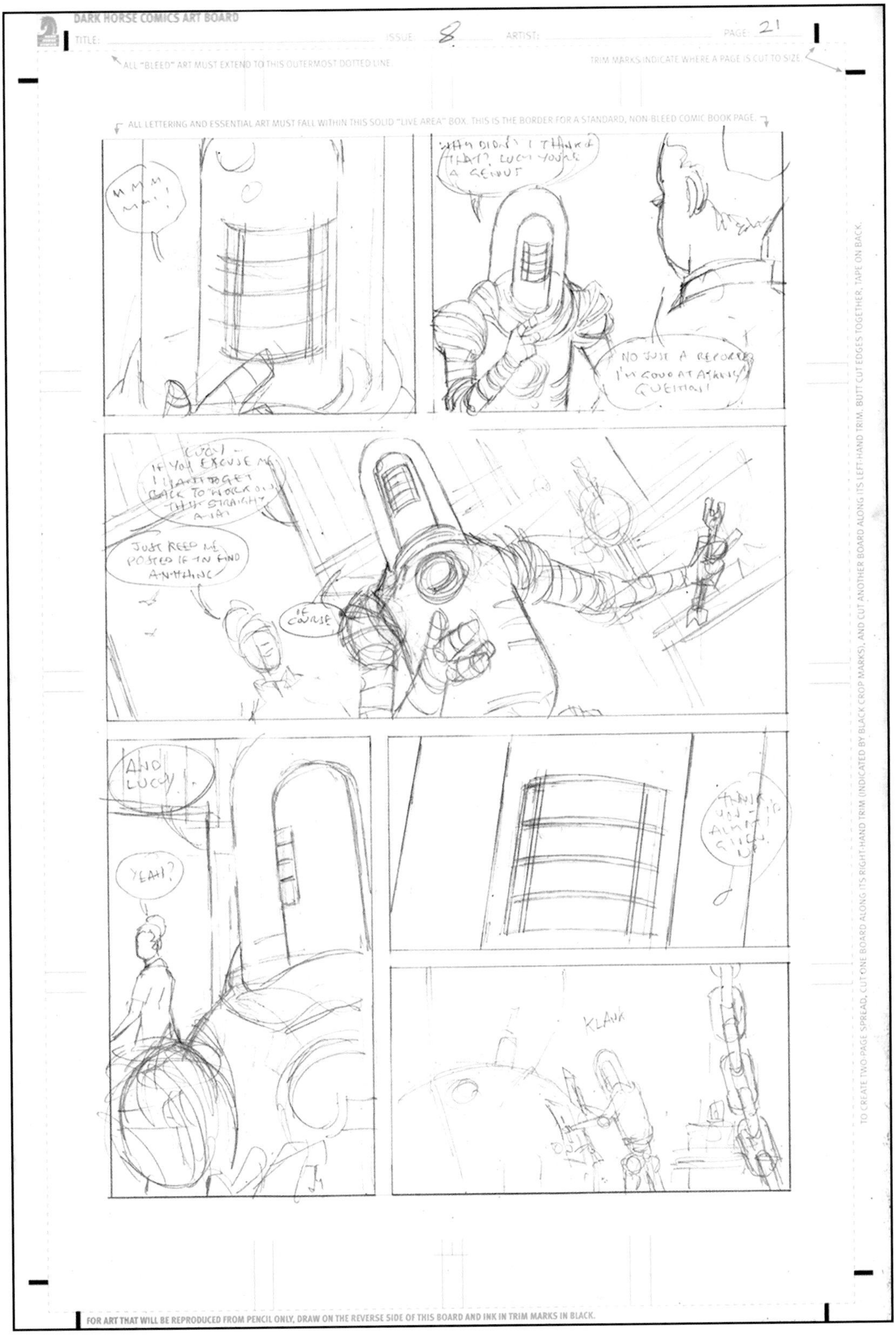

DARK HORSE COMICS ART BOARD
TITLE:
ISSUE: 8
ARTIST:
PAGE: 21
ALL "BLEED" ART MUST EXTEND TO THIS OUTERMOST DOTTED LINE.
TRIM MARKS INDICATE WHERE A PAGE IS CUT TO SIZE.
ALL LETTERING AND ESSENTIAL ART MUST FALL WITHIN THIS SOLID "LIVE AREA" BOX. THIS IS THE BORDER FOR A STANDARD, NON-BLEED COMIC BOOK PAGE.
MMM MM!
NO JUST A REPORTER. I'M GOOD AT ASKING QUESTIONS!
LUCY – IF YOU EXCUSE ME I WANT TO GET BACK TO WORK ON THIS STRAIGHT AWAY
JUST KEEP ME POSTED IF YOU FIND ANYTHING
OF COURSE
AND LUCY...
YEAH?
KLANK
TO CREATE TWO-PAGE SPREAD, CUT ONE BOARD ALONG ITS RIGHT-HAND TRIM (INDICATED BY BLACK CROP MARKS), AND CUT ANOTHER BOARD ALONG ITS LEFT HAND TRIM. BUTT CUT EDGES TOGETHER, TAPE ON BACK.
FOR ART THAT WILL BE REPRODUCED FROM PENCIL ONLY, DRAW ON THE REVERSE SIDE OF THIS BOARD AND INK IN TRIM MARKS IN BLACK.

KLANK!

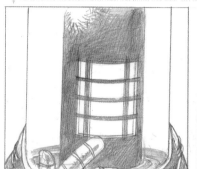

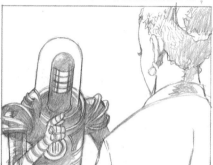

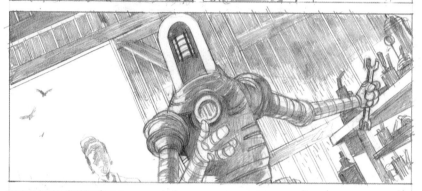

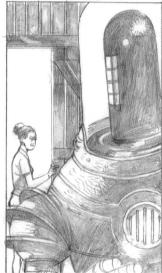

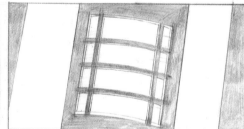

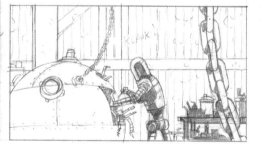

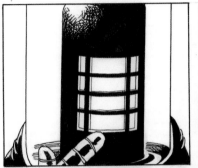

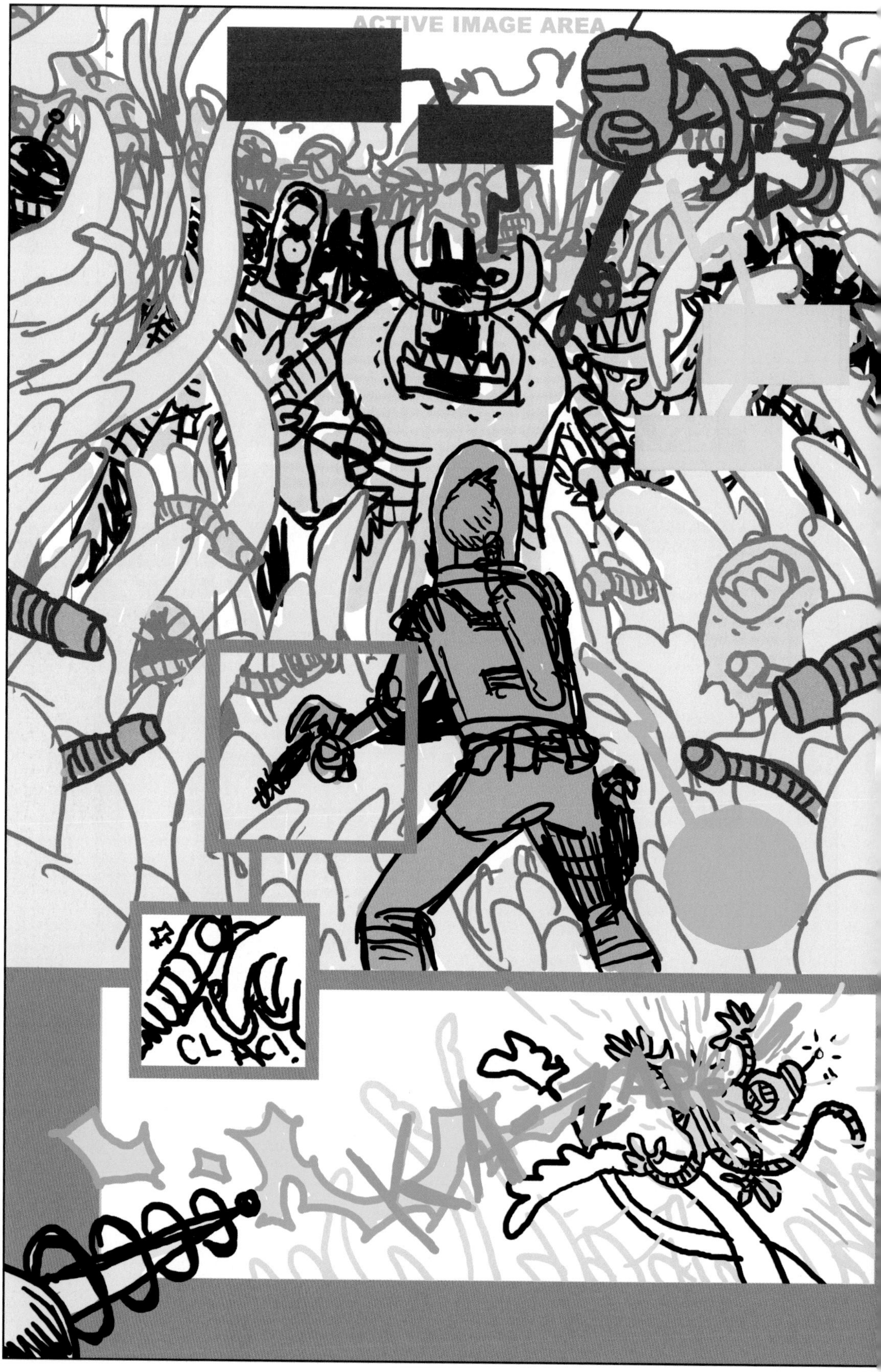
ACTIVE IMAGE AREA
CLAC!
KA-ZAP!

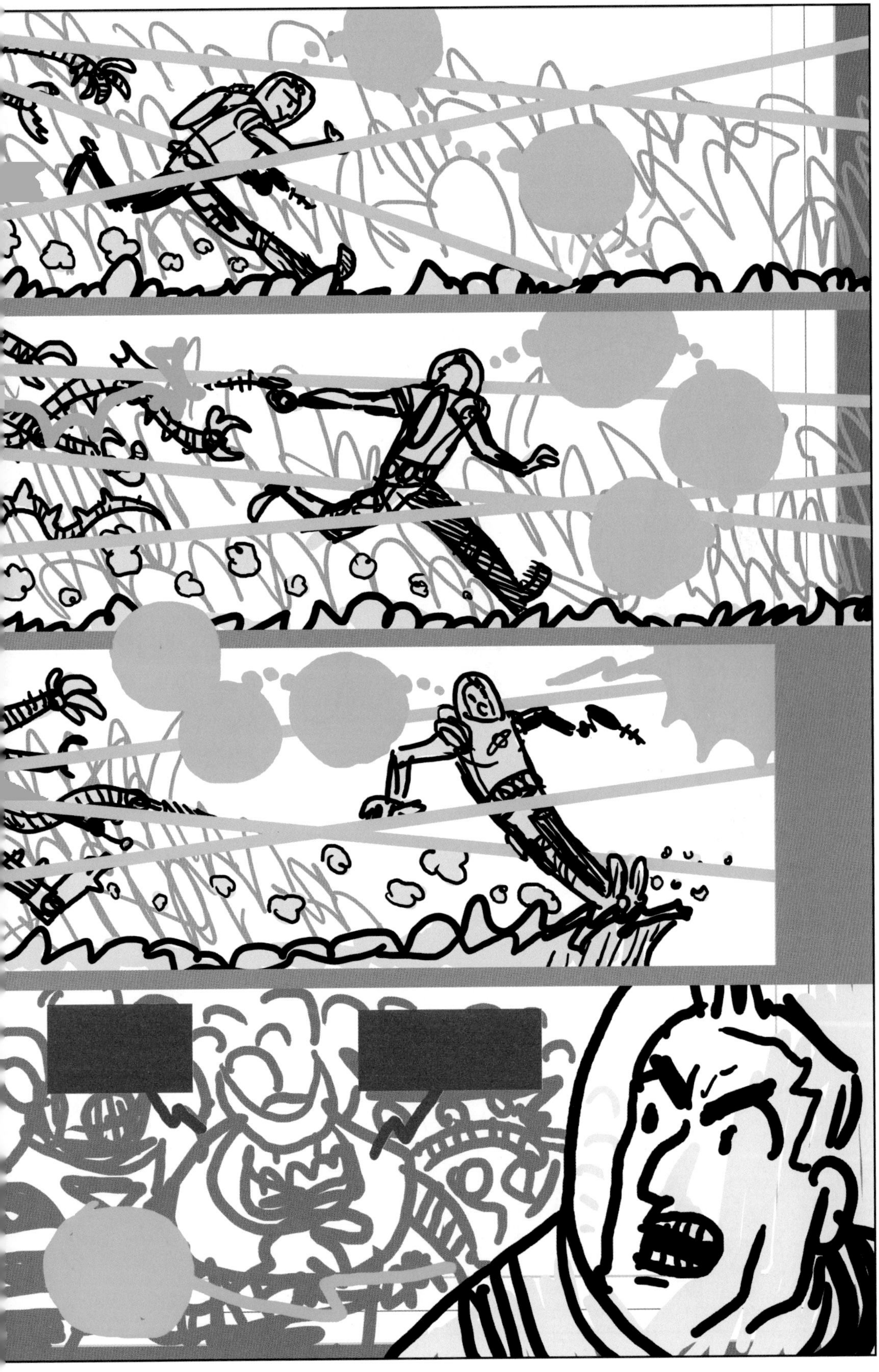

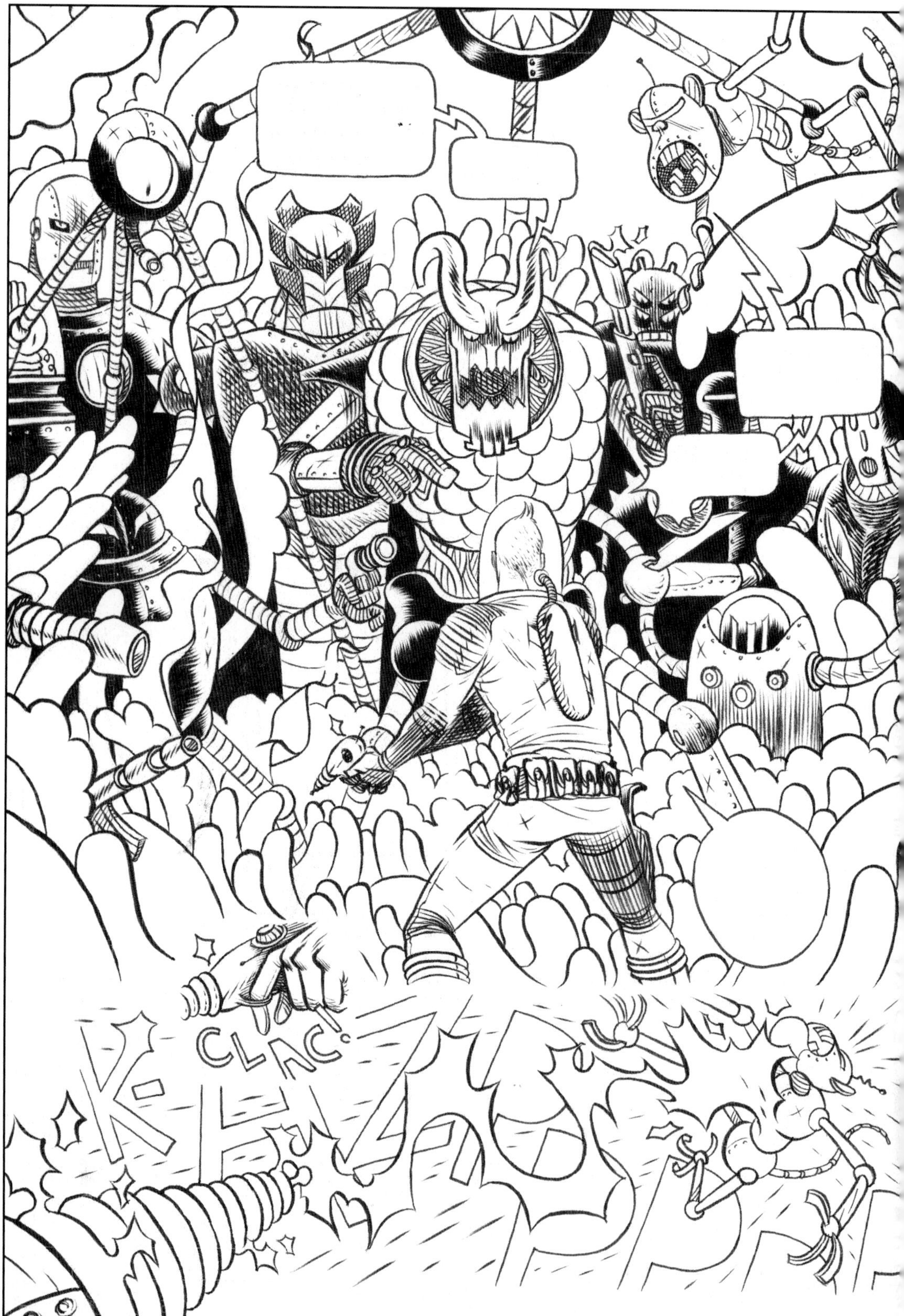
CLAC!

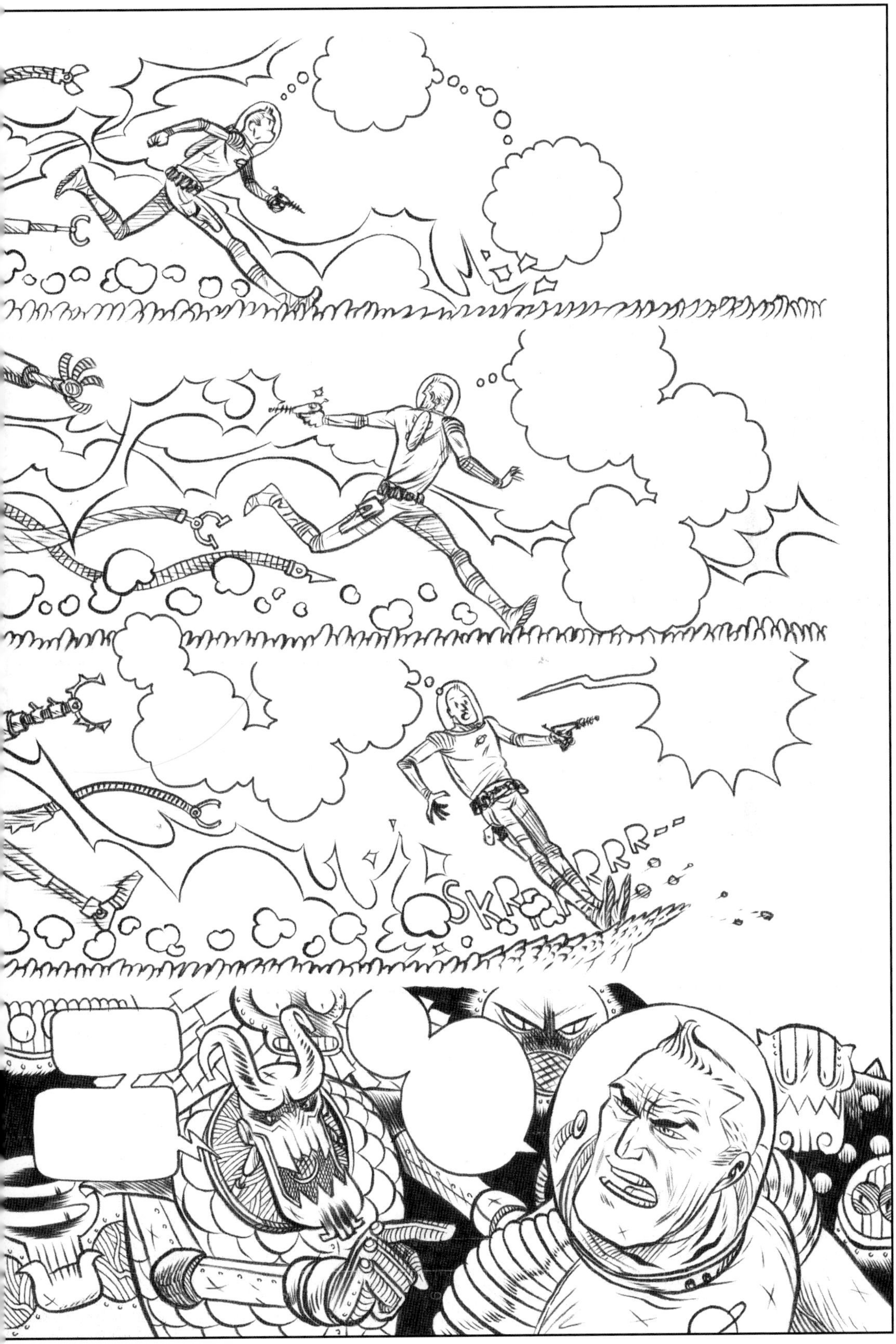
SKRRRRR--

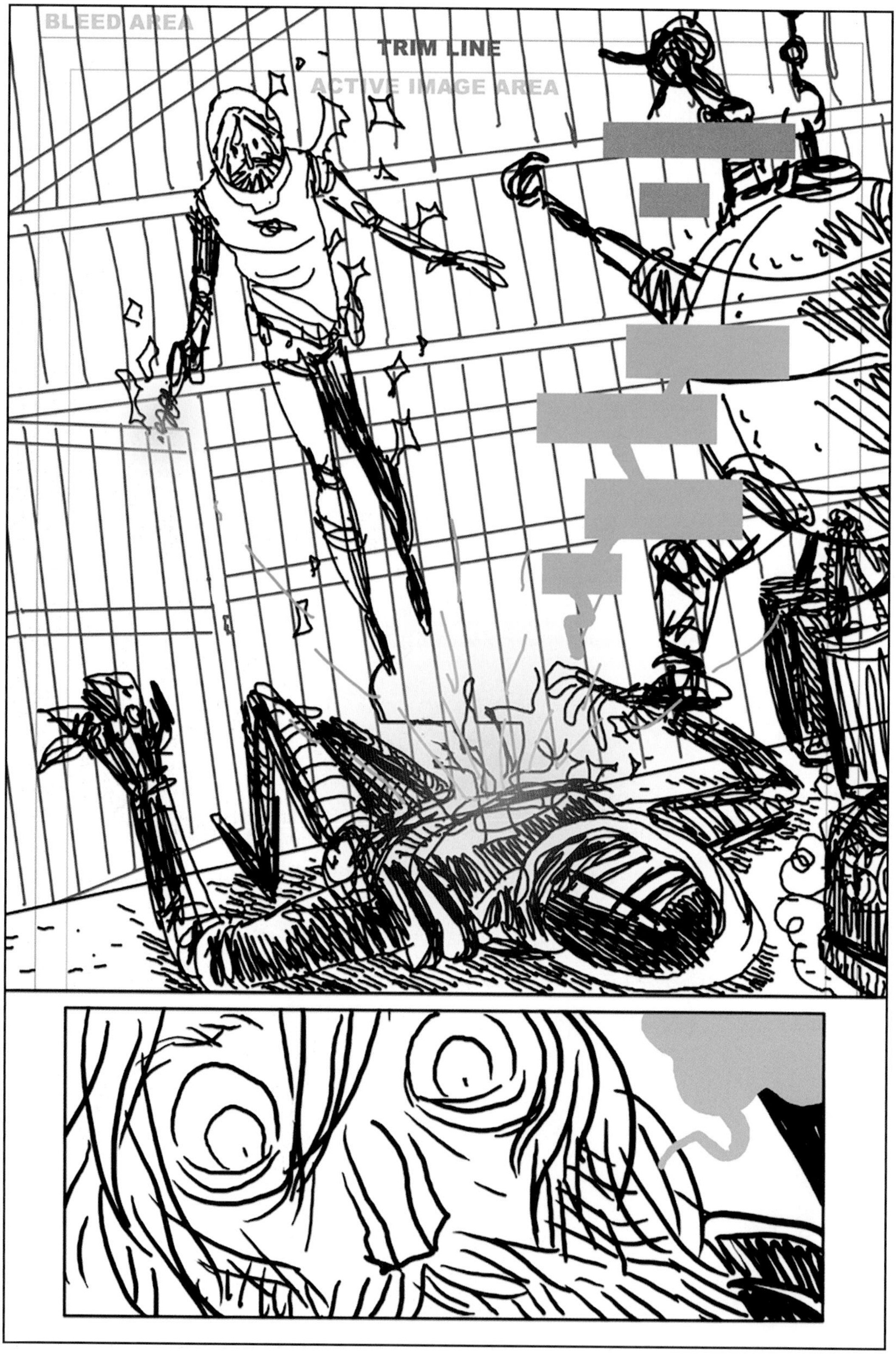
BLEED AREA
TRIM LINE
ACTIVE IMAGE AREA

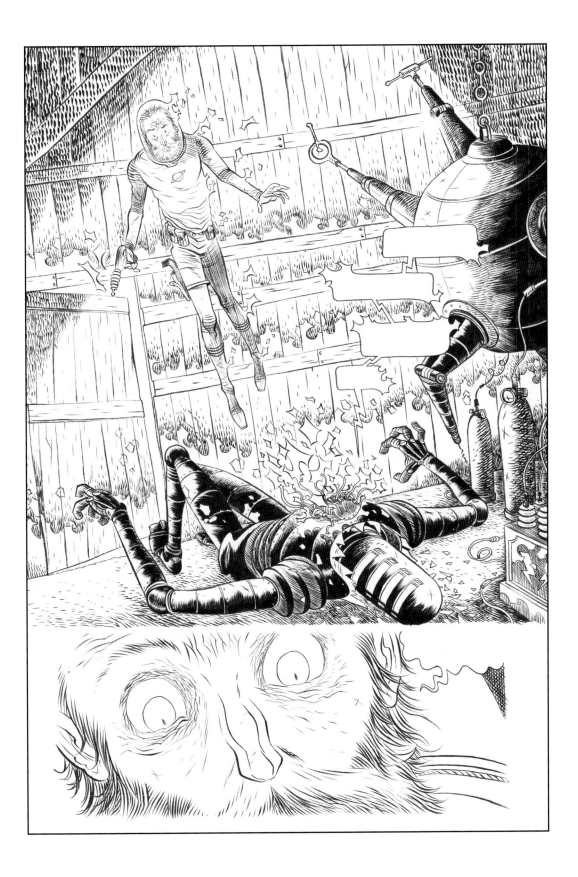

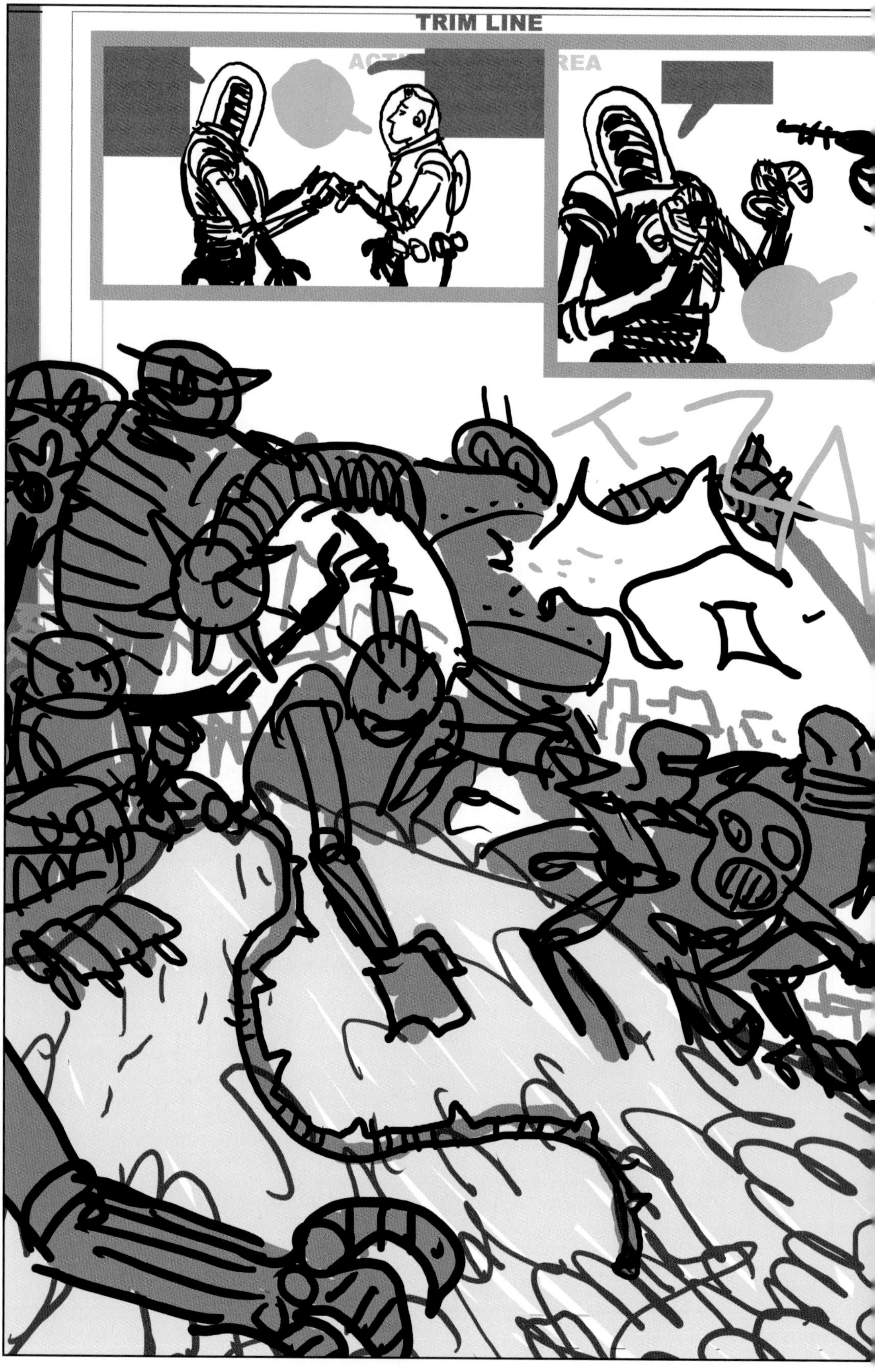
TRIM LINE

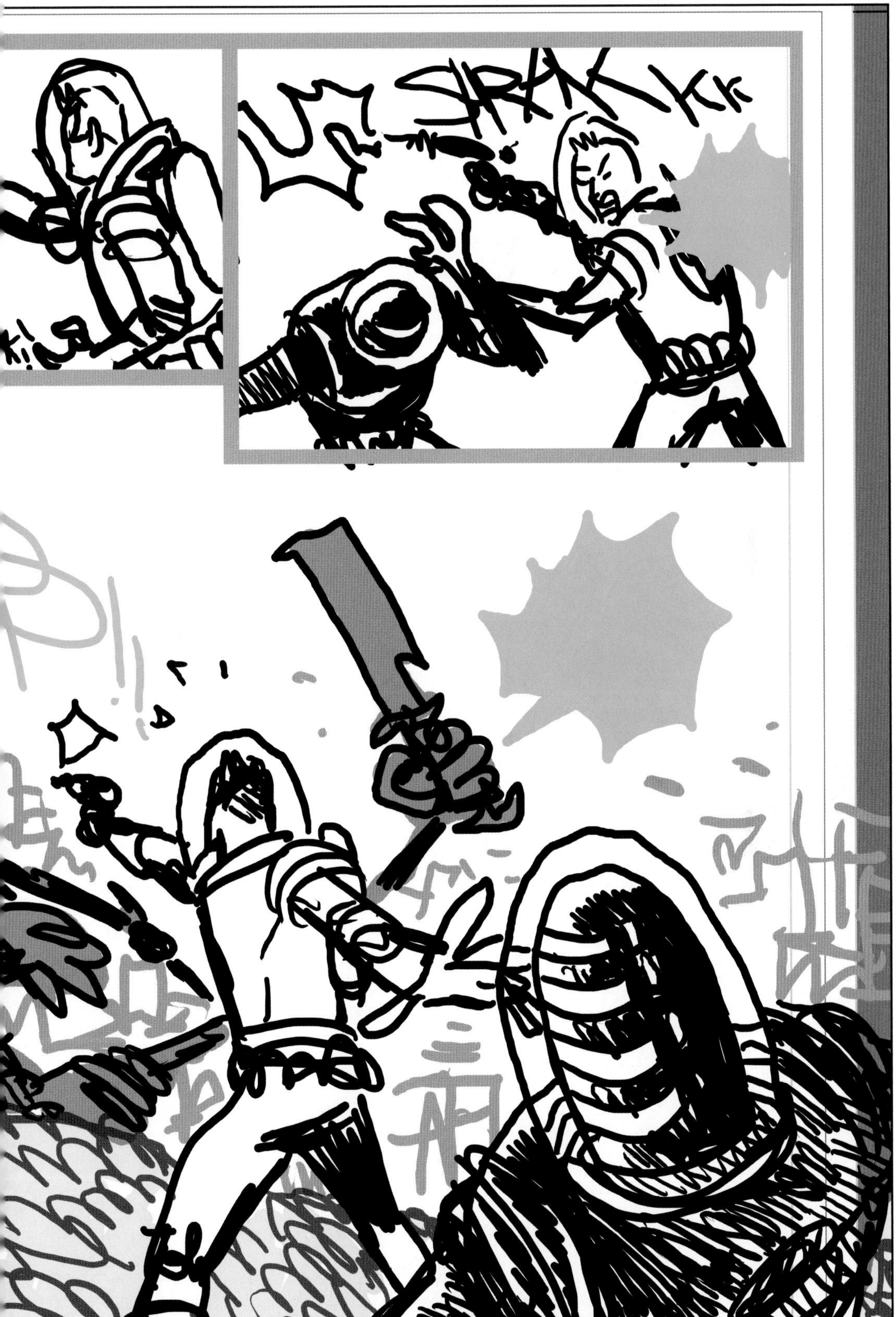

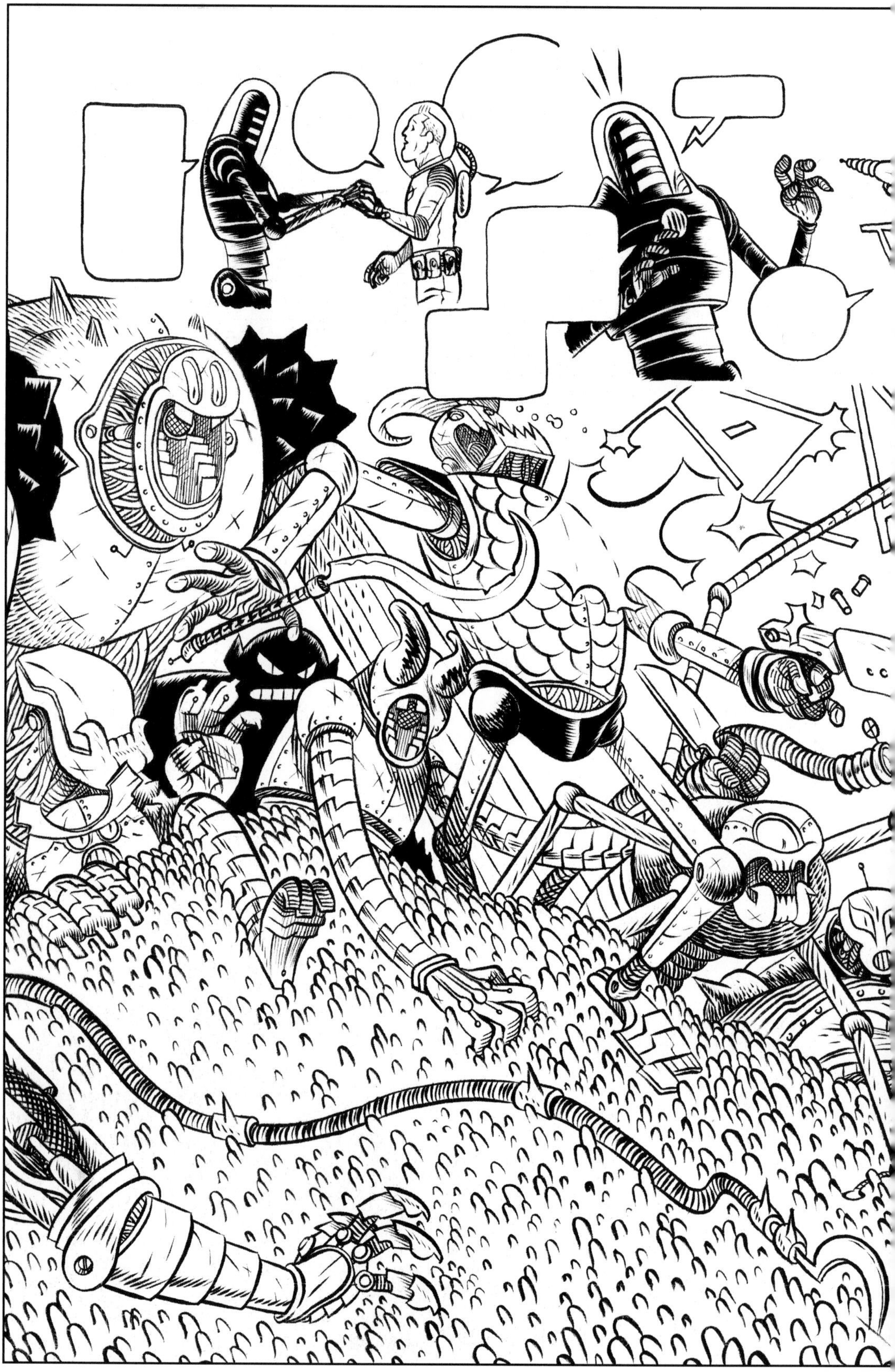

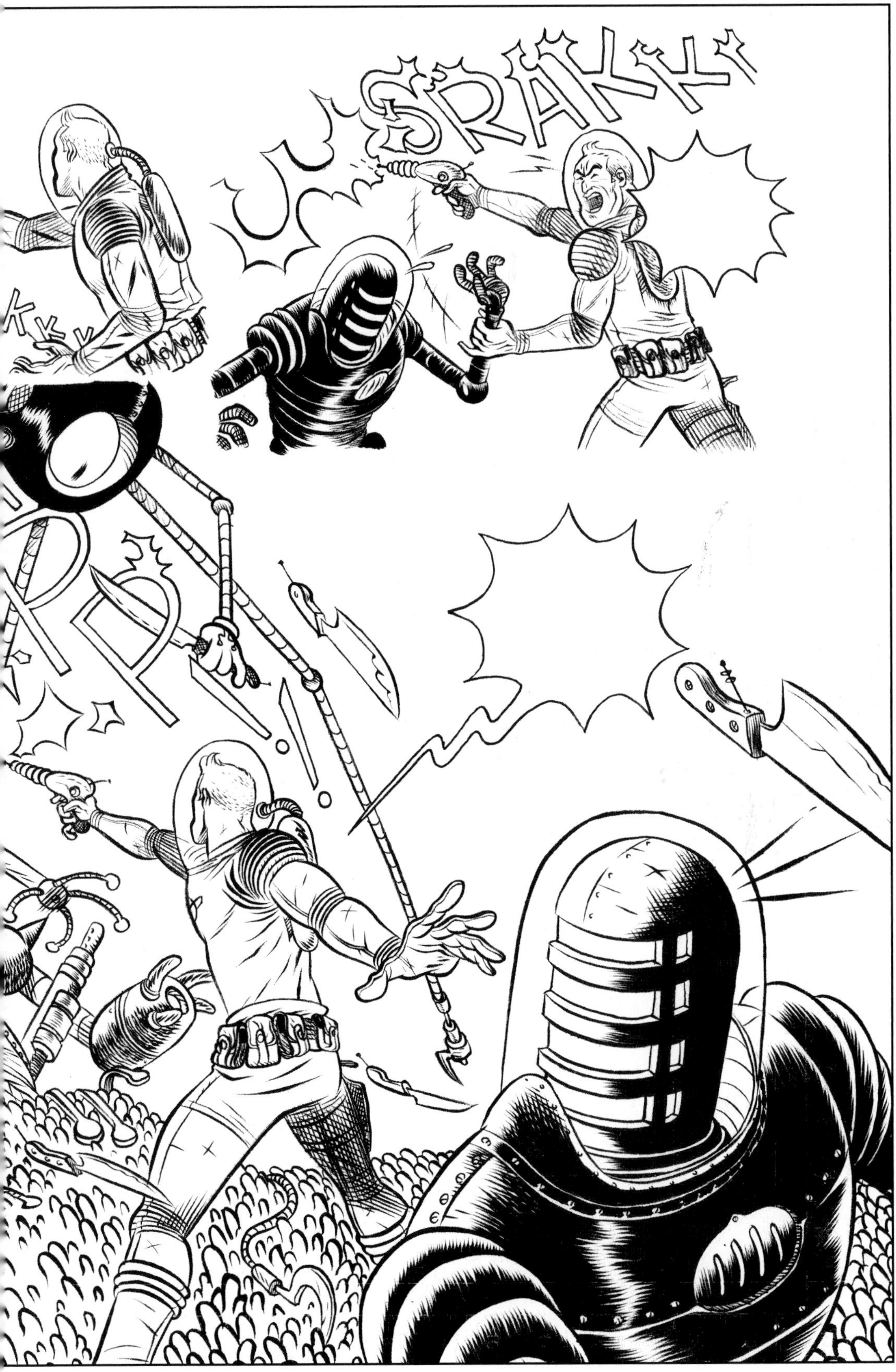
SRAKK!

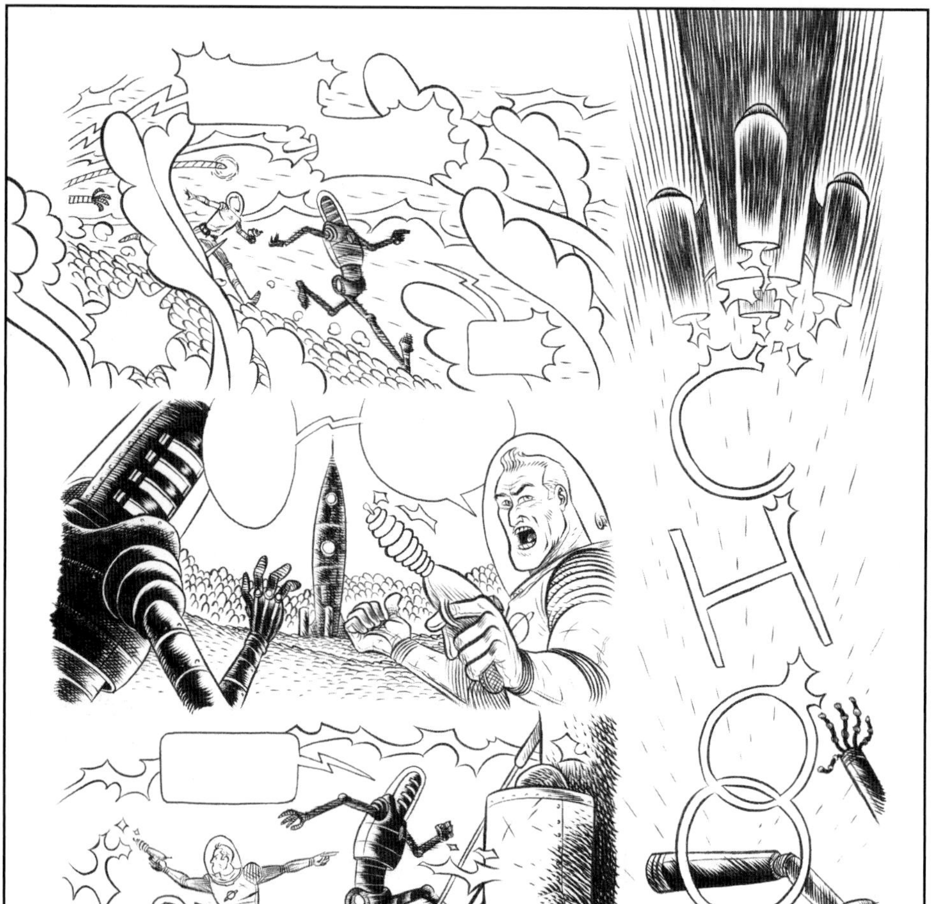
T-ZAP!
CHOOM
PUSH

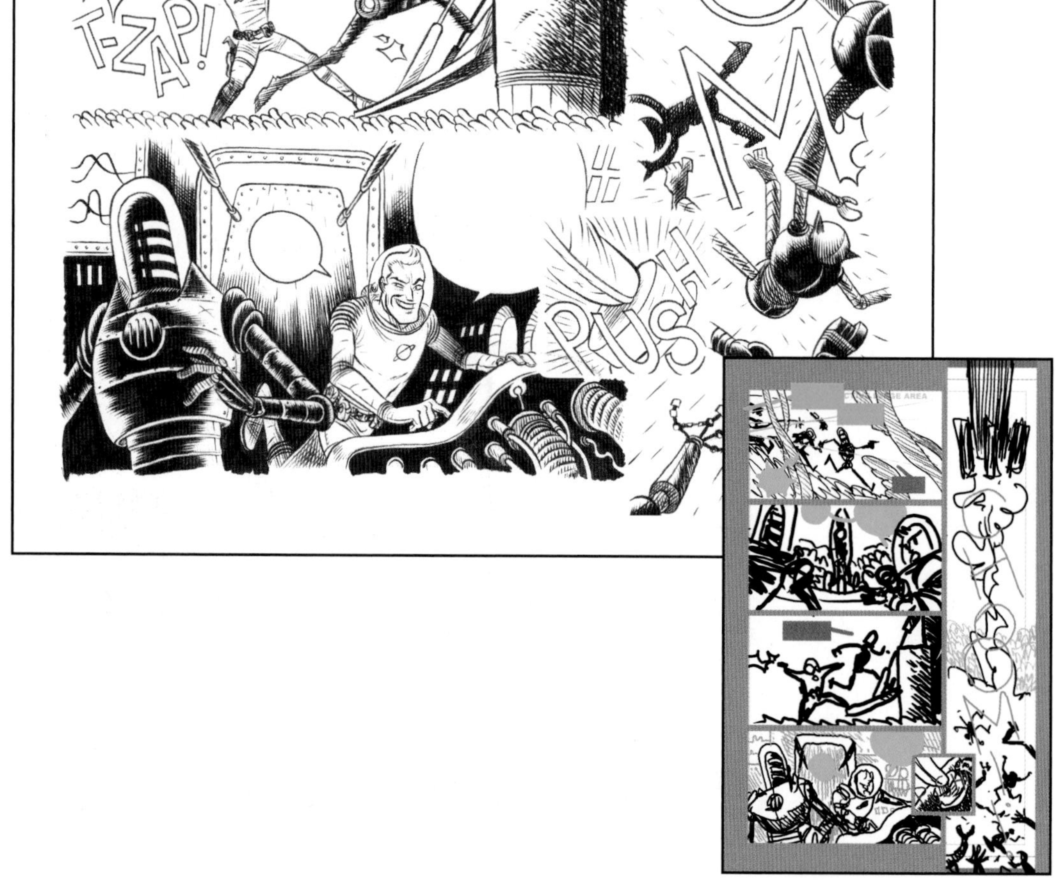

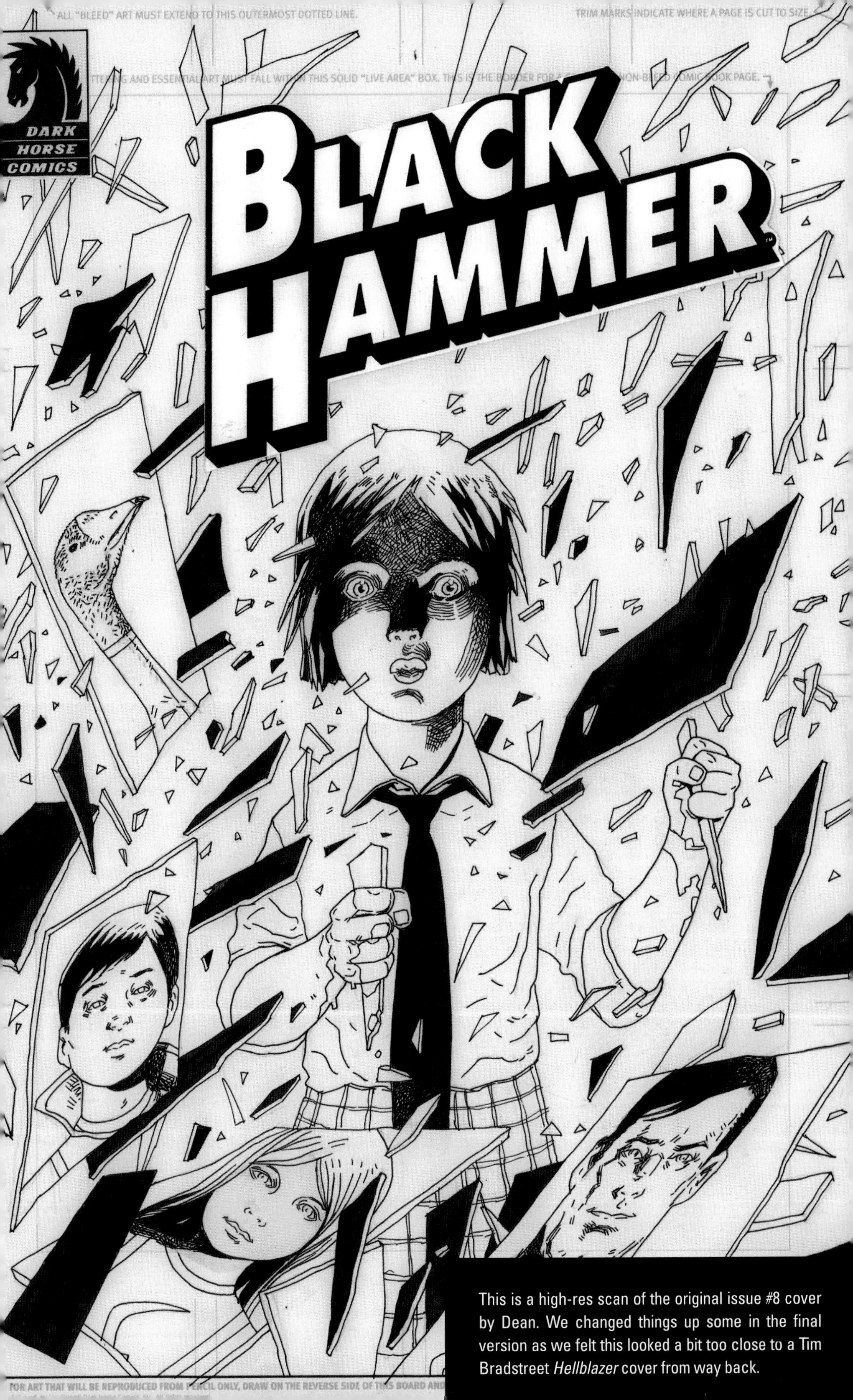
ALL "BLEED" ART MUST EXTEND TO THIS OUTERMOST DOTTED LINE.
TRIM MARKS INDICATE WHERE A PAGE IS CUT TO SIZE.
DARK HORSE COMICS
BLACK HAMMER

This is a high-res scan of the original issue #8 cover by Dean. We changed things up some in the final version as we felt this looked a bit too close to a Tim Bradstreet *Hellblazer* cover from way back.

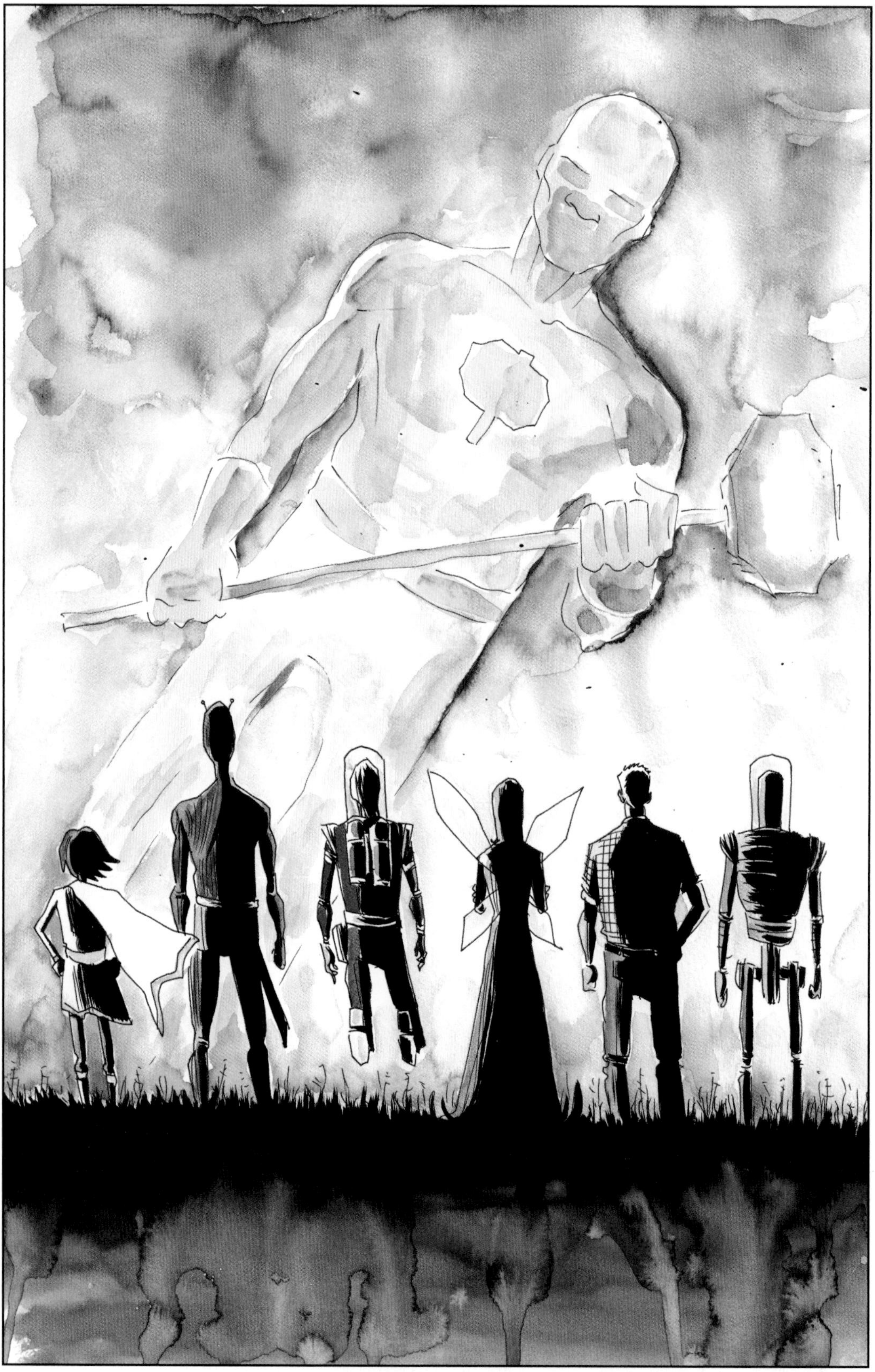

This page features art drawn by Jeff Lemire that was used as a special signed bookplate for comic book retailers. On the next page is a *Batman: The Dark Knight* #2 cover homage by Jeff that was used as a giveaway poster to comic retailers at San Diego Comic-Con 2017. I love that Jeff added the old-school Dark Horse logo here.

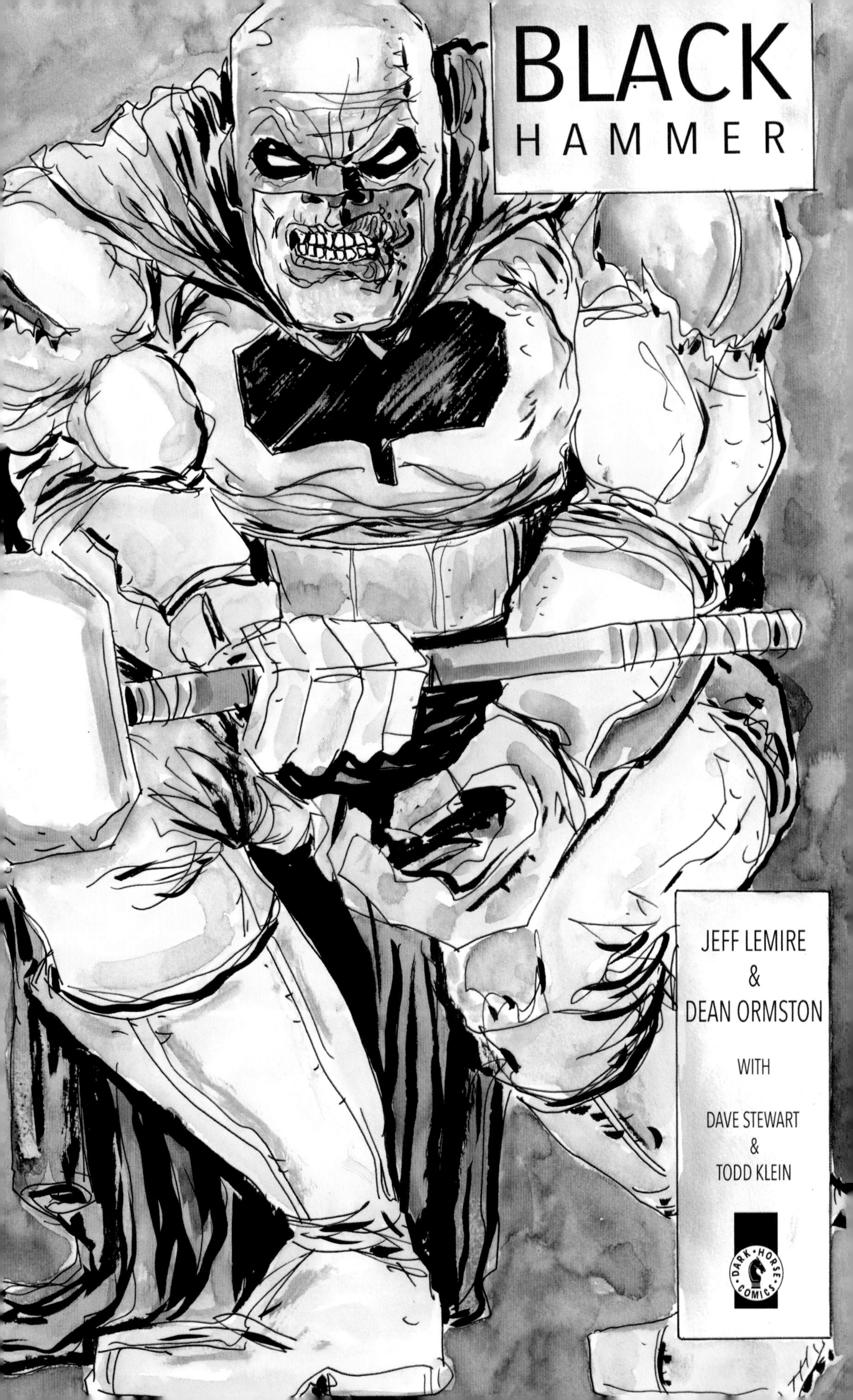
BLACK
HAMMER
JEFF LEMIRE
&
DEAN ORMSTON
WITH
DAVE STEWART
&
TODD KLEIN
DARK HORSE COMICS

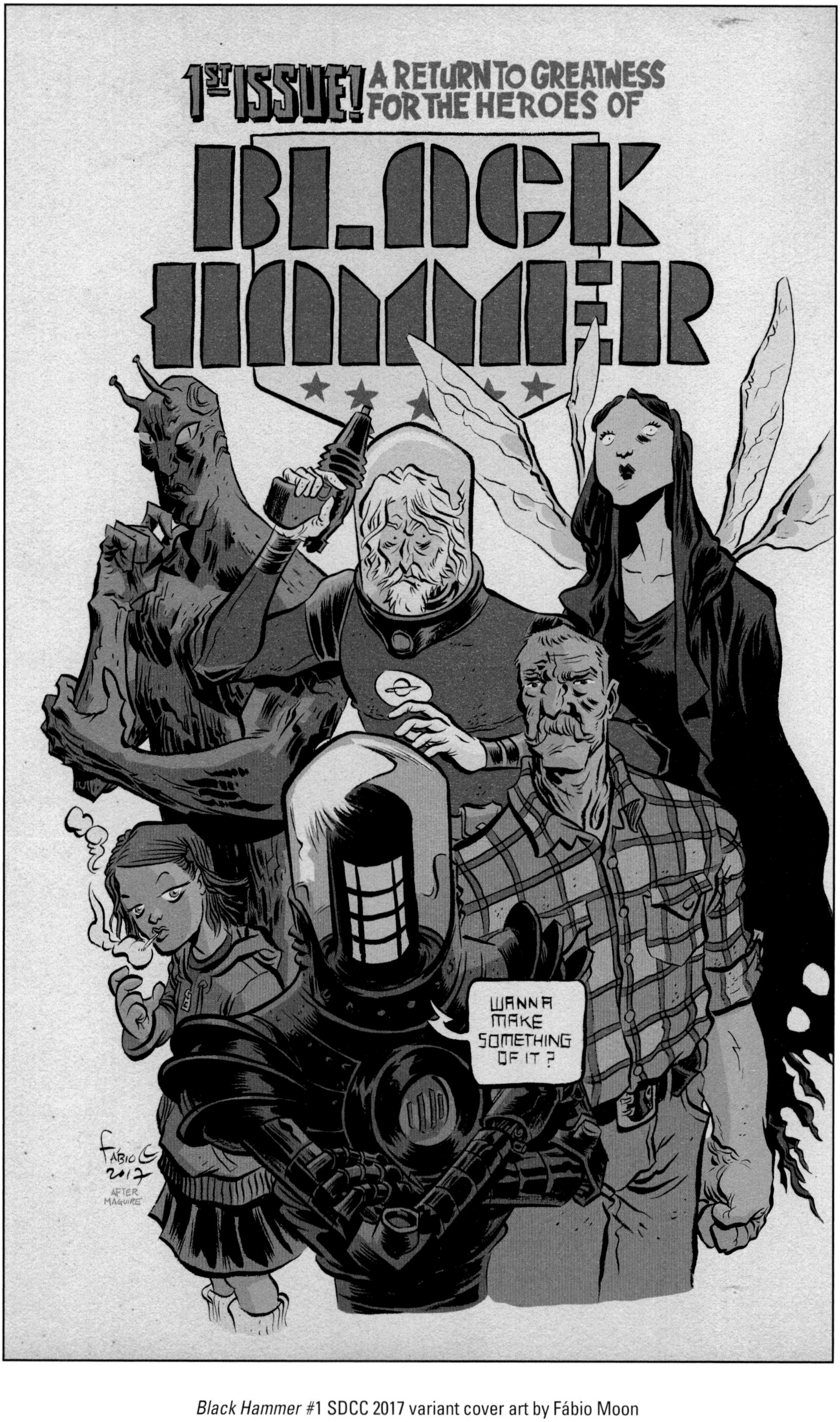
1ST ISSUE! A RETURN TO GREATNESS FOR THE HEROES OF
BLACK HAMMER
WANNA MAKE SOMETHING OF IT?
FÁBIO 2017 AFTER MAGUIRE

Black Hammer #1 SDCC 2017 variant cover art by Fábio Moon

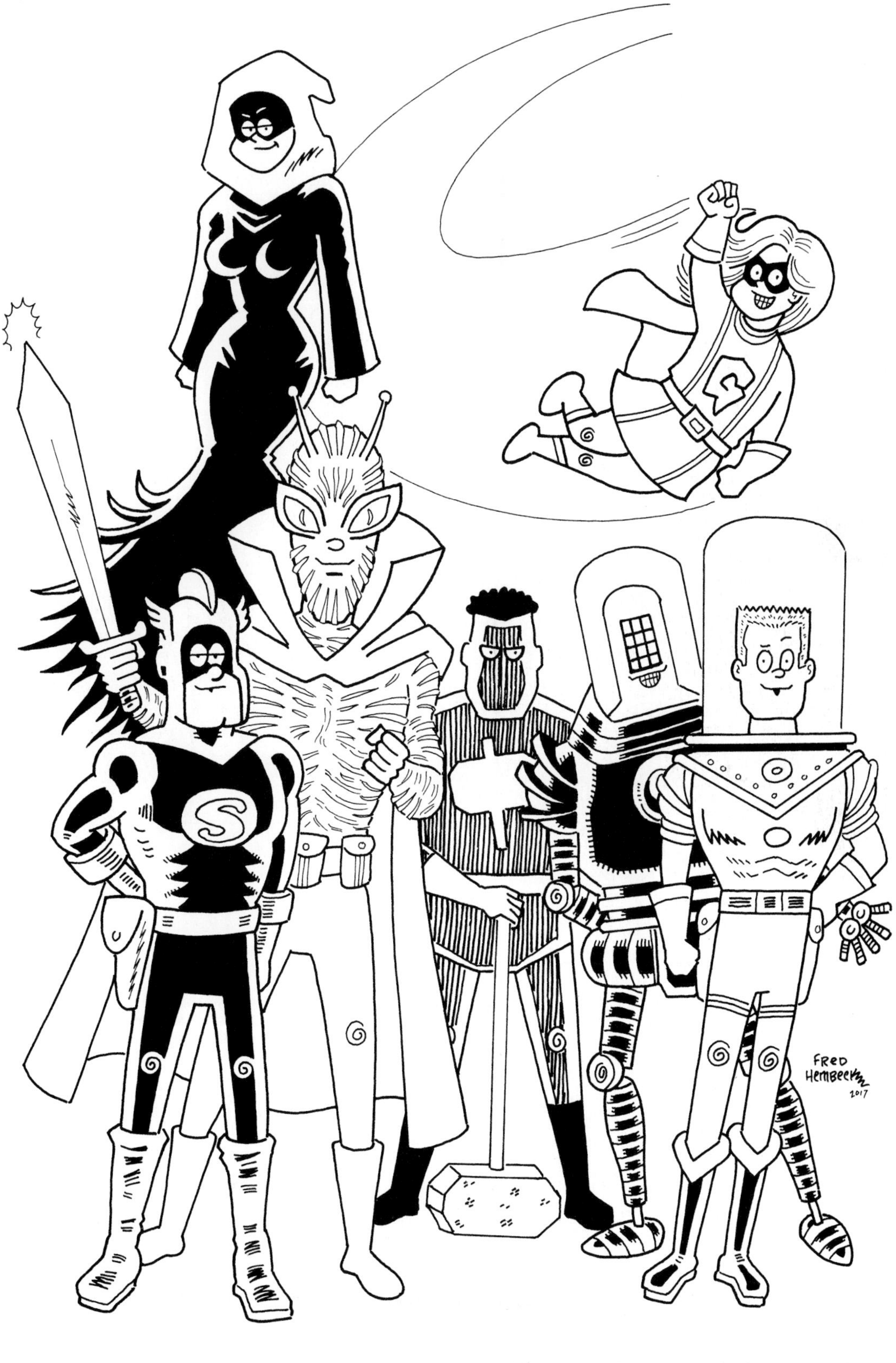
FRED HEMBECK 2017

Art by Fred Hembeck

BLACK HAMMER
Jeff Lemire and Dean Ormston

VOLUME 1: SECRET ORIGINS
ISBN 978-1-61655-786-7 | $14.99

VOLUME 2: THE EVENT
ISBN 978-1-50670-198-1 | $19.99

DREAM THIEF
Jai Nitz and Greg Smallwood

VOLUME 1
ISBN 978-1-61655-283-1 | $17.99

VOLUME 2: ESCAPE
ISBN 978-1-61655-513-9 | $17.99

THE BLACK BEETLE
Francesco Francavilla

NO WAY OUT
ISBN 978-1-61655-202-2 | $19.99

KARA BOCEK
ISBN 978-1-50670-537-8 | $12.99

THE ANSWER!
Mike Norton and Dennis Hopeless
ISBN 978-1-61655-197-1 | $12.99

BLOODHOUND
Dan Jolley, Leonard Kirk, and Robin Riggs

VOLUME 1: BRASS KNUCKLE PSYCHOLOGY
ISBN 978-1-61655-125-4 | $19.99

VOLUME 2: CROWBAR MEDICINE
ISBN 978-1-61655-352-4 | $19.99

MICHAEL AVON OEMING'S THE VICTORIES
Michael Avon Oeming

VOLUME 1: TOUCHED
ISBN 978-1-61655-100-1 | $9.99

VOLUME 2: TRANSHUMAN
ISBN 978-1-61655-214-5 | $17.99

VOLUME 3: POSTHUMAN
ISBN 978-1-61655-445-3 | $17.99

VOLUME 4: METAHUMAN
ISBN 978-1-61655-517-7 | $17.99

HELLBOY: SEED OF DESTRUCTION
(third edition)
Mike Mignola
ISBN 978-1-59307-094-6 | $17.99

ORIGINAL VISIONS—
THRILLING TALES!

"These superheroes ain't no boy scouts in spandex. They're a high-octane blend of the damaged, quixotic heroes of pulp and detective fiction and the do-gooders in capes from the Golden and Silver Ages." —Duane Swierczynski

AVAILABLE AT YOUR LOCAL COMICS SHOP OR BOOKSTORE! • To find a comics shop in your area, visit comicshoplocator.com.
For more information or to order direct visit DarkHorse.com or call 1-800-862-0052 Mon.–Fri. 9 a.m. to 5 p.m. Pacific Time. Prices and availability subject to change without notice.